THE COLLAPSE
OF COMMUNISM

THE
COLLAPSE
OF
COMMUNISM

Edited by Bernard Gwertzman
and Michael T. Kaufman

TIMES 𝕿 BOOKS

RANDOM HOUSE

Library of Congress Cataloging-in-Publication Data

The Collapse of communism / edited by Bernard
Gwertzman and Michael T. Kaufman.
       p.   cm.
  ISBN 0-8129-1872-X
  1. Communism—1945–   2. Communist countries—Economic conditions.
I. Gwertzman, Bernard M.   II. Kaufman, Michael T.
HX44.C6415   1990
335.43′09′048—dc20   90-10755

Manufactured in the United States of America

9 8 7 6 5 4 3 2

CONTENTS

INTRODUCTION
Bernard Gwertzman

The Communist countries of Europe underwent a stunning metamorphosis in 1989. A process of change which started slowly in countries already predisposed to reform snowballed by year's end to engulf the hard-line regimes in East Germany, Bulgaria, Czechoslovakia, and Rumania. Not only had Moscow given up its dominion in Eastern Europe, but there was a loss of control evident inside the Soviet Union as well. And perhaps more important, gone was the assumption that only the Communist Party could be entrusted with political power in Eastern Europe. Instead, the seeds of multiparty democracy had been sown throughout the former Soviet empire.

"Our jaws cannot drop any lower," said Ronald Linden of Radio Free Europe, expressing the sense of shock these upheavals had caused. Most astonishing was the behavior of Soviet leader Mikhail S. Gorbachev. Although he had earlier promised not to interfere in Eastern Europe, few in the East or West expected him to live up to his word and be so indifferent to the swirl around him.

At every turn, he either did nothing or actually appeared to support those in Eastern Europe seeking more freedom and an end to Communist domination. He ordered Soviet troops out of Afghanistan, urged the Vietnamese to depart from Cambodia and the Cubans from Angola, and seemed to lend his personal prestige to the ouster of such veteran Eastern European leaders as Erich Honecker in East Germany, Milos Jakes in Czechoslovakia, Todor Zhivkov in Bulgaria, and Nicolae Ceausescu in Rumania. He tolerated, if not encouraged, the opening of the Berlin Wall, Solidarity's taking over the government in Poland, and the Hungarian Communists' setting elections which may lead to their own political suicide. Gorbachev was also perceived by Chinese students during his trip to Beijing in China in May to be backing the student revolt which was ruthlessly put down with force in June by the leadership. Inevitably his attitude had repercussions within the Soviet Union. Members of restive nationality groups saw the East Europeans achieving with impunity the independence from Moscow they had sought for themselves.

The domino effect that President Eisenhower had once feared might topple nations one after another toward Communism was now clearly working in the opposite direction. As much as the changes themselves, it was the swiftness of the process that stunned the world. After all, there had been something comfortable about the cold war. Statesmen, journalists, novelists had become accustomed to the stability of the division of Europe. In truth, of course, the separation was less than total. The Iron Curtain had long ago showed signs of serious corrosion. In today's era of modern communications and technology, it was becoming increasingly difficult for the Communist leaders to immunize their peoples from contact with the outside world.

In fact, Communist leaders found themselves inept at taking advantage of the possibilities of the new high-tech era. And at a time of astonishing prosperity in the West, the Eastern bloc simply fell into an economic and moral slump to which there seemed no end in sight. It was this pressure for change from the outside combined with the disintegration on the inside that led to the rapidity of the collapse. The toughness of the Soviet bloc turned out to be very brittle indeed.

What follows is a summary of the background to the events country by country in Eastern Europe.

Poland

It was appropriate that the upheavals of 1989 began with Poland—the first nation to be compelled by the victorious Soviet Union to accept Communist domination at the end of World War Two. The Poles were always the most rebellious in the bloc, and from time to time were led by nationalist Communist leaders, such as Wladislaw Gomulka, who in 1956 sought to limit Moscow's direct control. But the Communists were always tainted in the eyes of Poles, both because of the Communists' allegiance to Moscow, and the hostility of the Catholic Church.

The rise of the trade union movement Solidarity in 1980 marked a new chapter in Poland, and in the bloc. It demonstrated that an opposition group could be formed which could challenge the Communists for leadership. The martial law crackdown in 1981 only thrust Poland into a worsening economic situation. A series of strikes in 1988 finally forced the regime of President Jaruzelski to hold round-table talks with Solidarity. That in turn led to a fateful agreement to hold free elections in Poland in June 1989.

Hungary

In the immediate aftermath of World War Two, Hungary was not immediately forced by the Red Army to become a Communist state. The Hungarians, in fact, had had an earlier brief Communist rule following World War One, under Bela Kun, which was not a happy period for most Hungarians. But after the conservative Smallholder party won 60 percent of the first election in November 1945, and the Communists only 17 percent, the Soviet authorities gradually began to force the country to adapt to their demands, so that by 1949 Hungary was considered a Soviet satellite.

The tumultuous days of the 1956 revolution under Imre Nagy showed the country's antipathy toward Communism and toward the Soviet Union. Nevertheless, Janos Kadar, who took over after Nagy's failed revolt, eventually won respect inside Hungary and began to open up his country to a more liberal internal system, known as "goulash Communism." For many years in the 1960's and 1970's, Kadar was probably one of the most popular of the world's Communist leaders. But in the 1980's an economic crisis and a lapse of confidence in the aging Kadar began to sweep the country. By 1987, demands for change were everywhere. In May 1988, Kadar was ousted from power and replaced by Karoly Grosz. By 1989, the splits within the ruling Communist Party—known officially as the Hungarian Socialist Workers' Party—had become pronounced.

If the changes in Poland and Hungary were carefully plotted and resulted, to a great extent, in public balloting, the upheavals that were to dominate the news in the latter part of 1989 came unexpectedly and from the streets.

East Germany

In the aftermath of World War Two, the division of Germany between East and West became the symbol of the cold war which was to dominate international relations for the next forty-five years. By 1948, after three years of trying to negotiate some way of uniting the occupation zones, the four powers in effect acknowledged their failure. The West created what became the Federal Republic of Germany, and the Soviet Union created the German Democratic Republic. The capital of the former, Berlin, was itself divided into zones. The eastern part of the city became the capital of the GDR. Bonn became the capital of West Germany, and West Berlin remained an outpost in the midst of East Germany—a symbol of Western determination to keep the city open despite a land and rail blockade in 1948.

In 1961, in the midst of a crisis in East-West relations, thousands of East Germans poured into the West through West Berlin. Nikita S. Khrushchev, the Soviet leader, ordered the East Germans to put up a wall to lock in the East German people. A succession of East-West accords in the 1970's seemed to make formal the division of Germany. The reunification of Germany, once the leading issue in East-West relations, faded into memory, to be revived in 1989.

Bulgaria

A Soviet satellite since the last days of World War Two, Bulgaria had one of the least imaginative Communist regimes in Europe. For thirty-five years, Todor Zhivkov was a virtual dictator. There was little inkling abroad or even in Bulgaria that his rule would come to an abrupt end in 1989.

Czechoslovakia

After World War Two, Czechoslovakia was permitted the freest multiparty democracy in Eastern Europe. In part, it was because there was a genuine sympathy for the Communists among the electorate. But by 1948, support for the Communist Party was eroding as tensions grew in Europe. Non-Communists in the government resigned to force new elections, which they thought they could win. But instead, the Communists organized a coup d'état in February 1948, and seized power through the unions and police. The "fall" of Czechoslovakia to the Communists and the death of the popular foreign minister Jan Masaryk (who either jumped or was pushed from a window) led President Truman to conclude that it was crucial for the West to rearm or face a new war. The cold war was launched.

In the mid-1960's, a cultural awakening occurred in Czechoslovakia, which had been one of the most repressive of the Communist regimes. In late 1967, demonstrations by students, combined with a bid for greater equality among the Slovaks and a continuing economic stagnation, led the party to replace Antonin Novotny with Alexander Dubcek. The developments in Prague in 1968, the "Prague Spring," presaged the events of 1989. In 1968, however, there was one major difference: the Soviet Union under Leonid I. Brezhnev was frightened by the liberal changes taking place, and in August it forced the other Warsaw Pact states (except Rumania) to join it in invading Czechoslovakia, crushing the new freedoms.

The new Czechoslovak regime was one of the most repressive in Eastern Europe. Yet dissident elements, led by Vaclav Havel, the playwright, staged frequent protests. Havel and others were frequently arrested. Demonstrations continued into early 1989, until in November they became irresistible.

Rumania

The Rumanians came out of World War Two at a certain advantage, since they had switched sides in the middle and thrown their support to the Russians after earlier fighting for the Nazis. But the Russians nevertheless imposed a Communist regime on the country, which had probably the weakest Communist Party in the region. The few Communists in Rumania were by and large non-Rumanian, and this caused them to be seen as largely alien. Moscow settled on Gheorge Gheorgiu-Dej, who was Rumanian, and Gheorgiu-Dej surprisingly took an independent tack in the early 1960's, emboldened by the withdrawal of Soviet troops in 1958. He sought to reduce Soviet control in his country.

That more independent course was advanced by his successor Ceausescu, who after taking over in 1965 became a maverick in the Communist world. He declined to join in the invasion of Czechoslovakia, curried favor with China when it was at odds with Russia, did not break ties with Israel after the 1967 war, and set out on an ambitious industrialization policy that eventually failed. But this dynamic leader, who was feted in Western capitals throughout the 1970's, became increasingly ruthless and dictatorial in the 1980's. He relied on nepotism. His wife, Elena, was made second in command, and his sons, brothers, and in-laws played key roles in running the country.

The developments that followed in these countries, along with those in Afghanistan and China, form the subject of this book. This is how the correspondents of *The New York Times* saw the momentous events of the year 1989.

THE COLLAPSE
OF COMMUNISM

WINTER 1988-89

As the year opened, it was already evident that as an ideology and as a formula for totalitarian rule Communism was in retreat, if not yet in outright decay. In a number of countries where Communism had been imposed, old orthodoxy was being challenged by deviant strains. In the name of reform, people who still called themselves Communist were countenancing, even advocating, private ownership and private enterprise. In Hungary, bonds were being traded on a stock market. In Poland, the once tightly censored official media was revealing more and more as it was forced to compete for credibility and readers with a vast network of independent clandestine publishers. In China, officials were advocating freer markets to encourage modernity, and in Moscow, Mikhail Gorbachev, the chief apostle of Communist reformation, was spearheading a move to introduce limited representative government on a western parliamentary model that not so long ago was reviled as bourgeois democracy. Amid such developments, what did it mean to be a Communist? Were there still basic tenets of belief that applied everywhere? Were Communists still supposed to believe in the teachings of Marx and Lenin if not the practice of Stalin and Mao? Did they still cling to the idea that Communism was inevitably destined to overwhelm and supersede capitalism? To find out, correspondents of The New York Times interviewed Communists from many countries, asking them such questions as who they considered to be their leaders and how specifically their views and hopes had changed. On the basis of these responses The Times published a series in January under the rubric "Communism Now: What Is It?" This is how it began.

In Hope and Dismay, Lenin's Heirs Speak
By Serge Schmemann

In the Communist world, the underground joke is often the best index of conditions. "What is Communism?" asks one that has recently been making the rounds.

"Communism," goes the reply, "is the longest and most painful route from capitalism to capitalism."

That joke, heard in Moscow, would be immediately understood in Beijing, Budapest or any other Communist-ruled capital where a battered economy, systematic repression and chronic corruption are prompting fundamental and wrenching reappraisal.

The process of reform, personified now by Mikhail S. Gorbachev, the Soviet leader, evokes both hope and dismay: hope that at last the millions who have lived through the tyrannies and chronic shortages endemic to Communist states could find some relief; dismay that so much of the terrible sacrifice, struggle and deprivation they have endured for so long must now be acknowledged to have been in vain, that the secular faith that once promised so much now stands revealed to its own adherents as a failure.

Nascent stock exchanges have opened in Shanghai and Budapest. State-owned companies in the Communist East are eagerly canvassing for joint ventures with capitalist behemoths from the West to gain access to post-industrial technology that has passed them by. The movement's once sacred history has been reopened to increasingly bold and brutal scrutiny. In this upheaval, what does it mean any more to be a Communist?

What remains of the old zeal and idealism, the sense of historical inevitability, of an inspired vanguard leading the masses to utopia? What, if anything, remains of the old faith?

To get a sense of how Communists now see themselves and their movement in a rapidly changing world, 26 correspondents of *The New York Times* had extensive interviews with 50 Communists from 23 countries. The aim was to hear the voices of individual Communists— leaders, intellectuals, ordinary party members, including some in countries where the Communists are out of power and still regard themselves as revolutionaries—to hear their reflections on the newly acknowledged moral and political failures that have beset their cause and to learn how they gauge its prospects.

In the broad diversity of their answers, in the degree of their faith or doubt, these Communists gave a human face to the plight of a formerly monolithic faith that once spread fear and hope throughout the world—a faith that now, according to the best available estimate, by the Hoover Institution at Stanford University, has 88.6 million adherents worldwide, 4.5 million of them living in non-Communist countries.

The sense of lost idealism common among old revolutionaries was expressed by Tran Bach Dang, a Vietnamese Communist who has spent most of his life hiding and fighting. "In the past, when fighting with the enemy, I enjoyed life more than now," he said. "For now we have to take responsibility for the fate of the entire society. The problems of peace are more complex than those of war."

More bluntly, a high-ranking Yugoslav official, Matjaz Kmecl, replied when asked what made him proud to be a Communist: "At the moment, nothing."

Even before the rise of Mr. Gorbachev in Moscow, China had renounced most of the Maoist creed that had defined its revolution. Hungary and Yugoslavia had experimented with new forms of economic management. But it was when the new Soviet leader raised the three banners of glasnost, perestroika and new thinking over the red ramparts of the Kremlin, the symbolic heart of the Communist universe, that the secular religion of Marx and Lenin was shaken to its core.

To the West, Mr. Gorbachev may seem merely pragmatic in admitting the profound "mistakes" of virtually all his predecessors since Lenin, in abandoning the dream of Communism in our lifetime, in acknowledging the legitimacy of other social systems, in withdrawing troops from Afghanistan or in seeking to inject competition, democratic debate and diversity into his society.

Yet in the process, he has also called into question the last surviving precepts of the faith he claims to defend—democratic centralism, class struggle, world revolution, party discipline and, finally, even the dominant role of the party itself. Saints have been toppled and heretics have been rehabilitated by the millions, usually posthumously.

"All happy families are alike, but an unhappy family is unhappy after its own fashion," wrote Leo Tolstoy. So too among the Communists in nations where the party won power in revolution, whether the Soviet Union, China or Vietnam: if the romantic early stages were filled with similar slogans, cameraderie and hope, the later hardships have been varied and the responses different.

Among Russians, the prevailing debate is predictably over Mr. Gorbachev. There are intellectuals like Erik M. Ametistov, a 54-year-old lawyer, who unabashedly described himself "a fervent supporter of Gorbachev" and as an equally fervent opponent of any vestiges of Stalinism. "I cannot accept that I share ideals with thousands who are guilty of mass repressions during the Stalin era," he declared with feeling.

Yet the excited praise for the "new thinking" clashes with the voice of a Nina A. Andreyeva, the Old Guard loyalist whose letter to the press last spring became the manifesto of conservative resistance to Mr. Gorbachev.

In her first interview with a Western reporter, Mrs. Andreyeva agreed with great reluctance that "mistakes" had been made under Stalin. But she said the assault on his rule marked the start of a total dismantling of the uncomplicated faith on which she was reared: "Next Lenin's teachings will be criticized, then they'll put into doubt socialism itself—which was built and defended in battle."

In China, from the perspective of a writer in his late 60's, Huang Gang expressed a similar regret that basic tenets and ideals are being eroded in the rush to modernize and Westernize. Increasingly, he said, the young are straying from "correct" understandings of socialism, and those like himself who rigorously protected the orthodox views are being pushed aside.

Mr. Huang, too, acknowledged "mistakes"—the universal Communist euphemism for the atrocities committed in the name of building a new world. In China, the epic "mistake" was the Cultural Revolution, under which party zealots were set loose to hound all who fell short of their radical standards. But it was party members, Mr. Huang insisted, who had righted the wrongs.

Those same "mistakes," however, profoundly shook the faith of Li Shuxian, a 53-year-old professor who is the wife of China's most prominent dissident, Fang Lizhi, an astrophysicist. She spoke poignantly of her loss of faith, which she said was common in the Chinese intelligentsia: "We had thought the party was so pure and clean, and maybe the top leaders simply didn't know what was happening in the country. But then in the Cultural Revolution everything came out."

The religious metaphors came up again and again. In its claim to be a comprehensive guide not only to economics and politics but also to morality, social organization and behavior—in its promise of a New Man—Marxism has become a caricature of the religion that its founder had declared an opiate.

In Vietnam, as in the Soviet Union, China and some other Communist lands, the death of a charismatic revolutionary leader marked the end of the romantic struggle, when crusaders for the faith could justify violence in the name of a grand future, and ushered in the gray realities of a flawed system.

In every land where Communists attained power, idealism and enthusiasm gave way to careerism and cynicism. Industrial powers watched their exports shrink as quality and innovation were throttled by vast central bureaucracies. Food supplies dwindled in inverse proportion to land collectivization.

Nations with great cultures found their writers and thinkers suppressed, jailed or exiled. Elemental rights and freedoms—travel, communication, information, religion—were denied in the name of the worker and a brave new world. And old truths were challenged as old alliances crumbled—the Chinese split with Russians, the Cubans split with both, and eventually Vietnam even stopped its summary and ritual rejection of American overtures.

As recently as 1960, Nikita S. Khrushchev could thump his shoe in the belief that the Soviet Union would overtake the West. But there was none of that bravado in the interviews of 1988–89. Many of the Communists seem defensive or ashamed of their party's history, or, in Mrs. Andreyeva's case, nostalgic for the old iron fist.

She spoke with dark suspicion of intellectuals—most of those she named were prominent Jews—and of the West. Yet in her nostalgia for a simpler past and an unquestioned order, in her invocation of the sacrifice of her precedessors and her faith in Lenin, she seemed to speak for many in her generation.

That reluctance to relinquish the faith is taking a different form in different lands. For people who live in China, the revolution is the antithesis of the corruption of the Nationalists and the backwardness of the past; for the Vietnamese, the memory of the struggle is still fresh.

In the Soviet Union, where it all began, there is no democratic tradition to fall back on, and too much blood has been spilled to abandon the cause. However discredited the ideology, Marxism remains the sole source of legitimacy for the state, and it is unthinkable for a party member not to invoke Lenin or Communism either in seeking or resisting change.

Mr. Gorbachev, for example, declared his perestroika and glasnost the only path to Lenin's true intent. Yet as glasnost rummages ever deeper in the Stalinist hell, it seems inevitable—as Mrs. Andreyeva feared—that some tarnish will begin to show on Lenin's halo.

And if Lenin is not secure, no demigod is. If Mao shared Lenin's revolutionary aura, he also shared Stalin's brutality. If the gods are falling, it is hard to see what remains of the old faith. Already the deadline for achieving utopia has been pushed far beyond the horizon, the once-damned West is revealed to be a viable model, global revolution is no longer certain or necessary, and glasnost is playing havoc with virtually every sacred myth.

On the economic front, Mr. Gorbachev has challenged presumptions on which generations of Soviet youths had been raised. State monopoly has been stripped of its sanctity and capitalism of its pointed tail. Long-scorned notions like flexible pricing, free trade, labor and capital markets, joint ventures, even competition were set loose on the land.

Private entrepreneurs, so recently caricatured as fat capitalists with silk top hats or as sleazy black-marketeers, were given respectability, though to maintain a proper Marxist facade their restaurants and services had to be called "cooperatives." Even that most fundamental bedrock of the Soviet social contract, cradle-to-grave security, came under threat in vague discussions of layoffs.

None of the Communists claimed a monopoly on truth or even social justice. At most, they viewed their party membership as a shared responsibility for vague humanitarian and social principles. To paraphrase Dwight D. Eisenhower, what matters is that you profess belief in Marx, and it doesn't matter what Marx you believe in.

Roy A. Medvedev, a Marxist historian who stood in the ranks of dissidents until Mr. Gorbachev came to power and is now much in demand in Moscow as a social and political critic, reported that members of the party who support the "new thinking" no longer like to speak of themselves as Communists.

"When I say I'm an adherent of socialism, it's clear that I'm a man who wants to build a humane society," he said. "But to be a Communist means to be a member of a party that lost considerable prestige, to be subject to its discipline.

"I think the time will come when nobody talks of 'Marxism-Leninism' anymore. Our system will be called something else, something like 'developed socialism.' " . . .

Mr. Gorbachev himself came from the generation of the "thaw," men and women who joined the party in the period of heady optimism that came with Mr. Khrushchev's condemnation of Stalin's crimes.

And now Mr. Gorbachev's own "thaw"—and the warming that has followed it in other Communist lands—is certain to profoundly affect those who now join or remain in the party. . . .

Other voices presented in the series belonged to people like Enrique Lister, an 81-year-old Spanish general, a veteran of the Civil War who

8

had outlived Franco and who while insisting that Marxism was a proven science claimed, "We have a long way to go yet; Communist society is yet to come." The manager of a Polish pencil company bragged about how much money he earns but complained that despite his windfall profits he could not buy his son the Yamaha motorbike that the teenager yearned for, and as a result the boy had misgivings about the system. A Sicilian editor who wears a ring made from the metal of a U.S. plane downed by the Vietnamese told of his disillusionment when the Italian party sought an alliance with Christian Democrats. Italy, he realized, is no longer "a country of poor folk with nothing to lose but their chains," but rather one in which people "now they have automobiles and houses."

From the third world came opinions of men like Gustavo Espinoza Montesinos of Peru, who defended the Soviet invasion of Czechoslovakia. There was also the anger of Safdar Hashmi, an Indian theater director, who deplored the then planned though not yet carried out Soviet withdrawal from Afghanistan. "We have defended the presence there of Soviet troops," he said. "Now you have the Soviets saying they have no business to be there. So what happens to the class struggle? Do you abandon Nicaragua and Ethiopia too? What will happen to them?" Soon after he offered his views, he was beaten to death by a gang after refusing to stop production of a political street play.

There was the testimony of the Nicaraguan Bayardo Arce, who said he read Henry Kissinger but could not get through Karl Marx. There was the Chilean architect who recalled wistfully that he had "entered adolescence together with a woman who was begining to mature and who was called the Cuban revolution." And finally, there was Mzala, a 32-year-old South African living in London for whom Communism essentially meant an ideology that he thought bound him in communion with comrades around the world but which also most alarmed his enemies, the architects and technicians of apartheid. "I think we are driven to our quest for Marxist theory by the South African Government itself because, from the time we became politically conscious in South Africa, the Government has been, and continues to be, at pains to show that, more than any other political entity, it opposes and it is afraid of the Communist Party."

• • •

The year's first dramatic reflection of Communism's attrition came when Moscow ordered the withdrawal of all Soviet troops from Af-

ghanistan. For nine years the Soviets had fought there to bolster successive Marxist regimes. During that span thousands of Soviet soldiers had been killed, more than 100,000 were wounded, and still others were captured in battles with sharpshooting Muslim warriors. In April of the previous year, the Soviet Union had agreed in Geneva to withdraw its forces by February 15, 1989. Such a pullback would mark the first time since the Second World War that Soviet Union was relinquishing territory it had sought to dominate.

Getting Out with Honor
By Bill Keller

MOSCOW, Feb. 2—As the last Soviet troops muster in Kabul for their convoy home from Afghanistan, the Kremlin has already turned its attention to a desperate salvage operation aimed at snatching as much honor as possible from the jaws of retreat.

With the hope of a last-ditch political settlement all but dissolved, and the search for any long-term lessons postponed to the future, Soviet officials have focused their diplomatic and military efforts on a set of more immediate goals.

"The main object of all this activity," a Western diplomat said, answering the question of what Moscow wants, "is to prevent the Soviet Union from being humiliated."

What Moscow seems to want, first, is to get out without further indignities avoiding heavy casualties as the final Soviet convoy moves north in the next few days.

To this end, the military has bombarded guerrilla strongholds along the main highway from Kabul to the Soviet Union, and Soviet diplomats have warned the opposition to hold its fire or risk reprisals.

Second, the Soviets want to demonstrate to their own people—and to clients elsewhere who may see the withdrawal as a betrayal of Communist solidarity—that they are doing all they can to prevent their clients from being quickly submerged in a bloodbath.

This means the diplomatic overtures aimed at forming a coalition government will continue, and perhaps intensify, after the troops have gone. Some diplomats say they believe it will also mean continued bombing runs from Soviet territory to help the Afghan Army, although this would draw protests from the West. The Soviet commander in Afghanistan has said this will not be done, but some diplomats believe that will depend on how the tide turns after the withdrawal.

10

Soviet officials seem to believe that the Afghan Government of President Najibullah will show greater staying power after the withdrawal than most Western diplomats expect, holding Kabul and perhaps some other major cities.

"I think the Soviets hope they can hold on to Kabul for at least six months while the negotiations continue," a Western diplomat said.

Third, the Soviets hope to salvage enough influence in the region to assure peaceful relations with their southern neighbor, whoever is in power, and to prevent Afghanistan from falling under the thrall of other powers, especially Pakistan. . . .

And fourth, Kremlin leaders are preparing to extract the remaining political benefits of the retreat, both at home and abroad.

At home, this means using the Afghanistan failure as an additional justification for cutting the military budget and diverting resources to shore up the fragile civilian economy.

Abroad, it means aggressively pursuing new opportunities for better relations with China and the Arab world, where the Afghan conflict has been a major diplomatic obstruction. Foreign Minister Eduard A. Shevardnadze was in Beijing today, laying plans for a Soviet-Chinese summit meeting that would have been impossible while Soviet troops were fighting in Afghanistan.

The mood in Moscow in the closing days of this nine-year misadventure is neither celebration nor defeat, but fatigue.

The Soviet public, having long since breathed its relief over the withdrawal and disinclined to dwell on the possible collapse of the Afghan regime, now seems eager to put the whole affair behind them.

"We are leaving as we arrived: neither victorious nor vanquished," Vladimir Bavin, who served with the Soviet Army in Afghanistan from 1984 to 1986, said in an interview this week at a club for war veterans. "So I don't think there will be a national holiday on February 15." That is the day the Soviet withdrawal is to be completed under the Geneva accords signed last April. . . .

Soviet officials have already set forth in general terms what they consider to be the broad lessons of Afghanistan.

Mr. Shevardnadze has cited the decision to send troops as evidence of the need for wider and more public discussion of foreign policy decisions, including involvement of the Soviet Parliament, which is supposed to be given new powers this year.

Mikhail S. Gorbachev, the Soviet leader, certainly had Afghanistan in mind when he told the United Nations General Assembly in December that the major powers should "totally rule out any outward-directed use of force," or even the threat of force, as an instrument of foreign policy.

By citing the cost of the war in Afghanistan as one culprit in a staggering Soviet budget deficit, Mr. Gorbachev has also made clear that he intends to use the war in pressing his case for cuts in the military budget.

"I think we will learn from Afghanistan the lesson you learned in Vietnam—that military force is a limited instrument of foreign policy," a Soviet journalist said today. "Given the state our economy is in right now, that happens to be a very timely lesson."

Pravda wrote on Wednesday that "it still remains for politicians and military historians" to explain what went wrong. It added, "Probably everything will be told, without secrets or evasions, even about what the leaders of the party and country have called 'sins.' "

A day later the Soviet press offered a new and thorough reckoning of old Soviet "sins."

Major Soviet Paper Says 20 Million Died as Victims of Stalin
By Bill Keller

MOSCOW, Feb. 3—A Soviet weekly newspaper today published the most detailed accounting of Stalin's victims yet presented to a mass audience here, indicating that about 20 million died in labor camps, forced collectivization, famine and executions.

The estimates, by the historian Roy Medvedev, were printed in the weekly tabloid *Argumenti i Fakti*, which has a circulation of more than 20 million.

The estimated number of deaths is about equal to the number of Soviet soldiers and civilians believed killed in World War II.

Mr. Medvedev's grim arithmetic was reported in a less detailed version last November in *Moscow News*, a limited-circulation weekly, which sells about 200,000 copies in Russian, but today's article marked the first time the numbers have been disclosed to a nationwide audience.

In all, Mr. Medvedev calculated about 40 million victims of Stalin's repressions, including those arrested, driven from their land or blacklisted.

Although the bookkeeping of Stalin's terror is an inexact and contentious science, Mr. Medvedev's estimates are generally in line with Western calculations that have long been disparaged by more official Soviet historians.

"It's important that they published it, although the numbers themselves are horrible," Mr. Medvedev said in an interview tonight. "Those numbers include my father."

Mr. Medvedev, a dissident Marxist who has recently been rescued from official obscurity and honored as a leading authority on dark corners of Soviet history, said the weekly newspaper solicited the article and presumably showed the contents to officials before publishing it.

Mr. Medvedev said he had no special access to official archives, but relied on his own compilations of material over the years and recent publications in the Soviet press.

Under a headline proclaiming "The Number of Victims of Stalinism Is About 40 Million People," in a terse, question-and-answer format, Mr. Medvedev cited the human cost of Stalin's leadership year by year, leaving it to the reader to complete the arithmetic.

Mr. Medvedev's accounting included these victims:

- One million imprisoned or exiled from 1927 to 1929, falsely accused of being saboteurs or members of opposition parties.
- Nine million to 11 million of the more prosperous peasants driven from their lands and another 2 million to 3 million arrested or exiled in the early 1930's campaign of forced farm collectivization. Many of these were believed to have been killed.
- Six million to 7 million killed in the punitive famine inflicted on peasants in 1932 and 1933.
- One million exiled from Moscow and Leningrad in 1935 for belonging to families of former nobility, merchants, capitalists and officials.
- About 1 million executed in the "great terror" of 1937–38, and another 4 million to 6 million sent to forced labor camps from which most, including Mr. Medvedev's father, did not return.
- Two million to 3 million sent to camps for violating absurdly strict labor laws imposed in 1940.
- At least 10 million to 12 million "repressed" in World War II, including millions of Soviet-Germans and other ethnic minorities forcibly relocated.
- More than 1 million arrested on political grounds from 1946 to Stalin's death in 1953.

The Soviet press has left little unsaid about Stalin's shortcomings, probing into sacred myths like his conduct of World War II, likening him to Hitler, dissecting his cruelties period by period. But official historians have shied away from putting a number to it all.

Mr. Medvedev acknowledged in *Argumenti i Fakti*, and repeated tonight, that many periods of repression will never be fully measured because records have been lost or never existed.

Meanwhile, as the withdrawal of troops continued, the Soviets virtually trumpeted their retreat.

Soviets Delighted to Survive
By Bill Keller

TERMEZ, U.S.S.R., Feb. 6—The Soviet Union marked the final stage of its withdrawal from Afghanistan with a show for the press today in this dusty border city.

Nine years and 41 days after troops parachuted into Afghanistan to support the Soviet-sponsored Government in Kabul, a token paratroop regiment rumbled back across a railroad bridge over the Amu Darya River, to be greeted by an anxious group of parents and fiancees, assorted minor dignitaries, 200 reporters from all over the world, and an all-girl, all-drum band from a Termez school.

The ceremony was more weary than festive, and just a bit premature.

Army officers here said this morning that as many as 20,000 Soviet soldiers were still in Afghanistan, awaiting airlift to Soviet territory or gathered in convoys converging on Termez or the western border crossing at Kushka.

But the authorities said the last soldiers had left Kabul and its environs, including the airport that had been a virtual Soviet military base. . . .

The display in Termez today was intended to show the world that the Soviet Union is abiding by its commitment to vacate Afghanistan before February 15, and to show the home audience that the Kremlin was not going to let its soldiers slink home as if no one cared.

The authorities flew in more than 100 foreign journalists from Moscow, and 45 more were allowed to ride in with the paratroopers from north of Mazar-i-Sharif.

Today's show took place at a dirt parade ground overlooking a railroad bridge named Friendship, which connects Termez with the Afghan town of Heiratan.

People in Termez, many wearing the quilted, multicolored robes traditional in Uzbekistan, came to feast on meat pies and kebab and to browse at tents selling chocolate bars, soap, toothpaste and other scarce items.

At about 11:30, the paratroopers climbed atop armored personel carriers and roared across the bridge from Heiratan, where they had spent the night bathing and watching a variety show.

Stepping up to a reviewing stand decorated with flags and a large, decidedly Asian-looking visage of Lenin, Lieut. Col. Aleksandr I. Skachkov, a regiment commander, announced to the local authorities that "the battalion, having fulfilled its international duty, has come home."

A military band played the Soviet national anthem, followed by a girl from the Termez school who recited a patriotic poem in high-pitched fervor.

One thing that did not seem staged was the joy of the 300 weary paratroopers chosen to symbolize the war's end for the world's cameras. They waved and grinned in happy exhaustion.

The soldiers said the convoy home was slowed by slick roads in the Salang Tunnel and mountain passes. An avalanche reportedly swept several vehicles into a ravine, killing three men. But they said they encountered no attacks from guerrillas.

Girls from Termez passed through the ranks on the parade ground with carnations, cigarettes and blank telegram forms for word to loved ones far away.

"I'm back home, I'm alive and well," Pavel Nochikov scrawled to his mother in the Komi region.

Reporters were given only half an hour to mingle with the troops before the men boarded their vehicles. In that time, traces of bitterness were evident along with relief.

Asked what he felt he and his comrades had accomplished in Afghanistan, one private paused a long time, shrugged, and said, "We survived."

Some waiting relatives were similarly candid. "They say it's a mistake, but when so many people die for a mistake, it's terrible," said Nina Peshkova, 27 years old, an officer's wife from Siberia who came for her husband's homecoming. She added: "I think the regime of

Najibullah has hardly any support. The people should decide for themselves."

Maria G. Sabriva, a tiny woman from the Termez region, found her grandson among the arriving soldiers and was quickly surrounded by reporters eager to record the moment. "At least he was healthy," Mrs. Sabriva said of her grandson, who had written her that he was in Mongolia so she would not worry.

More than 600,000 men have served in Afghanistan since the war began, and more than 13,000—by the last official count, not updated since May—have died there.

Meanwhile, in Warsaw, another group of people who had been strug-gling against Communist domination for about as long as the Afghan Mujahaddin were also making sudden gains. The Solidarity free trade union movement had been born when workers in Gdansk set off a wave of strikes that linked demands for better pay to calls for political liberty and civil rights. The movement was at first legalized, but then in 1981 General Wojciech Jaruzelski declared martial law and most of the union leaders were arrested. But enough escaped to build a nationwide conspiracy in which ordinary people increasingly acted like free men and women, meeting in churches, ignoring censorship and paying more attention to the leadership of Lech Walesa, the electrician who founded the union, than to the general who headed the party. For several years the Communists contended that Solidarity had had its day and was a spent force. But finally, as the country's economy worsened, they were forced to reckon with ideas they could not squelch and men they could not subdue.

Warsaw Opens Parley with Solidarity
By John Tagliabue

WARSAW, Feb. 6—The Government and the banned labor union Solidarity began discussions today on broad political and economic change in Poland. The Government offered to reinstate the union and give it a share of parliamentary power through "nonconfrontational elections" in exchange for Solidarity support of Government economic programs.

The Interior Minister, Gen. Czeslaw Kiszczak, said in a keynote address that such elections could lead to the formation of a broad coalition government to prevent Poland from degenerating into "the sick man of Europe."

One key issue facing Solidarity will be whether to accept what would in effect be rigged elections that the Government has suggested in the past would assure the union 30 percent to 40 percent of the seats in Parliament. That would not represent a dramatic shift in power, but would open the door to greater influence for the union and its poltical allies and create a base for further future change.

General Kiszczak, who headed the Government delegation, said an overhaul of Poland's political system was needed for economic and social change. But he said the restoration of Solidarity should rule out a return to the "anarchy and destruction" that marked its legal existence in 1980–81.

Speaking for Solidarity, the banned union's leader, Lech Walesa, called for a gradual dismantling of Poland's one-party state, asserting that such a process should commence with "the reinstatement of trade union pluralism, the reinstatement of Solidarity."

As part of an agreement to end a wave of strikes in August, the Government of Gen. Wojciech Jaruzelski promised to include Solidarity in discussions on Poland's problems, including a $38.9 billion debt and chronic consumer shortages. The Government banned Solidarity after martial law was declared in December 1981.

Fifty-seven delegates from the Government, the opposition and the Roman Catholic Church gathered for the round-table talks at the Governor's Palace

General Kiszczak proposed these three measures as a new "social accord":

- An increase in the opposition's representation in the Parliament, through what he called "nonconfrontational elections."
- A program of economic recovery, whose aim above all would be to stifle inflation, restructure industry and resolve Poland's pressing foreign debt.
- Resolution of the problem of trade union pluralism, through the legalization of Solidarity.

The delegates are expected to continue discussions in small groups this week before convening again in full session.

In their opening addresses, which were televised nationally this evening, both sides appeared to be staking maximalist positions, reflecting the Government's desire to retain the last word on political change, and Solidarity's wish to claim an area of independent activity within Polish society.

In his address, Mr. Walesa asserted that a "new law on associations should create real freedom of association for everyone."

"This must not depend on arbitrary decisions of administrative authorities," he added.

"In this way union and social pluralism will create an area of freedom that Poles need as much as they need air," he said.

Mr. Walesa also blamed the Communists for Poland's situation.

"We know it—the country is ruined," he said, "but it wasn't some elves who ruined it, but a system of exercising authority that detaches citizens from their rights and wastes the fruits of their labor."

Among the conclusions the Government has drawn from experience, General Kiszczak said, was that, "renewal requires social peace, the consideration and responsibility of all the partners, and the expansion of the social base of reforms and ruling."

But he added, "No national problem will be solved by denying the historical achievements and undermining the socialist shape of Poland."

As rivals talked in Poland, in Afghanistan the invaders departed.

Last Soviet Soldiers Leave Afghanistan After 9 Years, 15,000 Dead and Great Cost
By Bill Keller

MOSCOW, Feb. 15—The last Soviet soldier came home from Afghanistan this morning, the Soviet Union announced, leaving behind a war that had become a domestic burden and an international embarrassment for Moscow.

The final Soviet departure came on the day set as a deadline by the Geneva accords last April. It left two heavily armed adversaries, the Kremlin-backed Government of President Najibullah and a fractious but powerful array of Muslim insurgents, backed by the United States and Pakistan, to conclude their civil war on their own.

Lieut. Gen. Boris V. Gromov, the commander of the Soviet forces in Afghanistan, walked across the steel Friendship Bridge to the border city of Termez, in Uzbekistan, at 11:55 A.M. local time (1:55 A.M., Eastern time), 9 years and 50 days after Soviet troops intervened to support a coup by a Marxist ally.

"There is not a single Soviet soldier or officer left behind me," General Gromov told a Soviet television reporter waiting on the bridge. "Our nine-year stay ends with this."

Today's final departure is the end of a steady process of withdrawal since last spring, when Moscow says, there were 100,300 Soviet troops in Afghanistan. At the height of the Soviet commitment, according to Western intelligence estimates, there were 115,000 troops deployed.

This morning, as the last armored troop carriers rumbled home across the border, a Soviet newspaper carried the first report of atrocities committed in the war by the nation's military forces.

The weekly *Literaturnaya Gazeta* described the killing of a carload of Afghan civilians, including women and children, and the order by a commander to cover it up.

The article was a foretaste of recriminations expected in the months ahead.

The war cost the Soviet Union roughly 15,000 lives and undisclosed billions of rubles. It scarred a generation of young people and undermined the cherished image of an invincible Soviet army. Moscow's involvement in Afghanistan was often compared to the American experience in the Vietnam War, in which more than 58,000 Americans died.

The Soviet intervention, which received international condemnation, cast a pall over relations with China, the Muslim world and the West. It led to an American trade embargo and a Western boycott of the 1980 Olympic Games in Moscow.

"The day that millions of Soviet people have waited for has come," General Gromov said to an army rally in Termez, Reuters reported. "In spite of our sacrifices and losses, we have totally fulfilled our internationalist duty."

The official press agency Tass said the Defense Ministry presented all of the returning soldiers with wristwatches. . . .

At home, the Soviet Government now faces a period of reckoning with the roots and consequences of the war.

In Pravda, the authoritative Communist Party newspaper, a commentator insisted today that the intervention was carried out with the best intentions—including maintaining the security of the Soviet Union's southern border. But he said that the war was characterized by the mistakes and misjudgments of previous leaders.

"One can question the Brezhnev leadership's assessment of the military threat," the commentary said. "One can say that in the future such vital issues as the use of troops must not be decided in secrecy, without the approval of the country's Parliament." Other commentators, who have been constrained while Soviet soldiers were still fighting on Afghan territory, can now be expected to question more pointedly how the Soviet Union got into Afghanistan, what it did there, why it stayed so long and what lessons it has learned. . . .

And days after the Afghan pullout, there was news from Warsaw of another breakthrough, a seeming concession by the Communists to allow Solidarity a share of political power.

Solidarity May Win 40 Percent of Parliament
By John Tagliabue

WARSAW, Feb. 19—Two weeks after the start of talks between the Government and the outlawed opposition, both sides say they have reached "fundamental accord" on allowing the Solidarity-led opposition to control as many as two-fifths of the seats in Parliament through pre-arranged elections.

As outlined by a senior party official, the accord would allow Poland's Solidarity-based opposition roughly 40 percent of the seats in Parliament under an agreement by which the sides would divide electoral districts beforehand, then refrain from running candidates in each other's districts or "sabotaging" their campaigns.

In exchange, the officials said, Solidarity is being asked to provide popular support for unpopular Government economic policies. . . .

Both sides stressed that the accord could unravel before a final agreement is reached . . . but it appeared to represent major concessions by both sides. The Communist Party has never permitted more than token opposition in the largely rubber-stamp Parliament, and Solidarity has boycotted all Polish elections, denouncing them as hoaxes designed to cement party control. . . .

The impetus behind the political bargaining, which includes the Government, the party, Solidarity and the Church, as well as Communist-backed labor unions and other organizations, is a looming economic crisis that representatives of Government and Solidarity fear could provoke new outbursts of industrial strife.

But the proposals also reflected the broad political liberalization in several countries of East Europe, including Hungary and Yugoslavia. Both countries, in addition to Poland, are testing the waters of multiparty government.

A senior Church official said "free elections are impossible." But he and Solidarity strategists appeared to suggest that an infusion of opposition politicians into Parliament would favorably influence the development of democratic institutions and augment pressure on the Communist party for further change. . . .

It was hardly yet a contagion of freedom, but before winter loosened its grip there were remarkable stirrings along the Baltic, most notably among the Lithuanians. They were now Soviet citizens and their land was a Soviet Republic. But as with the Poles, to whom they once were linked in monarchial union, they were many among them openly yearning and striving to stand alone.

Lithuania Nationalists: A Fine and Fragile Line
By Bill Keller

VILNIUS, U.S.S.R., March 9—Ignoring damp snowflakes, Lithuanians by the thousands filed into the sylvan amphitheater of a Vilnius park the other day for an election rally.

They cheered the candidates of the popular movement called Sajudis, whistled their collective disdain for the Communist Party, listened stoically as their leaders appealed for calm in the face of official resistance, and then lifted perhaps 15,000 voices in the Sajudis oath: "Our goal is a free Lithuania!"

A few weeks ago these were words of nostalgia and bravado. But in the heat of an uninhibited Soviet election campaign, the notion of "free Lithuania"—free, that is, of the Soviet Union—has become a live and explosive issue.

In February, Sajudis, now a commanding political presence in this republic of 3.7 million people, took a daring step by announcing that its ultimate goal is to restore "an independent and neutral Lithuanian state in a demilitarized zone," like the nation that existed here between the two world wars, until the Soviet Union annexed the Baltic states in 1940.

The group had earlier called for a form of home rule, but stopped short of endorsing independence. But with the new declaration, including the statement that Lithuania had been "occupied" by the Red Army against its will, Sajudis portrayed itself as a lineal descendant of the partisans who waged armed resistance against Soviet power until 1953.

The declaration made Sajudis the first of the Baltic Popular Fronts to explicitly chart a separatist course, although similar groups in Estonia and Latvia include factions that favor full independence.

21

The group's leaders say their declaration was a statement of principle, not a short-term program. But some Sajudis members who are running for office in the election on March 26 are quite prepared to push for secession almost immediately.

The Lithuanian Communist Party leader, Algirdas Brazauskas, who had been nervously tolerant of the nationalist group, was called to Moscow for consultations last month, and returned with a new, firm set to his square jaw.

The party promptly announced new limits on Sajudis's independent press, purged several party and government officials considered sympathetic to the movement, and warned of a possible state of emergency if the separatist calls did not subside.

"We have told Sajudis that together we can approach that red line, but we, the official leadership, cannot cross it," Mr. Brazauskas said in an interview, adding that he "cannot imagine the consequences" if Sajudis pushes for secession.

"On the other side of the line, we can no longer remain friends or support their ideas," he said. "You can criticize us, you can mistrust us—whatever. But we won't cross that line."

What makes the debate especially pointed is the prospect that, thanks to the Soviet Union's first competitive elections, Sajudis is likely soon to acquire real power in the Lithuanian government.

The organization is backing candidates for 39 of Lithuania's 42 seats in a new national congress to be elected on March 26, and even party officials concede that the movement stands a good chance of winning most of them. The Popular Fronts in Latvia and Estonia are also backing candidates, but have not organized such complete slates. . . .

More important, Sajudis expects to win control of the republic's legislature in the next round of local elections. Already, Sajudis has gone up against the party in three special elections to fill vacant seats in the Lithuanian legislature and won all of them handily.

Alarmed that Sajudis members might use a majority in the legislature to formally declare Lithuanian independence, the Communist Party is now pressing to have the local legislative elections postponed from next fall until at least the following spring.

Both Sajudis and the Communist Party are divided about how to continue their troubled relationship.

Vytautas Landsbergis, the president of the independent movement, has tried to steer his group away from outright confrontation with the party. He and other Sajudis leaders say that if Lithuania is allowed to develop its own experimental economy—to shut down polluting heavy industries, develop private factories and farming, engage in free trade with the West, and create its own monetary system, then Lithuania can remain part of a Soviet federation, at least for now.

Separatist talk, the Sajudis moderates argue, simply provokes Moscow's anger, and in any case the republic will need perhaps 10 years of economic development before it is ready to stand on its own.

"The prevailing view, which I suppose you could call utopian, is that Lithuania should help the Soviet Union by providing an intelligent economic model," Mr. Landsbergis said. "The other view, which is the radical view, is to jump out of a sinking boat."

Keeping these two factions together in Sajudis "is my biggest problem," he added.

Others on the group's executive council, like Arvydas Juozaitis, a 32-year-old political scientist, say that Sajudis has taken the first logical step toward secession by proclaiming Lithuania an occupied country. Economic independence is another step on that road, he said.

"We know very well what it actually means to introduce private enterprise and a free economic zone in Lithuania," Mr. Juozaitis said. "In fact, it will be a decisive step toward seceding from the Soviet Union."

Even if Moscow gives Lithuania economic free range, the Kremlin is unlikely to tolerate another Sajudis demand—that the republic be removed from Soviet military jurisdiction.

Mr. Brazauskas, a former industrial planner regarded by Sajudis as a reasonable but indecisive moderate, has supported greater sovereignty for Lithuania within the framework of the Soviet Union. He argues that disengaging Lithuania economically is wildly impractical and that demilitarization is politically unthinkable.

The republic party leader made several concessions, including restoration of the old Lithuanian flag and a tough new language law that will require officials to speak basic Lithuanian within two years, and has promised that the republic will have vastly greater economic power next year.

"Compared with the other republics we have gone very far," he said. "Everyone wants to forget this and look ahead to see what is going to happen next."

The party leader warned that "extremist slogans" arouse the resentment of the Soviet Union's Russian-speaking majority and could undermine Mikhail S. Gorbachev, the nation's leader.

"Without a doubt, such demarches can influence society's opinion of Gorbachev's authority," he said.

Mr. Brazauskas seems to be under heavy pressure from Moscow, where some Kremlin leaders are alarmed at how quickly Lithuania is increasing its demands, and worried by signs that the nationalist sentiment is spreading to two much larger republics, the Ukraine and Byelorussia.

Last month, the Government banned Sajudis's weekly television show, a live call-in program that has provided some of the most astonishing moments in Soviet television. On one of last programs, on February 1, Julius Juzeliunas, a composer, praised the Lithuanian partisans who haunted the woods of the republic until 1953 picking off Soviet soldiers.

"This is the state television network, not a private company," Mr. Brazauskas said, defending the decision to cancel the program. He said the issue would be reconsidered after the elections.

Most Sajudis leaders are sympathetic to Mr. Brazauskas' predicament and see the need for conciliation.

"He's under a lot of pressure," said Romualdas Ozolas, editor of the main Sajudis newspaper. "I wouldn't want to be in his place."

Earlier this month, Sajudis candidates withdrew from the election districts where Mr. Brazauskas and the No. 2 two republic party leader are running, fearful that if the moderates were beaten, Moscow would replace them with hard-liners.

The people who make the movement's decisions are no scraggly band of dissidents, but solid civic leaders. The 35-member executive council that meets each Tuesday to map strategy includes prominent economists, lawyers, cultural figures and scholars, and a priest, indicating the tacit support of the Roman Catholic Church, which is still a power in this heavily Catholic republic.

Perhaps most surprising, 14 of the 35 Sajudis council members are also Communist Party members.

Lithuania was the last of the three Baltic states to form its independent political movement. Sajudis was organized in October after creation of the Popular Fronts in Estonia and Latvia.

But Sajudis has moved ahead of neighboring groups by making full use of the new election law.

Adolfas Uza, a journalist for the Lithuanian state press agency and a Sajudis spokesman, said the movement may have grown faster because Lithuania is less Russified than the other republics—80 percent of the people are ethnic Lithuanians, while the indigenous population is less than two-thirds in Estonia and about half in Latvia.

"We have to take the step first because we have the better demographic situation," Mr. Uza said. "Estonia and Latvia look to us with great hope. The further we go toward independence, the easier it will be for them."

Democracy—or at least a half measure called "democratization"—was also churning debate and hopes in the Soviet Union. As spring came, citizens there were preparing for the first time in their lives to vote clearly and unmistakably for the candidate they preferred and against those they disdained.

In Moscow's TV Political Debates, the Unspeakable Is Now Routine
By Bill Keller

MOSCOW, March 21—"Do you believe in God?" the moderator asked the candidates in one of Moscow's first televised campaign debates.

"I do not believe in God," replied Boris N. Yeltsin, the city's former Communist Party leader, smiling a wan smile at an audience estimated in the millions.

"I am an atheist," concurred his adversary, Yevgeny A. Brakov, an auto-factory director, who was visibly ill at ease.

It was the politically correct answer for two career members of the Communist Party, but not necessarily a vote-getter in a nation of many devout believers, and certainly not a question that party luminaries are accustomed to being asked on live television.

Since the beginning of March, the popular nightly program "Good Evening, Moscow" has been been subjecting candidates to questions submitted by viewers in preparation for the Soviet Union's first competitive national elections this coming Sunday.

The elections are to choose 1,500 territorial representatives to a new national Congress of People's Deputies, largely in contested races. Together with 750 deputies named directly by the Communist Party and other official organizations, they will set general policy and select a standing legislature and president from their ranks.

For voters accustomed to unopposed candidates with look-alike platforms, the uncensored programs have represented a crash course in the new Soviet approach to political pluralism.

The program has also caused one political tempest, when supporters of Mr. Yeltsin charged that hostile questions were planted on the show to embarrass their candidate.

The questions, phoned in beforehand by viewers and selected by Andrei G. Skryabin, the moderator of the debates, range from the brazenly personal—"How big is your apartment?"—to the politically provocative. Candidates can count on blunt questions about legalizing opposition political parties, abolishing the draft, banning nuclear power or slashing the space program.

"Not long ago, if somebody had come on my show and said one-tenth of the things that are said in these debates, at the very least I would be out of a job," said Mr. Skryabin, a fast-talking former science reporter.

Viewers frequently demand to know what magazines the candidates read, a favorite barometer of political inclinations.

Candidates in all 27 Moscow election districts have agreed to submit to the televised encounters, which, like American presidential debates, are really side-by-side interviews more than classic debates.

One Moscow candidate who escaped the televised cross-examination was Lev N. Zaikov, Mr. Yeltsin's successor as chief of the Moscow Communist Party organization. Along with Mikhail S. Gorbachev, the Soviet leader, and most other top party officials, Mr. Zaikov was named to the new congress as part of the party's slate, without opposition or a vote by the public.

Mr. Skryabin said the debates are without precedent and, as far as he knows, unique to Moscow. And in a campaign with no paid commercials and spotty Soviet press coverage, many believe that they could prove decisive.

If Ilya I. Zaslavsky, a 29-year-old campaigner from an unofficial association for the disabled, wins Sunday in his campaign to represent the Oktyabrsky region of Moscow, it may well be because he quietly dominated the televised debate against his better-known opponent, a popular television journalist named Aleksandr N. Krutov.

Mr. Zaslavsky, whose legs are withered as a result of a contaminated polio vaccination he received as a child, outlined a detailed program to improve health care, stiffen environmental protection and assist those on fixed incomes. Mr. Krutov lost points by making patronizing comments about the disabled and by declining to disavow an endorsement from the extreme Russian nationalist group Pamyat.

Valery M. Savitsky, a lawyer and highly regarded civil rights specialist, appearently damaged his campaign against a prominent economist when he bobbled a question about his ex-wife, the daughter of a top Soviet official.

"He hesitated and mumbled," as if apologizing for his marriage, Mr. Skryabin said. "It was not the way a man behaves toward his wife. It was an unquestionable defeat."

Mr. Skryabin said there are no reliable studies of how many people are watching the debates, but since about 30 million people can pick up the broadcasts, and since "Good Evening, Moscow" is one of the most popular programs on local television, it is likely that millions have tuned in.

The format of the program is simple: each candidate has six minutes to describe his platform, and then they take turns giving one-minute answers to the questions Mr. Skryabin has picked. The host sorts the hundreds of questions phoned in each day by viewers, selecting those that seem to reflect wide interest, and those that are the most pointed.

"I immediately discard questions like 'My dear Comrade Brakov! We greet you, we love you, you are our friend and brother,' " he said. "Next, I throw out questions of a personal nature: 'help us fix our roof.' "

The candidates are given the questions shortly before the program so they will not be caught totally by surprise. A few days after the Yeltsin debate, in which the former Moscow party chief fielded a number of unfriendly queries about his conflicts with party leaders, a commentator for the Novosti news-feature agency, a Yeltsin supporter, charged that he had tried to track down the authors of the questions and found that most did not exist.

Mr. Yeltsin and his backers alleged that this was part of an organized campaign to discredit the candidate.

Mr. Skryabin said producers of the show did their own investigation and located all but one of the questioners. It is true that Mr. Yeltsin drew the more aggressive questions, he said, but that was because he is controversial.

Mr. Skryabin said he could recall only once when his superiors at central television complained about the debates. The question about God, they told him, was out of bounds.

"Maybe it was a mistake to ask that question," he mused later. "It does not relate to their qualifications for public office. But what the devil, they didn't have to answer it."

After the campaign came the vote.

Soviets Savor Vote in Freest Election Since '17 Revolution

By Bill Keller

MOSCOW, March 26—Soviet voters today relished their freest elections in more than 70 years, choosing a new national Congress of Deputies that is to replace a legislature wholly subservient to the Communist Party.

In the race that some regarded as a plebiscite on the establishment, Boris N. Yeltsin, the deposed Moscow Communist Party leader, appeared headed for a victory over a candidate backed by the Moscow party machine.

Mr. Yeltsin, campaigning against party privileges and for greater political pluralism, seemed to have overwhelming support over Yevgeny A. Brakov, the director of the Zil limousine factory, in a contest to represent the city in the congress.

An informal sampling by Western news organizations of more than 2,300 voters at polling places around the city found that more than 90 percent had supported Mr. Yeltsin's comeback. The first official tallies from scattered polling places also pointed to a Yeltsin landslide.

Today's voting was the first nationwide, competitive election since the autumn of 1917, when Lenin's Bolshevik party was outpolled by the Socialist Revolutionaries. The following July, Lenin ousted the rival party from the Government and began the one-party state that exists to this day.

The new congress and the standing legislature it must appoint within two months are certain to be dominated by the Communist Party on all major policy questions. But voters appeared likely to elect enough independent-minded deputies to make open clashes of ideas highly likely.

Soviet citizens seemed to revel in their first opportunity to vote for candidates like Mr. Yeltsin, who promised to accelerate the pace of change and railed against the bureaucrats and power brokers.

One woman may have embodied the national mood when, asked by a Soviet television crew how she had voted, she replied firmly, "Against what we have now."

Mikhail S. Gorbachev, the Soviet leader, while declining to say how he had voted, cautioned against the impatience evident among Mr. Yeltsin's army of supporters.

"We must not commit stupidities, attempt great leaps forward, or overreach ourselves because we could put the people's future at risk,"

Mr. Gorbachev said after casting his ballot at the headquarters of the Association of Soviet Chemists. . . .

Mr. Gorbachev, who is expected to be named to an enhanced position of President when the new congress convenes, was also asked how he felt about the widespread discussion of a multiparty system that has arisen during the campaign.

The Soviet leader, who not long ago dismissed the idea as "rubbish," today seemed to soften his longstanding opposition to the prospect of genuine political competition. He repeated his contention that creating more parties "is not a solution," but he stopped short of condemning the idea. . . .

Mr. Yeltsin, considered a popular figure but a temperamental administrator, resigned from the ruling Politburo in 1987, complaining of obstruction by Yegor K. Ligachev, then the party ideologist.

He was drummed out of his Moscow party leadership after a ritual denunciation by his comrades but allowed to keep a high-ranking post in the Construction Ministry, which he must forfeit when he assumes his legislative post.

His campaign to win the congressional seat in what is known officially as National District No. 1 became a vehicle for a multitude of public discontents.

Among intellectuals, many had misgivings about Mr. Yeltsin's maverick qualities, his upbringing as a Communist Party apparatchik, and his suspiciousness on such issues as private business. But in these circles, his candidacy represented the seed of an opposition that would goad the party leadership toward wider civil rights and pluralism.

"Perhaps he does not represent the democratic ideal, but he represents the hope for change," said Viktoriya O. Chalikova, a sociologist interviewed after voting for Mr. Yeltsin at a polling station in south Moscow. . . .

"I hope this is all for real," said Boris Mamedov, a court clerk, at his voting place in south Moscow. "We've never had anything like it before— discussions, debates, fighting. Before people dropped a piece of paper in a slot. You couldn't describe it as a choice." Aleksandr A. Sokolov, an artist interviewed after voting in the city center, added: "The real test of this election is whether the people we elect stick to their principles and ideals. If not, this will turn out to be just like all the elections in the past."

The voters, having been given the right of choice and discretion, apparently used it.

Soviet Voters Deal Humiliating Blow to Party Officials

By Bill Keller

MOSCOW, March 27—The Soviet electorate has dealt a mortifying rebuke to the high and mighty in elections for a new national congress, including stunning upsets of a Politburo member and several other senior Communist Party officials who ran without opposition.

Results piling up today from the freest nationwide elections since 1917 showed that the mayor and the second-ranking Communist official of Moscow, the Communist Party leader in Leningrad, the commander of the Northern Fleet, the President and Premier of Lithuania, the Estonian K.G.B. chief, the commander of Soviet troops in East Germany and other prominent officials were defeated by candidates promising more rapid change.

The elections on Sunday, for the new and theoretically powerful Congress of People's Deputies, swept in a substantial minority of independent candidates, planting the seeds of the first national opposition since the time of Lenin. . . .

The more independent candidates have, almost without exception, pledged their loyalty to Mr. Gorbachev and his program of political and economic change.

The Soviet leader may thus use his new parliament—which he is expected to head from the newly enhanced post of President—to push his program faster than hard-liners the party would like.

But Mr. Gorbachev may also find that a free-thinking legislature will make his life more difficult, with some nationalist deputies threatening to bolt from the Soviet Union and reformers impatient for more radical change than even he wants.

The best known of the victorious candidates in Sunday's elections, Mr. Yeltsin, fell from Mr. Gorbachev's favor because he became impatient with change, and Mr. Gorbachev on election day pointedly warned against "great leaps."

The campaign over, Mr. Gorbachev went on the first of what were to be several foreign visits, a voyage to Cuba. As elsewhere he was widely seen an apostle for liberalized Communism, something that Fidel Castro, his host, found reproachful.

Gorbachev-Castro Face-Off: A Clash of Style and Policies
By Bill Keller

HAVANA, April 1—The guest is Mikhail S. Gorbachev, the smooth salesman of new Communist pragmatism, who preaches economic experimentation, social liberalization and peaceful coexistence.

The host is Fidel Castro, the khaki-clad revolutionary ideologue, who has said of Mr. Gorbachev's new doctrine: "Perestroika is another man's wife. I don't want to get involved."

Their meeting, which is to begin Sunday with a carefully staged welcome by half a million Cubans in the streets of Havana, will be Mr. Gorbachev's diplomatic debut in America's tropical backyard.

The Soviet leader's task will be to see if Cuba—long an outpost of Leninist orthodoxy and an agent of international revolution—can be made a partner in spreading the Gorbachev image of Communism in Latin America.

According to Soviet officials, Mr. Gorbachev would like to encourage domestic changes in Cuba that would ease the burden of bankrolling Mr. Castro's vision of Communism.

By American estimates, Moscow pays $6 billion to $8 billion a year to arm Mr. Castro's military and to prop up Cuba's economy, mostly by buying sugar at inflated prices and selling Soviet oil at a discount. . . .

Gorbachev Begins His Visit to Cuba with Castro's Hug
By Bill Keller

HAVANA, April 2—Mikhail S. Gorbachev arrived in Cuba tonight to an effusive welcome from one of his prickliest allies, Fidel Castro.

On his first diplomatic venture to Latin America, the Soviet leader was greeted with a bear hug and kisses by Mr. Castro, who depends heavily on Soviet subsidies but has little use for Mr. Gorbachev's more flexible brand of Communism.

Mr. Castro turned out much of Havana for the occasion and turned on the charm, clearly hoping to dispel any impression of friction.

Mr. Gorbachev's mission is apparently to reassure the Cuban leader of continued friendship while enlisting his support for economic restructuring and detente diplomacy. . . .

For many Cubans, the visit and speeches will be their first detailed exposure to the Soviet leader.

Mr. Gorbachev's speeches and programs are reported selectively here in the Government-controlled press. Spanish-language Soviet publications are difficult to come by, and many residents profess only scant knowledge of the competitive elections, the freer debate and the market-oriented economic experiments under way in the Soviet Union.

"It is not permitted," said one worshiper this morning at Corpus Christi Roman Catholic Church in the Miromar neighborhood of Havana. "Nothing is permitted here."

As the ten o'clock Mass ended, several parishioners stood by the pews of the church, and after assuring themselves that visiting American reporters were not state security policemen, they spoke excitedly of their hopes that Mr. Gorbachev's visit would inspire a political liberalization, including greater religious freedom.

Parishioners said they had gotten most of their news about Mr. Gorbachev from Radio Marti, the United States Government station that Mr. Castro regards as a vehicle of imperialist propaganda.

"Cuba needs perestroika and glasnost," said one woman, who asked that her name not be used because "you will leave, but we have to stay."

"God has put Gorbachev in the world, and we are grateful," she added.

Silvia Valdez, a teacher of Spanish literature, hailed Mr. Gorbachev as "a man who understands that his country has problems, and he is doing things to change it."

"We hope he will bring about a change in Cuba, to make it more democratic," she said. . . .

Sitting with friends on the crowded beach at the city's eastern edge, Armando Ramos, a young warehouse worker, said: "I understand very well Mr. Gorbachev's reforms. But I also understand the process here. In the future I think we will probably have the same process here as they have in the Soviet Union. But not now. We're not at the same stage of development. We have a long way to go." . . .

Gorbachev Signs Treaty with Cuba
By Bill Keller

HAVANA, April 4—Mikhail S. Gorbachev called today for an end to all outside military aid to Latin America, and signed a friendship treaty with Cuba condemning the use of force as an instrument of foreign policy.

In a speech to the Cuban National Assembly that had been billed as the high point of his first visit to the region, Mr. Gorbachev presented no specific new initiatives, confounding speculation that he would outline a peace plan for Central America or would cancel Cuba's huge debt.

The Soviet leader was upstaged by his host, Fidel Castro, who turned his introductory remarks into a blistering anti-American diatribe that seemed to raise serious doubt about whether the two Communist leaders had come to a meeting of the minds. Mr. Castro spoke for 45 minutes, almost as long as Mr. Gorbachev.

While praising Mr. Gorbachev as a peacemaker and reformer, Mr. Castro left little doubt that he did not intend to follow Mr. Gorbachev's conciliatory approach to the United States or his formula for internal economic and political change. . . .

In Warsaw the round-table talks between Communists and those who had challenged them under the banner of Solidarity were proving remarkably fruitful. Government officials and people they had imprisoned were exchanging handshakes and were making progress on a plan for free elections that went beyond anything ever put forth in any Communist country.

Poland Sets Free Vote in June, First Since '45; Solidarity Reinstated
By John Tagliabue

WARSAW, April 5—The leaders of Solidarity signed accords with the Government today restoring the banned union's legal status and providing for the first free and open elections in this country since World War II.

If carried out, the accords could markedly change the political system in this country, one of the first to be put under Soviet domination after the war. The political structure in Poland was more or less followed in the other countries that one by one were attached to the Soviet bloc in the late 1940's.

Poland was the first Soviet-dominated satellite to achieve a measure of independence in 1956, and it now appears that Poles, driven by economic disaster, have taken advantage of the changes wrought in the Soviet Union by Mikhail S. Gorbachev to forge new agreements that go well beyond anything current in the bloc.

These will be the most immediate effects of the accords:

- Restoration of Solidarity, the trade union that was formed in 1980 and then crushed after martial law was imposed in December 1981. The farmers union, Rural Solidarity, and the Independent Student Association, will also be restored to legal status.
- Elections in June for a two-house parliament, in which 35 percent of the 460 seats in the newly structured lower house will be allocated to delegates of the Solidarity-based opposition. The Communists will have another 38 percent, and parties formerly aligned with the Communists the rest.
- Restoration of Poland's upper house of Parliament, which was disbanded after World War II. It will have 100 members, who will be chosen in free and open elections. The upper house will be able to veto legislation of the lower house.
- Establishment of the post of president of the republic; the holder will be elected by the two houses of Parliament for a six-year term. The President will have broad powers to dissolve Parliament, and to veto laws passed by the lower house. The lower house can overturn vetoes by a two-third vote.
- Broad changes in the running of the economy, including the installment of a wage indexing plan, by which workers and retired people will receive compensation to 80 percent of any increase in the cost of living.

The announcement of the accords was broadcast on national television, a measure of the change already wrought since the Government began serious talks with Solidarity last August, after years of repression that culminated last year in two serious waves of labor unrest.

The current Sejm, or Parliament, is expected to meet on Friday to make the agreements into law.

Today's developments came at a formal closing session of the round-table talks, which began eight weeks ago. The ceremony today involved the Interior Minister, Gen. Czeslaw Kiszczak, and Lech Walesa, the Nobel Peace laureate and leader of Solidarity.

Mr. Walesa endorsed the accords in a 10-minute speech after General Kiszczak addressed the round table.

For Mr. Walesa it was an almost dizzying moment of triumph: The union leader congratulating the Communist official who, together with Gen. Wojciech Jaruzelski, was one of the people who engineered the imposition of martial law on December 13, 1981, and ordered the imprisonment of nearly all the union leaders, Mr. Walesa included.

The most ambitious gains, after the union's legalization, appeared to have come in the political agreement. It announced that the authorities would cede 35 percent of the 460 seats of the lower house of Parliament, leaving the Communist Party with only 38 percent, a minority for the first time since 1944. The remainder of the seats will fall to small parties that until now have been faithful allies of the Communists in a ruling coalition.

Perhaps the most startling concession, however, was the Government's agreement to restore Poland's upper house of Parliament with free and open elections. The upper house was abolished in 1946 in a rigged referendum, although some of the elections that year were free. The Government also agreed to create the office of president, who will be elected by a joint session of both houses. It is generally accepted that General Jaruzelski will be chosen the first president, for a six-year term, with the possibility of one more term. . . .

The Government also agreed to make the state-controlled press available to Solidarity by allowing the union a half hour of air time weekly on television and one hour weekly of radio time. In addition the union will be allowed its own daily national newspaper and regional weekly papers. Government censorship is to be eased, though not abolished.

The agreements require the Government to make broad changes to assure the independence of judges and the courts, to assure that Poles can freely form associations and clubs, though not political parties, and to bring about an overhaul of the economy. . . .

Mr. Walesa, a 45-year-old shipyard electrician who in August 1980 founded Solidarity, said: "I have to emphasize that for the first time we have talked to each other using the force of arguments, and not arguments of force. It bids well for the future, I believe, that the round-table discussions can become the beginning of the road for democracy and a free Poland."

"Either we'll be able to build Poland as a nation in a peaceful way, independent, sovereign and safe, with equal alliances," he said, "or we'll sink in the chaos of demagogy, which could result in civil war in which there will be no victors."

General Kiszczak seemed to be playing down the notion that the Government had surrendered substantial ground. "There's only one victor, the nation, our fatherland," he said.

Walesa Isn't Among Candidates Solidarity Lists for June Elections
By John Tagliabue

WARSAW, April 13—Solidarity spokesmen said today that several of the union's most prominent national advisers would lead its slate in open elections for Parliament.

The slate is to include Adam Michnik, an influential theoretician of Solidarity; Jacek Kuron, a former Communist and leading dissident whom Mr. Michnik has often described as his mentor, and Ryszard Bugaj, one of the union's leading economic strategists.

At a news conference in Gdansk, Lech Walesa, the Nobel Peace Prize winner and founder of the union, said that despite "strong pressure" for him to run, he did not intend to be a candidate for office in the coming elections, which essentially pit the ruling Communists against the Solidarity-based opposition.

Instead, Mr. Walesa told reporters of his intention to run in 1995 for President of Poland, an office that is to be restored under the accords last week between the authorities and Solidarity. . . .

For those Poles who had been waging an anti-totalitarian struggle, it was a time of both jubilation and confusion. They had battled and sacrificed for the idea of democracy, but few had ever experienced it in practice. They had been excellent dissidents, which meant standing up, telling the truth and if necessary, going to jail. Now, however, what was needed were politicians, not dissidents, and politics has to do largely with compromise. In the transformation an underground paper that had defied censorship was turned into a legal journal that accepted restrictions, and men who had been sent to prison were campaigning to to enter a parliament that seemed destined to be dominated by the same men who had imprisoned them.

For Paper, Jungle (and Censor) Await
By John Tagliabue

WARSAW, April 21—This month, the most influential source of un-censored information in Poland was laid to rest. Next month it will be reborn as the first independently published daily newspaper in the East bloc.

The new national daily, which will be the election campaign publi-cation of Poland's newly legalized Solidarity trade union, will be under Government censorship as it prepares voters for democratic elections in June. The paper, which has no name, will probably be called simply *Gazeta*.

The weekly it is replacing is *Tygodnik Mazowsze*, or Weekly of Mazowia, in central Poland. The weekly was founded in 1982 and became one of hundreds of underground publications, from a chil-dren's magazine to scholarly quarterlies, that shielded the flame of Solidarity.

Despite raids and arrests, *Tygodnik Mazowsze* became an institu-tion, with an average printing that opposition sources said was around 15,000 copies. But the new paper, unlike the old one, will be subject to censorship, a condition demanded by Government negotiators at the recent round-table talks with Solidarity that produced the legal-ization of the union and an agreemnent on sweeping political and economic change in Poland.

"How do we justify it?" asked Helena Luczywo, a principal editor of *Tygodnik Mazowsze*, who will be responsible for running the new paper. "It will be a daily paper with much bigger circulation, much bigger access. We could stay underground. I do think others might stay underground. But it's an opportunity, because 500,000 copies can be published daily and sold legally in the kiosks."

Adam Michnik, one of the opposition movement's most influential intellectuals, will be editor in chief and bear final responsibility. But Mrs. Luczywo, who began her career in opposition journalism in 1977 at Robotnik, an underground publication, will head day-to-day opera-tions.

"It is impossible to have a daily newspaper in Poland without censorship," said Mrs. Luczywo, who gained familiarity with Ameri-can newspapers while at Radcliffe in 1986.

"But here I will be pragmatic," she added, sipping tea in her apartment, which is also the site of editorial meetings. "In a sense this is what we did at the round-table talks. You give up something to get something. It's a calculation."

Mrs. Luczywo said the first edition, scheduled to appear in early May, will have eight pages in tabloid format, which may be supplemented later by an advertising insert. The layout, she said, was developed with the help of French designers on loan from the Parisian daily *Liberation*.

"The main problem," she said, "will be the reliability of information. We think a staff of around 50 people will be enough, and there is a small Solidarity news agency. But there is not a good tradition of reliable information." . . .

Seasoned underground reporters like Mrs. Luczywo recall that *Tygodnik Mazowsze*, over its 290 issues, changed format several times according to supplies, missing a week or even two and at times even appearing on green paper once.

Technologically, too, Mrs. Luczywo acknowledged, legalization will be a setback. In recent years the underground weekly has been published on personal computers with laser printers. But the printing house assigned to the above-ground weekly, which it will share with the Communist Party's own daily, *Trybuna Ludu*, has no such sophisticated equipment. . . .

Slogans Ready, Solidarity Takes Stab at the Hustings
By John Tagliabue

CRACOW, Poland, May 7—In a concrete schoolyard in the Nowa Huta district of Cracow, Mieczyslaw Gil's jabbing hand seemed to be poking a hole in a wall of popular doubt about Poland's coming elections.

Three years ago, Mr. Gil sat in prison, serving a four-year term handed down by a military court for his role in setting up Solidarity in 1980 as the East bloc's first free trade union.

Roughly a year ago, fleeing the police and finding shelter in colleagues' apartments and church cellars, Mr. Gil steered the strikes that crippled Nowa Huta's enormous steel mill, ultimately pressuring the Government to recognize Solidarity and introduce sweeping political and economic changes.

Today the burly 45-year-old steel worker is Soldarity candidate in cantankerous Nowa Huta, a Solidarity stronghold, struggling to convince workers that acceptance of elections that are not entirely free—

though the freest Poland has known since World War II—was the politically correct answer to the Government's offer to restore Solidarity.

"These are not yet entirely free elections," Mr. Gil shouted to several hundred Solidarity stalwarts. "In '81 they first legalized us, then crushed us. There will be more seasonal gestures, and we fear that the same thing can happen again. So we are creating democratic institutions to make it less likely."

Glancing over at Edward Nowak, a lanky 39-year-old steelman and Solidarity veteran who shared the platform, Mr. Gil said, "When we sat in the same cell in jail, we never thought we'd be candidates together."

Most of the crowd of several hundred Solidarity supporters would have shared Mr. Gil's incredulity, for in the last few weeks, as the campaign warms up for the elections next month, the unheard of has become the routine. . . .

In at least three areas of Poland, Solidarity has accused the police of tearing down Solidarity campaign posters, and last week Solidarity's national spokesman, Janusz Onyszkiewicz, said the union was dissatisfied with the party's observance of agreements on the number of seats the opposition can contest.

But in Cracow and neighboring towns, large white posters urge: "Vote for Solidarity: Elections '89." Newsstands in Cracow, including those in the principal hotels, sell copies of a local Solidarity weekly, *Glos Wyborczy Solidarnosci*, or Solidarity's Election Voice, whose first issue printed the schedule of Solidarity radio programs.

Poles have already grown used to seeing Solidarity leaders in televised debates, though the union's leaders say coverage by the state television can still be manipulative. Last week, when the union strategist, Adam Michnik, debated the campaign in Gdansk, television broadcast only snippets of remarks highly flattering to the Polish leader, Gen. Wojciech Jaruzelski.

An editorial in the Cracow paper's first issue—published over a cartoon of Karl Marx begging on a streetcorner, hat in outstretched hand—said, "Poland Returns to Europe." . . . Over tripe soup and a pork schnitzel, Mr. Gil reflected on the campaign. "Most difficult to answer are the basic questions involving trust and doubt," he said. "They still don't really believe in it."

"But slowly, slowly a mood is building," he went on. "People are becoming aware of enormous changes."

At the rally Saturday in Nowa Huta, Mr. Nowak got the most

applause when he summed up his view of Communist Poland since the war.

"For forty years we've been driving in one car," he said. "They're trying to paint it, to fix it, repair it. We have to change to another car."

SPRING 1989

Something was stirring in China. On April 15, Hu Yaobang, the maverick who had sought to steer China away from Communist orthodoxy, died at the age of 73. He had reportedly suffered a heart attack at a politburo meeting a week earlier. He had been on the Long March in 1934 and 1935 and he lived through the Cultural Revolution, when his head was shaved and he was sent to the countryside to tend livestock. But then after Mao died in 1977, he and his mentor Deng Xiaoping mounted a slow but steady return to power. Then in 1987 he was again forced out of the innermost circles of leadership after a siege of student demonstrations. More than any of the Chinese oligarchs, he had captured the hearts of young people, and within days of his death, students at Beijing University sneaked off at night to hang up illegal posters that expressed sadness and guilt. In the middle of April, Nicholas D. Kristoff wrote in **The Times** that "The common theme in the posters was that the wrong leader had died." Among the messages he noted in the poster campaign were "Xiaoping is still healthy at the age of 84. Yaobang, only 73 years old, has died first," and, "When you were deprived of your post, why didn't we stand up? We feel guilty. Our conscience bleeds." In the last two weeks of April the students became bolder with each passing day, moving out from the campuses onto the streets. Their marches grew steadily in size, surging ever closer to the seat of political power.

Urging Chinese Democracy, 100,000 Surge Past Police

By Nicholas D. Kristof

BEIJING, May 4—A defiant and enthusiastic crowd of more than 100,000 workers and students forced its way through police cordons in the capital today to demand more democracy, and smaller demonstrations were held in many other cities around China.

The occasion for the marches today was the 70th anniversary of famous nationalist demonstrations in Beijing that led to the May 4 Movement, which led a generation of Chinese intellectuals to seek a major re-examination of Chinese society. The movement also foreshadowed the rise of the Communist Party.

By far the largest demonstration outside Beijing was in Shanghai, China's largest city, where the crowd suddenly swelled tonight to perhaps 20,000 or more, said a Western resident of the city who witnessed the march.

The flurry of demonstrations was among the largest in Communist China's history, and in Beijing the protest appeared to draw record numbers of workers.

While the nucleus of the crowd was still students, they were easily outnumbered by the young workers who came to express dissatisfaction with the inflation, corruption and other frustrations that most bother them. Inflation is running at a rate of about 27 percent a year.

"I hope student demonstrations will make the Government do something about inflation," said Yuan Jun, an iron worker who came from out of town to join in the demonstration. "But even if the students don't bring up the inflation problem, I'll still support them. They demand press freedom, which is something we need, too. Now we have no freedom at all."

Worker participation in the recent unrest has been one of the Government's greatest fears, but today the workers still seemed to be coalescing around the students rather than forming their own organizations. This is likely to give the Government some reprieve, particularly as most of the students seem to be planning to end their class boycott and focus their attention once more on their books.

Wuer Kaixi, a student leader, told the crowd that the students reserved the right to hold further demonstrations, but for now there was no clear issue that seemed likely to send large numbers of them into the streets.

Their protests began as mourning for Hu Yaobang, the dismissed Communist Party leader who died April 15, and then drew inspiration in the approach to today's anniversary of the founding of the May 4 Movement.

Important anniversaries often carry more political significance and resonance in China than they would in the West. Because the original May 4 protesters—numbering only 3,000—have been sanctified by history, both the Government and the students have been jostling to gain the legitimacy that comes with being seen as the rightful inheritors of the May 4 legacy.

The Communist Party held its own parades and festivals today to commemmorate the anniversary, but they paled beside the outpouring for the students' illegal march.

In the northeastern city of Changchun, 8,000 to 10,000 student demonstrators gathered at the provincial headquarters this afternoon, while in the port city of Dalian more than 2,000 students from several universities marched for democracy, a Western diplomat said tonight.

In addition, the diplomat said, student demonstrators in the northeastern cities of Shenyang and Harbin were locked into their campuses and not allowed to march onto the streets.

Other small demonstrations also occurred today in the cities of Changsha, Nanjing, Wuhan and Xian, reports reaching Beijing said.

The protests today were a display of support for the students and their demands—particularly freedom of the press, which has become an increasingly important issue in the last few weeks. But the march in Beijing lacked the drama and fervor of the protest a week ago, which is already being viewed as a historic occasion by students and intellectuals in China.

On that occasion, a crackdown seemed imminent, and army troops had been called in to stop the students. Some thought that the demonstration would fizzle completely, and yet more than 150,000 protesters, applauded by hundreds of thousands of cheering onlookers, swept through the city like a liberating army, forcing the Government to back away from the repression that had apparently been planned.

Perhaps it was only a sign of how much has changed in the last two weeks that today a crowd of more than 100,000 could roll through police lines to take over Tiananmen Square, the political focal point of the nation, without anyone registering much surprise.

"The Government can't crack down on us," said a worker in a radio factory who took part in today's march, "because 90 percent of the population supports the students."

Several hundred journalists for official publications gathered today in front of the official New China News Agency to protest false and biased reporting and to call for the reinstatement of Qin Benli, the editor of a Shanghai newspaper and one of the boldest journalists in the country. Mr. Qin was dismissed last week after insisting on publishing comments that supported student demonstrators.

Students were delighted to receive support from the journalists, and as they marched by they shouted, "Long live journalists with a conscience!"

The journalists shouted back: "We support you! Long live the students!"

The audacity of the students was spreading. In early May, more and more workers were joining in the marches and journalists were also finding their voices.

China Newspapers Try New Openness
By Sheryl WuDunn

BEIJING, May 5—After studiously ignoring pro-democracy protests for the last two weeks, China's official newspapers seemed today to display a new openness in their reports of a mass demonstration held here on Thursday.

Photographs of streets filled with students waving banners as far as the eye could see ran on the front pages of most newspapers. The newspapers also reported details of demonstrations not only in the capital but in many other cities. Some of those demonstrations had not previously been reported.

The largest demonstration was in Beijing, where 100,000 people gathered in the central square to call for greater democracy and an end to corruption.

China Youth News reported demonstrations in at least 11 cities outside Beijing, and reported that in Shanghai, Xian and Wuhan, more than 10,000 students took part. The other cities were Changsha, Hangzhou, Nanjing, Taiyuan, Chengdu, Chongqing, Lanzhou, and Xining.

More accurate reporting has been one of the demonstrators' principal demands, and today's articles and photos seemed to be a move to satisfy the demand. While the articles were not as comprehensive as the students would have liked, the surprise was that they appeared at all.

The articles noted that the demonstrations were called on the occasion of the 70th anniversary of the nationalist demonstrations that led to the May 4 Movement. The movement called for China's political and cultural modernization and led to the birth of the Chinese Communist Party. To some extent, the articles tried to portray the demonstrators as patriotic citizens commemorating a historic occasion.

But the articles also referred explicitly to the demands of the student demonstrators who blanketed Tiananmen Square for an afternoon of speeches, chanting and singing.

"Several hundred thousand spectators watched the students marching along the streets, and many of them donated cold drinks and food," read part of an article from the official People's Daily. "As long as there is corruption, this country will never be stable," the article quoted a banner as saying.

Such articles were unusual only given the Government's previous determination to avoid references to the demonstrations. It is not clear if today's articles and photos in the official press mark a permanent step toward openness that will let Chinese people learn about events as they happen.

Today's newspapers also quoted the Communist Party General Secretary, Zhao Ziyang, as saying that corruption occurs partly because there is a "lack of openness in the system of work." That seemed to be another call for more openness in Chinese society, one of the major student demands.

University students said today that they had no immediate plans for further demonstrations.

From the outset, the students in China, like the Polish workers in Solidarity, had stressed nonviolence, but in Beijing the demonstrators were evolving their own specific form of petition and protest.

A Chinese Lesson in Polite Protest
By Nicholas D. Kristof

BEIJING, May 6—For anyone tempted to think that rebellious Chinese students must be fighting for capitalism and multi-party democracy, a banner fluttering over People's University marchers on Thursday was a rude shock. It read, "We firmly support the correct leadership of the Communist Party."

If South Korean university students are at the militant extreme, totally rejecting the Government and battering lines of police with firebombs and wooden staves, then Chinese demonstrators are at the peaceful extreme.

They sometimes go out of their way to say nice things about the Communist Party, even when it is clear they do not believe them, and they overwhelm the police as much with courtesy as with force.

When approaching lines of the police, the students try to ingratiate themselves by chanting, "The people love the people's police; the people's police love the people." After some hard pushing, but never any blows, the police usually give way to the students.

That is when the demonstrators pause to bellow, "Thank you, police." A few students are even assigned to pick up any shoes lost in the shoving and return them to their owners, be they police or protesters.

Such tactics, which resemble those employed in the Philippine uprising rather than those in South Korea, have been enormously successful so far. It has been difficult for the Communist Party to crack down on those who politely call on the party to uphold its own ideals of honesty and democracy. And the students' charm has won grins and support from many ordinary workers.

Student comments in favor of Communist rule are perhaps more difficult to decipher, but interviews with dozens of students in the last two weeks suggest that they are partly tactical and partly sincere. Early last week, when the Government seemed about to proclaim a crackdown against students who it said wanted to overthrow the socialist system and Communist rule, many student leaders seemed to feel that their best defense was to deny the charges and wage their struggle for more democracy in the guise of a devoted attempt to cleanse the party of its faults.

The fiercest slogans—like "Overthrow the dictatorship!"—were mostly replaced by slogans like "Down with graft!" Students also began to wave pro-Communist banners, rather like amulets intended to ward off the police.

Yet the slogans are not only a form of protection, for many students genuinely believe in Communist Party rule. Or, perhaps more accurately, they genuinely believe that there is no alternative any time soon to Communist Party rule.

"In an ideal world, a multi-party system would be better," said Xia A. P., a graduate student in politics who has taken part in the demonstrations. "But it's not feasible now. We want what is practical."

"It would be difficult for the Communist Party to move forward without a push," Mr. Xia added. "The aim of the student movement is to give the Communist Party an outside push so that it can reform itself."

Several of the student movement's leaders have said that they would consider joining the Communist Party at some point in their careers. Even Wang Dan, the Beijing University student leader who is regarded as among the most aggressive in the movement, scarcely paused when he was asked if he supported the leading role of the Communist Party in China.

"You can say I support correct leadership by the Communist Party," Mr. Wang said, putting emphasis on the word "correct." He seemed to mean that he was willing to tolerate the leading role of the party, so long as it was upright and permitted greater democracy.

When a group of students at Qinghua University was asked if they opposed the Communist Party, they mustered as much indignation as possible.

"The reason we demonstrate is that we still have some faith in the Communist Party," one said.

Another added: "We're not against the Government, just against the way it is run. It's a question of the party atmosphere, of corruption and of the bureaucracy."

Then the students looked a bit uneasy, as if they might be giving a foreign reporter the wrong idea about their goals. One ventured: "Remember, though, we can't always say what we think."

In private, students express almost no interest in socialism or communism as an ideology, and say instead that they favor whatever will make China strong and rich. But in the absence of any realistic alternative, and to avoid being labeled as counterrevolutionaries, they are willing to say they support the Communist Party.

Even this degree of consensus seems to break down when students contemplate the economy. When they are asked if they favor capitalism or socialism, the overwhelming majority of students reply that they do not know.

"I haven't thought about that," said Xiong Wei, a 22-year-old electrical engineer and student leader.

As the protests mounted, the old men who ruled China intensified their deliberations on whether to try to accommodate the demands, co-opt, divert, or crush those who were raising them. As an atmosphere of crisis thickened, the advocates of gentler approaches clashed with those who argued for harsh responses.

China Party Chief Appears to Gain in Power Struggle

By Nicholas D. Kristof

BEIJING, May 13—An unannounced Politburo meeting has endorsed the moderate line of the Communist Party leader, Zhao Ziyang, toward student demonstrators, including more discussions with the students and limited steps toward greater democracy, Chinese with high party connections say.

The situation remains extremely unsettled, as the debate over recent student demonstrations continues to reverberate through the leadership and exacerbate the power struggle here. However, three Chinese familiar with the Politburo proceedings say that the result of a tense meeting held on Wednesday and Thursday in the capital was to strengthen Mr. Zhao's faction, favoring more rapid economic and political change over one preferring a more cautious path.

The result, at least for now, is a reversal in the fortunes of Mr. Zhao, whose influence had slipped greatly over the last year and reached its nadir at the beginning of the student protests last month. Many of the students had worried that their demonstrations might lead to his dismissal.

The eventual outcome of the party's internal conflicts remains uncertain, however, and officials say that further student demonstrations might affect the competition and possibly hurt Mr. Zhao. Today, students continued their protests by taking a new tactic and going on a hunger strike to back their demands for more democracy and a meaningful dialogue with the nation's leaders.

More than 20,000 spectators watched in Beijing's Tiananmen Square as more than 1,000 university students staged the strike in the middle of the square. Some students said they would remain until Mikhail S. Gorbachev, the Soviet leader, arrives on Monday for the first Chinese-Soviet summit meeting in 30 years. . . .

And indeed, Mr. Gorbachev was once again being cast in the role of a catalyst. The apostle of economic modernization and some greater though still limited freedom of expression was being hailed in China as a man pointing the way out of a fossilized system just as he had been welcomed on earlier trips abroad to such places as Hungary and Czechoslovakia.

China's Hero of Democracy: Gorbachev

By Nicholas D. Kristof

BEIJING, May 13—When Mikhail S. Gorbachev arrives on Monday for four days of talks designed to restore normal relations between China and the Soviet Union, he will be cast in the unusual role of champion of democracy.

It is the role that American Presidents like to fill, but there is much more anticipation in China's democratic movement today than there was on the eve of President Bush's visit in February. Almost everybody seems to think that the Soviet leader's visit will do more for democracy in China than Mr. Bush's trip did, and some believe that the Soviet Union will do more than the United States to inspire political liberalization in China.

"China used to be afraid of influence from the West," said Yan Jiaqi, a prominent political scientist and supporter of greater democracy. "Now we are afraid of influence from the Soviet Union.

"If we want to keep out Western influence, we can say we're against 'bourgeois liberalization,' or against 'total Westernization,' " Mr. Yan added. "But we can't use that pretext against Soviet influence. Nobody, not even Deng Xiaoping, can resist the Soviet influence, because there is no ideological concept to resist it."

The perception of Mr. Gorbachev as an evangelist for democracy might surprise some political dissidents in the Soviet Union, and it has little to do with the real purposes of his talks with Chinese leaders from Monday through Thursday. The agenda of the summit includes trade, economic cooperation and the Cambodian conflict, not democracy and human rights.

Nonetheless, the enthusiasm for Mr. Gorbachev is a tribute to the extent to which he has opened up the political system in the Soviet Union. It is a commonplace, here as well as abroad, that China has gone further than the Soviet Union in economic liberalization but that the Soviet Union has done much more in political liberalization.

The result is not quite Soviet fever, for most intellectuals here seem much more interested in visiting New York than Leningrad. Many seem to regard the Soviet restructuring less as a model to be meticulously examined than as a key debating point to push for change in China.

The support for Mr. Gorbachev is a deep embarrassment for the man who otherwise might well regard the summit as a personal triumph: Deng Xiaoping. Mr.Gorbachev is coming to Beijing mostly on Mr. Deng's terms, having withdrawn troops from Afghanistan, reduced Soviet forces on the Chinese border and brought pressure on Vietnam to end its occupation of Cambodia. Moreover, this may be one of Mr. Deng's last major acts, for the capital is full of rumors of his impending retirement.

Mr. Deng, however, has been humiliated by the recent student demonstrations, and by the successful defiance of his order last month that they be suppressed. After having made his career as a daring reformer, Mr. Deng is suddenly made to look like a stodgy old man outshined by the strong young socialist dynamo from Moscow.

The contrasts have been evident even in the Chinese press. The *China Youth News* published a long account in which a Soviet citizen was quoted as saying that before Mr. Gorbachev "our country was run by old and sickly people who need help to walk, who lack the breath to speak, whose minds are stiff and muddled." In a country where criticisms are always made indirectly, this appeared to be a comment on Mr. Deng and a call for "a young and strong leader," as the article described Mr. Gorbachev.

The differences are also evident on China's campuses, where the talk is often bitterly critical of Mr. Deng these days. At Beijing University, the most important institution in the country, thousands of students have signed an open letter inviting Mr. Gorbachev to speak at the school. The authorities have said that Mr. Gorbachev's schedule is full, but the gesture was an indication that many students who dislike their own leader regard Mr. Gorbachev as a hero. . . .

The arrival of Mr. Gorbachev in Peking, on a visit that had been scheduled long before, would have been historic even without the growing uproar in the streets. The Soviet leader had come to signal an end to the split between the world's two most powerful Communist states. But the noises and shouts raised by ordinary people were clearly being heard in the chambers where the leaders meeting.

Gorbachev Meets Deng in Beijing; Protest Goes On
By Nicholas D. Kristof

BEIJING, Tuesday, May 16—Deng Xiaoping and Mikhail S. Gorbachev shook hands today to signal the formal end of three decades of hostility between China and the Soviet Union.

The two leaders then met for two and a half hours. Afterward, Mr. Deng was the host at a banquet for the Soviet President.

The 84-year-old Mr. Deng, whose frailty and stumbling speech contrasted with the strength and vigor of the 58-year-old Mr. Gorbachev, said as they met that several years ago he had noted a new mood in the Soviet Union and had hoped for the summit meeting. Mr. Deng added that he believed the new Soviet outlook held the potential to help resolve what he described as the central problem in international affairs, the Soviet-American relationship.

"For a long time, cold war and confrontation have made the international situation tense," Mr. Deng, the foremost Chinese leader, said. "This leads nowhere."

The summit meeting, the first between the two countries since 1959, is described by both sides as marking the beginning of normalization of relations. However, the domestic atmosphere in Beijing was decidedly abnormal because of continuing protests.

In a major loss of face for the Chinese leadership, Monday's itinerary had to be repeatedly adjusted to avoid 150,000 students and spectators who took over Tiananmen Square. While Mr. Gorbachev, the Soviet leader, did not directly refer to the student demonstrations in his meeting on Monday with President Yang Shangkun, the entire day seemed to be an exotic dance in which the Chinese side tried to shield Mr. Gorbachev from the protesters.

The demonstrations were doubly embarrassing for the Chinese leaders because of the obvious enthusiasm that many of the protesters felt for Mr. Gorbachev. Several had prepared banners in Russian hailing him as a great reformer, and a crowd of workers and bicyclists applauded when he drove past them on his way to the Great Hall of the People.

Mr. Gorbachev was to lay a wreath at a monument in the center of the square, but because of the crowds of protesters occupying the area, the Chinese Government canceled the event this morning.

Because of the demonstrations, the Chinese Government held its welcoming ceremony for Mr. Gorbachev at the airport, instead of on the edge of the square where the students gathered. Officials then had to drive Mr. Gorbachev by a back road to his guest house when students blocked the avenue that had been decked with Soviet and Chinese flags in preparation for Mr. Gorbachev's entry.

Later, the Chinese postponed the discussions between Mr. Gorbachev and President Yang by two hours, and then changed the site of his arrival at the Great Hall of the People from the main entrance first to a side door and then to a back door.

Despite the adjustments and confusion, Mr. Gorbachev seemed in good spirits on Monday on the few occasions when it was possible to catch a glimpse of him. His plane touched down at noon, and he and his wife, Raisa, stepped out to a 21-gun salute and a welcome from the Moscow-educated Mr. Yang, who later practiced his rusty Russian on the Soviet leader. When driving around the capital, Mr. Gorbachev was grinning broadly as he waved to bystanders along the roads.

The meeting and banquet with President Yang, an 81-year-old veteran revolutionary whose post is largely honorary, was cordial and took as its tone the need to forget past differences and begin a new chapter in bilateral relations.

"There is no need for us to recollect the past," Mr. Yang said, quoting Mr. Deng. Mr. Gorbachev agreed, saying, "That is an approach that we welcome."

The meetings of leaders were having an impact on the streets.

150,000 Lift Their Voices for Change
By Sheryl WuDunn

BEIJING, May 15—One after another today, groups of teachers, professors, museum workers, factory workers, writers, artists, scholars, entrepreneurs, low-level officials, middle-school students, and even journalists from the official *People's Daily* paraded into Tiananmen Square behind their own wide, colorful banners.

They sang the "Internationale" and chanted anti-Government slogans, while inside in the adjacent Great Hall of the People, President Yang Shangkun held a banquet this evening for the Soviet leader, Mikhail S. Gorbachev.

The ebullient crowd of about 150,000 protesters and spectators rallied to show support for a hunger strike on the opening day of the first Chinese-Soviet summit meeting in 30 years. . . .

"In the Soviet Union, they have Gorbachev," read a banner carried by students. "In China, we have whom?" . . .

"Sell the Mercedes-Benzes to pay the national debt!" shouted several thousand citizens as they marched into Tiananmen Square, where the hunger strikers, visibly weakened on their third day without food, lay sprawled in one corner under the scorching sun.

"This day will go down in history," said Zhao Xiaoyan, a reporter with *Science and Technology Daily*, who marched to the square with a large group of journalists. "Today, we have gone beyond the students. It it clear that the Chinese people believe that the Communist Party cannot continue to adopt the kind of attitude it takes toward its people."

The diplomatic business was completed.

Soviets and China Resuming Normal Ties After 30 Years; Beijing Pledges "Democracy"
By Bill Keller

BEIJING, May 16—If Mikhail S. Gorbachev were to stray from his diplomatically constrained itinerary for a visit to the unofficial festival of democracy under way on Tiananmen Square, he would surely be flattered by the banners in Chinese and Russian hailing him as a champion of political liberty.

But as a Soviet consumer, he might be more impressed by the slogans in Japanese—Nikon, Panasonic, Ricoh, Olympus—displayed on the cameras and tape recorders wielded in profusion by the protesting Chinese students and their sympathizers.

While Mr. Gorbachev and China's leaders learn to like each other better, the citizens of the two giant neighbors are beginning to envy each other. Russia is getting freer, China is getting richer, and at the human level far below the meeting of the leaders, the people of each country are demanding more of what the other has.

The experts have long recognized that economic change—the breakup of collective farming, the growth of private commerce, the decentralization of industry—has progressed a good deal farther in China, while political liberalization—a less inhibited press, a measure of democracy, a promise of civil rights—is far more advanced in the Soviet Union.

Mr. Gorbachev's visit here has helped advertise this to the ordinary citizens of each country, and has also raised hopes that each can learn something from the other.

In Moscow, extensive and positive press coverage has been given to China's experiments with private farming and stock markets, as Soviet journalists decided that Mr. Gorbachev's visit made China topical.

And in Beijing, a consumer attuned to the paucity of Soviet consumer choice can only marvel at the things money will buy.

Within earshot of the student brass band that blared the "Internationale" for the occupiers of central Beijing this afternoon, a shopper finds stores stacked to the ceilings with Chinese and imported electronics, private shops displaying stylish shoes turned out by China-Hong Kong joint ventures, street vendors peddling strawberries and watermelons, and restaurants where the meals are cheap and decent. What is more, there is often quick and cordial service, something as exotic to Muscovites as the Forbidden City.

A bit of that in Moscow, and Mr. Gorbachev would be almost as popular at home as he is on Tiananmen Square.

In Beijing, the student bullhorns and bicycle brigades have quickly spread the word that the Soviet Union is a center of something vaguely known as political reform.

The students, joined each day by droves of journalists, intellectuals and factory workers, demand greater press freedom, free speech, the recognition of their independent students' unions, an attack on official corruption and legal safeguards against an authoritarian Government.

"We have rice, but we need laws," said a Beijing University language student who was pleased to learn from a Chinese television documentary this week that Mr. Gorbachev graduated from law school. "Many, many laws."

Mr. Gorbachev is less the inspiration for this movement than an opportunity to flaunt its demands in a way the leadership cannot ignore.

"As a great political reformer, we urge Mikhail Gorbachev to talk to the Government on our behalf, for humanitarian reasons," Wang Dan, a student leader from Beijing University, said at a news conference today. . . .

According to Zhang Binjiu, a research scholar at Beijing University, another Gorbachev-era event that struck a powerful chord here in this corruption-conscious society was the bribery trial last December of the son-in-law of Leonid I. Brezhnev, the former Soviet leader.

Most Chinese know few details of the Soviet experiment, but they declare with pride that given the chance they will quickly surpass it.

"The flowers of political reform blossom in the Soviet Union," Mr. Zhang said. "But the tree will bear fruit in China."

In truth, the grass is not as green in either China or Russia as it seems from across the border.

The chanting crowds in the center of Beijing might be disillusioned to learn that similar demonstrations in the Soviet Union are some-times set upon by riot policemen, that Moscow intellectuals consider their democracy still tenuous and halfway, and that some of the new Soviet laws impose new restrictions on protest and expression.

The Muscovite, in turn, might be disenchanted to learn that the VCR's freely available in Chinese cities cost an average worker's annual paycheck, to see the occasional run on the banks when a wave of inflation fever hits, or to visit the squalid, tenement-style dormito-ries in which the protesting students live six to a room.

The disparity in the two countries' routes from Communist or-thodoxy has its reasons. Deng Xiaoping, the senior Chinese leader, introduced his version of perestroika, called gaige, 10 years ago by freeing peasants to be private farmers. China started so far behind that things could hardly help but get demonstrably better.

The Soviet Union has implemented perestroika piecemeal, mostly in the last two years, and many of the proclaimed revisions have been thwarted by the dead weight of an outmoded industrial economy.

The Chinese, in turn, felt no pressure to democratize, and the aging leadership had no inclination to share the Communist Party's power.

Mr. Gorbachev, on the other hand, recognized that his sluggish and authoritarian bureaucracy was the worst impediment to moderniza-tion. That is why the Soviet leader came more quickly to the view that political and economic change must go hand in hand.

The Soviet Union, most Russians would agree, has not yet proved his point.

But the respective discontents of the Chinese and Soviet people have proven that neither economic freedom nor political freedom is wholly satisfying by itself.

Gorbachev Praises the Students and Declares Reform Is Necessary
By Bill Keller

BEIJING, May 17—Mikhail S. Gorbachev today portrayed the popu-lar uprising that has engulfed the Chinese capital as part of a painful but healthy worldwide upheaval in Communist countries.

In his most extensive comments on the demonstrations that have disrupted and overshadowed the Chinese-Soviet reconciliation here, Mr. Gorbachev cautiously praised the students who began the huge vigil for greater democracy and repeatedly declared that economic change was impossible without political reform.

"I am convinced that we are participating in a very serious turning point in the development of world socialism," the Soviet leader said at a news conference when asked to assess the unrest here and in his own country.

All Communist countries, he said, are headed at different paces toward greater freedom of expression, democracy and individual rights.

"These processes are painful, but they are necessary," he said.

The Soviet leader was careful not to be seen taking sides in the domestic political struggle provoked by the unrest, but it now appears clear he has used his three days in Beijing to encourage political liberalization and indirectly to do what he could to promote the aspirations of the self-styled reformer, Zhao Ziyang, the Chinese Communist Party leader, in an internal power struggle.

Mr. Gorbachev's comments today, in a speech to Chinese intellectuals, a televised interview and the news conference, also included calls for patience and discipline, but he avoided any direct criticism of the students.

In a meeting with Mr. Zhao on Tuesday, Mr. Gorbachev reportedly expressed his distaste for "hotheads" who demand that change be accomplished overnight. Today he said he had received a letter from the students praising the Soviet moves toward political liberalization, and added, "I value their position."

He commended the Chinese leadership for opening a political dialogue with the students, a conciliatory approach that initially met firm resistance from some senior Chinese leaders. . . .

Those within the Chinese leadership who might have been hoping that Mr. Gorbachev's visit and the declarations of restored amity with Moscow would appease or divert the protesters had their hopes dashed very quickly. Instead of quieting down, the crowds became even more insistent.

A Million Chinese March, Adding Pressure for Change

By Sheryl WuDunn

BEIJING, May 17—Sirens wailed as ambulances whizzed by, carrying hunger strikers who have fainted after five days without eating, when the gray-haired schoolteacher suddenly pulled out her handkerchief and cried.

"Our hearts bleed when we hear the sound of ambulances," she said, her voice breaking. "They are no longer children. They are the hope of China."

The teacher, like more than a million other people in the capital, had taken to the streets to support the hunger-striking students and express her demands for democracy. When a group of students approached, passing around a cardboard box to collect money for their cause, she reached into her faded purse and pulled out the equivalent of $5—a week's wages for her—and put it into the box.

"I want to thank them," she said, sniffling. "They represent our hearts. They represent our hopes." Scenes like that near Tiananmen Square—the Square of the Gate of Heavenly Peace—occurred all over central Beijing today, as office clerks, factory workers, bank tellers, journalists and taxicab drivers fought through vast seas of people to get near the enclave of hunger-striking students, now the center of China's swelling democracy movement.

The twist and tangle of people, bicycles, pedicabs, cars and banners froze the steady flow of traffic, and when protesters had no room to march, they cheerfully walked around in circles.

But as confusion bordering on chaos spread across the capital, with more and more people leaving their dank offices and small homes for the open air, a certain order is evident on the streets, revealing the touch of a tightly run organization of students.

Specially designated students used long ropes to keep a single lane free on the otherwise jammed Avenue of Eternal Peace and on Tiananmen Square, so that spectators did not get in the way of ambulances carrying hunger strikers.

The result is that the ambulances dash by at 40 miles an hour, while all around them are pedestrians who struggle even to inch forward through the mass of demonstrators.

Just a week or two ago, many Beijing residents patronized the students, saying they were a bit too idealistic and too inclined to tie up traffic with their demonstrations. But now the city's citizens, from the young entrepreneurs in business suits to the old ladies sitting in front of their homes, compete in praising the students.

"The student movement is terrific!" an elderly police officer shouted to a group of high school students and workers who had gathered to listen. "If the Government commands a crackdown, will I obey their order? No, I will go against it."

Marchers and spectators, chanting and singing and screaming, shoved their way back and forth on the Avenue of Eternal Peace in front of Zhongnanhai, the Communist Party headquarters, where the country's leaders live. Even late at night, the entrance was packed with 2,000 workers, students, and other protesters shouting for the Prime Minister: "Li Peng, come out! Li Peng, come out!" In the afternoon, students formed a semicircular human fence to protect the leaders' compound from the possibility of being stormed by angry workers. Just inside the human ring, but outside the doorway, students turned the area into a place for resting and eating.

Deep in the heart of Tiananmen Square, the nation's political center that the democracy fighters have now invaded, inside several rings of students, is a heavily guarded, peaceful, airy enclave where the senior student leaders confer with the hunger strikers and where the containers of water and stacks of medicines—glucose and aspirins and salt tablets—are dispensed.

Here, the nearly 3,000 strikers—sprawling on the ground from exhaustion, heat, lack of food and sleep—are fainting more frequently as the sun sears the square throughout the day.

Every so often, bicycle riders carting wagons of soda water and bread are allowed to penetrate the outer layers of the rings to bring in nourishment for students who are eating but still showing their support by occupying a spot on the square 24 hours a day. Some rise in the early morning, carrying old, dirty banners that they use to help sweep away the litter of the previous day's thousands of spectators.

A makeshift loudspeaker system allows them to announce news of their latest plans or supporters—how much money they have raised, the condition of strikers, a letter of sympathy. They have a copying machine, and every time they distribute a stack of pamphlets, spectators fight for every scrap of paper.

The outpouring of sympathy stretches two miles in either direction, from the faces that peer out of office buildings, to the posters hanging out the windows, to the cars whose passengers lean out to wave banners or pictures of Zhou Enlai, the former Prime Minister who is now a hero for many young people.

Sensing that this is a historic time that they want to play a part in, many workers have come to help. Often that means buying food and drink for students, even if they don't ask for it.

"We're very moved by the people coming out to support us," said T. F. Wang, a Beijing University student who was carrying a watermelon and box of Popsicles that people had handed to him. "This turnout adds to the pressure on the leadership to come out and talk to us."

In the days that followed Mr. Gorbachev's departure the tempo of China's upheaval quickened and a sense of menace grew.

Crowds in Street Ask Deng's Ouster
By Nicholas D. Kristof

BEIJING, May 18—More than a million Chinese took to the streets of Beijing Wednesday in an extraordinary outpouring of support for more democracy.

The protests, amounting almost to a general strike, continued this morning and greatly increased the pressure on the Government to sacrifice one or more top officials and speed political liberalization.

In an attempt to defuse the situation, several of the nation's top leaders visited hospitalized students on a hunger strike early this morning to show their concern. But the crowds this morning seemed at least as militant as those on Wednesday, and many people said they would be satisfied only with the removal of the country's senior leader, Deng Xiaoping, or Prime Miniser Li Peng. . . .

Chinese Premier Issues a Warning to the Protesters
By Nicholas D. Kristof

BEIJING, Friday, May 19—Prime Minister Li Peng warned Thursday that chaos in Beijing was spreading all over the country, but his demand for restraint was ignored by up to a million people who braved a driving rain to demonstrate once more for greater democracy.

To defuse the situation, the Government capitulated on a key student demand by arranging a nationally televised meeting between Mr.

Li and leaders of the students' pro-democracy movement.

In another gesture of conciliation, Mr. Li and the Communist Party leader, Zhao Ziyang, went to Tiananmen Square in central Beijing before dawn today to visit some of the 3,000 hunger strikers whose protest has galvanized the nation into mass demonstrations of support.

"We've come too late," Mr. Zhao told the students, according to the official New China News Agency. "You have good intentions. You want our country to become better. The problems you have raised will eventually be resolved. But things are complicated, and there must be a process to resolve these problems."

Mr. Zhao added that "the whole of Beijing" was discussing the hunger strike, and he called on the students to end the fast. . . .

The Chinese leadership has been split about how to handle the challenge from the students. Mr. Zhao's comments appeared to be an attempt to win support from demonstrators and to put blame on other leaders for adopting a harder line and thereby complicating the situation.

The meeting today in Tiananmen Square appeared to be much more cordial than the students' televised encounter with Mr. Li on Thursday, in which the Prime Minister refused to discuss issues raised by the students and hinted at a crackdown if the disorder continued. . . .

"Most people didn't do any work today," said a graying, heavily callused worker of Beijing's No. 2 Chemical Factory. "You can call it a strike, and it will continue until the Government responds to our demands. We're terribly angry, because the Government won't agree to a meaningful dialogue with the students. What kind of a Government do we have?. . . ."

The demonstration in the capital on Thursday was noteworthy not only for the numbers of people who braved the rain, but also for the degree of organization. Many workers clearly had the support of their work units, for they carried the official banners of their factories. Several said Communist Party cadres had approved of the protest.

The degree of organization did not necessarily indicate some hidden hand encouraging the demonstrators to benefit a faction in China's leadership. The workers all denied that this was the case, and some said their local Communist Party cells had simply become sufficiently independent of the central party organization that they did not worry about disobeying higher officials.

As on Wednesday, the organizations represented in the demonstrations included an array of institutions that are close to the party and the Government. A few units from the army arrived in the square, and so did others from the police and several Government ministries.

The army was called in. Was this a prelude for a violent crackdown like the tank-led invasions that had crushed the Budapest uprising of 1956 or Prague's liberal spring in 1968? Or were the Chinese getting ready to spring the trap of martial law as Poland's General Jaruzelski had done in December of 1981, when thousands of members of Solidarity suddenly found themselves detained?

China Hard-Liners Send Troops to Beijing
By Nicholas D. Kristof

BEIJING, Saturday, May 20—The Government called troops into the capital this morning and imposed martial law in parts of the city to crack down on China's growing democracy movement. But tens of thousands of people rushed out of their homes to block troops from reaching student demonstrators in the central square.

"We must adopt firm and resolute measures to end the turmoil swiftly," Prime Minister Li Peng said in a speech broadcast shortly after midnight. "If we fail to put an end to such chaos immediately and let it go unchecked, it will very likely lead to a situation which none of us want to see."

Chinese with access to information at the highest level said the Communist Party leader, Zhao Ziyang, had been stripped of all power but retained his title of General Secretary of the party.

Mr. Zhao was apparently deprived of his authority because he was too conciliatory toward the demonstrators and because he lost a power struggle with Mr. Li. Chinese said the nation's senior leader, Deng Xiaoping, removed Mr. Zhao and put Mr. Li in charge of the party as well as the Government.

The Beijing municipal authorities imposed strict limits on the activities of foreign journalists, banning interviews or taping on the streets or at government offices, schools, factories and mines. "Any violators will be stopped according to the law," the order said.

The Government ordered the Cable News Network to halt transmissions, a move that also shut down transmissions by NBC News, which was sharing equipment with the cable network. CBS News and ABC News reported similar restrictions.

In mid-morning, loudspeakers on Tiananmen Square in the center of Beijing announced that martial law had been imposed in some parts of the capital. The announcement said this meant restrictions on movement within the city, but it did not give details. The crowd of workers and students in the square had welled by then to about 200,000. . . .

The announcement of a crackdown set the stage for a confrontation between the Government and the vast numbers of people who have joined demonstrations for more democracy in the capital and more than 20 other cities.

More than one million people demonstrated in Beijing this week for greater democracy—often calling for the resignations of Mr. Li and Mr. Deng—and many students seemed to think that the next few days would see an enormous uprising against the Government.

"This is a people's revolution, and the people will win," Z. G. Yang, a history scholar, said as he stood near the trucks immobilized at the western outskirts. "We will stay here around the clock, and we won't let them leave."

Many others were less optimistic about a short-run victory. A 33-year-old army engineer who had rushed out of his home to block the troops, said, "If the Government is determined to resort to violence, the people can't stop the army."

Before dawn, citizens hurried to Tiananmen Square or to places where they had heard that army convoys were approaching. Groups of students set up roadblocks every few hundred yards on the Avenue of Eternal Peace to stop private cars and demand a ride to the site where the soldiers were blocked. . . .

Sad but Defiant, Chinese Stand Up to Troops
By Sheryl WuDunn

BEIJING, Saturday, May 20—The 1,000 troops looked out in bewilderment from their immobilized convoy of 21 trucks in western Beijing today to find that their world had been turned upside down.

Rather than dispersing student demonstrators, as they had apparently been sent to do, they found themselves protected by students from throngs of residents who wanted to climb on the vehicles and let air out of the tires. The students linked arms and refused to let people through, except a handful who were assigned the task of making speeches imploring the soldiers to join the cause.

"You are our army," said a Chinese businesswoman who gave her name as Linda Liu and seemed near tears as she went from truck to truck pleading with the soldiers. "You are our brothers and sisters. You are Chinese. Our interests are the same as yours. We believe you have a conscience. You must not crush the movement."

Prime Minister Li Peng's speech calling for "resolute and powerful measures to curb turmoil" had barely concluded when students rushed from all parts of the capital to the central square and vowed they would continue their fight for democracy. Later in the day there were reports of violence in the outskirts of the city, but early this morning the confrontations were peaceful.

"Even if there is bloodshed, we are not afraid," said a 27-year-old teacher from Beijing University who then joined in singing the "Internationale" as he linked arms with his colleagues.

Throughout the capital before dawn today, tens of thousands of people, stunned and worried, emerged from their homes after seeing the speech on television—parents with children, workers on trucks, teachers, intellectuals and party officials. As they wiped their blurry eyes and clasped jackets around their nightgowns, many said that they would do what they could to overcome the planned crackdown.

"We're ordinary people, but we heard the speech and we decided we had to do something," said a young man whose body was one link in the human chain formed on Beijing's outer road to keep troops from passing through. "We'll keep this barricade up, because students are protesting for the things we want, and we must protect them."

Those forming the human cordon seemed somewhat disappointed that no troops were to be seen. All over the city, citizens were hailing down cars and trucks to take them to the site of the troops who they were told would remain in Beijing for at least a few days.

Chinese were treated to a rare scene on television in the early hours today. A usually calm and expressionless Mr. Li had given his sternest speech yet, clenching his fists at times and tensing his face in a display of emotion that few ordinary people had seen in him before. Throughout the day on Friday, the television had replayed portions of a critical speech by Mr. Li to hunger-striking students in a Thursday discussion.

The atmosphere all night was tense and excited, as workers defied the Government by jumping into trucks to stage demonstrations of support, shouting slogans and waving banners. Teachers rushed to Tiananmen Square to watch over the weakened hunger strikers and throw warm blankets over the students.

As the Prime Minister's speech blared again and again, the city's residents rushed to and fro in large packs, tilting their ears to catch a word from the nearest orator or passing on the latest rumor about the Communist Party leader, Zhao Ziyang, who had apparently fallen from power.

Many gathered in small groups at intersections or on the edge of Tiananmen Square to guess what might happen next and to denounce the Government action.

"This Government is crazy," said a law professor whose face was flushed with anger. "How does it think it can go against such a clear demonstration of the people's will? The more blood that is shed, the angrier people will get and the faster the Government will be overthrown. This Government is not worth dying for."

In the streets, along the human picket lines, in the tangles of bicycles, people were discussing the fate of the student movement and what it would mean for the battles the people seemed to have won for press freedom and the freedom to demonstrate and organize.

"China has a long history of submissiveness, and so the progress of this movement came as a surprise to many people," said Q. X. Chen, who had listened to Mr. Li's speech over the official loudspeaker in the central square. "But the people have gained confidence in the last few days, and they will not keep silent anymore."

Facing the People, the Soldiers Fall Back
By Sheryl WuDunn

BEIJING, May 20—When a small convoy of military trucks used to launch tear gas and to spray water on rioters rolled through eastern Beijing early this morning, the soldiers met their first unexpected challenge. An old woman street cleaner rushed up and lay down on the road in front of the trucks.

Several hundred students immediately dashed toward the convoy, and the soldiers found themselves surrounded by Beijing residents who showered them with questions about why they wanted to repress a democratic movement. The residents also offered the troops breakfast: bread, Coca-Cola and Popsicles.

"We absolutely won't repress the people," an officer told the crowd. "We are the people's soldiers." And then the soldiers, so moved that several were crying quietly, drove back the way they had come.

In an awakening of sorts, the Chinese people are tapping the only weapon they can to defend themselves and their struggle for democracy against the tens of thousands of military troops ordered by the Government to move into the city: what many residents were calling "people power."

Martial law in some sectors of Beijing went into effect at 10 A.M. today. But by late tonight none of the special troops that have been brought in from outside Beijing had made much progress into the city. All over the capital, China's "desperados" and "kamikazes"—as they call themselves—were emerging from their silence and standing up for the university students' protest for democracy.

"We have towels for tear gas and maybe buckets of cement to make road blocks, but besides that, we come just as we are—people," said Kong Lingqi, a 39-year-old worker at Capital Iron and Steel Company.

Mr. Kong and the people around him in the Haidian district of Beijing were preparing for the coming of the troops, who they said were based about seven miles away. They were hoping that every inch of the seven miles would be lined with people prepared to bodily block the convoy of military trucks.

The residents tried to obstruct the soldiers with persuasion. They tried to engage soldiers in discussions about the democracy movement, and often they found that the troops had no idea at all of their cause. At least some of the troops said they had been told by their leaders not to read recent newspapers or watch television news.

Flush with exuberance, crowds have massed along roads they think the troops may use to approach Tiananmen Square, the nation's political center. When five military helicopters encircled the area above Tiananmen Square today, thousands of fists went up in the air and angry shouts rose against the Government.

The crowd swelled at many intersections, and the hum of the crowd's voices rose into shrill shouts every so often when someone believed he had spotted the troops.

"We will lie beneath the wheels," said Wang Gang, a 30-year-old leader of a new workers' organization whose members have taken an oath to risk their lives for the students. These 300 "desperados," as they call themselves, wear white bandannas to distinguish themselves from the 400 "deputies" who wear red bandannas and take fewer risks because they have families to protect.

"We are not afraid of guns or bullets," Mr. Wang said. "But we are not allowed to smash glasses, flatten the trucks' tires or beat the drivers."

Mr. Wang, a sweater factory designer who has spent most of the last few days at Tiananmen Square, spent this morning planning where the men in his organization should be placed.

Similar volunteer groups have sprung up all over the capital as angry residents form neighborhood teams that link up with others to protect the area from soldiers.

Often these teams form spontaneously. In the predawn hours today in the southern suburbs of Beijing, 48 armed personnel carriers and 17 trucks holding about 850 policemen found their path impeded by a truck driver who parked his large vehicle right in front of them and then ran around the neighborhood to get the help of neighbors, witnesses said.

"I'll never come again," a lieutenant in the convoy was quoted as saying. "I'll never touch a hair of a student's head."

When troops parked three supply trucks near the Beijing Steel Institute, students drained the gas from the tanks and deflated the tires of the trucks.

This evening, people were out on the streets discussing the political state of affairs and waiting for the troops to come.

In the Xizhimen district, thousands of people crowded around the train station because they had heard that the soldiers may be forced to come in by train since they were having difficulty entering by truck or tank.

"We are waiting here," said a film worker, Wu Jianping, "because we hear there are tens of thousands of troops coming in by train."

Biggest Beijing Crowds So Far Keep Troops from City Center; Party Reported in Bitter Fight
By Nicholas D. Kristof

BEIJING, May 20—Huge throngs, possibly amounting to more than one million Chinese, took to the streets today to defy martial law and block troops from reaching the center of the capital, effectively delaying or preventing the planned crackdown on China's democracy movement.

Troops approaching Beijing on at least five major roads were halted or turned back by the largest crowds to have gathered so far in a month of almost continuous protests. Students and ordinary citizens erected roadblocks or lay in the path of army trucks, while others let the air out of their tires.

Reports from around the country indicated growing support for the democracy movement. The city of Xian was reportedly brought to a standstill by 300,000 protesters, and rallies were reported in Shanghai, Canton and at least half a dozen other cities, and even small villages.

A few clashes were reported, but the confrontations seemed to be mostly peaceful. More troops were reported to be making their way toward Beijing, however, and it was not clear that the people could continue to keep the soldiers out. So far, the troops have not tried very hard to enter Beijing, and a more concerted effort backed by the use of tear gas would almost certainly succeed. But after a full day of confrontation, questions were increasingly raised about the army's readiness to quell the protests. Prime Minister Li Peng, who early this morning ordered the military crackdown on the democracy movement, did not make an appearance or comment later today. Television stations repeatedly broadcast his speech calling for the military crackdown.

As the military crackdown seemed increasingly uncertain, there were signs that the Communist Party General Secretary, Zhao Ziyang, still had a chance of recovering his authority and elbowing aside Mr. Li and the senior leader, Deng Xiaoping, to become China's next leader in an intense and increasingly bitter power struggle within the Communist Party.

Communist Party officials with access to information at the highest level say Mr. Deng has stripped Mr. Zhao of his powers while leaving him with his title. In addition, they say a meeting of the Central Military Commission on Thursday effectively stripped him of his right to order troop movements.

Mr. Zhao submitted his resignation on May 17, after being out-voted 4 to 1 on the Standing Committee of the Politburo on his proposals to grant most student demands, the official said. The resignation was withdrawn the next day before it was acted upon. . . .

"Li Peng is now in charge of the party, so he'll be scheduling the meetings," an official said. "So if he thinks he might lose, he will delay holding a meeting." The harshness of Mr. Li's speech seems to have galvanized much of Beijing's population to support the student democracy movement, and Mr. Li and Mr. Deng are now openly referred to as public enemies.

Protesters in Shanghai today carried banners reading "Li Peng does not represent us" and "Li Peng, do not use the people's army against the people," Reuters reported. In most parts of Beijing, neither the police nor army troops could be seen today, but residents were in an exuberant frenzy to protect themselves from the threat of what is regarded as virtually an enemy invasion. All major intersections have been taken over by local residents who stand guard, waiting impatiently for the troops to arrive so they can implement careful plans to erect barricades and summon help.

"With the people behind us, we'll succeed," said Xu Shiyi, a student from Henan Province who has come to Beijing to support the movement. "No Government can survive by using the army against its own citizens." . . .

Truck drivers drove their vehicles in front of military convoys to block their way, and ordinary citizens lay down on the ground in front of army trucks. Many seemed to remember these tactics from the Philippine military coup that ousted President Ferdinand E. Marcos. Television footage of the "people power" revolution of the Philippines was widely shown in China at the time and now workers delight in saying that people power will defeat Prime Minister Li.

The most serious of the scattered clashes reported today occurred on a road in western Beijing, according to students, who said about 150 police officers used cattle prods to beat about 45 students blocking military trucks. . . . Nearly 100,000 people seemed prepared this evening to wait all night in central Tiananmen Square to protect student protesters from attack by troops. Even though there was no evidence of hostile troops within miles, many waited expectantly with cloths over their faces for the clouds of tear gas they have been told to expect.

The readiness to help has taken other forms. The Government today cut off the water supply to Tiananmen Square, but as word spread that the water fountains and taps in the area were no longer working, private business people from all over the capital contributed their motorcycles to carry buckets of water to the students.

There are still nearly 3,000 students engaged in a hunger strike on the square to back their demands for a dialogue with Government officials and for reappraisal of the student movement. After the harshness of Mr. Li's speech, the lack of any strong military follow-through has raised questions about the extent to which the Prime Minister can force his will. About 30,000 troops from Inner Mongolia and Shanxi Province reportedly have been deployed, but they are vastly outnumbered by the more than one million people who took to the streets today.

Some of the troops today could be seen with tear gas canisters, and some reportedly had guns, but they seemed decidedly pacifist. Most of the soldiers seemed unwilling to openly violate their orders to advance on Beijing, but they seemed quite happy to be blocked along the way.

Beijing Throngs Again Thwart Advances by Troops Amid Signs Military Balks at Crackdown
By Nicholas D. Kristof

BEIJING, Monday, May 22—Workers and students blocked new advances by army convoys today, preventing a military crackdown on China's democracy movement from taking effect, and several dozen top legislators quietly began preparing a strategy to revoke martial law.

There was exhilaration as well as exhaustion on central Tiananmen Square as dawn broke this morning, for many of the tens of thousands of students occupying the square had earlier written their wills after widespread rumors that brutal repression would begin during the night.

While many still fear that there will be violence, there is a sense of triumph in the capital that ordinary citizens have been able to prevent the Government from carrying out martial law more than two days after Prime Minister Li Peng ordered it.

It is not clear why the troops have not moved more aggressively to put martial law into effect. Several knowledgeable Chinese said the army did indeed plan a crackdown on Sunday night, and there are growing suspicions that the army's slowness has more to do with its own reluctance than with Prime Minister Li's.

The crowd this morning bellowed out a new slogan referring to the architects of martial law, Mr. Li and Deng Xiaoping, the senior leader: "Step down, or we will keep coming every day!" . . .

"Tiananmen Square has become a holy spot for Chinese democracy," a student leader, Wang Dan, told the crowd today. "If we stay here longer, we will contribute more to China's democratization and increase our influence. If we withdraw, we will let down the citizens who have defended us. We will stay until our victory."

Since Martial Law, Protest Crackles with Fury at Deng

By Sheryl WuDunn

BEIJING, May 21—As daylight wanes, a defiant exuberance seems to swell among the throngs clogging the intersections along roadways leading to Beijing's central square. But in the small homes of the capital, in the moments shared by friends away from the comfort of the masses, the darker side of what it means to live under martial law emerges.

"Don't you dare go out tonight," an official in a Communist Party organization said, his voice shaking, as he scolded his younger brother, who until Saturday had fasted for democracy with his university classmates.

"Mom spent her whole life raising us. The Government, those troops, if they come out, they will have no mercy," the official said as his brother, sinking into his chair, nodded. But the elder brother was planning to go to the square and spend several hours to support the students there.

Streets all over the capital were jammed with hundreds of thousands of citizens, many of whom were awakened politically by the call for greater democracy in China by hunger-striking students. . . .

The idea that tens of thousands or even hundreds of thousands of army troops, possibly carrying tear gas or guns, might close in on the unarmed students in and around Tiananmen Square is deeply troubling to many citizens. Some have forsaken sleep to spend the night on the streets waiting for the troops to arrive. Others have tried to persuade the students to be more careful.

"Please, those of you students who have no brothers or sisters, go home," a teacher implored his students on the square. "You must be prepared for the worst."

"I do not want to see these students killed by guns," said Li Xiaodong, a 22-year-old Government official. Like many other citizens, he accepted an assignment from the student organization to keep a lookout for troops at a particular location. "I was stationed at the Golden Water Bridge yesterday and I will be there again tonight," he said. "If and when the troops begin their action, they probably will come out over the bridge. We will perhaps be killed there, so we at least will die before the students." . . .

As tension grew, strategic concerns overtook idealistic visions.

70

Reporter's Notebook

By Nicholas D. Kristof

BEIJING, May 22—Throughout the capital, neighborhood residents have taken charge of local intersections. The people stay up all night, passing the time by exchanging increasingly implausible rumors about the imminent arrival and undoubted brutality of enormous numbers of troops.

Most of the corner-watchers are people who live nearby, but a few are sent by the central student organizing committee to make sure that all intersections are covered. The main strategy, if the troops come, is to block their path with people and obstructions like bicycles, bricks and anything else available. They also speak to the soldiers and try to convince them that they should not attack their fellow countrymen.

The students' latest concern is that the Government will use soldiers from remote areas because they speak different languages and may be unable to understand the students' pleas for retreat. So the student organizing committee now sends members of minority nationalities to all the major roads where it expects troops may arrive, so that they can function as translators and persuade soldiers to leave in any tongue.

"We can convince any group of soldiers not to attack us," Pa Hardin, a member of the Uighur minority, said the other day as he waited in front of the Beijing train station. He had been assigned to stand there in case Uighur soldiers emerged from the station to attack the students.

Another tactic has been adopted by the "kamikaze" group of workers who roam around the capital all night looking for invading army convoys to halt. Many of the kamikazes now carry knives, so they can puncture truck tires, and they often travel with their wives or girlfriends. The idea is that the woman will distract the soldiers while the man slashes the tires. . . .

Before the Communist victory in China in 1949, Mao Zedong and Zhou Enlai were famous for their accessibility and common touch.

When they conquered Beijing, they moved into the walled Zhongnanhai compound in the center of the capital, but for the first few years, ordinary Chinese could still stroll around the leaders' compound. As time passed, not only were ordinary Chinese barred, but a complex system of passes was devised so that permission was required to go from one part of the compound to another.

The students on Tiananmen Square have adopted a similar system.

The outside of the square is cordoned off by students, supposedly to protect those who are resting inside. Then there are several inner circles, each cordoned off by student guards who demand a pass to go through. To see the student organization's top leaders, a visitor must be escorted through four different checkpoints and present identification at each.

"We need to have a good system of discipline and organization," a student leader explained this evening. "Otherwise the Government will say we encourage chaos."

As the the size of the crowds in the square rose and fell from day to day, so did the power struggle within the leadership. Seven military commanders warned against the use of military force by the soldiers who were still massing. But Li Peng, the known advocate of toughness, was seemingly gaining. For the fully committed students, the time for caution had passed, but for those who had spent their working lives aware of limits, the new conditions required a certain nimbleness.

Boldly and Subtly, China's Press Tests Limits . . .
By Sheryl WuDunn

BEIJING, May 23—Not many Chinese follow Italian politics, so perhaps it was a bit surprising for *People's Daily* to carry a small front-page article Sunday on the resignation of the Italian Government.

But in China, where subtlety is a way of journalism as of life, the message was obvious: China's Government should think about resigning as well. . . .

In the last five weeks, news organizations witnessed a startling transformation to what was for a Communist country a remarkably independent press. Then, on Saturday morning, came martial law, and all bets were off.

News organizations suddenly assumed a more cautious attitude, printing fewer articles that were not authorized, but it was not a full-scale retreat. Instead of openly criticizing the Government, newspapers tried more subtle tactics.

People's Daily on Monday published a front-page article about a Hungarian leader objecting to the use of army troops to solve domestic problems. That was a slap at Prime Minister Li Peng after his attempt to call army troops to the capital to suppress the democracy movement.

A journalist at the newspaper confirmed that the placement of the article was intended as a criticism of Prime Minister Li and his policies. He recalled the glee in the newsroom when the Hungarian leader's comment was found, and it was realized that it could be printed on the front page.

Television news and radio broadcasts have recently included daily reports on the student protests. In a subtle indication that army troops are dissatisfied with their mission to quell students, the television news today carried an illuminating interview with an officer in the military. The news tonight was clearly trying to embarrass Mr. Li by undermining the likelihood that his order for martial law would be carried out.

"As soldiers, it is our bounden duty to obey orders," the major told the reporter for the Central China Television news agency. "But we will never fire at the people."

Then, the television reporter asked the kind of leading question that is rarely seen, "Haven't you received an order to move away?"

The major answered, "Retreat, retreat."

As May entered its last week, successive headlines reflected how impasse was inching toward a violent resolution, how hopes were giving way to fears, and how the harsh counsel of Li Peng was holding sway.

Tide Turns Toward Chinese Hard-Liner

Students Plan for Hurdle: Zhao's Fall

Wishful Thinkers?

Chinese Hard-Liner Tightens Grip as Attacks on His Rival Multiply

Then the students, who had been massed in large but tensely quiet numbers, moved once more.

Students Renew Call for Change in Beijing March
By Nicholas D. Kristof

BEIJING, May 28—About 100,000 people on foot and on bicycles streamed through the capital today to demand more democracy and the resignation of Prime Minister Li Peng. The police and soldiers made no move to interfere despite martial law restrictions and the Government's strict warnings against demonstrations.

The students, who are increasingly aware of support from Chinese around the world, hailed the protest as part of an "international Chinese people's demonstration day" to put pressure on the Government. Other demonstrations were held in several Chinese cities, including the economic capital, Shanghai, as well as in Taiwan, Hong Kong, Australia and the United States.

One of the largest protests was in Hong Kong, which held a political rally with a crowd estimated at more than 300,000. Such protests are likely to put new pressure on the Chinese authorities, who are sensitive to turbulence in Hong Kong in the years before they inherit the British territory in 1997.

In Beijing, the demonstrators paraded along five different routes intended to maximize their exposure to the city's residents. Separate columns of protesters—mostly students but including some workers—passed by the Zhongnanhai compound, where Mr. Li lives, as well as the Dianmen neighborhood home of the 84-year-old senior leader, Deng Xiaoping.

"We love our country, but we do not love the puppet government of Li Peng," chanted the demonstrators as they waved red banners and sang songs that mocked the nation's leadership.

The demonstration in the capital was smaller than several previous marches, although it was difficult to calculate since the students took different routes and did not all pass by central Tiananmen Square. In particular, fewer workers joined in, although those who lined the route cheered the students and seemed enthusiastic.

"I see hope for China, which I didn't see before," said Yang Mei, an artist who joined the protesters. "The students already have won, because they have support from 90 percent of the population. And the greatest climax is yet to come. This is sowing time, and the harvest will come when Deng Xiaoping dies."

The demonstrations were smaller today for two reasons. The first is that the Government has been putting intense pressure on factories and universities to curb protests, and factory managers have warned workers that they will lose their bonuses and maybe their jobs if they join the students.

The second is that there is an air of apprehension in the nation these days, a fear that a violent crackdown and major political realignment will be announced in the next few days.

The demonstration today was not reported by the television news or the New China News Agency, a sign that the Government is tightening its control over the media. The official news media here have covered previous demonstrations, although with less and less interest in the last week following Prime Minister Li's announcement of martial law on May 20.

The Communist Party newspaper, *People's Daily*, was represented in today's march by a small group of journalists who demanded press freedom, but most journalists seem to have battened the hatches of their aspirations, in expectation of rough weather ahead.

"There's a spirit of depression that probably the conservatives have won and that there will be a settling of accounts," said a Western diplomat. "The mood is that there's trouble ahead."

Fates were being decided in party meetings but consciousness was being shaped on the street. Thousands of young people were living through events and emotions that they would one day tell to children as yet unborn.

In Quest for Democracy, a Mini-City Is Born
By Sheryl WuDunn

BEIJING, May 30—A few hundred yards from the center of Chinese bureaucracy, where the Communist Party leadership is engaged in a bitter power struggle, a smaller group of less experienced bureaucrats on Tiananmen Square is building its own society, a virtual city of protest.

The several thousand students who are occupying the square as a pro-democracy demonstration have established their own mini-government: a secretariat, a printing office, a financial affairs ministry, a goods and resources ministry, a propaganda ministry, a liaison ministry, a picket squad, a special action squad, a small loudspeaker broadcast station, a pharmacy and three clinics.

Instead of the nation's five-star flag, the students have hung a kaleidoscope of red, blue and white school flags from tall poles to represent their federation of universities from all over the country. Presiding over the scene is a large mascot, a 27-foot-high replica of the Statue of Liberty positioned so that it faces a large portrait of Mao Zedong.

"This is a holy land for democracy," said Zhou Chihui, a 22-year-old mathematics student from the central Chinese city of Wuhan. "It takes a lot of courage to continue to stay on Tiananmen Square. And we need to manage a life here."

Three rings of student picket lines surround the headquarters that house the ministries, and in the times of tight security, there were several types of special passes that students had to show to pass through deeper rings of student police. Even now, it is rare to be allowed to speak with any of the student leaders.

But if the students consider their own society on the square a battleground in the struggle for freedom and democracy, they have not produced defenses against the thousands of military troops on the outskirts of the capital.

The students say they plan to rely on local citizens to help them should there be a confrontation. If a military crackdown occurred quietly in the middle of the night, they acknowledge that they would probably be defeated, but they say this would anger citizens the next day and generate more support.

Even if the troops do not invade the square, it is not clear how long the students' small society can last. Already the numbers are dwindling sharply. Only a few thousand students are now camping on the square. While the students say they will maintain their occupation at least until June 20, when the standing committee of the National People's Congress is due to meet, the numbers are likely to shrink even more by then.

Because they have so effectively sheltered themselves from the Beijing authorities, the students have also lost some of the benefits from the city's social services, like garbage collection, continuous electricity and water supply. All this has made the square a less habitable place.

The ministries hardly resemble the halls of Government offices. Most of them are housed in red or light blue plastic tents that were sent as donations from Hong Kong. But also unlike the nation's formal ministries, these offices are open 24 hours a day.

Already, the financial affairs office has the equivalent of nearly $40,000 under its management, which it will begin spending more quickly as donations of food, drink and other supplies come in more slowly from local residents.

Money has been raised throughout the world for the students, and in one instance, a rock concert in Hong Kong reportedly raised the equivalent of more than $1 million for the students. But the students say they have not been able to receive money sent from overseas through the Government postal system, a common financial intermediary.

As a result, the student money managers have shied from parking their money in the Government banks or post offices. Instead, they keep it hidden in a place outside the square. They also plan to issue financial reports through posters, news conferences and loudspeaker broadcasts.

"You can say this place is like a city," said Mi Weizhuo, a 21-year-old statistics student from Hebei University who is in charge of financial supervision in the financial affairs office. "But it is a purely consumer's society because we don't produce anything."

Mr. Mi has helped allocate the money for food purchases, which the resources department is responsible for purchasing. To control how much food is bought daily, delegates from each university on the square are required to show the resources department the student identification cards of their students living on the square.

Even then, the food is mainly bread and drink. Students have already complained that they lack various vitamins and vegetables, as well as adequate hygiene. While the clinics are much emptier now than they were during a hunger strike two weeks ago, when tens of thousands more students lived on the square to show their support, most of the patients have minor ailments like the common cold, a sore throat or fatigue.

The clinics also have their specialties, according to their facilities and supplies. At one small clinic, which like the others is under the Red Cross, physicians mainly administer first aid. Severe cases are sent to the square's emergency clinic.

The pharmacy dispenses both Western and Chinese medicines that have been donated by factories. Many of the hundred-odd boxes of medicine that line the pharmacy tent have not been opened, and since the hunger strike, the supplies of glucose water, salt water and a popular Chinese nutritional medicine have hardly been used.

The anxieties and fears that were gripping Beijing were not limited to just one side of the conflict.

Why Deng Trembles: A Leader Equates Protest and Chaos
By Nicholas D. Kristof

BEIJING, May 31—For many Chinese and foreign viewers of the latest upheavals, China's script in the last few weeks has resembled a Greek tragedy: Deng Xiaoping is cast as the once-heroic leader whose intolerance and hubris caused him to destroy much of what he has accomplished.

What impels a man like Mr. Deng, China's senior leader, to undermine in a few weeks what took him a decade to achieve: a stable political order, respect in Hong Kong for China's good intentions, the preparations for a succession of power?

Mr. Deng's critics—and these days they are numerous—often assume that his decision to dismiss his chosen successor, Zhao Ziyang, and summon troops to crack down on the democracy movement simply reflects the tenacity of his ambition, an unwillingness or inability to share power. Mr. Deng is undoubtedly reluctant to give up the power he has grown used to, but there is an additional explanation to account for his horror of the democracy movement.

"If our country were plunged into disorder and our nation reduced to a heap of loose sand, how could we ever prosper?" Mr. Deng asked in a speech more than two years ago, on the eve of his last crackdown on a student movement. "The reason the imperialists were able to bully us in the past was precisely that we were a heap of loose sand."

He and others of his generation spent the first half of their lives in a China racked by division and chaos, where the hopes of modernizing movements always seemed frustrated by the country's disorder.

The lessons about chaos were burned into their psyches again when the Cultural Revolution began in 1966 and led to hundreds of thousands of deaths and other personal tragedies in their families.

"They have a deep-seated allergy to any form of disorder," a Western diplomat said recently in Beijing. "They have an intense belief that they need stability in order to have development."

The distaste for student unrest is perhaps accentuated because Mr. Deng's oldest son, Deng Pufang, was permanently paralyzed after being pushed from a window at Beijing University by student militants during the Cultural Revolution.

"While Westerners have tended to think of China as under firm rule, Deng tends to see the potential for chaos, and may often feel the central Government is hanging on by its fingernails," explained Kenneth G. Lieberthal, director of the Center for Chinese Studies at the University of Michigan. "He wants reform but not at the price of chaos."

While Mr. Deng is best known for his efforts to open China's economy, and, to a lesser extent, its political system, these are simply means to achieve his most cherished aim: modernization. And Mr.

Deng has made clear that he regards political protest as inimical to modernization. He seems to see bubbles of discontent not as a sign of China's resilience but as a sign of its growing malaise and weakness.

In a speech early in 1979, when he was cracking down on an earlier democracy movement, Mr. Deng warned that if it was allowed to continue, it would "inevitably lead to the unchecked spread of ultra-democracy and anarchism, to the complete disruption of political stability and unity, and to the total failure of our modernization campaign."

"China will once again be plunged into chaos, division, retrogression and darkness, and the Chinese people will be deprived of all hope," he said.

In addition to this fear of chaos, there seems to have been a naked fear of losing power. For a group of old revolutionaries, men in their 80's who have held power for four decades and see their interests as virtually identical with their country's interests, there was a deep-seated alarm at the possibility that the Communist Party would crumble the way that Chinese dynasties have fallen.

"To retreat means our downfall," President Yang Shangkun said in a speech to the Politburo now being circulated among party officials. "To retreat means the downfall of the People's Republic of China and the restoration of capitalism."

There is also evident in the leadership a deep resentment against Mr. Zhao's unwillingness to play by the rules. The old leaders constructed China according to their vision, and Mr. Zhao apparently came to threaten not only that vision but also their personal hold on power. Respect for the elderly is fundamental practice in China, and yet Mr. Zhao openly disagreed with Mr. Deng and other senior officials. While they warned of the dangers of unrest, Mr. Zhao hailed the patriotic spirit of student demonstrators.

President Yang, an 82-year-old veteran military figure, suggested in the speech that one of Mr. Zhao's offenses was a simple lack of respect, an unwillingness to be subdued even in the presence of Mr. Deng.

"He insisted on his own idea," President Yang complained in the speech, a copy of which was obtained from students and has been verified by people who heard it read in party meetings. "When Comrade Deng Xiaoping attended the meeting, he still insisted on his idea."

For Communist Party leaders, who for decades have felt secure when a single voice emanated from the party, there has been something deeply troubling about Mr. Zhao's unwillingness to be quiet. Mr. Zhao in his speeches never openly broke with his colleagues, but his televised speeches were more conciliatory toward the protesters than those of other officials, and President Yang appears convinced that this is what stimulated the democracy movement.

The old revolutionaries seem to regard the public as having little or no independent vitality, but are simply a weather vane to be directed by the force of the Communist Party or the force of opposing "bourgeois liberalism," whichever is greater. Their fear is that divisions within the party will strengthen the enemy.

China's former President, Li Xiannian, complained that "there are two headquarters" in the party, and that this confused people and encouraged unrest. While in the West there is a political tradition that glorifies the lone dissenter who sticks to his principles, in the Politburo Mr. Zhao's persistence came across as impudence and treachery.

Indeed, there may be more to the situation than is now known, and no one can rule out the possibility of Mr. Zhao plotting against Mr. Deng. A member of Mr. Zhao's camp confirmed that the party General Secretary had directly challenged Mr. Deng's authority, and there are some hints that Mr. Zhao's aides may have tried to stir up unrest in the belief that it would help their man.

In 1976, when it was to his advantage, Mr. Zhao reacted to the purge of Mr. Deng by calling on the masses to "thoroughly expose and criticize the crimes of Deng Xiaoping." On this occasion, once again, his own interests may have crossed Mr. Deng's.

Mr. Deng and his comrades may have felt they had little choice but to take the actions they did, if they were to hold on to the power they had grown used to. It was not necessarily a blunder—a miscalculation of the impact of suppression on Hong Kong, on the succession plans or on China's domestic political stability—but a response to a higher imperative, from the perspective of the old revolutionaries. They felt that it came down to the need to preserve their own power, and also the need to save China.

Few people, in China or abroad, seem to agree with Mr. Deng that his actions have helped. But even many of his detractors believe it was such calculations that drove him to rise in a fury and turn on his protégé and uproot the carefully laid plans for political stability and succession that previously had won him such acclaim.

Mr. Deng's actions have probably already cost him his reputation in China, for he is increasingly resented and disliked in the country he leads. Now the central question, which the coming months are likely to answer, will be whether his forceful intervention has staved off the chaos he dreads or merely worsened it.

Some troops started to move and the supporters of the students moved to parry them.

Beijing Residents Block Army Move Near City Center
By Nicholas D. Kristof

BEIJING, Saturday, June 3—Tens of thousands of Beijing students and workers surged onto the streets early this morning to turn back more than 2,000 troops who were marching toward Tiananmen Square.

It was the biggest outpouring of citizen support for the demonstrating students in more than a week, and it seemed possible that it would rekindle the student movement and present a new challenge to the Government.

The confrontation underscored the fragile and volatile nature of the situation in Beijing just when the turmoil here seemed to be subsiding after seven weeks of demonstrations by students and workers for democracy and against corruption.

[The Associated Press, in a report from Beijing today, said about 800 riot police officers fired tear gas to clear an area outside the Communist Party headquarters, just west of the square. Witnesses reported at least 30 people outside the Beijing Hotel were beaten by the police, who were said to be armed with truncheons and knives, the A.P. said.]

Students and local residents were convinced that the army troops planned to clear Tiananmen Square, which students have occupied for three weeks. All along Changan Avenue, the main east-west thoroughfare, local residents emerged in the pre-dawn hours to block nearby intersections and prevent troops from passing, after more than a week in which the streets were clear of such roadblocks. . . .

Local residents stopped every police and military truck they could find along Changan Avenue. They barricaded the vehicles and let the air out of their tires. Some also drove trucks across the avenue to create roadblocks.

Thousands of students and local residents also gathered at the site of the car accident, but the police left the scene and there were no conflicts.

The number of students occupying the square is down to a few thousand from the tens of thousands who camped there just a week ago. But on Friday evening, more than 100,000 people had gathered in Tiananmen Square to listen to a pop singer, Hou Dejian, who began a 48-hour hunger strike in support of the students. Mr. Hou was joined by two young scholars and an officer of a major computer company who were planning a 72-hour fast.

As a group, the students had made a powerful impression on a world that watched the mounting confrontation until television was prevented from transmitting its images abroad. They had appeared on screens all over the world speaking intensely, if often naively. They all made it clear that they were only spokesmen, not leaders, and with their modesty, it was hard to hear specific voices and accounts of individual lives.

A Portrait of a Young Man as a Beijing Student Leader
By Sheryl WuDunn

BEIJING, June 2—Four months ago a scrawny, scraggly-haired student gave speeches about human rights that baffled his classmates, who wondered how anyone could harbor such a passion for what was then a remote concept like democracy.

Now, Wang Dan, a 20-year-old history student at Beijing University, is a national figure. He carries a beeper and is accompanied by two bodyguards, signs of his new status as perhaps the single most prominent leader of the student democracy movement that has thrust the Government into a political crisis.

He is rather embarrassed to talk about how his personal life has changed. But when his mail is given to him, he lets on that he has already received a dozen love letters. Certainly he has been the subject of some wild rumors. Some people say he has taken part in Politburo meetings, while others say he has been martyred in various grim ways.

Two students from the eastern city of Suzhou, who arrived in Beijing the other day, were surprised to learn that Mr. Wang was still alive. They said they had held a ceremony in Suzhou to mourn his passing.

What emerges from the last seven weeks is a picture of a survivor: an intellectual lacking charisma or oratorical skill, but bold enough and determined enough to remain a student leader despite factional bickering and Government criticisms.

While other student leaders focus on tactics and mundane matters like where to obtain megaphones, Mr. Wang stands out as the leader who dares to articulate a world very unlike China today.

"I'm not afraid," Mr. Wang said. "I've nothing to be afraid of. I don't think they will be able to imprison me for as long as Wei Jingsheng." Mr. Wei is a dissident who was sentenced a decade ago to 15 years in prison.

There are other prominent student leaders, like Wuer Kaixi and Chai Ling from Beijing Normal University, but it is Mr. Wang who seems to have had the greatest influence. Mr. Wuer's popularity tumbled 10 days ago when he proposed leaving the square, and Miss Chai's role seems limited to the students now occupying the square.

Mr. Wang refuses to evaluate his own role as a leader, but admits there have been mistakes and lessons.

"I have one regret," Mr. Wang said. "I failed to persuade the elite intellectuals to give us direct support." Intellectuals should have been more involved in helping to lead the movement, he says.

Mr. Wang believes that the intellectuals joined too late, and he suggests that one of the results of this is that the students did not have coherent goals.

"I think that the student movements in the future should be firmly based on something solid, such as the democratization of campus life or the realization of civil rights according to the Constitution," Mr. Wang said. "Otherwise, the result is chaos."

Although many of the students' demands—press freedom, direct talks with the Government and the uprooting of corruption among officials—were more practical than in past demonstrations, they had no framework.

While certain themes, like opposition to official corruption, gained the support of workers, Mr. Wang says he believes the movement is not ready for worker participation because the principles of democracy must first be absorbed by students and intellectuals before they can be spread to others.

The recent student movement went way beyond just ideas, and Mr. Wang has learned that there are limits to how one can apply those ideas, especially the concept of democracy.

When students went on their hunger strike, any policy decision that was made had to be voted in unanimously by all the fasting students, whose numbers grew from 1,000 to 3,000.

Another difficulty was the election of a student leadership.

"You can't have direct democracy where everyone is electing leaders and trying to get involved because it only results in frequent changes of leaders and causes disorder," Mr. Wang said.

Another problem that hampered the student movement was the bickering among leaders. Most recently, a debate centered on whether to stay at or leave Tiananmen Square, which students invaded more than two weeks ago.

Mr. Wang and his fellow students from Beijing University and other colleges in the capital have essentially retreated from the square, which has lately been occupied mainly by students from outside Beijing.

Through all this, Mr. Wang has remained a leader, partly because he is from Beijing University, the nation's most prestigious school, and partly because he has become a nationwide figure who has been involved all along, from the hunger strike to the talks with the Government.

In part Mr. Wang seems to have held on to his constituency because he has learned to sense how far his supporters are willing to go.

Other times, he displayed a knack for public relations. Mr. Wang says he did not spearhead the hunger strike, but when the idea became popular and a list of participants was posted, his name was the first on the list.

"The hunger strike was significant," Mr. Wang said, "because it brought out the ordinary people's enthusiasm."

And then the army stormed the heart of the city, firing at protesters who tried to fight back as best they could.

Troops Attack and Crush Beijing Protest; Thousands Fight Back, Scores Are Killed
By Nicholas D. Kristof

BEIJING, Sunday, June 4—Tens of thousands of Chinese troops retook the center of the capital early this morning from pro-democracy protesters, killing scores of students and workers and wounding hundreds more as they fired submachine guns at crowds of people who tried to resist.

Troops marched along the main roads surrounding central Tiananmen Square, sometimes firing in the air and sometimes firing directly at crowds of men and women who refused to move out of the way.

Early this morning, the troops finally cleared the square after first sweeping the area around it. Several thousand students who had remained on the square throughout the shooting left peacefully, still waving the banners of their universities. Several armed personnel carriers ran over their tents and destroyed the encampment.

Reports on the number of dead were sketchy. Three Beijing hospitals reported receiving at least 68 corpses of civilians and said many others had not been picked up from the scene. Four other hospitals said they had received bodies of civilians but declined to disclose how many. Students said, however, that at least 500 people may have been killed in the crackdown.

Most of the dead had been shot, but some had been run over by armored personnel carriers that forced their way through barricades erected by local residents.

The official news programs this morning reported that the People's Liberation Army had crushed a "counterrevolutionary rebellion" in the capital. They said that more than 1,000 police and troops had been injured and some killed, and that civilians had been killed, but did not give details.

Changan Avenue, or the Avenue of Eternal Peace, Beijing's main east-west thoroughfare, echoed with screams this morning as young people carried the bodies of their friends away from the front lines. The dead or seriously wounded were heaped on the backs of bicycles or tricycle rickshaws and supported by friends who rushed through the crowds, sometimes sobbing as they ran.

The avenue was lit by the glow of several trucks and two armed personnel carriers that students and workers set afire, and bullets swooshed overhead or glanced off buildings. The air crackled almost constantly with gunfire and tear gas grenades.

"General strike!" people roared, in bitterness and outrage, as they ran from Tiananmen Square, which pro-democracy demonstrators had occupied for three weeks. "General strike!"

While hundreds of thousands of people had turned out to the streets Saturday and early today to show support for the democracy movement, it was not clear if the call for a general strike would be successful. The Government had been fearful that a crackdown on the movement would lead to strikes, but its willingness to shoot students suggested that it was also capable of putting considerable pressure on workers to stay on the job.

The morning radio news program reported that it would be "very difficult" to hold a meeting of the National People's Congress standing committee as scheduled. The committee, which had been scheduled to meet June 20, has the power to revoke martial law and oversee the Government, and many members of the panel are known to be deeply upset by the crackdown.

The announcement by the Beijing news program suggested that Prime Minister Li Peng, who is backed by hard-liners in the Communist Party, was still on top in his power struggle for control of the Chinese leadership. The violent suppression of the student movement also suggested that for now, the hard-liners are firmly in control, and that those who favor conciliation, like party leader Zhao Ziyang, at least temporarily have little influence on policy.

It was too early to tell if the crackdown would be followed by arrests of student leaders, intellectuals who have been critical of the Party, or members of Mr. Zhao's faction. Blacklists have been widely rumored, and many people have been worried about the possibility of arrest.

Students and workers tried to resist the crackdown, and destroyed at least sixteen trucks and two armored personnel carriers. Scores of students and workers ran alongside the personnel carriers, hurling concrete blocks and wooden staves into the treads until they ground to a halt. They then threw firebombs at one until it caught fire, and set the other alight after first covering it with blankets soaked in gasoline.

The drivers escaped, but were beaten by students. A young American man, who could not be immediately identified, was also beaten by the crowd after he tried to intervene and protect one of the drivers.

Clutching iron pipes and stones, groups of students periodically advanced toward the soldiers. Some threw bricks and firebombs at the lines of soldiers, apparently wounding many of them.

Many of those killed were throwing bricks at the soldiers, but others were simply watching passively or standing at barricades when soldiers fired directly at them.

Two groups of young people commandeered city buses to attack the troops. About 10 people were in each bus, and they held firebombs or sticks in their hands as they drove toward lines of armored personnel carriers and troops. Teenage boys, with scarves wrapped around their mouths to protect themselves from tear gas, were behind the steering wheels and gunned the engines as they weaved around the debris to approach the troops.

The first bus was soon stopped by machine-gun fire, and only one person—a young man who jumped out of a back window and ran away—was seen getting out. Gunfire also stopped the second bus, and it quickly caught fire, perhaps ignited by the firebomb of someone inside. No one appeared to escape.

It was also impossible to determine how many civilians had been killed or injured. Beijing Fuxing Hospital, 3.3 miles to the west of Tiananmen Square, reported more than 38 deaths and more than 100 wounded, and said that many more bodies had yet to be taken to its morgue. A doctor at the Beijing Union Medical College Hospital, two miles northeast of the square, reported 17 deaths. Beijing Tongren Hospital, one mile southeast of the square, reported 13 deaths and more than 100 critically wounded.

"As doctors, we often see deaths," said a doctor at the Tongren Hospital. "But we've never seen such a tragedy like this. Every room in the hospital is covered with blood. We are terribly short of blood, but citizens are lining up outside to give blood."

Four other hospitals also reported receiving bodies, but refused to say how many.

In addition, this reporter saw five people killed by gunfire and many more wounded on the east side of the square. Witnesses described at least six more people who had been run over by armored personnel carriers, and about 25 more who had been shot to death in the area. It was not known how many bodies remained on the square or how many people had been killed in other parts of the capital.

It was unclear whether the violence would mark the extinction of the seven-week-old democracy movement, or would prompt a new phase in the uprising, like a general strike. The violence in the capital ended a period of remarkable restraint by both sides, and seemed certain to arouse new bitterness and antagonism among both ordinary people and Communist Party officials for the Government of Prime Minister Li Peng.

"Our Government is already done with," said a young worker who held a rock in his hand, as he gazed at the army forces across Tiananmen Square. "Nothing can show more clearly that it does not represent the people."

Another young man, an art student, was nearly incoherent with grief and anger as he watched the body of a student being carted away, his head blown away by bullets.

"Maybe we'll fail today," he said. "Maybe we'll fail tomorrow. But someday we'll succeed. It's a historical inevitability."

On Saturday the police had used tear gas and beat dozens of demonstrators near the Communist Party headquarters in Zhongnanhai, while soldiers and workers hurled bricks at each other behind the Great Hall of the People. Dozens of people were wounded, but exact numbers could not be confirmed.

It appeared to be the first use of tear gas ever in the Chinese capital, and the violence seemed to radicalize the crowds that filled Tiananmen Square and Changan Avenue in the center of the city. The clashes also appeared to contribute to the public bitterness against the Government of Prime Minister Li.

The violence on both sides seemed to mark a milestone in the democracy movement, and the streets in the center of the city were a kaleidescope of scenes rarely if ever seen in the Chinese capital: furious crowds smashed and overturned army vehicles in front of Zhongnanhai, and then stoned the Great Hall of the People; grimfaced young soldiers clutching submachine guns tried to push their way through thick crowds of demonstrators near the Beijing train station; and the police charged a crowd near Zhongnanhai and used truncheons to beat men and women disabled by tear gas.

"In 1949, we welcomed the army into Beijing," said an old man on the Jianguomenwai bridge, referring to the crowds who hailed the arrival of Communist troops at the end of the Communist revolution. Then he waved toward a line of 50 army trucks that were blocked in a sea of more than 10,000 angry men and women, and added, "Now we're fighting to keep them out."

Most Chinese seemed convinced that the tanks and troops had been ordered into the city to crush the pro-democracy demonstrations once and for all. The immediate result of the first clashes was to revitalize the pro-democracy movement, which had been losing momentum over the last 10 days, and to erase the sense that life in the capital was returning to normal. But the use of tanks and guns came later, and it was not clear if they would succeed in ending the movement or would lead to such measures as a general strike.

The tension was exacerbated by an extraordinary announcement on television Saturday night, ordering citizens to "stay at home to protect your lives." In particular, the announcement ordered people to stay off the streets and away from Tiananmen Square.

"The situation in Beijing at present is very serious," the Government warned in another urgent notice read on television. "A handful of ruffians are wantonly making rumors to instigate the masses to openly insult, denounce, beat and kidnap soldiers in the People's Liberation Army, to seize arms, surround and block Zhongnanhai, attack the Great Hall of the People, and attempt to gather together various forces. More serious riots can occur at any time."

There were some reports that the Communist Party's ruling Politburo had met Friday and given the Beijing municipality the authority to clear the square and end the protests. The *People's Daily* and the television news on Saturday took a hard line against the unrest, and the evening news warned that "armed police and troops have the right to use all means to dispose of troublemakers who act willfully to defy the law."

The clashes and enormous outpouring of support for the students were an unexpected turnaround for the democracy movement. Just a few days ago, the number of students occupying Tiananmen Square had dropped to a few thousand, and students seemed to be having difficulty mobilizing large numbers of citizens to take to the streets. The Government's strategy, of waiting for the students to become bored and go home, seemed to be leading to the possibility of a resolution to the difficulty.

Then a police van crashed into four bicyclists late Friday night, generating new outrage against the Government. One cyclist was killed instantly, and two died in the hospital Saturday, while the fourth seemed less seriously hurt.

Rumors were less meticulous about detail, and word spread early Saturday morning through the capital that four people had been killed by the police. Tens of thousands of people took to the streets to protest, and immediately found themselves confronting more than 2,000 unarmed troops who were marching toward Tiananmen Square.

The troops retreated, but that confrontation seemed to set the tone for the massive demonstrations later Saturday and early today.

Crackdown in Beijing; In the Streets, Anguish, Fury and Tears

By Sheryl WuDunn

BEIJING, Sunday, June 4—As the crackle of automatic weapons filled the air today on the Avenue of Eternal Peace, tens of thousands of

Beijing residents, even elderly men and women, rushed out to see what they could do to turn back the troops.

"The citizens have gone crazy," said a driver watching as a tank plowed its way down the main thoroughfare. "They throw themselves in front of the tank, and only when they see it won't stop, they scatter."

The driver himself was shaken by what he had seen: A tank had rammed into an army truck used as a barricade. As the truck turned over, it crushed a man to death. Elsewhere, he had seen three bloodied bodies lying in the street. Several soldiers still standing in their trucks were crying.

Students and workers threw beer bottles, gasoline bombs, lead pipes, whatever they could find, at the tanks and armed personnel trucks, which nevertheless continued rumbling down the avenue. One truck drove back and forth along the east side of Changan Avenue, as the Avenue of Eternal Peace is known in Chinese, and did not stop when people stood in its path.

Amazement had already turned to fear and defiance earlier in the evening as citizens saw the military convoys entering the city. Some troops from other provinces practically paraded their AK-47 rifles as they stood in their trucks, stranded by the human blockades that had formed around the trucks.

By dark, tensions had soared throughout the city. Hundreds of thousands of people were impelled outdoors by their disbelief and anger, yet brought back to their homes by fear of the violence. The sound of tanks whizzing by and reports of open firing fanned their fears.

"You beasts! You beasts!" shouted the people at the troops.

Around a convoy of about 45 military trucks in the eastern part of the city, people pushed and shoved their way to the troops, shouting and urging them to consider their role as fellow citizens. But the sympathy that had characterized the troops last week was gone; the soldiers seemed to have a certain resolve.

"Will you shoot at us if they order you to?" was a question asked by many of the people surrounding the truck. The soldiers gave weak assurances to the people that they would not fire, but they also admitted that they had to follow orders.

"We have to obey orders because we are soldiers," said one uniformed trooper who was driving a truck. "Otherwise, we will be punished. In any case, there's no way they will order us to shoot the people."

His platoon commander was firm. "We don't fear being beaten by you people," he said as he climbed out of the truck. "We just fear that our guns will be taken and then we will have chaos." Everywhere in the vicinity of the convoy was the sound of hissing, as people let out the air from the tires of as many trucks as they could.

"Why do you have guns?" shouted one man.

"A man is not a soldier without his gun, is he?" came the reply of a soldier carrying an AK-47 automatic rifle.

An old man took up the cause. "I tell you, there will be no good end for you if you follow your order loyally," he screamed as though his life depended upon it. "You have parents, you have brothers and sisters. You should not beat your fellow citizens under any circumstances."

The nearly crazed citizens were climbing onto the trucks, trying to intimidate the soldier. But everywhere in the vicinity, anger was mixed with horror as the people saw how the soldiers handled their rifles and watched as several tanks pulled up.

"Is this the way Li Peng shows how martial law protects the people?" said an old man sitting on a rail.

Another young man said, "When they shoot with real bullets, it will be doomsday." Only hours later did the troops open fire.

In the afternoon, the scene near the walled-in Communist Party compound, where about 30 tear-gas bombs were released, had been the first site of violence. But now that seemed tame. A 20-minute conflict between 300 to 400 riot policemen and hundreds of citizens seemed to have galvanized the citizens. They began to believe that the Government was willing to use force—rubber bullets, broken bricks, truncheons—against the people.

"I couldn't keep my eyes open because of the dense tear gas," said Lu Baochun, a 26-year-old assistant engineer. "It was the troops that first used bricks and tiles to attack, and the citizens fought back."

Mr. Lu had rushed back out to the scene, a chaotic swirl of thousands of people darting back and forth inspecting broken bricks and glass and examining the white powder-like splotches on the street apparently from the tear gas.

"When I went into the house of a nearby citizen to wash my eyes with fresh water, I saw several children lying on their stomachs on a bed," said Mr. Lu, whose own face and neck were reddened from the gas. "They had wet towels covering their mouths, and an old woman was beside them weeping."

He was standing at the Communist Party headquarters shouting with rage now at the two dozen military troops with long truncheons and green helmets, sweating in their heavy green uniforms under the pelting sun.

Some citizens gathered in small huddles around people they thought had been witnesses to the attack. Others crowded together discussing the event, many apprehensive about how far the Government would go.

"They are simply ruffians and bandits," said a young well-dressed woman who had gotten caught in the cross fire of bricks and stones as she was on her way to the office. "They bit people just like mad dogs."

A Chinese journalist was trying to comfort her. "We are shocked," he said. "We thought that this kind of thing only happened during the reign of the corrupt Government of the Kuomintang. Yet this happened in our People's Republic. The troops and the police, they are supposed to be our brothers."

"Please, Tell the World," Students Beg
By Nicholas D. Kristof

BEIJING, Sunday, June 4—The violence against students and workers in Tiananmen Square was most obvious today, because for the most part they were the ones getting killed. But they, too, were violent against the police and army troops, although less effectively so.

Clutching iron bars and bricks, the students glared at soldiers 100 yards away on the other side of the square. It was dark, although the fire from an armed personnel carrier that students had set ablaze cast an eerie glow over part of the square, and the troops and their rows of vehicles could be dimly discerned in the haze.

From time to time, a group of them would advance on the soldiers to throw rocks and otherwise harass them. And then often, they would be shot and killed. It was an unequal competition.

Whenever the students got their chance, spotting an unarmed group of soldiers, they attacked with bricks and iron bars. However, the soldiers, most of whom had guns, tended to stick together.

Until now, students had emphasized the need for nonviolent tactics, and today some still begged their friends to put down their bricks and iron bars. But many students seemed to have crossed their personal Rubicon today, and those who previously had clutched leaflets and megaphones today picked up firebombs.

To be an American on the square this morning was to be the object of fervent hope and inarticulate pleas for help.

"We appeal to your country," a university student begged as bullets careened overhead. "Our Government is mad. We need help from abroad, especially America. There must be something that America can do."

Enraged and desperate as they saw their friends fall and crimson stains grow on their chests, students and workers rushed to any foreigner they could find to express such appeals for help. Almost nobody had any idea what the United States could do, and perhaps it was more a cry of outrage than a plea for help. But this sometimes wordless craving for an international response seemed almost universal on Tiananmen Square.

It was not that students wanted or expected foreign forces to actively intervene. Rather, it seemed to be a moral judgment that they sought, and especially the hope that the news of the bloodshed would reach the outside world and not be covered up.

Most were convinced that the Chinese authorities would never report an accurate toll of the dead and wounded, nor explain what had truly happened in the capital. The morning news programs seemed to justify their skepticism: a brief report said little more than that soldiers had successfully crushed a "counterrevolutionary rebellion."

Denied recognition at home, it became all the more important that the blood and sorrow and bitterness somehow find expression abroad. Even if it did not reverberate back home, students said, at least it could give some meaning to the sacrifices. And so they sought out foreign journalists, tugging them toward the corpses, showing them the blood on the pavement, and begging them to write about what had happened.

"You must tell the world what is happening," a long-haired university student urged, nearly incoherent with fury, "because otherwise all this counts for nothing."

Many asked that their appeals be transmitted to the United Nations, although none had a clear idea of what the United Nations could possibly do to help.

"Maybe it can discuss this situation," a student said impatiently. "Anyway, we have to do something."

While reassurances to the rest of the world that China welcomes foreign tourists and investment presumably remain a consideration, such matters seemed to take a back seat in this morning's military crackdown.

The diplomatic quarter in Beijing was roused from slumber this morning by the almost deafening rumble of seven armed personnel carriers rolling by on the way to Tiananmen Square. Then, truckloads of soldiers arrived and, directly in front of the Jianguomenwai diplomatic compound where many diplomats live, began firing their submachine guns in the air.

In front of the Friendship Store, where tourists go to buy souvenirs, students and workers had turned over an army van and set it ablaze. In the Sanlitun diplomatic compound to the north, opponents of the Government expressed their outrage by setting a police station on fire.

In the lobby of the Beijing Hotel, undercover police officers searched photographers for film they had taken of the clashes, and one photographer was beaten when he refused to hand it over.

While there were no direct attacks on foreigners, there seemed to be a hostility in the air from the Government toward Western influences that had helped the democracy movement. Student demonstrators may appeal to Americans for help, but the Government is suggesting that Americans keep their distance.

Beijing Death Toll at Least 300; Army Tightens Control of City but Angry Resistance Goes On
By Nicholas D. Kristof

BEIJING, Monday, June 5—Army units tightened their hold on the center of the Chinese capital on Sunday, moving in large convoys on some of the main thoroughfares and firing indiscriminately at crowds as outraged citizens continued to attack and burn army vehicles.

It was clear that at least 300 people had been killed since the troops first opened fire shortly after midnight on Sunday morning but the toll may be much higher. Word-of-mouth estimates continued to soar, some reaching far into the thousands. Outbreaks of firing continued today, as more convoys of troops moved through the city.

The bloodshed stunned Beijing and seemed to traumatize its citizens. Normal life halted as armored personnel carriers and troop trucks rumbled along debris-filled roads, with soldiers firing their automatic weapons in every direction. Smoke filled the sky as workers and students vented frustration and outrage by burning army vehicles wherever they found them separated from major convoys, in side streets or at intersections.

The area around central Tiananmen Square was completely sealed by troops who periodically responded with bursts of automatic-weapons fire whenever crowds drew close to the square.

By ordering soldiers to fire on the unarmed crowds, the Chinese leadership has created an incident that almost surely will haunt the Government for years to come. It is believed here that after the bloodshed of this weekend, it will be incomparably more difficult to rule China.

Many fewer people than normal were in the streets Sunday and today, and some of them ended up in the hospitals or in the morgues. The number of casualties may never be known, because the Government has asked hospitals not to report any numbers on deaths or injuries. However, based on accounts pieced together from doctors at several hospitals, it seems that at least 200 died in the hospitals and that many other corpses were probably left in the hands of the military.

'We had to concentrate on those who were still living," one doctor said today. "We had to leave behind most of those who already were dead."

When troops finally seized Tiananmen Square early Sunday morning, they allowed the student occupiers who held on to the center of the square for three weeks to leave and then sent tanks to run over the tents and makeshift encampment that demonstrators had set up. Unconfirmed reports rapidly spread that some students had remained in the tents and were crushed to death.

The troops sealed off Tiananmen Square and started a huge bonfire. Many Beijing residents drew the conclusion, again impossible to verify, that the soldiers cremated corpses to destroy the evidence.

The student organization that coordinated the long protests continued to function and announced today that 2,600 students were believed to have been killed. Several doctors said that, based on their discussions with ambulance drivers and colleagues who had been on Tiananmen Square, they estimated that at least 2,000 had died. But some of these estimates, based principally on antipathy for the Government, appeared to be high.

Soldiers also beat and bayonetted students and workers after daybreak on Sunday, witnesses said, usually after some provocation but sometimes entirely at random.

"I saw a young woman tell the soldiers that they are the people's army, and that they mustn't hurt the people," a young doctor said after returning from one clash Sunday. "Then the soldiers shot her, and ran up and bayonetted her. I ran away, so I couldn't tell if she lived or died."

News of the killings quickly spread to other parts of China, principally by radio reports from the Voice of America and the British Broadcasting Corporation.

Chinese-language broadcasts have been jammed recently, but not on all frequencies.

In Shanghai, some supporters of the democracy movement reacted to the killings in Beijing by going on strike, a diplomat there said in a telephone interview. However, few factories are open on Sundays, so the real test of a strike will come today, and many people doubt that a strike will be successful because of a lack of organization among workers.

In addition, Shanghai residents expressed protest by erecting barricades throughout the city to block traffic.

In northeastern China, small demonstrations to protest the killings in Beijing were held in Shenyang, Dalian and Changchun. However, in those areas there has not been much talk of a general strike, a diplomat said.

Huge convoys of scores of army vehicles, led by tanks, continued to roll through the main roads of Beijing this morning and early afternoon, skirting trucks that had been set on fire by civilians with Molotov cocktails. Troops in the vehicles fired their submachine guns constantly, mostly in the air. However, some casualties were reported.

Troops still fired periodically when clusters of people gathered near the Beijing Hotel, and several people were reported killed and injured. Among them was a middle-aged Western man who was hit in the leg and stomach, according to a witness. He could not be immediately identified and his condition was not known.

In a sign that the troops' mission is not over, the television news today broadcast a letter from the army headquarters to the soldiers, congratulating them on their "everlasting historic exploits in defending our republic" and warning that "the struggle is a long and complicated one."

"Arriving at the scheduled positions and restoring order at the square is only the first elementary victory we have achieved," the letter added, without elaborating. "More difficult and challenging tasks remain before us."

China's television news on Sunday night showed the army knocking down a replica of the Statue of Liberty that students had put in place on the square. The broadcast hailed troops for "victoriously crushing this counterrevolutionary rebellion."

The broadcast did not mention civilian casualties, but said that three soldiers had been killed and two were missing.

In fact, one of the three, a man who was described as "beaten dead by ruffians on Jianguomen Bridge," had actually been run over by an armored personnel carrier.

The official news also indicated that people had destroyed 31 military trucks, 23 police cars, two armored personnel carriers and 31 buses. But those numbers seemed much too low, for everywhere in Beijing people reacted to the killings by torching vehicles and creating blockades. The troops controlled only a few major thoroughfares, and elsewhere citizens continued to control the streets.

One soldier who had shot a young child was overpowered by a large crowd in the Chongwenmen district early Sunday, and then hanged and burned him as he dangled from a bridge. Troops later arrived at the scene and cut down his smoking corpse.

The Government issued an announcement calling for the return of weapons it said had been taken from the army, as well as demanding that "kidnapped" troops be returned. The announcement could be interpreted as preparing the way for an attack on several universities, on the ground of recovering stolen weapons.

Student leaders apparently have some submachine guns that were taken from soldiers or from supply trucks, but at least so far they have seemed more interested in displaying the weapons than in using them. Students at People's University also seized an armored personnel carrier this afternoon and drove it around their neighborhood, but there was no indication that they planned to use them against troops.

There was no announcement from the senior leader, Deng Xiaoping, Prime Minister Li Peng or other officials who presumably ordered the military attack on student demonstrators. Mr. Li is believed to be winning so far in a major power struggle with the Communist Party General Secretary, Zhao Ziyang, who favors a more moderate line toward protesters.

Some accounts had Mr. Deng in poor health, and even in a hospital, but diplomats noted that such rumors invariably surface whenever the 84-year-old leader has been absent from view for a period of time. Mr. Deng has not appeared in public since he met the Soviet President, Mikhail S. Gorbachev, on May 16. . . .

In Beijing, Rage and Despair over the Soldiers' Brutality

By Sheryl WuDunn

BEIJING, June 4—Her world collapsed early this morning, when she got a phone call that her husband was in the hospital fighting to survive the bullets that ripped through his midriff.

"He was convinced that by staying in the Communist Party, he was in a better position to contribute to the reforms," said the 30-year-old woman, whose puffed red eyes betrayed hours of weeping. "At the time, he said such a party could never hurt the people. But he was wrong. And so many party members think the same way he does. They are all deluded."

Despair seemed to silence the woman's sobs as she sat on an old bench outside the intensive care unit where her husband lay. The despair was accompanied by a fear that kept her from disclosing her name.

Throughout the capital today, untold numbers of people found their lives shattered by a similar grief. Their tales were all different, but they were bound by a common source of tragedy—the military crackdown against China's democracy movement—and by a common rage at the Government. Beijing today was nothing so much as a city of sorrow.

The woman's husband, a 31-year-old engineer who has seven Chinese patents to his name, had sensed that something would happen Saturday night, and he had made sure to carry a piece of paper with his name, address and phone number on it.

Early in the night, the two of them had gone out together and seen the troops chatting rather comfortably with local residents. She went home at 11 P.M. to care for their 4-year-old son and to wait for her husband. He returned around midnight after the first shots were fired at the crowd, but he left again almost immediately.

"There is violence out there and the students are poor and weak," she recalled him saying. "I must go out and help them."

Finally, at 3 A.M. this morning the Beijing Union Medical College Hospital called to say that her husband needed emergency surgery. It lasted seven hours.

The hospitals this afternoon were calmer than in the early morning, when wounded students and workers were brought in every few minutes. Several stretchers are still splotched with bloodstains, but the pools of blood on the hospital floors are gone and the frenzy has subsided.

The possibility that the bloodshed may continue alarms doctors, however.

"We have no more blood," said one doctor at the Union Medical College Hospital. "If there are many more wounded again in the next couple of days, we won't be able to handle them."

The growing expectation of a widespread crackdown frightens some hospital employees from revealing details about their patients or the number of deaths, and doctors at several hospitals say they have been told that visitors other than kin or close friends are not allowed through the gates.

This afternoon, sympathetic workmen led a reporter into the Union Medical College Hospital by an underground passage, past the guards at the gate.

A small crowd gathered in the center of one of the special wards, where the bloodied young men and women lay side by side on mattresses on the floor. Wives bent down over their wounded husbands to loosen a shoelace or just to reassure their loved one that the wounds would heal.

Citizens carried or carted to the hospitals many of the wounded found on the outskirts of the square, but ambulances were needed to enter parts of the Tiananmen Square area to pick up the wounded.

Doctors at different hospitals said today that they had often been restricted in collecting the wounded. Without the cooperation of the army, it was difficult to enter or leave certain parts of the Tiananmen area with the wounded.

One doctor who traveled in his hospital's ambulance to Tiananmen Square said machine guns raked the sides of the ambulance when it was making its way out of the square with several wounded citizens. He showed the bullet holes in the vehicle.

Everywhere in the hospital corridors there were stories of dashed hopes and lives that had been changed forever by a moment on Tiananmen Square.

A 24-year-old Government official was fleeing from a volley of bullets on a side street just northeast of the square when three men near him were hit with bullets. He went to help them, but a People's Liberation Army officer stopped him from tending the wounded.

"Don't stir or you will be dead," a soldier said as he pointed a rifle at the official's head. The official said a dozen soldiers then surrounded him and beat him with bricks, truncheons and the butts of their rifles.

"I never thought they would be so brutal," said the official, still wearing his bloodied clothes at a hospital where he is recovering from wounds all over his body. A friend had spent the afternoon with him, and now they were taking a walk around an area of the dark corridor, his friend supporting him.

A 28-year-old Government official stayed at home during the night and wandered out only at daylight to see what happened. When he strolled over at 9 A.M. to the Beijing Hotel, a few hundred yards east of the square, he was shot in the hip.

"I feel as though my leg isn't there," he moaned to a doctor beside him. The doctor assured him that he would survive, although she said nothing about his leg.

"I thought the Government would use only rubber bullets," he added, as his wife moved closer to comfort him.

One young man who had spent hours helping out at a hospital early in the morning returned home this afternoon only to find that his wife's younger brother had been beaten to death by the troops.

Shoppers on a major side street this afternoon also were shot simply because they were in the line of view when troops decided to open fire on Wangfujing, one of Beijing's most popular shopping districts.

A Chinese student studying in Japan had returned home to visit his wife and son. When he crossed the street, soldiers shot him in the back. Doctors say he will be paralyzed forever.

A Student's Body Is Honored with Tears of Horror and Cries for Revenge
By Sheryl WuDunn

BEIJING, June 5—For the dozen student pallbearers who walked solemnly into the university hall, it was a grim scene: The body of a friend lay wrapped in a red cloth and nestled in a bed of ice on a table.

The students, their heads bowed in silence, circled the table while another student with a megaphone tried to clear the crowds away. Next to the body someone had placed a white "A01" license plate, the code for a high-ranking military vehicle and now, for the students, a spoil of war.

"I want to take revenge," said a 22-year-old student, his voice choking and his eyes beginning to tear beneath his wire-rim glasses. "It will be blood for blood."

Hundreds of people had come to see the macabre exhibit, which the students had erected to expose the atrocities they say the Government has committed against its citizens. Students wept, and in hushed voices they constantly asked each other one question: How could the Government commit such a horror?

The air was heavy with the smell of death and the floor splotched with pools of water where ice had melted. The body, along with four others, had been carried by workers Sunday morning from central Tiananmen Square to a small alley in the western part of the city. From there, the bodies were transported by car to the dark, empty front hall at the University of Politics and Law, where the last one now remained.

For the visiting students, who were from the University of Aerospace and Aeronautics, the body was confirmation that their friend had been martyred for the democracy movement. The whereabouts of two other students, out of 100 in the department of engineering dynamics, are still not known.

Students say more than 2,000 of their classmates from universities all over the capital are missing and feared dead. Some may have gone home to the provinces, and some may have stayed with family or friends in central Beijing. Some may have been killed and their bodies burned by troops to destroy the evidence.

Throughout the universities in the capital, the color and zest of the protest movement has turned to deep bitterness. Now white banners of mourning cover the campuses, and black cloths frame the front entrances of the universities, where people have come to seek solace.

"The soil of our nation is fertilized by blood," read a banner at Beijing University. "In all the world, there is nothing more cruel than this."

Students hovered in small groups, sharing expressions of horror over the army's massacre and trying to dispel their anger and anxiety over rumors that the universities will be the targets of the next military attack.

At Beijing University today, teachers were urged by school officials to spread the word among the students not to stage any demonstrations. The university clinic was asked to prepare for first aid, and teachers and students were warned not to go out at night.

The authorities said troops had been ordered to kill anyone who tries to stop the army from entering the school, according to a teacher who attended the meeting. For those still at the universities, there was no place to hide.

"Many students have left the campus because it is dangerous here," said another young teacher, who spoke as she nervously fiddled with her bicycle in the center of the campus. The absence of so many students makes it difficult to account for those who may have been killed. Some teachers say that only one death of a Beijing University student has been confirmed, and some estimates put the number of those missing from the university at more than 200.

"The Government won't let Beijing University alone, because it knows that this university is a hotbed of activism," the teacher said. The prestigious school traditionally has been the focus of many student political movements.

"What can we do?" she asked. "We have nowhere to escape."

Artillery Firing in Suburbs Adds to Tensions in Beijing; Mystery on Leaders Grows
By Nicholas D. Kristof

BEIJING, Wednesday, June 7—Artillery fire reverberated through the capital Tuesday, and there were continued reports of clashes among rival military units.

The security situation seemed to continue to deteriorate, and today there were the first direct moves against foreign residents of the capital. Troops fired at the Qijiayuan Diplomatic Compound, where many diplomats and foreign journalists live, witnesses said, but no one was known to be injured.

This afternoon, troops sealed off the nearby Jianguomenwai Diplomatic Compound, which also houses thousands of foreign diplomats and journalists. Several soldiers with submachine guns guarded each entrance and refused to allow people to enter or leave.

Embassies of several countries were trying to arrange evacuations of their nationals in the compound, but it was not immediately clear if they would be successful.

Witnesses also said that soldiers had stopped two diplomatic cars on Beijing's third ring road, forced the foreign occupants of the car out at gunpoint and robbed them of all their belongings.

The sounds of artillery fire appeared to be coming from the western outskirts of the city, the general direction of the headquarters of the Beijing military region. But it could not be determined if the headquarters was involved in the fighting or who was firing the shells. Most diplomats and Chinese said they assumed that the shelling involved competing army units seeking a military solution to China's power struggle.

The evening news program denounced as "purely rumor" the reports of fighting between military units near the military airport in southern Beijing. It also offered an unusual denial of a report that Deng Xiaoping, China's senior leader, had died.

"That's a sheer fabrication intended to poison people's minds," the newscaster said, without shedding any light on Mr. Deng's situation or whereabouts. . . .

The air of unreality in the capital has been increased by the mysteries in the press. The newspapers have not appeared in several days, and state television has been growing increasingly peculiar. Tuesday's evening television news program never showed the faces of the news readers, for example, as if they were embarrassed to be seen. The English-language news was canceled, and all programming ended early.

Nobody interviewed seems to believe the Government propaganda, and it is so discredited that it seems to make most people even angrier than they were.

The Government spokesman said in his estimate of casualties that more than 5,000 soldiers had been wounded, compared with 2,000 citizens wounded. He said that the number of 300 killed included "troops, thugs and spectators," but did not indicate which were most numerous. But he said that only 23 students were known to have died. . . .

Foreboding Grasps Beijing; Army Units Crisscross City; Foreigners Hurry to Leave
By Nicholas D. Kristof

BEIJING, Thursday, June 8—As reports of clashes between military units on the outskirts of Beijing continued, a major convoy of tanks and trucks returned to the capital early today, dashing hopes that the unit responsible for large-scale killing might be withdrawing.

On Wednesday, three tank-led convoys headed out of the city toward the east. All were assumed to belong to the 27th Army, the unit most responsible for the killing of hundreds or possibly thousands of protesters and bystanders here since Sunday. Clashes were then reported in Tongxian County, about 20 miles east of Beijing, but like most such reports they could not be confirmed.

The crisscrossing of the capital by nervous military units compounded the sense of urgency at foreign embassies. The United States and other countries ordered an evacuation of diplomats' families, and some embassies said they would also be sending staff members home. . . .

Everything about China is tinged with the surreal these days, even the troop movements.

"Down with chaos!" several thousand troops shouted in unison on Wednesday as they marched east along the Avenue of Eternal Peace, accompanied by scores of military vehicles. "Down with corruption! Fight the counterrevolutionaries! Fight the fascists!"

And then, fueling the chaos around them, the troops simultaneously began firing their submachine guns into the air, creating a deafening thunder that lasted several minutes and sent people diving to the ground. It was not clear if they were firing as a show of strength, to clear the streets of spectators, or for some other reason.

This morning, shortly before dawn, tanks escorted scores of troop trucks west along the Avenue of Eternal Peace toward Tiananmen Square, the clatter of tank treads softened slightly by a gentle rain. It was no clearer why the convoy was now heading west than why it had gone east the previous day.

It was similarly unclear who, if anyone, is running China. The country's pre-eminent leader, Deng Xiaoping, was last seen on May 16, and there were rumors that he is dead or dying. But the morning news programs and the Communist Party newspaper, *People's Daily*, which reappeared for the first time in several days, reported that Prime Minister Li Peng had held a meeting, suggesting that he still is in authority. . . .

The Government issued a statement attacking the decision to give refuge in the American Embassy to Fang Lizhi, the astrophysicist, who is China's best-known dissident.

"The refuge provided to Fang by the U.S. Embassy in Beijing is an interference in China's internal affairs," read the statement, issued by the official New China News Agency.

On the Surface, Beijing Starts to Appear Normal
By Sheryl WuDunn

BEIJING, June 8—A bitter memory lingers on a narrow street where soldiers opened fire on scores of citizens last Sunday, but even here on South Pond Street, life today seemed to be gradually returning to normal.

A man selling bananas now stands where neighbors say an old man was shot in the head Sunday morning, and part of the street has become a nursery for children who chase each other in circles a block away from the Avenue of Eternal Peace, or Changan Avenue, which is still controlled by troops.

Neighbors took their turns walking gingerly toward the avenue to peer beyond the police barricade at the troops. Just days before, few of them dared to venture that far.

The rumble of tank treads and the sporadic crackle of machine-gun fire continued in the capital today. But the atmosphere of fear and apprehension that cast a pall over Beijing earlier this week seemed to fade today as people on bicycles flooded the streets, mail trucks began to resume their rounds, and many Government offices resumed operation. People answered the phone at more than half of 26 Government offices called today. Today, much more than in previous days, there seemed a genuine possibility that life would soon return to normal— although there remains a deep bitterness against the Government.

But this calm may be only superficial. While people's activities may hint of normalcy, many citizens, like the residents of South Pond Street, still harbor a deep anger against the Government.

"The blood of those who were killed has already hardened on the gate down the road," said one woman.

The Government has blamed the chaos that has stricken the city on "a very small number" of counterrevolutionaries and thugs whom it accuses of conspiring to overthrow the Government.

"We are all counterrevolutionaries," said a 30-year-old woman, with some bitterness. "We are all thugs now."

Next to her, a young man said, "Only a very small number of people support the Government."

Although garbage lay scattered in the streets, the authorities had towed away many of the burned-out vehicles and buses that citizens used to make road blocks. Tonight's news program also showed soldiers sweeping the streets of debris from recent fighting.

For the first time since the military crackdown, troops even allowed citizens on Changan Avenue and on the north side of Tiananmen Square early this morning for about half an hour. The square had been the campsite of pro-democracy student demonstrators until soldiers cleared the area Sunday morning. Now the square is an encampment for thousands of soldiers and their tanks and trucks.

When the area was sealed off again this morning, it was by the police rather than by army troops, and the atmosphere seemed much less tense than before. Leaving one's home to buy vegetables still involves a risk, but it is smaller than it was a few days ago, and residents seemed to have stopped building barricades at intersections.

Groups of troops still patrolled the capital, as they marched in formation through neighborhood streets, and gunfire echoed periodically. But along major roads and bridges where armed soldiers had set up camp, citizens of all ages gathered and chatted with them.

The fervor of their appeals was gone, and instead the citizens were restrained and polite, taking care not to taunt or anger the armed soldiers.

"We hope you think of yourselves as the army for the people," a young man said calmly to one of the soldiers. "We hope you will protect, and not harm, us."

Some of the soldiers listened silently to the pleas of the people, while others laughed and joked. This group of troops said it was from the 39th Army, from the northeastern city of Shenyang, and some soldiers even said they did not approve of the massacre committed Sunday by troops widely believed to be from the 27th Army.

"They have tarnished the image of the army," said one soldier to a small crowd of citizens plying him with questions about his views on the 27th Army.

"We wouldn't kill people," said another soldier. "We are the people's army." But a woman hearing this turned away in disgust.

"That's what they've been saying all along, but look what happened," she said as she walked away. . . .

Democracy Movement: Over, for the Time Being
By Nicholas D. Kristof

BEIJING, June 11—The bloodstains are scarcely visible on the pavement now, the once ubiquitous posters calling for greater freedom are now only tattered shreds, and no one dares protest as the prisons open up for those who sought change.

The democracy movement, which in just eight weeks convulsed China and awakened aspirations throughout the nation for a more open political system, seems finally to have collapsed, for now. Even in cities around the country where protest reached a peak last week in reaction to the shooting of hundreds or possibly thousands of demonstrators in Beijing, resistance has collapsed and protesters are awaiting their fates.

The collapse of the movement suggests the difficulties that Chinese dissidents face in sustaining any organized opposition to the Government. The authorities apparently retain the loyalty of the security apparatus and the army, and the result is that they can intimidate an active opposition into at least a sullen acquiescence.

In the pre-dawn hours on June 4, when soldiers were firing their guns on demonstrators and the crowd was retreating down Beijing's Changan Avenue, anguished young men carried the bloodied corpses of their friends and bellowed their response: "Strike! Strike! Strike!" But there was no general strike. People stayed away from work for a few days—mostly because of fear of stray bullets—but there was never an organized strike. Now workers are returning to their factories.

Last week, many Chinese also hoped that some military units were ready to attack the 27th Army, which was responsible for most of the bloodshed, and depose the elements in the leadership that had launched the crackdown. There were some murky reports of military skirmishes, but it now seems increasingly unlikely that the army will intervene in support of democracy.

"There is no hope," said a Beijing University student who has been active in the democracy movement. A few weeks ago, he would have been happy to be quoted by name; now he is afraid to allow his name to be used.

"The movement is over," he continued. "Maybe it can come back later on, maybe there can be some underground organization, but essentially everyone is terrified into submission. Who can resist guns?"

The democracy movement has several times risen after what seemed to be fatal blows, and the situation in China is unstable. But for now, intimidation seems to prevail.

The tangible achievements of the last two months—a freer press, a network of student organizations, an unofficial student newspaper, an unofficial labor union, an immense number of ad hoc bulletin boards where people posted essays and articles from foreign newspapers—all have vanished. The exhilaration and boldness of the last two months have been replaced by pain and panic.

The university campuses are empty, the loudspeakers quiet, and the student organizations disbanded. Since all the students have gone home, it would be difficult to revive the student movement even if the atmosphere were more tolerant.

Still, beneath the surface and beyond the superficial expressions of assent there is a profound rage and bitterness at the nation's aging leadership. In some past crackdowns, such as the 1957 anti-rightist campaign, there was a reservoir of good will toward the Government, and so people wondered if maybe the leadership was right even when it did things that seemed on their face to be bad. But the good will has long since dissipated, and it is virtually impossible to find somebody who in private has anything positive to say about the Government.

Even if the democracy movement has lost this battle, this rage is likely to resurface. Both Chinese and foreign experts note that there has been a regular pattern of a period of growing tolerance followed by a crackdown and then crackdown followed by a steady increase in tolerance and democracy, followed by a new crackdown. Each time the flowering of ideas and enthusiasm for democracy has been greater than the previous one, and so most people expect that after a few months or years, the movement will re-emerge as vigorous as ever.

"Democracy is now engraved in people's hearts, so you can't say the movement is washed up," said a young worker who sympathized with the recent demonstrations but was not much involved himself. "Even ordinary people who don't really understand what the students want, they feel in their hearts a hatred for the Government that makes them support the students."

While most people believe that the democracy movement, as a mass campaign, has definitely lost the first round, many say the present leadership is unstable and could still be ousted by other elements within the Communist Party. The leadership still has not summoned a Central Committee meeting to ratify the dismissal of the party General Secretary, Zhao Ziyang, and most people believe that Mr. Zhao has a number of silent supporters on the Central Committee.

It is not yet clear how the provinces and localities will react to the political furor in Beijing, but so far they seem to be unenthusiastic about a retreat to the purges of the Maoist era.

Two years ago, the campaign against "bourgeois liberalization" collapsed partly because provinces did little to implement it. Now Chinese intellectuals are hoping that the same will happen this year, and they are fleeing to the provinces because they feel they are safer than the capital.

Almost anything seems possible, including some kind of a power play or revolt within the leadership that would bring less hard-line elements to the fore. And if this does not happen, many believe that the political problems and economic challenges that the Government faces will be so severe that Prime Minister Li Peng will be hard pressed to last a year.

SUMMER 1989

As *the enthusiasm on the streets of China was turning into anxiety and then to despair, people in Poland, who had been through similar emotional cycles over the past decade, were embarking on something that had never happened before under Communism—openly contested elections for a parliament that was to be more than a rubber stamp. As agreed in the round-table talks held during the winter, the elections were organized in such a way as to assure the Communists a bloc of seats in the lower house, which along with those allotted to their docile allied parties would assure them a majority. In the newly reconstituted Senate, however, all 100 seats were up for grabs, and there, it was thought, the Solidarity-backed candidates would make the largest gains. From Solidarity's perspective the election turned out considerably better than this. As summer approached and the cherries blossomed, revolutionary élan was giving way to energetic political campaigning of the sort that had never been seen within any Communist country. Even though there was little tumult in the streets, it was nevertheless a remarkable season. People who until very recently had been in prison or hiding as fugitives were running for the highest offices as heroes of the nation. At the same time the leaders of the party were relinquishing power and prerogatives and were virtually shrinking in full view as the election approached.*

Communist Wallflowers Join Democracy's Dance
By John Tagliabue

WARSAW, May 23—The Communist Party's candidates held an open house Saturday, and they were selling warm Coca-Cola, toilet paper and biographies of President Bush.

The Coke was a kind of refreshment. The toilet paper, a notoriously scarce commodity in present-day Poland, was a come-on for indifferent voters, and the Bush biographies were being autographed by the author, Longin Pastusiak, a Communist Party candidate for the Senate and one of the country's best-known America scholars.

For the first time since early postwar years, Poland's Communist Party is waging an election campaign, one that essentially pits it against the Solidarity trade union movement. But while Solidarity is fighting aggressively, the party has been a wallflower, trying to interest Poles in a party most of them hold responsible for 40 years of repression and mismanagement.

"I'll probably lose," said Jerzy Wojtysiak, a 46-year-old building contractor who is running on the independent list, which the Communist leadership hopes will siphon votes from Solidarity. "You know about the Roman Emperor Caligula, how they elected his horse to the Senate?" he asks. "Well, here, if they brought a cow with a sign that said Solidarity, it would get elected."

At a rally that was billed as an occasion to meet the candidates, Mr. Wojtysiak stood in a schoolyard out in the Wola district of Warsaw, amid gray apartment buildings, where children played games, sipped Coke and heard a group wail an American country-and-western tune that went, "I hope your dreams come true." None of the Solidarity people showed up since the union rarely sends candidates to such rallies because they seldom offer a chance for debate and the union resists giving any semblance of support to the party and its allies.

Few voters came, and those who did appeared very much more interested in toilet paper than politics.

Ireneusz Szrajner, a Communist candidate from a Wola housing project, uses none of the signs, symbols or slogans of the party. There are no endorsements from smiling party bosses, no mention of Gen. Wojciech Jaruzelski or the Prime Minister, Mieczyslaw Rakowski, on any posters or leaflets. The party organization in Warsaw has eschewed the hammer and sickle on streetcar advertisements, choosing instead a bright red-and-white stylized figure of a mermaid, the symbol of Warsaw, waving a Polish flag.

Mr. Szrajner, a 42-year-old engineer, is down-to-earth. "Do you want to have a telephone?" his election leaflets ask. "Then vote for Ireneusz Szrajner." That is because in his neighborhood, a cluster of high-rises housing 6,500 families, there are 200 telephones.

To offset the unpopularity of its leaders and record, the party has sought popular figures from the stage, television and public life. Poland's first astronaut, Miroslaw Hermaszewski, an Army officer who rode in a Soviet craft, is running for the Senate. In Wroclaw, an industrial center in Silesia, the local zookeeper, who also stars with his wife in a popular television show about animals, is a Communist candidate.

Whatever the outcome of the election, the party hardly forfeits its primacy. Though elections to the 100-seat Senate will be entirely open, the Communists and their allies in two smaller parties are guaranteed 65 percent of the seats in the more powerful lower chamber.

While in Warsaw, where Mr. Szrajner is running, the local party apparatus decreed that any party member who obtained 3,000 signatures would be on the ballot, party leaders in other regions established a process to assure selection of the party's preferred candidate.

Competitive caucuses and competition as in Warsaw were the means preferred by the party leader, General Jaruzelski, who appears to be following the lead of Mikhail S. Gorbachev in exploiting such competition to weed out old faces and inject new vigor into the prostrate party.

"The process is important not only for the elections, but also for the party," said Ludwik Krasucki, a leading party ideologist. "We need changes, and this creates a possibility for volunteers to come forward."

Fired by successes in these pre-election caucuses, liberal party thinkers like Mr. Krasucki, who is also the deputy editor of the party's ideological journal, muse about the day when the party may evolve into a "modern left-wing party."

The anguish over all this among the party's conservatives is threatening to split its ranks. Their anger is raised by Solidarity's campaign claim to an agreement the union says was struck with the authorities that while the present elections are limited, those in four years will be entirely free.

As the campaign heats up, those in the party averse to change show signs of the party striking back. In Warsaw today, a court angered students by refusing to fulfill agreements reached between the Communist authorities and Solidarity and register a Solidarity-affiliated student union. Some 200 students chanting anti-Government slogans tried to march on central Warsaw, and some fought with the police and shouted "Down with Communism!" About 20 protesters were detained.

This evening, television viewers were startled to discover that Solidarity's weekly election campaign program had been struck from the listing and replaced with a song-and-dance show. A speaker on the screen announced laconically that the program offended "the policy of reconciliation."

Mr. Krasucki said internal party studies showed about 10 to 12 percent of party members reject the changes represented by the balloting, while 23 to 25 percent fully supported them. "The majority are in the middle, and they are waiting to see whether the reforms will succeed," he said. "If they succeed, they will be with us."

"Both clear tendencies are playing a bigger role than the persons in the middle," he said. "What Poland needs is a return to the middle."

But if the still-ruling party was undergoing stress in the process, there were other Poles who were clearly euphoric as they watched their candidates campaign openly with speeches that a year earlier could have only appeared in the clandestine press.

In an Unpredictable Land, the Pariah as Candidate
By John Tagliabue

WARSAW, June 1—The indictment in Jacek Kuron's trial for anti-Government activity in 1983 describes him this way: "Not working, no estate, no decorations, nonassociated." Despite such meager qualifications, Mr. Kuron has been a favorite target of official repression over the years.

Twice he was ejected from the Communist Party: the first time in 1953, after six months' membership, for refusal to submit to self-criticism, and again in 1964. Once he was beaten senseless by the police and left with a concussion.

All told, the 56-year-old Solidarity leader has spent nearly nine years in prison for crimes ranging from attempting to overthrow the system to undermining the alliance with Moscow. Now he is a Solidarity candidate in the election on Sunday, Poland's first experiment in competitive elections in nearly half a century.

Yet Mr. Kuron's race is unusual for reasons other than his background, which has produced charges that he is a Communist and anti-Semitic slurs although he is not a Jew. It is perhaps the most intensely watched and compelling match in the country because his opponent is one of Poland's most distinguished lawyers and defenders of human rights causes, Wladyslaw Sila-Nowicki. Mr. Sila-Nowicki, once a chief Solidarity adviser, enjoys strong backing from some of Poland's Roman Catholic bishops.

On Wednesday night, the burly Mr. Kuron, clad typically in T-shirt, blue jeans and denim jacket, and clutching a microphone, paced like an aging warhorse in the cavernous basement of St. Zygmunt's Church, a cluster of concrete spires in Warsaw's lately patrician Zoliborz district. It is here that he is running against Mr. Sila-Nowicki.

The tall, 76-year-old lawyer fell from favor three years ago after agreeing to join an advisory council to Gen. Wojciech Jaruzelski, when the opposition was still boycotting the Communist leader. Though Solidarity is assured 35 percent of the 460-seat Parliament, it has declared the balloting for its seats free and democratic, opening the door to challengers like Mr. Sila-Nowicki, who for his part says he is running to give Solidarity voters a clear choice.

In response to the challenge, Mr. Kuron has plunged into a grueling campaign, rousing crowds that, night after night, jam local movie houses and church basements with impassioned defenses of his record and his vision of Poland's future.

The campaign tactics of the race are strikingly up-to-date by Western standards. Andrzej Anusz, a 24-year-old history student, commands an army of 100 volunteers, high school and college students who wallpapered Zoliborz with red and white posters proclaiming the time and place of Mr. Kuron's twice-daily public appearances. Others depict the burly, balding candidate side by side with Solidarity's leader, Lech Walesa. A minibus cruises the neighborhood, loudspeakers on its roof blaring the Kuron message.

Although he lacks the broad appeal of leaders like Mr. Walesa, Mr. Kuron has been called the godfather of Solidarity. A veteran of the Workers' Defense Committee in the 1970's, he organized an information service during the strikes that spawned Solidarity in 1980, and again last year during the labor unrest that led to its return, to keep reporters abreast of events. Last year, he was arrested.

Solidarity's intellectual roots go back to elaborate strategies Mr. Kuron developed in the 1970's with other independent leaders, like the essayist Adam Michnik, who calls Mr. Kuron a spiritual mentor.

These themes echo at his rallies. In response to a woman's question whether elections will be truly free in four years, as promised, he said: "Political agreements in which political forces divide power are not worth the paper they're written on. If an agreement is real, not fictitious, it is worth the strength of the partners that sign it."

"With the army, the militia and the bureaucracy, the party has about 65 percent of the power," he said, only half-joking, "and the accords we reached with the authorities take into account those circumstances. But those accords give us a chance to organize ourselves. In four years, we will create a new balance. Then we can approach a new agreement with a new balance."

"Is there any certainty?" he asks. "No. But we have a 35 percent chance."

Mr. Kuron spends much of his time seeking to exorcise what many Solidarity supporters see as the greatest sin of his past—his membership in the Communist Party. He explains that he was young—"I stemmed from a very strongly socialist family, my father was a socialist"—and how his membership in the party ended in 1965 when he was sent to prison for the heresy of charging that Poland was run by a "dictatorship of the political bureaucracy" that exploited workers under Communism as the capitalists had done earlier.

Some Zoliborz voters are unhappy about his professed agnosticism. Pamphlets that appear to have been the work of Solidarity's radical student wing, which opposes accommodation with the Communist Party, have appeared, denouncing "the Jew Kuron." Mr. Kuron's campaign managers believe them to be counterfeit, the work of the Government's security police.

For the authorities, Mr. Kuron has evolved from a dangerous enemy into something of a reasonable negotiator and supporter of compromise with the Communists. Still, a victory by Mr. Sila-Nowicki would not be unwelcome, weakening the opposition as it enters Parliament.

Yet Poland is an unpredictable place. Witold Trzeciakowski, a Solidarity economist who shares the Solidarity ticket with Mr. Kuron, gets up to tell one of the few jokes, a flash of black humor, that the campaign has spawned. "Kuron and Kiszczak are taking a walk," the economist says, referring to Gen. Mieczyslaw Kiszczak, the Interior Minister and the Government's negotiator with Solidarity.

"Kuron reproaches Kiszczak: 'Why did you have to demand 65 percent of Parliament?'

"Kiszczak replies, 'Why did you have to demand wage indexing?'

"A voice speaks out," Mr. Trzeciakowski says, " 'Recreation's over. Back to your cells.' "

Everyone, including Mr. Kuron, laughs.

On the very day that Chinese troops were shooting into demonstrators calling for democracy, Poles were lining up to vote in the freest elections ever held under Communism. By the time they ended, Solidarity-backed candidates had been swept in and the party was repudiated. In the weeks and months ahead, the processes unleashed by the elections would go so far that Jacek Kuron, former critic and gadfly of social change, was serving as Minister of Labor in a non-Communist government. But that is getting ahead of the story.

Poland Flirts with Pluralism Today

By John Tagliabue

WARSAW, June 3—Solidarity, born in 1980 as an independent trade union, is being reborn on Sunday as an all-but-official opposition party in the first openly contested election in Eastern Europe in more than four decades.

Four years from now, the movement's banners proclaim, Poland will see a genuinely free election. By implication, Solidarity is campaigning for votes this weekend by promising that limited power is within reach now while the prospect of real power is at least within sight.

For now, with only the Communist Party and its allies formally recognized as political parties, the union must field its candidates as independents, but there are 261 candidates running under a loosely knit organization called the Citizens' Committee of Lech Walesa, named after the union's leader. Mr. Walesa is not running himself, but appears to be waiting in the wings to negotiate for Solidarity in the likely event that the movement emerges with something of a parliamentary veto over the Government's initiatives.

Behind Solidarity's dramatic return to the political stage was the Government's realization that the country's economic problems are so severe that they cannot be resolved without the help of the union. But within Solidarity are conflicting views of how to deal with the crisis.

"Solidarity is itself a child of the system," said Marian Drozdowski, a historian at the Polish Academy of Sciences and a Solidarity supporter. "At heart, there is some kind of belief in a powerful state at the center of the economy."

Echoing other observers of the movement, Mr. Drozdowski predicted that "after the elections there will be a disintegration," as

Solidarity strategists more in favor of market economic solutions find it increasingly difficult to support the mainstream labor union orientation, with its focus on job security and maintaining standards of living.

In fact, since its restoration to legal status in April, Solidarity has been slow to sign up new members. It now counts about one million members, compared with the seven million it boasted when martial law was imposed in December 1981.

According to Jan Litynski, a Warsaw union leader who is running on the Solidarity list, this is partly because Solidarity has thrust its limited resources into running the election campaign. He conceded, however, that the relatively low membership is also partly a reflection of a stronger mood of caution and diminished optimism among workers burned once by the use of military force.

Mikolaj Kozakiewicz, a distinguished sociologist and incumbent Parliament deputy who is running for the lower house on the so-called national list of candidates proposed by the Communist-led bloc, believes that divisions after the election will not be limited to Solidarity.

"We can expect after the elections some kind of shifts within all the movements, including the Communist Party, maybe reaching a level as it was before the war when we had 12 to 15 parties," he said.

"As is normal, some will then die out, others will create new alliances, until a more reasonable number emerges at the next elections in four years' time," he added.

Mr. Kozakiewicz believes that Solidarity itself will split into separate groups, one carrying on the functions of a party while another focuses on trade union functions. Mr. Walesa is expected to seek his future in the union wing of Solidarity.

On the Government side, it appears that the Communist Party leader, Gen. Wojciech Jaruzelski, hopes that the balloting process sweeps away apparatchiks resistant to change so that new blood can be pumped into the party—a process employed by President Mikhail S. Gorbachev in March's voting in the Soviet Union.

But the balloting could have the opposite effect of dealing a serious blow to the party's liberal, change-oriented wing. That is because 35 leaders of the Communist-led bloc, including the Prime Minister, Mieczyslaw Rakowski, and Gen. Czeslaw Kiszczak, the Interior Minister who was the chief negotiator with Solidarity, have been put on a national list of candidates.

To win, these unopposed candidates must obtain the support of at least 50 percent of the voters, who must express their preference by not crossing out the candidates' names. Solidarity has mounted a campaign to have voters cross off Communist nominees.

Under sweeping accords concluded in April between Solidarity and the Communists, the union's candidates are in theory capable of sweeping all 100 seats in the Senate, where voting is open and competitive, and can win 35 percent of the lower house, where seats have been apportioned according to a complex formula agreed to at the negotiations this year between Solidarity and the authorities.

The Communist Party will have another 38 percent and parties aligned until now with the Communists the rest.

Runoff elections June 18 will decide any seats not won outright in the first round. Within days of that vote, a joint session of both houses is expected to select a President of the Republic for a six-year term. Given the Communist-bloc majority in the lower house, Gen. Jaruzelski is expected to be chosen. The bold experiment in democracy poses no immediate threat to the Communist Party's monopoly on power, but it will provide Poles with a clear public referendum on the Communists, who have ruled Poland since the country became the first in Eastern Europe to fall under Soviet domination after the war.

Understandably, the campaign has provoked varying official reactions throughout the Eastern bloc, deepening the ideological divide between countries fired more or less by the momentum for change coming from the Soviet Union.

In Hungary, where moves toward change are apace of those in Poland, attention in the official press and television has been rapt. Opposition forces in Hungary reached agreement this week to begin talks with the Communist leadership that could lead to balloting comparable to Poland's.

In East Germany and Czechoslovakia, where resistance to change is strong, reports on Poland were limited and hostile. East Berlin's Communist Party daily, *Neues Deutschland*, has published one report in the last two weeks, reprinting an article from Poland's Communist Party daily that scathingly attacked Solidarity. *Rude Pravo*, the Czechoslovak party daily, has contented itself with reprinting aggressively polemical reports from the Polish Communist press on Solidarity and its allies in the Roman Catholic Church.

The first major step toward institutionalizing democracy in the East bloc came in the Polish elections. Other steps were soon to follow, first in Poland, then Hungary, and then in those very countries whose leaders had been so contemptuous of Polish reforms—East Germany, Czechoslovakia, Bulgaria and Rumania. But as summer approached, Poland was out in front.

Big Solidarity Victory Seen in Poland
By John Tagliabue

WARSAW, June 4—In their first chance to express at the ballot box their feelings about 44 years of Communist rule, Polish voters today appeared to have voted overwhelmingly for candidates endorsed by the Solidarity opposition and to have endangered many unopposed Communists whose election was thought to have been insured by the intricate election rules.

Informal samplings by foreign journalists and exit polls conducted by the opposition raised the prospect that the Communists could fall short, in what would be a crushing setback, of the majority of 65 percent of the seats in the Parliament's lower house that had been guaranteed to them and their supporters by their agreement with Solidarity.

Communist candidates and their allies, running unopposed and on a separate election list from opposition and independent candidates, appeared to be failing in many cases to get the 50 percent of the votes cast that is required for their election to be certified. If they fail to get 50 percent, their seats are supposed to be declared vacant.

Although the system of separate lists was contrived to minimize comparisons between support for the Communists and support for Solidarity, it seemed clear that many more votes were cast for opposition candidates than for supporters of the regime.

By contrast, candidates endorsed by the Solidarity movement—which became a legal organization again less than two months ago—appeared to be rolling up huge majorities in races for the lower house, called the Sejm (Assembly), and the Senate.

The contest for the 100 seats in the Senate was an open one, conducted with a single list of candidates, and there Solidarity's nominees appeared to be on their way to a solid majority in the most open election the Soviet bloc has seen in more than four decades.

Official results were not expected until later in the week, but if the results for the Communists and their allies were as poor as the samplings and exit polls indicated, the opposition may have exceeded its expectations to such an extent as to endanger Solidarity's agreement with the regime of Gen. Wojciech Jaruzelski.

Under the agreement, the governing party needs its guaranteed 299 seats in the 460-member Assembly to assure General Jaruzelski's election as President in an indirect vote by the Parliament's two chambers. Communist officials have hinted that they might then seek to block the convening of the Parliament on constitutional grounds, pointing to a requirement that all 460 seats in the Assembly be filled.

The Solidarity leader, Lech Walesa, who was not standing as a candidate, expressed anxiety about the effects of lopsided results in favor of his movement. "I think that too big a percentage of our people getting through would be disturbing and might force a fight on us," Mr. Walesa said after casting his vote in the Oliwa district of Gdansk, his hometown, according to Reuters.

Though the day was sunny, voter turnout appeared low. The Government said that turnout by 7:30 P.M. varied considerably by province. Low attendance was marked in Lodz, where only 40.9 percent voted, and Bialystok, 50 percent. The largest turnout, according to a Communist Party spokesman, Jan Bisztyga, was in Wloclawek, in central Poland, at 70 percent.

Adam Szostkiewicz, the spokesman for Solidarity's organizing committee in Cracow, said by phone that an informal exit poll of about 100 people in each of the city's nearly 20 districts showed that 75 percent to 80 percent had voted for the union's candidates.

The Government appeared nervous that some of its best-known candidates, running unopposed on the so-called national list, might fail to receive the required 50 percent.

Major losses on the national list would be a blow to General Jaruzelski, who has sought to use the vote to sweep reform-minded leaders into key posts. Speaking in Gdansk, Mr. Walesa said one of the Communist candidates he had chosen was Tadeusz Fiszbach, the Gdansk party leader in the years 1980–81, when the accords that gave birth to Solidarity were signed. Mr. Fiszbach later left office in disgrace and was named Ambassador to Finland after hard-line party factions prevailed.

General Jaruzelski, while declining to say how he had voted, said he hoped that Poland "will get peace from these elections."

"This is a huge step toward democracy," the Polish leader said after casting his vote.

First partial returns were expected to begin arriving on Monday, but official results in most election districts were not expected until later this week, after hand counting of the ballots.

It was as Mr. Walesa feared. Solidarity's people had won everywhere. Moreover, many of the leading Communists who were running unopposed failed to get enough votes to assure victory. Now Solidarity's gravest problem was that society would be expecting their people to bring about real and rapid improvements in daily life, while technically power still lay with the party.

Stunning Vote Casts Poles into Uncharted Waters

By John Tagliabue

WARSAW, June 5—As the breadth and depth of Solidarity's overwhelming victory over the Communists in Poland's freest election in more than four decades emerged today, both the Communist leadership and Solidarity faced questions never confronted before in a Communist-ruled Eastern European country.

To be sure, the Communists have never relied on parliamentary majorities to maintain control. Yet neither had Communists ever resorted to competitive elections before.

For the Government, there was the question of how to continue governing when the results of the elections, though only partial and not official, showed that Solidarity enjoyed the support of the broad majority of Poles. . . .

What appeared to most upset the Communist leadership, as well as some of Solidarity's senior strategists, was the danger to a large bloc of unopposed Communist candidates whose election was supposed to have been assured under the intricate election rules. . . .

Thus the immediate concern was how to get these candidates into the lower house despite the results. To the end, senior Solidarity advisers were hoping they would surmount the 50 percent hurdle. "We would prefer they got 50.5 percent," a Solidarity strategist in Warsaw acknowledged.

"We are trying to shift the focus of power from the party to the Parliament," he explained, "and for that we need these people in Parliament. . . ."

Warsaw Accepts Solidarity Sweep and Humiliating Losses by Party

By John Tagliabue

WARSAW, June 8—As Government and Solidarity negotiators sat down tonight to map out potential fields of political collaboration, the

Government announced the official returns showing the extent of Solidarity's success in Sunday's national elections.

At the start of the talks with Solidarity this evening, Gen. Czeslaw Kiszczak, the Interior Minister who signed the arrest order for the union leader, Lech Walesa, when the Government imposed martial law to crush the movement in 1981, now shook his hand, and told him, "Lech, my hearty congratulations on your election success."

Mr. Walesa, who traveled by train to the talks from his home in the Baltic seaport of Gdansk, replied, "I want to use it for the benefit of Poland."

General Kiszczak, along with the Prime Minister, Mieczyslaw Rakowski, and other members of the Communist Party elite, failed to win seats in Parliament, although they ran as unopposed candidates whose election was thought to have been assured by the complex voting. The same humiliation befell six other members of the party's 17-member ruling Politburo.

According to the official figures, the vote swept in 92 of Solidarity's candidates to the 100-seat Senate, which was contested in open balloting. Eight seats in which none of the competing candidates obtained 50 percent of the votes will be contested in runoffs June 18. There appears to be only one seat, in Slupsk, in northern Poland, where the Communist candidate, a successful private businessman named Henryk Stoklosa, who made a fortune running what is reputed to be Poland's largest private enterprise producing animal fodder, is given a good chance.

In voting for the 161 seats accorded Solidarity in the lower house, the Sejm, only one of the union-endorsed candidates failed to be elected in the first round, necessitating a runoff.

By contrast, the electorate dealt a mortifying rebuke to the Communist Party and its allies. None of those candidates were elected outright to the Senate, and only three obtained enough votes to be certified the winners in the elections to the lower house, in which a complex apportionment assures the Communist-led bloc 65 percent.

Moreover, only two of the Communist-bloc candidates on a list of 35 unopposed nominees to the lower house took the requisite 50 percent of the vote to take their seats. One of them, Mikolaj Kozakiewicz, is a leader of the small Peasant Party, allied with the Communists. Mr. Kozakiewicz, a respected sociologist, has been one of the most scathing critics of the Communist regime in the present Parliament.

The second, Adam Zielinski, is a little-known law professor and chief judge of Poland's highest administrative court. One Communist Party official speculated that Mr. Zielinski may have been elected inadvertently, since his name stood at the bottom of the 35-place alphabetical listing, and some voters may have missed it as they crossed out the names by making a large "x" on the ballot.

Voters in most of the 108 districts gave the Communists dismal returns, ranging from 25 percent down to 5 percent or lower. In one of the most striking defeats, the Government's former spokesman, Jerzy Urban, who is widely known from regular television appearances, ran as an independent for the lower house head-on against a popular Solidarity-endorsed actor, Andrzej Lapicki, and suffered defeat with 15.6 percent of the vote, against his opponent's 77.8 percent.

Among Solidarity's candidates, some of the more prominent to win seats in the Senate included Adam Michnik, the essayist and a leading intellectual light of the opposition, and in the lower house, Jacek Kuron, whom Mr. Michnik has often described as his mentor, who got 65.8 percent of the vote to defeat his opponent, the human rights lawyer Wladyslaw Sila-Nowicki, with 21 percent.

The election paved the way for a bizarre period of parliamentary bickering and maneuver. Finding themselves with a larger and more powerful bloc in Parliament then they had anticipated, the Solidarity-backed representatives were divided as to how to proceed. There were some who wanted to use their new muscle to punish the Communists, for example, to defeat their old nemesis General Wojciech Jaruzelski as he sought parliamentary election to the new post of President. But there were others who cautioned that the still-fragile quest they were embarked upon would require the support of Jaruzelski and the army he commanded. They claimed that the old party liberals were needed to protect the process from party hard-liners who would love to topple it. In the end, Jaruzelski was elected to the post by one vote but only with the help of key abstentions by Solidarity members. Another debate among the Solidarity bloc concerned how they should use their wind-fall from the elections. Should they remain as an opposition for a while, learning parliamentary practices, or should they immediately vie for real power?

Solidarity Takes Its Elected Place in the Parliament
By Henry Kamm

WARSAW, July 4—Solidarity, vilified and outlawed for eight years until April, jubilantly entered Parliament today as the first freely elected opposition party to do so in a Communist country.

As the Assembly opened its session at noon, Lech Walesa, the Solidarity leader, sat in the place of honor of Poland's newest political institution—the opposition front bench. On the Communist front bench sat Gen. Wojciech Jaruzelski, the man who imposed martial law in 1981 to crush the movement Mr. Walesa founded and put him and his companions in prison.

Later in the day, the two men sat next to one another in the Senate. But at this first meeting, in the lower house, the general sat stolid and unsmiling, barely speaking to those near him and occasionally applauding politely. The Nobel Prize–winning union leader, at ease and visibly enjoying every moment, carried on an animated conversation throughout the formalities with his movement's parliamentary leader, Bronislaw Geremek, and occasionally exchanged jokes with those behind him. Mr. Walesa and General Jaruzelski took no note of one another.

The Solidarity deputies and senators, most of whom still sported the badges bearing the familiar red and white logo on their suits or dresses, took visible satisfaction in reflecting on how far their movement had come. They recalled its birth in the strikes of 1980.

They spoke of the national exhilaration that followed the union's legalization in August 1980 and its crushing and banning by the declaration of martial law in December 1981.

There was a sense of having earned the rebirth of their movement last year in the crucible of renewed labor unrest, which forced the Government to extend implicit and finally explicit recognition of the fact that Solidarity had never ceased to exist.

Today was for the Solidarity members a day of quiet but full triumph. Janusz Onyszkiewicz said this evening at an Independence Day reception at the American Embassy that "the big day for us was the opening of the round-table, when we forced them to talk with us after all these years."

In the afternoon, when the newly created Senate gathered for the first time in the same hall as the Assembly, Gen. Jaruzelski and Mr. Walesa sat together in the front row as guests of honor, smiling and chatting for a moment before proceedings began. The Senate offered no Communist bench to accommodate Gen. Jaruzelski, the party's leader, because Solidarity swept 99 of the 100 seats, losing one to an independent.

Neither General Jaruzelski nor Mr. Walesa ran in the general elections last month.

Many who did watched from the visitors' gallery, among them Prime Minister Mieczyslaw Rakowski, Interior Minister Czeslaw Kiszczak, Defense Minister Florian Siwicki, the official trade union chief Alfred Miodowicz, and several other Politburo members. The voters denied them the right to sit as members, striking their names from the list of 35 unopposed candidates that had been thought sure of election to the lower house.

The union movement won, in addition to 99 seats in the newly created Senate, all 161 seats in the Assembly that it was permitted to contest under the agreement reached with the Communist Party in April.

The losers sat quietly, occasionally conversing with one another and unsmilingly enduring the cameras that were constantly trained on them from the adjoining press box.

They looked down on those whom until recently their party and government had jailed as "dissidents." Elevated to the legitimate status of opposition deputies were such prominent former political prisoners as Jacek Kuron, Adam Michnik and Janusz Onyszkiewicz, as well as Mr. Geremek.

In the Senate, the Solidarity leaders who were honored by the presence of their former jailers as they were sworn in included Bogdan Lis, Karol Modzelewski and Jan Jozef Lipski. Andrzej Wajda, the noted film and stage director, also took the oath of office.

In Parliament today, Mr. Michnik, who unlike his colleagues continued to eschew suit and tie and took his oath in jeans and an open-necked shirt, challenged the lower house's Communist majority when it presented only one candidate for the post of marshal, the officer who presides over sessions.

"Let's have elections here and not just voting," he said in his first appearance at the speaker's rostrum. His demand for more candidates was ignored and the single nominee, Mikolaj Kozakiewicz of the Peasant Party, the only survivor from the "national list," was chosen.

Mr. Kuron, whose friends said he had worn a suit only once, to meet President Bush earlier this year, astonished supporters by appearing in unaccustomed elegance.

The new deputy strayed from the routine of the inaugural session by attacking the Government for Poland's dire economic crisis and denouncing its recent raising of a wide range of consumer prices. "This chaotic policy of the Government is alone responsible for social disturbances and deep public unease," Mr. Kuron said.

Although the Communists intend the "round-table" agreement to safeguard their party's control until fully free elections in 1993, the structure of the new two-chamber Parliament does not guarantee it. The Senate has the right to veto decisions of the lower house. The veto can be overridden by two-thirds, or 306 votes, of the 460-member Assembly. The Communists and their coalition partners, the Democratic and Peasant parties, hold only 299 seats.

As the new Parliament went about its business of establishing a government, it grew more and more apparent that the Communists would not be able to rule on their own. The small, once docile parties that associated with the Communists for so long were finding it advantageous to cut deals with the Solidarity bloc, thus depriving the Communists of the edge they needed to form a government. In this situation the Communists were hoping to entice the Solidarity people—including many they had arrested—to support them as junior partners in a coalition.

Walesa Rejects Offer of Coalition
By John Tagliabue

WARSAW, July 25—The Solidarity leader, Lech Walesa, said today that his movement would not join a grand coalition with the Communist Party, but would prepare instead for the "inevitable" day when it would form a government on its own.

In a two-hour meeting with President Wojciech Jaruzelski, Mr. Walesa spurned the general's offer of a Solidarity-Communist coalition, presenting a statement asserting that in the face of Poland's "continuously deteriorating economic situation," the "only reasonable decision" for the Communists and their minor-party partners would be to hand over running of the Government to Solidarity, which he described as "those forces that enjoy the support of a majority of society."

"Everything indicates, however, that the coalition exercising power now is not ready to accept such a solution," Mr. Walesa said. "In this situation, it must, as a result, take over the whole responsibility for forming a Government.'. . .

"Our philosophy, our attitudes toward the Government, are different," he said. In a Communist-led coalition, Mr. Walesa said, Solidarity would be a "mere floral decoration."

"We would take responsibility for many bad things, we would try to lead the country to reform and we would be buried," he said. . . .

The headlines of the days that followed told the story of a deepening parliamentary crisis and political impasse.

Jaruzelski Says Warsaw Pact Opposes a Solidarity Premier
By John Tagliabue

WARSAW, July 26—President Wojciech Jaruzelski has told Solidarity that he cannot allow it to form a government because Poland's Communist neighbors "would look at this askance," a Solidarity official who attended talks with him said today.

The official, Jozef Slisz, head of Solidarity's rural wing, said General Jaruzelski, in the talks on Tuesday, mentioned "in particular" the Soviet Union, East Germany and Czechoslovakia as opposing the formation of a Solidarity Government or the naming of a Solidarity leader as Prime Minister. . . .

Jaruzelski Quits as Party Leader
By John Tagliabue

WARSAW, July 29—President Wojciech Jaruzelski resigned today as the leader of Poland's Communist Party and was replaced by his close associate, Prime Minister Mieczyslaw Rakowski, the Government press agency said.

At the same meeting, the party's Central Committee shook up its leadership. Besides accepting the resignation of General Jaruzelski, it dismissed 4 others from the 17-member Politburo and 5 of the 9 high-ranking party secretaries.

General Jaruzelski's resignation from the post of First Secretary was expected; he had pledged to step down if elected to the new office of President. When he became President, he gained powers greater than those he held as party secretary. . . .

General Chosen as Polish Prime Minister

By John Tagliabue

WARSAW, July 31—The newly elected Polish Communist Party leader, Mieczyslaw Rakowski, nominated the Interior Minister today to be his successor as Prime Minister, the nation's official press agency said.

The choice of Interior Minister Czeslaw Kiszczak comes as Poland braces for a possible round of sharp food-price increases in the wake of a Government decision to move Tuesday to make food and other essential goods subject to free-market forces. Price increases are a particularly sensitive political matter here, for they set off riots or strikes that toppled party leaders in 1956, 1970 and 1980.

The selection of General Kiszczak was announced by Mr. Rakowski to the Communist parliamentary caucus. Afterward, the floor leader of the Solidarity opposition in Parliament, Bronislaw Geremek, met with General Kiszczak and told him that Solidarity would refuse to provide Cabinet ministers for his Government. . . .

Solidarity Seeks to Oust Warsaw Premier

By John Tagliabue

WARSAW, Aug. 7—Solidarity mounted an effort today to oust the newly elected Prime Minister, Czeslaw Kiszczak, by appealing to small parties allied with the Communists in Parliament to swing their allegiance to an anti-Communist coalition.

Solidarity appears to believe that it can persuade the small Peasant and Democratic parties, whose loyalty to the Communists has been wavering, to withdraw support from General Kiszczak and throw it behind a Solidarity nominee for Prime Minister. Lech Walesa, the Solidarity leader, said efforts by General Kiszczak to assemble a Communist-led cabinet had worsened "the crisis of confidence" and "reaffirmed society's fears that essentially nothing has changed, that hope for the future is nonexistent."

In a statement released to news agencies, the union leader said, "I once again categorically oppose the formation of a new Government by General Czeslaw Kiszczak.". . .

Peasant Party: New Kingmakers for a New Poland
By John Tagliabue

WARSAW, Aug. 10—The newly complicated task of forming a Polish cabinet has turned a little-noticed political party that was a steady satellite of the Communists into a maverick force familiar to millions of Poles.

Today, officials of the party, the United Peasant Alliance, met with leaders of the Solidarity opposition to explore Lech Walesa's appeal this week for the Peasants to desert the Communists and switch to the opposition. Afterward, the two sides announced only that they intended to meet again.

On Wednesday, Aleksander Bentkowski, the Peasants' floor leader in Parliament, shocked Poles by announcing on state television that when it came to a vote, his group could be expected to oppose a cabinet assembled by the Communist Prime Minister, Gen. Czeslaw Kiszczak. . . .

Poland's Premier Offering to Yield to Non-Communist
By John Tagliabue

WARSAW, Aug. 14—Under increasing Soviet pressure for an end to Poland's Government crisis, Prime Minister Czeslaw Kiszczak said today that he would resign and ask that the leader of a small party traditionally allied with the Communists be allowed to form a cabinet.

In a statement read on state television, General Kiszczak said a "new situation has arisen" that appeared to provide a chance for the leader of the United Peasant Alliance, Roman Malinowski, to form a Cabinet "in which representatives of all forces in Parliament would be included."

On the basis of that new situation, General Kiszczak said he would ask that President Wojciech Jaruzelski "draw the appropriate conclusion.". . .

Senior Solidarity Aide Says He Is Being Named Premier
By John Tagliabue

WARSAW, Aug. 18—A senior Solidarity official said today that he would be nominated as Poland's Prime Minister. He would be the first non-Communist head of government in Eastern Europe since the early postwar years.

Various reports in the capital said that the official, Tadeusz Mazowiecki, would be formally nominated by President Wojciech Jaruzelski on Saturday. The nomination would then face a vote in Parliament.

Mr. Mazowiecki, a close aide to the Solidarity founder Lech Walesa, met with General Jaruzelski today and said afterward that he expected to be nominated and that he would accept. . . .

And finally, there came the word that Mr. Mazowiecki, a prominent Catholic editor and Solidarity organizer, had indeed become the first non-Communist to head a government in Eastern Europe since Stalin had imposed Soviet-style Communism there after the Second World War.

Jaruzelski, Moved By "Needs and Aspirations" of Poland, Names Walesa Aide Premier
By John Tagliabue

WARSAW, Aug. 19—The Communist President, Wojciech Jaruzelski, today designated a senior Solidarity official, Tadeusz Mazowiecki, to be the first non-Communist Prime Minister of Poland since the early postwar years.

"The President believes," said a statement issued by General Jaruzelski's office, that the formation of a Government headed by Mr. Mazowiecki would be "conducive to expeditiously overcoming economic difficulties, continuing reforms . . . and satisfying the needs and aspirations of Polish society."

Recalling the year of Solidarity's birth, Mr. Mazowiecki said, "I think there are a great many historic moments in our life, in my lifetime, and I can mention here 1980, that show we can still achieve a lot.

"I think we can gather our strength from within ourselves," he said. "This is not easy, but it is possible if everyone begins to realize and to feel that we are now on our own, and that it all has some sense and can lead somewhere."

The nomination of Mr. Mazowiecki was expected. He is a 62-year-old journalist, a devout Roman Catholic and a close adviser to the Solidarity leader, Lech Walesa, since the union's birth nine years ago.

If he succeeds in assembling a cabinet, it will be a substantial change in the type of rule found in the Soviet bloc since World War II.

Bush Administration officials welcomed the selection of Mr. Mazowiecki as a historic step, but their reaction was muted rather than jubilant as they noted the immense economic challenges he faces. "There is no sense of gloating here," said a State Department official. The nomination was another major success in a series of Solidarity victories that began last year when the outlawed union led nationwide strikes against economic conditions. The strikes led to the union's legalization, to negotiations with the Communist Government, and that led in turn to the June elections in which Solidarity soundly defeated Communist candidates for the Parliament. This success made it impossible for the Communists to form a government and led to President Jaruzelski's decision to agree to a Solidarity Prime Minister. Earlier this week, Mr. Walesa rejected offers to take the post himself and proposed his old ally, Mr. Mazowiecki. . . .

The political structure in Poland was one of the first to be put under Soviet domination after the war. It now appears that General Jaruzelski, pressed by the prospect of political and economic chaos and taking advantage of liberal policies of the Soviet leadership under Mikhail S. Gorbachev, has decided to take the step that will push Poland's political system beyond anything being attempted elsewhere in the East bloc.

The Government's announcement came as the Communist Party Central Committee met in Warsaw to consider the changes.

Tonight, the Communist Party let it be known it intends to fight for more than just the two Cabinet seats Solidarity says it is willing to give it—the posts of Defense Minister and Interior Minister.

Slawomir Wiatr, a Central Committee secretary, said "two portfolios do not constitute a coalition."

Addressing a news conference after the session, Mr. Wiatr said the party favored a grand coalition, athough he did not explain how this differed from what Solidarity was about to assemble. The Central Committee session, he said, discussed the substance of policy, not the division of cabinet seats.

The Government announcement came in a statement released in English by the official Polish press agency reporting that President Jaruzelski, "as a result of talks and consultations with parliamentary and nonparliamentary representatives of social and political groups," had nominated Mr. Mazowiecki, who is the editor in chief of *Tygod-*

nik Solidarnosci, the Solidarity weekly newspaper.

The statement was later read in Polish on national television, a stunning event for Poles who have never seen opposition to Communist Party rule countenanced in the postwar history of their country.

Earlier, the press agency reported that the President had accepted the resignation of the incumbent Prime Minister, Czeslaw Kiszczak, whose efforts to form a cabinet stumbled over Solidarity's bitter resistance to the former Interior Minister. Many Solidarity supporters reject him for his role in engineering the imposition of martial law on December 13, 1981, and hunting down nearly all the union leaders.

In his statement, the President described Mr. Mazowiecki as a "longtime Catholic activist," who he said had been a deputy in the assembly from 1961 to 1972.

"Later he began his activities in Solidarity," the statement went on, describing the nominee as "one of the leading activists of this organization," and the editor of its weekly newspaper.

Mr. Mazowiecki, a graying man with an angular face and a dry sense of humor, spent the day in the gardens of a home for the blind in Laski, west of the capital, run by Franciscan sisters. He said he had gone "to concentrate a bit before facing what awaits me.". . .

In Moscow, Tone Is a Studied Calm
By Bill Keller

MOSCOW, Aug. 17—The Soviet Union reacted with deliberate equanimity today to Poland's movement toward a government led by non-Communists, declaring that developments there were strictly an internal affair.

"This is entirely a matter to be decided by Poland," declared Yevgeny M. Primakov, a chief legislative deputy to President Mikhail S. Gorbachev, when asked by a visiting United States Congressional delegation about the possibility of a Polish coalition government excluding the Communists.

Mr. Primakov described the proposal for a coalition involving Solidarity and two smaller non-Communist parties as "reasonable."

Yuri A. Gremitskikh, a Foreign Ministry spokesman, said, "We can only hope that the outcome will be in the best interests of the Polish people." He declined to make a detailed comment on the ground that events in Poland were its own business.

Western diplomats who have taken soundings among senior officials said they received nothing but clear signals that Moscow's policy of noninterference was firm.

Mr. Gorbachev has repeatedly disavowed intervention in Eastern Europe, and surely realizes that any Soviet interference in Poland would endanger the warm relations with the West on which his hope of a domestic economic recovery depends. . . .

As Poland was leading the way, Hungary was not far behind in moving toward pluralistic political institutions. One major obstacle was what to do about the recent past, notably the 1956 uprising against Soviet and Communist domination. Until very recently the party line had been that the uprising, which cost an estimated 30,000 lives, had been a counterrevolution and that those who led it were justifiably executed as criminals. They were buried in unmarked graves in an overgrown corner of a Budapest cemetery, and just two years earlier, people who put flowers on the mounds faced police interrogation.

Hungarian Who Led '56 Revolt Is Buried as a Hero
By Henry Kamm

BUDAPEST, June 16—Thirty-one years after he was hanged and his body thrown into a prison grave, Imre Nagy, who led the 1956 uprising against Soviet domination, was given a solemn funeral today on Budapest's largest square, followed by a hero's burial.

The ceremonies were organized by the opposition, which worships the former Prime Minister as a national hero, but four leading members of the ruling Communist Party came to pay tribute.

They were announced to the crowd by their Government titles, because it had been made clear that they would not have been welcome as party representatives. The Interior Ministry estimated the crowd at 100,000, nowhere near the quarter of a million the organizers had expected.

The four top party officials, Prime Minister Miklos Nemeth, Minister of State Imre Pozsgay, Deputy Prime Minister Peter Megyessy and Matyas Szuros, the president of Parliament, laid wreaths and stood briefly as honorary pallbearers flanking Mr. Nagy's coffin.

They left before a succession of eulogies to Imre Nagy that were unsparing in their condemnation of the Communist Party and its ally, the Soviet Union.

The Soviet Army crushed the uprising after feigning a withdrawal from Hungary on November 4, 1956. Its tanks began rolling after Mr. Nagy, yielding to an aroused nation, formed a coalition government to replace one-party rule, declared Hungary's neutrality and withdrew from the Warsaw Pact.

Moscow secretly put Janos Kadar, whom Mr. Nagy had earlier freed from prison, in full charge of the country, which he dominated until he was deposed last year. Mr. Kadar has been relegated to oblivion by his successor, Karoly Grosz, and is said by the party that for 32 years did his bidding to be physically and mentally ill.

Many in the crowd looked up in shock and seemed to be holding their breath to hear at so public a ceremony, in so sumptuous a setting, words of such astonishing candor. The Government network televised the ceremony live from 9 A.M. to 6 P.M.

Victor Orban, a spokesman for the Federation of Young Democrats, paid tribute to Mr. Nagy as a man who, although a Communist, "identified himself with the wishes of the Hungarian nation to put an end to the Communist taboos, blind obedience to the Russian empire and the dictatorship of a single party."

As though speaking of the party leaders who shortly before had bowed before the coffins of Mr. Nagy and his colleagues, Mr. Orban continued: "We cannot understand that those who were eager to slander the revolution and its Prime Minister have suddenly changed into great supporters and followers of Imre Nagy. Nor can we understand that the party leaders, who made us study from books that falsified the revolution, now rush to touch the coffins as if they were charms of good luck."

Sandor Racz, who led the Budapest Workers' Council during the uprising and spent seven years in prison, condemned the Soviet Army and the Communist Party as "obstacles for Hungarian society."

Looking toward the coffins, covered in wreaths and bouquets, as well as single flowers laid on them by a long procession of mourners, Mr. Racz said, "These coffins are a result of the presence of Russian troops on our territory."

He said the party was "clinging fearfully to power," although it was clear that "what it failed to achieve in the last 44 years cannot be remedied now." He continued, "They are responsible for the past. They are responsible for the damaged lives of Hungarians."

Budapest experienced a day full of anomalies and contradictions. No state funeral could have been more solemnly and publicly marked or held in a more prestigious setting, but for the Hungarian Government and the ruling party, Mr. Nagy and the four companions who were sentenced to death and now reburied with him remain traitors and counterrevolutionaries.

A review of their trial is under way, and after today's rites it can hardly end with anything short of restoration of their civil dignity and full rehabilitation as victims of judicial murder. But their sentences still stand.

As recently as earlier this year, Mr. Grosz still ruled out Mr. Nagy's rehabilitation. On the thirtieth anniversary of the hangings last year, the police broke up with considerable violence a small tribute organized by dissidents on a Budapest square.

It was an anomaly also that the Soviet Union and Hungary's other Communist friends sent diplomats, but not their ambassadors, to attend the ceremony, although it had no official character that would have obliged them to be there. But other Communist countries—China, North Korea, Rumania and Albania—stayed away.

The Heroes Square ceremony was staged, in one more irony, by the son of another executed Communist, Laszlo Rajk, who was Interior and Foreign Minister. Mr. Rajk, a loyal Communist, was hanged after a show trial in 1949 at the eight of the Stalinist period.

The younger Laszlo Rajk, an architect and movie set designer, draped the neoclassical facade of the art museum and a tall column in the center of the square's vast expanse fully in black and white, traditional mourning colors among the Hungarians of Transylvania, annexed by Rumania.

He devised strikingly modern wood and metal structures as a setting on which to display the five coffins, as well as a sixth, empty one commemorating the more than 300 victims of judicial retribution after the uprising.

Tall, flaming torches stood between the coffins, and a permanent rotation of honorary pallbearers—including widows, children and other relatives of the five victims being buried—flanked them. Each coffin was inscribed with the name of the executed man and his dates, all ending in 1958.

Like all of the victims, Mr. Nagy was a lifelong Communist and friend of the Soviet Union, where he spent nearly one-third of his 62 years. The others were his Defense Minister, Gen. Pal Maleter; Minister of State Geza Losonczy; Jozsef Szilagyi, the head of the Prime Minister's staff, and Miklos Gimes, a leading journalist and close associate of Mr. Nagy.

General Maleter and Mr. Gimes were executed with Mr. Nagy, Mr. Szilagyi was tried and put to death separately, and Mr. Losonczy died in prison.

Mr. Nagy was buried in secret in a prison lot while his wife and daughter were interned in Rumania. He was reburied, again in secret and in an unmarked grave, a few years later and exhumed this year when the party leadership finally yielded to demands for a decent burial.

Today, after the wreath-laying and eulogies, a procession of hearses, followed by cars and buses, set out for the huge public cemetery next to the prison where the hangings took place.

Plot 301, the once desolate potter's field that contains the graves of perhaps 260 of the victims, had been turned in recent weeks, since the reburial had been decided on, into a landscaped funeral park.

Fresh grass and trees now grow where only weeks ago there were only dirt and weeds. Paved paths led through the field to five open graves aligned in a row that had been dug for Mr. Nagy's companions and for the symbolic coffin.

Beyond them, in an adjoining field full of mainly unmarked graves, a tomb had been dug for Mr. Nagy. His daughter had requested that he be laid to rest amid the bulk of those who paid with their lives for following his lead.

Two actors read in alphabetical order the names of the 260 victims, who were executed from 1956 to 1961, their occupations and their ages. At each name, a torchbearer stepped forward, held high the flame and replied, "He lives in us; he has not gone."

When the name of one of the five was called, surname first, in the Hungarian fashion, like "Nagy Imre, Prime Minister, 62 years," his coffin was carried to the grave and a friend delivered a eulogy. Then, supporting one another, his nearest relatives stepped to the grave to put down flowers and stand, with bowed heads, allowed for the first time to mourn in public, together with those who share their grief.

The Hungarian summer rolled on and with it came the steady erosion of Communist power. First, the party leadership elected a four-man presidency, and then it virtually stripped one of the four, Karoly Grosz, who had succeeded Janos Kadar as party leader, of most his authority. The so-called party liberals were on the rise, while outside the party a variety of dissidents, cultural activists, defenders of the ecology and cultural nationalists were forming embryonic parties and coalitions for pluralistic free elections that many believed would take place in

1990. Indeed, such elections were later scheduled and by fall, the Communists were meeting to discuss the liquidation of party's assets and the changing of its name.

• • •

In the Soviet Union, the social trends set in motion by both glasnost and perestroika were also continuing through the summer. Some unfolded in troubling ways, while others offered hope of positive change. New institutions and beliefs were forming; old monoliths were weakening.

Enrollment Problems Increasing, Soviet Communist Party Admits
By Bill Keller

MOSCOW, July 11—The Soviet Communist Party is troubled by dwindling recruitment and a steep decline in prestige, according to an unusually candid collection of articles and letters published today in Moscow's main party newspaper.

The material included an article by a teacher at a top party training school who reported that many of the most active young party candidates are defecting to join informal political organizations, where the activities are "more relevant and effective."

Occasional letters expressing anguish about the condition of the party began to creep into the press last year, but the hand-wringing has become more pronounced since March, when many prominent party figures were trounced in the first competitive elections for a new national legislature.

In another sign of the party's distress, Mikhail S. Gorbachev, the President and party leader, today went to Leningrad, where voters rejected the six top Communists in the city's party organization. The defeated Leningrad officials have refused to give up their party leadership positions.

At the time of the elections, Mr. Gorbachev said the outcome was not a repudiation of the party. Emphasizing that nearly 90 percent of the winners were party members, he said the elections were a victory of fresher and more progressive Communists over conservative party functionaries.

But the party-controlled press is beginning to admit that the party itself is held in low repute.

The declining prestige of the party is most evident in statistics showing plummeting enrollment of new party members, despite the fact that membership has traditionally brought career advancement and privileges.

According to data published recently in the journal of the party Central Committee, induction of new members began to fall off in 1987, and last year plunged 20 percent. After years of steady growth, the total party membership barely held steady at 19.5 million.

The party does not publish statistics on the number of people who quit, but the letters published today in *Moskovskaya Pravda* indicated that this, too, has become a growing problem.

One writer, the party secretary at a Moscow metallurgical factory, reported that in the first six months of this year more workers in that factory had quit the party than had joined.

"The most active Communists often leave to 'do their own thing'— that is, they join more lively and flexible, more relevant and effective voluntary movements," wrote the teacher at the party training school.

Several writers said the greatest blow to the party's prestige was its decision to reserve 100 seats in the new 2,250-member Congress for deputies chosen by the party without a vote of the general public.

"No matter which way you look at it, the party still retains Stalin's pattern, a rigid, command-administrative structure," the teacher wrote. "It lags behind the changes in life. It cannot prevent undesirable changes and it lags behind the positive ones."

Among the older institutions still active under glasnost was the censor.

The Life of a Soviet Censor: Anything Goes? Not Just Yet
By Bill Keller

MOSCOW, July 17—Suppose an inquisitive Soviet reporter were to unearth evidence that a member of the Communist Party Politburo had a mistress. Could he publish it?

Vladimir A. Boldyrev, the chief censor of the Soviet Union, ponders the question for a long time. A very long time.

"Well, I think the answer is, yes, we are now approaching the stage where personal details can be made public that it was not customary to publish before," he replied at last.

Then he added, with a nervous laugh that suggested that the verdict was not final, "I hope this is just a hypothetical question."

Mr. Boldyrev is the keeper of a shrinking but still formidable catalogue of what the press cannot write, the publishing houses cannot publish, the movies cannot show, the libraries cannot put on public display, and the post office cannot deliver.

In his three years as chairman of Glavlit—the Administration for the Protection of State Secrets in the Press—Mr. Boldyrev boasts that he has cut the list by half, lifting the ban on such diverse secrets as the works of Aleksandr Solzhenitsyn, the bunnies of *Playboy* magazine, and the crime rate.

Indeed, it is difficult to extract from Mr. Boldyrev exactly what is forbidden anymore in the Soviet Union, in part because the boundary is moving so fast and in part because the idea of censorship has become so unfashionable in the day of glasnost that even the censor in chief finds the subject a bit distasteful.

"In the classical sense, it is no longer really correct to call us censors," he insisted in an interview at his office midway between the Kremlin and the K.G.B. headquarters. "Today we do not impose limits of a purely political or ideological character, which was one of our duties before."

Still, there is much room for discretion in Glavlit's current standard of what is prohibited, which Mr. Boldyrev recently elaborated to the newspaper *Izvestia* as follows: "The use of the press for purposes of undermining or eliminating the established socialist system in the U.S.S.R., to propagandize war, to preach racial or national exclusivity or hatred and violence on a national, religious or other basis, to damage the country's security interests or defense capability or public order, or to publish materials incompatible with the requirements of public morality and protecting the population's health."

Mr. Boldyrev said most of the thick catalogue of forbidden themes—a document that is itself restricted to a narrow circle of editors and publishers—consists of military and industrial secrets.

Glavlit's clout is such that it has occasionally overruled the Defense Ministry on what constitutes a secret, Mr. Boldyrev said, although it has never found occasion to overrule the K.G.B., the state security police.

His agency is also responsible for preventing the dissemination of pornography, which like many arbiters of official taste he has trouble defining.

"You probably have to see it," said the censor, who is 59 years old and an economist by training. Once resolutely puritanical, Glavlit has become more permissive. Soft-core erotica is now considered acceptable in films and publications, and formerly taboo themes like homosexuality can be discussed in a positive light, although an article on that subject is almost certain to pass Mr. Boldyrev's desk before it reaches the readers.

Despite his disclaimer about politics and ideology, Glavlit is also empowered to decide that hostile literature poses a danger to the state.

Mr. Boldyrev said Glavlit ruled last year that the works of Mr. Solzhenitsyn, the fiercely anti-Communist Russian living in exile in Vermont, were no longer a threat. Mr. Solzhenitsyn's epic labor camp memoir, *The Gulag Archipelago,* is to be excerpted next month in the magazine *Novy Mir*, and a publishing house has announced plans to publish seven volumes of selected Solzhenitsyn works.

"Regarding Solzhenitsyn, all debates are over," the censor said. "We released all of his works from the closed archives, and our publishing houses have the right to publish them—of course, without violating the copyright."

Mr. Boldyrev said the vast bulk of writings by émigrés and exiles, once banned automatically regardless of their content, have now been removed from the closed archives of libraries, and the rest are to be reviewed by the end of the year.

The liberated writers include some of the bitterest critics of Soviet authority, among them such émigré novelists as Vladimir N. Voinovich, Vladimir Maximov—who once damned Communism as "an evil ideology"—and Viktor Nekrasov, and the non-émigré Vasily Grossman, whose thinly fictionalized attack on Lenin, "Forever Flowing," was published last month in the magazine *Oktyabr*.

The books written by Trotsky before he was expelled from the country as a Bolshevik heretic are now open, but what he wrote in exile is still under review.

Also locked away are foreign works that Glavlit feels might "undermine" Soviet power or outrage public sensibilities.

Mein Kampf, the Hitler manifesto widely studied in other countries as a model of political pathology, is here banned as an offense to memories of the Great Patriotic War Against Fascism.

"I think it will eventually be published, but first we have to live through a certain period of time to absorb what is being done today," Mr. Boldyrev said of the book. "It would be wrong to overfeed the public."

The limits of contemporary writing are murkier.

"If some paper wants to publish a call to arms to overthrow the authorities, we will not allow it to be published," he said.

And what about a scathing satire of President Mikhail S. Gorbachev? Not likely, Mr. Boldyrev said.

"This affects not only the prestige of our country, but perestroika itself," he said. "If we trample on the leader of perestroika, how can we make any progress?"

He added, however, that an attack on the Soviet leader would probably be squelched long before it reached his desk. While Glavlit is the supreme court of censorship, the Soviet system has countless less formal ways of saying "nyet."

A magazine, for example, depends on the good will of the officially sanctioned organization that sponsors it, of the ideology department of the Communist Party, of the state committee that controls printing presses and newsprint, of the official writers' union, and of local authorities who sometimes block distribution of publications approved in Moscow.

Editors who rise in this system have cultivated a keen sense of protective self-censorship.

Thus while Glavlit says it has imposed no limits on writing about the recent bloody events in China, no Soviet publication has dared criticize the Chinese regime. On matters of foreign policy, editors take their cues from the party and Government leadership, which has been carefully nurturing its recently normalized relations with Beijing.

Mr. Boldyrev estimates that about half of the information dispensed for public consumption in the Soviet Union is reviewed in advance by Glavlit's agents. The rest—including reprints of literary classics, many local and regional newspapers of scant circulation, certain reference works, and publications with a demonstrated devotion to self-censorship—do not undergo prior review, but are spot-checked.

Periodicals that suddenly develop a free spirit may find themselves back under Glavlit's wing. That happened this year to *Twentieth Century and Peace*, a long-quiescent little magazine that fell into the hands of a free-thinking editor and began publishing critiques of the K.G.B.

Mr. Boldyrev explained to the disbelieving editors that the publication had been leashed because it wrote about disarmament, raising the risk that it would disclose some privileged detail of a Soviet negotiating position.

The reins on the press may be loosened further when the new legislature approves a long-awaited law on the rights and responsibilities of the press. But legislators say the new law is unlikely to curtail Glavlit's authority seriously or to permit a truly independent press. Mr. Boldyrev is not worried about job security.

"The system of protecting secrets was created by people who are not completely unreasonable," he said. "It was built up over time, and it has its rationale."

Much more troubling for Gorbachev than the drift from Communism of his Polish and Hungarian allies were the separatist feelings being articulated within his country's borders.

Annexation Void, Lithuanians Say
By Bill Keller

MOSCOW, Aug. 22—In a move that could lay the legal foundation for eventual secession from the Soviet Union, a commission of the Lithuanian Parliament declared today that Moscow's annexation of the republic in 1940 was invalid.

The commission, the first official body to challenge directly the legitimacy of Soviet rule in the Baltic republics, charged that Lithuania and its neighbors, Latvia and Estonia, were occupied and absorbed against their will as a result of a secret agreement between Stalin and Hitler.

The statement was published today in Lithuanian newspapers, as all three Baltic republics prepared mass demonstrations to mark the fiftieth anniversary of the accord.

The full Lithuanian legislature is expected to vote on the commission's declaration at its next session in early September, and approval is considered virtually certain.

"Stalinism and Hitlerism destroyed independent states by secret deals," the commission's statement released today said. "The independence of many of these states has been restored, but Lithuania, Latvia and Estonia still have not reacquired their independence."

The nonaggression pact reached in August 1939 by the Soviet Foreign Minister, Vyacheslav M. Molotov, and his Nazi counterpart, Joachim von Ribbentrop, included a secret protocol dividing Europe into Soviet and German spheres of influence, splitting Poland and giving the Soviets a free hand in Latvia, Estonia and part of Rumania.

A second secret protocol a month later refined the spheres of influence in Poland and gave the Soviets predominance in Lithuania, as well.

During the war, the Soviet Union annexed the three Baltic states and forced their puppet parliaments to seek admission to the Soviet Union.

The declaration made by the Lithuanians today directly contradicted the latest Moscow position on the Stalin-Hitler pact and its protocols. After decades of denying the existence of the secret deal, Communist Party officials now concede that such an agreement was signed, but they say that it had no bearing on the annexation of the Baltic states.

On Friday, Aleksandr N. Yakovlev, an influential Politburo member who is also chairman of a Government commission examining the history of the Stalin-Hitler pact, insisted that it was "farfetched to see some kind of interconnection between the present status of the three republics and the nonaggression treaty."

In an interview published on Monday, Valentin M. Falin, chief of the international department of the Communist Party Central Committee, warned that attempts to redraw the boundaries of Eastern Europe could have a dangerous destabilizing effect.

"If the striving to divide what cannot be divided continues, as was characteristic of the period before the previous two world wars, if lands and frontiers are being recarved while the lives and safety of people are neglected, the worst, and this time, the final disaster will be brought on," he predicted.

Residents of the Baltic republics are divided about the wisdom of separating completely from the Soviet Union, but there seems to be overwhelming agreement in the republics that their membership in a Soviet federation must be on their own terms.

The Soviet Constitution guarantees republics the right to secede, but this has always been regarded as symbolic and few doubt that Moscow would resist.

Popular Front groups that have amassed broad followings in the three republics have campaigned for invalidating the Soviet annexation, after which some favor a loose affiliation with the Soviet Union while others want independence.

Tonight in Vilnius, the Lithuanian capital, a crowd estimated in the tens of thousands roared approval as Vytautas Landsbergis, president of Sajudis, a Popular Front group, called for "a free Lithuania."

According to a Sajudis spokesman, Mr. Landsbergis rejected the Communist Party's proposal for a revamped confederation giving republics more, but still limited, freedom.

The sentiment for secession has grown with each expression of Moscow's resistance. Although the Soviet national legislature has approved in principle Baltic plans to experiment with market-style economies, the authorities have insisted that the republics be bound by the Soviet Constitution and laws.

Today, in laying the basis for a possible separation from the Soviet Union, the Lithuanian legislature said in conclusion: "The declaration of the People's Assembly of 21 July 1940 on the entry of Lithuania into the U.S.S.R., and the law of the Supreme Soviet of the U.S.S.R. of 3 August 1940 on the incorporation of the Lithuanian Soviet Socialist Republic into the U.S.S.R. are illegal."

AUTUMN 1989

T*roublesome as they were, the secessionist impulses in the Baltic were at least still largely a matter of debate and discussion. That was not so in the south, where the Kremlin was confronted with a bloody conflict between groups of citizens with very old grudges against each other.*

A Deadly Feud Tears at Enclave on Gorbachev's Southern Flank
By Bill Keller

BADARA, U.S.S.R., Aug. 29—From the windows of her living room, Galya Israelyan can look down over the rooftops of this Armenian village, out to the green and gold mountains and the clearing where a few days ago her husband, Ruben, was shot dead.

He was 32 years old and the father of five, including a newborn daughter, when he became a casualty in the Soviet Union's fiercest and most intractable nationalist feud in recent years.

Although the police say their investigation is unfinished, the victim's brother, a witness, identified the killer as an Azerbaijani farmhand from the neighboring settlement of Lesnoye.

"He had been a guest in our house for dinner," the widow recalled in a monotone bitter and hopeless from a dispute that is now more tribal than political.

This is Mikhail S. Gorbachev's Lebanon, his Cyprus: Nagorno-Karabakh—wild mountains of rugged beauty, riven by mutual hatred, partitioned by military force and governed, in reality, by no one.

In the 18 months since Armenians and Azerbaijanis began their struggle for custody of Nagorno-Karabakh, a predominantly Armenian enclave surrounded by the southern republic of Azerbaijan, the dispute has frustrated every attempt at settlement. Some say the demonstration of official impotence has encouraged outbreaks of unrest in other regions of the Soviet Union.

145

Military and civilian authorities sent from Moscow to oversee the territory say their greatest accomplishment has been to prevent all-out war between the two adjoining republics, Christian Armenia and Muslim Azerbaijan.

Now that nationalist tensions seem to tear at every corner of the Soviet Union, and the Communist Party awaits a special meeting to address the issue, Nagorno-Karabakh is a reminder of how limited Soviet power can be in the face of ethnic passion.

"For now, only Allah or God knows the answer," Mr. Gorbachev's special administrator in Nagorno-Karabakh, Arkady I. Volsky, told a reporter who was allowed a four-day visit to the tightly restricted region.

After a fresh outbreak of gun battles and highway ambushes, the Ministry of Internal Affairs moved in more troops in recent days to buy time while Mr. Volsky embarked without great optimism on the search for a new compromise.

For centuries before Nagorno-Karabakh became Mr. Gorbachev's affliction, the ancestors of today's Armenians and Azerbaijanis contested this mountainous land.

The successive masters of the region—the czarist empire, the Turkish Army, the British authorities after World War I, and then the Soviets—have placed Nagorno-Karabakh under Azerbaijani rule, primarily because of its geographic isolation from Armenia and its rail and economic links to Baku, the capital of Azerbaijan.

But the Armenian majority has usually retained a limited autonomy within the region, and has periodically defied Azerbaijani rule. Armenian passions are heightened by memories of the killings, starvation and forced resettlement inflicted on Armenian civilians in 1915 by the Ottoman Turks, the Azerbaijanis' ethnic cousins. The Armenians suffered losses on a scale that shocked the world, even during World War I. Inspired by Mr. Gorbachev's promise of greater democracy and by rising Armenian nationalism, Nagorno-Karabakh early last year demanded unification with the Armenian Republic.

Moscow, sensitive to the authority of Azerbaijan and the precedent of redrawing boundaries, refused and condemned the instigators as extremists. Tensions mounted. In February 1988, while the Azerbaijani authorities looked the other way, anti-Armenian riots broke out in the Azerbaijani port of Sumgait, on the Caspian Sea. This began a violent chain reaction that has left more than 100 people dead by official count—many more by unofficial estimates.

In hindsight, Armenians see Sumgait as a signal—and not just to Armenians—that Soviet power could not or would not protect them, that safety lay in the clan, the tribe.

Fearful minorities by the hundreds of thousands have fled the two republics, including a continuing Armenian evacuation of Baku, once a cosmopolitan, multinational city.

Trains and buses carrying refugees are regularly stoned as they pass through alien territory.

In Nagorno-Karabakh itself, there have been paralyzing strikes and huge demonstrations but, remarkably, no serious violence in the six months after the Sumgait killings.

Then last September, on two terror-filled nights, the neighboring cities of Stepanakert and Shusha erupted.

Scores of Azerbaijani homes were ransacked and burned in Stepanakert and scores of Armenian apartments in Shusha were destroyed before armored caravans escorted the two peoples to neutral corners.

Each side blames the other for the rampages. Each side insists it is the guiltless victim of a conspiracy.

"What happened here?" a visitor asked a group of Armenian men sharing a bottle on the sidewalk across from a burned-out Azerbaijani house in Stepanakert.

"The Azerbaijanis did it," one replied, "so the Armenians would get the blame."

Today, the 186,000 residents of Nagorno-Karabakh, about 80 percent of them Armenian, are almost completely polarized into Armenian and Azerbaijani sectors. They are guarded by troops of the Internal Affairs Ministry and by vigilante patrols, and ruled by a jumble of competing jurisdictions.

Stepanakert, the regional capital, is almost entirely Armenian, and is gradually cutting its ties to Baku.

Local factories that once worked as subsidiaries of larger enterprises in Baku have begun to realign themselves with Armenian companies in Yerevan, capital of the neighboring Armenian republic.

"Baku was just skimming off our profits, like tribute to the Azerbaijanis," said Boris S. Arushanyan, director of a lighting-fixture factory that now flies an Armenian flag over its main workshop.

The strike that had idled most of the city's factories since May ended a few days ago at the urging of Armenian nationalists, who decided that the tactic was self-defeating.

But the city is plagued by shortages of food, fuel and building materials. Supplies are delivered by armed convoy and airlift from Yerevan, the Armenian Republic's capital.

The seedy Hotel Karabakh is crowded with newly arrived refugees and shirtless soldiers, who roam the steamy corridors wearing their sidearms.

"We'll give it a year," said Lena Shakhgeldyan, who fled from Baku in December and now lives with her husband, mother and three children in a single room of a Stepanakert refugee hostel. "Then if it's still bad, we'll apply to go to America."

Four miles up the mountain, past a military checkpoint, is the main Azerbaijani stronghold, Shusha. Once it was a vacation mecca prized for its mountain springs and fresh air. Now the shady mountainside pavilion where Armenian and Azerbaijani Communist officials used to share long lunches is empty. The Armenian church and graveyard have been vandalized, and the holiday camps have been converted to refugee centers that fester with anger.

A children's camp on the outskirts of town is home for 100 Azerbaijani families who say they were driven forcibly from their farms in Armenia a year and a half ago.

They live jobless and in squalor, several generations packed into each small room, cooking communal meals over hot plates and washing at buckets because, local officials say, their water is often cut off at Armenian-controlled pumping stations.

They flock around a visitor, shouting their indignation. A current object of wrath is the United States Senate, which recently adopted a resolution expressing support for Soviet Armenians in the Nagorno-Karabakh dispute.

"If these young men were to take up guns and go off today to shoot Armenians, I could not sincerely tell them 'Don't do it,' " said Zakhid Abbasov, a local party official.

Not long ago, a Russian official in Stepanakert said, a reporter from the Soviet satirical weekly *Krokodil* visited Shusha, and word got out that he had an Armenian name. He was sitting in the office of the city's mayor when four men burst into the room, beat him to the floor and kicked him.

Local Azerbaijani officials abruptly canceled plans to let two visiting American journalists spend the night in Shusha when they learned that the photographer had an Armenian last name.

"You must understand we cannot guarantee your safety," said Rena A. Allakhverdieva, the Communist Party ideology chief for the

148

Shusha region. "When they see the name on your passport, the fact that you are American will not save you. It is out of our hands."

On the winding roads and in the mountain hollows, periods of false calm are followed by periods of reprisal.

"You cannot say who starts it, or who is more to blame," said Maj. Gen. Vladislav F. Safonov, the Internal Affairs Ministry troop commander in the region.

Early one morning, a bus from Yerevan, the Armenian capital, limped into Stepanakert with bullet holes in the side, and shattered windows.

The hysterically frightened Armenian passengers, huddled with their baggage in the lobby of the Hotel Karabakh, said they had been delayed at an Azerbaijani police post at Mir-Bashir, on the northeast border.

"It was a trap," one passenger said. "Young Azerbaijanis began arriving by the carload. Then someone shot at us from the roof of a garage, and the stones started flying. We screamed until the troops came."

The Armenians pointed to bloodstains on their clothes and held out rocks and handfuls of broken window glass they had scooped up as evidence of their ordeal.

"If the troops had not happened by, they would have burned the bus with us in it," a woman said.

In fact, General Safonov said, it was the outnumbered Azerbaijani police who called the special troops to rescue the Armenians. But no Armenian here seems to believe it.

The story spread quickly, and soon separate groups of Armenians and Azerbaijanis were on the highway armed with rocks and raising the level of violence, even stoning the military patrols sent to clear the roads. By the day's end, the authorities said the Armenians had smashed four buses, and each side had damaged a number of cars.

"We have a policy of not being the first to attack, but every action should have a concrete response," said Robert Kucharyan, the head of a local Armenian nationalist group, approving the day's reprisals.

"We know throwing rocks is not a civilized approach, but our neighbors are not civilized and they don't understand civilized language," he said. "From many years of living together, we learned to eat their bread and drink their wine. This month we've learned how to throw rocks at cars."

The next day, the commander of all troops of the Soviet Internal

Affairs Ministry, Col. Gen. Yuri V. Shatalin, arrived to survey the situation and announced plans to supplement the 4,500 soldiers in Nagorno-Karabakh with additional forces, mostly stationed in adjacent regions of Azerbaijan.

"The conflict has to be resolved by the two republics," he said in an interview. "There are two choices: begin talks or begin the bloodshed. And believe me, the number of victims would be in the hundreds."

In the mountains, villagers on both sides say they live in constant fear. Although the authorities have confiscated more than 3,000 hunting rifles and other weapons since the conflict began, enough remain in private hands to give the region a Wild West character.

In Lesnoye, a village of dilapidated houses isolated at the end of a road that passes through Armenian territory, 380 Azerbaijanis have lived the last year in a state of siege.

Once, the villagers say, they worked alongside Armenians in the nearby collective farm and in a woodworking shop. But after the "events" in Shusha and Stepanakert, Azerbaijanis say they were driven from their jobs.

Residents of Lesnoye get their flour, sugar and tea by helicopter from Azerbaijani authorities in Agdam, just east of Nagorno-Karabakh. Armenians are convinced they get weapons that way, too.

It is a war of attrition with the neighboring Armenian settlement of Badara. The villagers who used to attend each other's weddings now kill each other's livestock, stone each other's cars, cut each other's utility lines, and occasionally exchange gunfire in the woods.

A few days ago, Youssef Orudzhov was killed by an Armenian policeman at a makeshift guardpost at the edge of Lesnoye. The Azerbaijanis say that Mr. Orudzhov was shot in the back while fleeing into the woods so that the police would not confiscate his weapon. The police say it was a gun battle. Alysh M. Alyshev, a 39-year-old schoolteacher and Lesnoye spokesman, told a visitor that the Armenian policeman would be repaid.

"If I don't get him, the wife will, or the daughter will," he said calmly as he served tea and local honey. "If someone has to die, so be it."

A few miles away in Badara, the 850 Armenians seem more prosperous—the homes are well kept and a condenser factory in Stepanakert has just opened a branch here—but they are about equal in the purity of their hatred, in their determination to yield not an inch.

They have just buried Ruben Israelyan, and they mutter angrily that his killer will be "a national hero" in Azerbaijan.

Arshak Israelyan wears a snapshot of his dead brother pinned to his shirt.

"It is ridiculous to speak of peace," he said. "Maybe the only thing left is to poison the water and kill everybody.". . .

If old enmities and old yearnings for autonomy were surfacing through fissures pried open as a consequence of glasnost, there were also some basic institutional changes occurring. Among the more bizarre of these was the public relations drive to improve the image of spies and secret police.

The Soviets Proudly Present Their Friendly K.G.B. Agent
By Bill Keller

MOSCOW, Sept. 13—The K.G.B. stepped up its charm offensive today with the premiere of a new film on the benign patriotism and just-folks life-styles of the Soviet secret police.

The screening, before an audience consisting of a favorite K.G.B. target, the foreign press corps, was followed by a rare opportunity to question the chief of the K.G.B. investigations department and the operative who handled the agency's most stellar recruit, Kim Philby, the British spy who worked as a double agent before fleeing to the Soviet Union.

Neither the film nor the news conference provided any hard new information about the secret police, although afterward Mr. Philby's K.G.B. handler, a white-goateed colonel named Yuri Modin, told the correspondent for *The Independent*, a London newspaper, that there was an uncaught fifth mole in the Philby spy network. This information—or was it disinformation?—is sure to cause a minor tempest in London, where Mr. Philby, who defected in 1963 and died here last year, and "fifth man" conspiracy theories are subjects of boundless fascination.

The film, *The K.G.B. Today*, was intended to convince Soviet and foreign audiences that the agency long feared as an engine of repression has transformed itself into a rather likable law enforcement agency.

Today's skeptical full house reacted with smiles and occasional gales of laughter to the homespun glimpses of daily K.G.B. life.

K.G.B. cooking tips: Col. Igor N. Prelin, the K.G.B. press officer, escorts the camera crew through Lefortovo Prison, pausing at the kitchen where, viewers are told, the crew prepares a choice of vegetarian and nonvegetarian cuisine for lucky inmates.

"How do you manage to cook pearl barley this good?" Colonel Prelin inquires, dipping a spoon into an enormous vat of porridge. "Do you cook it over steam?" "Yes, I do," burbles the flattered chef. "I cook everything this way."

"I'll tell you one thing: my wife cannot do it right," the colonel confides as the cook ladles him a glutinous second helping.

K.G.B. grooming: "Is your haircut your own invention?" the narrator inquires of Sergei Savichev, a K.G.B. captain whose brush cut bears an eerie resemblance to the look of a recently liberated labor camp prisoner.

"I think it is the best for my head," the young officer explains.

And K.G.B. poetry: Colonel Prelin, an occasional scribbler of verse, recites for the camera his couplets about the crazy, cruel ironies of intelligence work: We wage a war with no rules / A snowstorm with no end. / We share a bottle with a foe / Or get a bullet from a friend.

Other highlights include a martial arts class at the K.G.B. Higher School; a clip of Mathias Rust, the young West German pilot who landed his Cessna uninvited in Red Square, giving a tour of his prison cell; and a seeming reenactment of the K.G.B. capture of an accused American diplomat-spymaster in Moscow.

The Novosti press agency, which produced the film, hopes for wide commercial distribution overseas. American television companies who inquired today were told that the opening asking price for North American rights was $100,000.

The 55-minute film will also be shown domestically in hopes of countering the outpouring of revelations here about repressions carried out during the decades of Soviet power.

"The K.G.B. is not what it used to be in the infamous 1930's," said Colonel-General Gennadi Ageyev, a K.G.B deputy director interviewed in the film. "Not a single member of the K.G.B. today has had anything to do with the events of that period."

Asked after the screening about the K.G.B.'s more recent role in repression of dissidents in the 1960's, 70's and 80's, Colonel Prelin neither denied nor apologized, saying all of those activities were conducted within Soviet law.

Col. Oleg Dobrovolsky, chief of the K.G.B. investigations department, also sidestepped questions about the agency's supposed use to this day of telephone taps and informants to monitor Soviet citizens of unorthodox views.

The K.G.B. officials declined to answer questions about the number of K.G.B. employees, the structure of the organization or K.G.B. methods.

Today's event was part of an intensive campaign to humanize the image of the K.G.B. and underscore its work against drug smugglers, terrorists and organized crime.

In recent months, the K.G.B. director, Vladimir A. Kryuchkov, has made himself briefly available to Western journalists and has met with the American ambassador in Moscow, Jack F. Matlock Jr., and with Robert M. Gates, a former deputy director of the Central Intelligence Agency.

In appearances before the new Soviet Parliament and in the Soviet press, the K.G.B. chief has sung the praises of glasnost, as President Mikhail S. Gorbachev calls his campaign for greater openness.

Colonel Prelin, who heads the K.G.B.'s recently opened press office, said today that the K.G.B. is cooperating in the production of two documentary films lionizing Mr. Philby and George Blake, another British intelligence officer who secretly served the K.G.B.

A recurring theme of the film released today is that all countries carry out intelligence work, and the K.G.B. is no worse—in fact, is more moral—than its Western rivals.

Using film clips and what appeared to be a reenactment, the film recounted the arrest of an American couple, Lon D. Augustenborg, a diplomat, and his wife, Denise, who were expelled from Moscow in 1983 on charges of collecting espionage data on the Soviet Navy.

The case received unusually detailed coverage in the Soviet press at the time, when the Soviets were intent on justifying their shooting down of a Korean Air Lines 747 that they suspected of a spy mission.

To accompany its movie, Novosti filmed the reaction of the K.G.B. director himself, Mr. Kryuchkov, who delightedly predicted the movie would help "to project an objective image of our work both at home and abroad."

With summer giving way to fall, people all over Europe were returning as they always did from their holidays. This time, however, the annual retreat was to lead to massive migrations and shifts of populations that changed governments and altered the political map of the continent. It began in Hungary, where for many years East Germans and West Germans would meet at vacation spots along Lake Balaton. In the past, the Hungarian border guards made sure that the East Germans went home to East Germany. This was the year when that changed.

East Germans Put Hungary in a Bind

By Henry Kamm

BUDAPEST, Sept. 1—At least 3,000 East German tourists, and possibly many more, are waiting in Budapest for permission from Hungary to cross into Austria on the way to West Germany.

Many say that if permission is denied, they intend to cross "the green border." This is a German expression for migrating illegally, through the forest.

Since the summer vacation period began, an estimated 6,000 East Germans have made it to the West German Embassy in Vienna in this way, passing under the willfully averted eyes of Hungarian border guards.

But as the vacation period ends and the tourists confront the choice between returning in time for the reopening of factories and schools or not returning, a diffuse flow has become a concentration and a diplomatic quandary that Hungary cannot pretend to ignore.

Officials from the West German Embassy here, which Bonn closed last month when it could no longer cope with an occupation by East Germans seeking to emigrate, have joined with a West German Catholic relief organization in an ad hoc refugee operation at the Roman Catholic Parish Church.

The tree-shaded streets around the church in the garden suburb of Zugliget are lined with hundreds of small cars with East German plates, and as one gets closer to the church, flashier cars from West Germany are mingled among them.

In the churchyard, about 600 East Germans, including the owners of the parked cars, are camping out under tents. At least 2,000 more are waiting in two other informal camps as well as in private accommodations.

This afternoon, the Hungarian Red Cross told West German reporters that a new camp was being opened on Lake Balaton, a favorite vacation area southwest of here.

Hungary appears to have conferred a kind of informal extraterritoriality on the spacious grounds around the neo-Gothic church, where the latest act in the drama of defying East German borders is being acted out. Few Hungarians are to be seen, and the prevailing language is German in the strong accents of Saxony and Berlin, whose people make up the bulk of East Germany's population.

To Budapest's embarrassment, thousands of East Germans are taking advantage of Hungary's new era of tolerance and its recent relaxation of controls along the Austrian border to turn their vacation trips to a fellow Communist country into permanent departures, by way of Austria, to the richer and freer Germany.

In addition to those who have declared their intention not to return home, more than 100,000 other East German tourists are thought to be in Hungary. How many of them will seek to join the mass migration is unknown.

The situation puts Hungary in a diplomatic bind. It is caught between its treaty obligation to East Germany not to allow East Germans to leave here for anywhere but home, and its need not to offend West Germany, its biggest Western creditor and trading partner, as well as its principal hope for future economic support.

Although Hungary calls it a problem for the Germans to resolve, Prime Minister Miklos Nemeth and Foreign Minister Gyula Horn visited Chancellor Helmut Kohl in Bonn last week in an effort to seek a solution. On Thursday Mr. Horn paid an unannounced visit to the East German Foreign Minister, Oskar Fischer.

No agreements were announced, although West German Government and opposition officials disclosed on Thursday that Bonn and Budapest had worked out a plan to let out all the East Germans who want to leave.

In addition, the Hungarian Interior Minister, Istvan Horvath, said in an interview with West German television on Thursday that he hoped "an acceptable solution, conforming to European norms and culture," would be found.

"We find the present situation at the country's borders highly unpleasant and inconvenient," said the minister, who is in charge of border forces.

Some would-be refugees took heart when told by a reporter that Mr. Horvath had said it was certain that Hungary would not return them to their country. In the East German penal code, "flight from the republic" is punished by long prison terms and followed by harsh discrimination in professional and social life.

"If nothing else works, our State Security Service does," a 27-year-old mechanic from Karl-Marx-Stadt said.

In a garage to the rear of the church, West German consuls, surrounded by a patient crowd of men and women shushing their bored and cranky children, are accepting applications for passports and, after a few days' delay, issuing them. Despite their valid passports, however, Hungary feels restrained from recognizing them because they lack entry stamps. The tourists entered Hungary with an East German travel permit valid only for this country.

East Germany demands that Hungary live up to the formal understanding between Warsaw Pact members not to abet "defection" of their citizens to the West.

The steady trickle of East Germans making their way to West Germany by way of Hungary intensified when ten days later the Hungarians removed the barbed-wire barriers at the crossing point to Austria and permitted East Germans to cross that frontier easily. The East Germans responded by limiting the access their citizens had to Hungary. At that point East Germans, mostly young, began showing up at the West German Embassy in Prague. Czechoslovakia was one of the few places in the world where East Germans could travel without hard-to-get documents, and more and more of them were flocking to the West German Embassy in hopes that they would be permitted to go to West Germany.

More Than 6,000 East Germans Swell Tide of Refugees to the West
By Serge Schmemann

HOF, WEST GERMANY, Oct. 1—From early this morning, packed East German trains pulled into this border junction town at three-hour intervals, disgorging exhausted East Germans whose departure had been allowed only the day before through an extraordinary face-saving arrangement reportedly approved by Erich Honecker, the East German leader.

By day's end, more than 5,500 East Germans who had taken refuge at the West German embassy in Prague and 800 more from Bonn's embassy in Warsaw arrived at Hof, near the juncture of West Germany's borders with East Germany and Czechoslovakia, after a 10-hour trip that took them back through the country they were leaving.

In Prague, several hundred more East Germans eluded the Czechoslovak police to gain sanctuary at the embassy. It was not clear whether the new arrivals would be covered by the agreement.

West German officials said the device that finally enabled East Germany to approve the departure was the detour through East Germany, proposed by Foreign Minister Hans-Dietrich Genscher on Friday. The arrangement enabled East Berlin to contend that the refugees had first come home, as it had repeatedly demanded of them, and on Saturday morning, the Communist Government agreed.

The deal also permitted stops in Dresden and Karl-Marx-Stadt, where more émigrés managed to climb aboard the train. According to the refugees, other East Germans gathered to wave as they sped past.

"This was the most moving hour in my political career," said Mr. Genscher, who himself fled from East Germany in the 1950s, in describing his trip to Prague Saturday night to tell the East Germans of their impending release. "You can see what people will go through so that they can live like we do—not in the material sense, but to have the right to decide for themselves what to do with their lives."

The development suggested that the summer-long exodus of East Germans and the occupation of West German embassies was far from over. "Our embassies will not be walled shut," a West German Interior Ministry official, Horst Waffenschmidt, said.

The arrangement to free the East Germans underscored the problem facing both Germanys as a result of the exodus, which began when Hungary dismantled the barbed wire from its border with Austria. More than 30,000 East Germans have fled illegally, most of them crossing from Hungary since September 10, when the Budapest Government lifted restrictions on westward travel. Those who arrived in Hof today were bleary after a sleepless night. For most there were still hours to go as they waited for trasnportation to reception camps.

Some had spent weeks at the embassy. Others had made the move at the eleventh hour. Heike Schubert, a 22-year-old hairdresser from Halle, and her boyfriend, Andreas Stolz, 20, took the plunge Saturday night on hearing on the radio that the Germans in Prague had been allowed to leave.

Miss Schubert, crying on Mr. Stolz's shoulder, described how they rushed to her parents, who were at a party, and how the parents had said: "You go on. We'd do the same if we were young and had the possibility." . . .

For East Germany, the flight has been a painful blow, for which any solution—whether to seal off borders with its East European neighbors or to allow the flow to continue—have been similarly untenable.

For West Germany, the flight has meant a flood of new settlers at a time when the country's capacity has already been strained by tens of thousands of ethnic Germans arriving from the Soviet Union and East European countries, as well as an estimated 100,000 East Germans expected to emigrate this year legally.

It is an article of political and constitutional faith in West Germany, however, that all East Germans are fellow Germans eligible for the benefits and privileges of West German citizenship.

Thus, while the exodus has provided something of a political boom to Chancellor Helmut Kohl and Mr. Genscher, it has also challenged the standing policy of seeking a gradual improvement in relations with East Germany.

The East German expectation that the flight of their young people would taper off were quickly proved wrong. The trail to the embassy in Prague grew congested as people made their way to sanctuary at the embassy. Eventually more special trains were organized. But as the numbers of refugees grew, the demands of those they left behind also grew more strident. Freedom of travel had been the first cry, but now people were taking to the street shouting that they wanted to stay but in a different sort of country than the one they lived in. In East Berlin, in Dresden, but most particularly in Leipzig, the calls for reform and democratic changes were being raised more and more loudly by greater and greater throngs. The headlines of early autumn reflect the feverish pace.

East Germans Line Émigré Routes, Some in Hope of Their Own Exit

By Serge Schmemann

EAST BERLIN, Oct. 4—Thousands of East Germans flocked to stations and junctions along the railroad line taking their compatriots from Prague to West Germany today in hopes of sneaking aboard. Conditions became so hectic that police had to clear the Dresden terminal by force and the doors of the trains were sealed from the outside to block them.

Security Forces Storm Protesters in East Germany
By Serge Schmemann

DRESDEN, Oct. 8—Protesters clashed with the police and security forces today in cities throughout East Germany as the Communist Government's efforts to celebrate its fortieth anniversary ignited rallies and demonstrations urging changes in the country's hard-line system.

Spurred on in part by the presence of the Soviet President, Mikhail S. Gorbachev, who came for the celebrations, protesters took to the streets late Saturday and again today, often mingling their calls for greater freedom with chants of "Gorby! Gorby!"

"In East Berlin, Dresden, Leipzig and elsewhere, the police beat back defiant protesters, swinging riot sticks and menacing them with water cannon. In East Berlin tonight, a candlelight vigil was broken up by the security police, who set upon some of the nearly 1,500 people there as the protesters shouted, "No violence!" and "We're staying here!" . . .

Two days later, the police stood by without interfering as large rallies took place. New Forum, an organization that arose out of the rallies, uniting people who wanted democratic change but who had little if any experience as dissidents, was gaining cohesion. The furor was mounting and the besieged party tried to sacrifice its leadership to save itself.

East Germany Removes Honecker and His Protégé Takes His Place
By Serge Schmemann

WEST BERLIN, Oct. 18—Confronted with increasing demands for change, the East German Communist Party today ousted Erich Honecker, its hard-line leader of 18 years, and named his 52-year-old protégé to replace him .

The new leader, Egon Krenz, had been the Politburo member charged with security and youth affairs. He was named to Mr. Honecker's three positions—party chief, head of state and chairman of the Defense Council—granting him the broad powers Mr. Honecker spent years accumulating.

Though the youngest member of the Politburo, Mr. Krenz is generally regarded as a tough and conservative leader in Mr. Honecker's mold but 25 years younger, more sophisticated and probably better aware of the scope and sources of popular discontent. . . .

Mr. Krenz underscored his difference in style from Mr. Honecker, who usually restricted public appearances to stiff, formal rituals, with an appearance on television shortly after his appointment. Smiling, Mr. Krenz said: "My motto remains work, work, work and more work, but work that should be pleasant and serve all the people."

In the evening Mr. Krenz delivered an hour-long nationally televised address in which he reaffirmed the standing policy of "continuity and renewal," but added that "within these bounds, the door is wide open for earnest political dialogue."

"It is clear that we have not realistically appraised the social developments in our country in recent months, and we have not drawn the right conclusions quickly enough," Mr. Krenz said. "We see the seriousness of the situation. But we also sense and recognize the major opportunity we have opened for ourselves to define the policies in dialogue with our citizens, policies that will bring us to the verge of the next century." . . .

It may not have been what Mr. Krenz had in mind, but an emboldened populace continued to speak out in large numbers. As reported in **The Times** *on October 19, meetings were being held at which people were publicly calling for the resignation of all the old guard and assailing the credibility of Mr. Krenz. At one meeting outside East Berlin's City Hall, citizens repeatedly challenged and attacked once-powerful figures, who listened meekly. One man stood facing the East Berlin party chief, Gunter Schabowski, and shouted, "You are finished! Give us Free Election!" Under such pressure something—in fact, many things—would have to give, among them the leadership and wall that symbolized the system that erected it to divide the continent.*

• • •

In early autumn, most of the world's attention was focused on East and West Germany. But the continuing erosion of Communist power was also occurring elsewhere. In Hungary, for example, the Communist leadership met with leaders of dissident groups and together they endorsed a plan calling for multiparty elections. Then, in anticipation that they would not do very well running as Communists against anti-Communists, the Communist party met in early October and decided to redefine itself.

Communist Party in Hungary Votes for Radical Shift

By Henry Kamm

BUDAPEST, Oct. 7—The Hungarian Communist Party voted today to transform itself into a socialist party and said it would strive to bridge the gulf between doctrinaire Marxism and European democratic socialism.

In a series of votes to change the party's name to the Hungarian Socialist Party and set general party direction, the delegates at an extraordinary party congress here greatly raised expectations that the reform-oriented leadership's entire program to overhaul the party would be adopted. Among the changes expected are more democratic procedures for choosing the leadership.

With Poland, Hungary is at the forefront of change in the Eastern bloc. But unlike Poland, where the Solidarity union has taken the reins of power with the Communist Party largely unchanged, Hungary is pushing through radical change from within its Communist Party. . . .

In a news conference before the voting, Imre Pozsgay, a member of Hungary's collective presidency and a leader of those advocating major change, said an overwhelming majority of the delegates supported the leadership's program so that the party can better confront new, independently formed parties in free parliamentary elections due to be held by next June. . . .

One key aspect of the changes in Budapest dealt largely with a semantic issue.

What's in a Name? Just Ask the Hungarians

By Henry Kamm

BUDAPEST, Oct. 10—Attila Agh, until last weekend a leading "reform Communist," was asked today what party members should be called now that their organization has become the Socialist Party. "Radical Socialists," he replied. For the first time in a Communist country, a ruling party has formally abandoned Communism.

In a four-day congress that ended on Monday, the party changed its name and structure, modeled closely on that of the Soviet Communist Party, and declared its eagerness to open friendly relations with reform-oriented Communist parties of East and West and beyond that with all leftist parties.

It expressed hope for contacts even with the organization that Communists demonize as an ideological enemy, the Socialist International.

The split between evolutionary and revolutionary Socialists after the Bolshevik Revolution of 1917 arrayed Communists in the Third International and Socialists and social democrats in the Socialist International.

Nonetheless, the Hungarian party president, Rezso Nyers, announced after his election Monday night that President Mikhail S. Gorbachev of the Soviet Union had waited only an hour or two to telegraph his congratulations.

Mr. Agh, a political scientist and drafter of the document embracing socialism, said that the new stance toward foreign parties showed how earnestly the newly baptized Socialists meant their break with Communism.

"We have given up the whole terminology of brotherly parties," he said.

Dogmatic Soviet and East European Communists take the terminology and protocol of their movement seriously, and consider it a faux pas to address a Communist as "Mister" rather than "Comrade." Such hard-liners are likely to consider the Hungarian party's turnabout as an act of treason.

Casual conversations with Hungarians, however, indicate that many remain unconvinced that the outward changes represent a change of heart of the party that under two earlier names has been the absolute ruler of their country since World War II.

At a news conference today, spokesmen for the Democratic Forum, considered the principal opposition party in the first free presidential and parliamentary elections to be held by next spring, made sport of the name change. With heavy irony, the opposition leaders showed their disbelief in the Communists' name change and conversion.

"It's strange, we are all liberals now," said Dean Geza Jeszenszky of the School of Social and Political Science at Karl Marx University, a leader of the Democratic Forum. "Their program is not just socialist, it's more liberal than that of traditional social democrats. As an admirer of nineteenth-century liberalism, I welcome this."

But, Mr. Jeszenszky said, the reform Communists needed to compromise with more dogmatic Communists to create the new Socialist

Party. Referring to Marx, he said, "They think the teaching of a nineteenth-century philosopher is still valid today." As an opponent, he said he welcomed the outcome of the congress because the party had not changed enough to win credibility with the voters.

Mr. Agh, however, said he was convinced that the majority of Hungary's 725,000 Communists accepted the conversion and that, little by little, symbols of Communism like red stars and portraits of Lenin would disappear.

He said he and his friends would have been happier had Mr. Nyers, who is regarded as a moderate reformer, adopted a stronger line against conservative party members and provoked more of them to leave.

Party officials estimate that about a third of the membership will choose not to register in the new group.

"If we are lucky, those who leave will found a big Communist Party," Mr. Agh said. "It will give us political credentials."

Mr. Agh said that only three of the new party Presidium's 23 elected members "may have a past," meaning a former association with more dogmatic Communism. "We have a very solid voting majority," he said.

And farther to the east, Mikhail S. Gorbachev was once again leading by retreating. This time it was in Finland that he delivered an unexpected message.

Gorbachev in Finland, Disavows Any Right of Regional Intervention
By Bill Keller

HELSINKI, FINLAND, Oct. 25—President Mikhail S. Gorbachev declared today that the Soviet Union has no moral or political right to interfere in the affairs of its East European neighbors, and held up neutral Finland as a model of stability in stormy Europe.

His spokesman embroidered the theme jokingly, saying that Moscow had adopted "the Sinatra doctrine" in Eastern Europe. "You know the Frank Sinatra song, 'I Did It My Way'?" said Gennadi I. Gerasimov to reporters. "Hungary and Poland are doing it their way."

"I think the Brezhnev doctrine is dead," he added, using the Western term for the previous Soviet policy of armed intervention to prevent changes in the Communist governments of the Warsaw Pact. In talks with Finland's President, Mauno Koivisto, at the beginning of a three-day state visit, Mr. Gorbachev was reported to have said that the current political upheavals in the East bloc must be allowed to run their course.

Mr. Gorbachev has repeatedly pledged a policy of noninterference, but his emphasis on the point—and his lauding of the Finnish example—were striking in a week when Hungary was joining Poland in a retreat from orthodox Communist rule and East Germany was boiling with demands for political liberty.

"The events that are now taking place in the countries of Eastern Europe concern the countries and people of that region," the Soviet leader told the Finnish President, according to Mr. Gerasimov, whose formal position is that of spokesman for the Soviet Foreign Ministry. "We have no right, moral or political right, to interfere in events happening there. We assume others will not interfere either."

Finland, once an autonomous part of czarist Russia, gained its independence in 1917. It was invaded by the Soviet Union late in 1939, after the formal outbreak of World War II, and was forced to cede some territory to the Russians. The Karelian Autonomous Republic, which borders on Finland, is largely populated by Finnish speakers.

Today, as Mr. Gorbachev moved through largely friendly crowds, there were some cries of "Give us back Karelia," but no indication that he heard them.

Mr. Gerasimov, who served for many years as a correspondent for the Soviet news-feature agency Novosti in New York, has used the "Sinatra doctrine" expression before to explain the willingness of the Soviet Union to allow its allies to follow different political lines.

Mr. Gerasimov declined a direct answer when asked how Moscow would respond if its allies wanted to move toward neutrality. He noted that Hungary and Poland still have obligations as members of military and economic alliances with the Soviet Union.

"We may witness a change of government in Warsaw or Budapest, but international obligations do not necessarily go away with a change of government," Mr. Gerasimov said.

He added that Moscow has long proposed a mutual breakup of both the North Atlantic Treaty Organization and the Warsaw Pact, but he did not say how the Kremlin would react if the Warsaw Pact showed signs of breaking up on its own.

Still, Mr. Gorbachev's remarks today seemed to suggest that Moscow is open to more fundamental changes in its relations with East bloc allies.

Both Poland and Hungary have said they do not plan to leave the alliance, but some officials in both countries favor drastic military changes, including withdrawal of Soviet forces now based on their soil.

In recent months, Finland—with a largely free-market economy but reliant on Soviet trade, formally neutral but always attentive to Soviet security concerns—has loomed large in the minds of East bloc countries. Hungary has sent several delegations to study Finland's economy, its laws and its relations with Moscow.

Asked during a brief walk in downtown Helsinki this evening whether he considered Finland a model for countries in Eastern Europe, Mr. Gorbachev replied, "To me, Finland is a model of relations between a big country and a small country, a model of relations between states with different social systems, a model of relations between neighbors."

As if to underscore the advantages of good-neighborly relations, Soviet officials this week are to sign an agreement to sharply reduce sulfur emissions that have been poisoning Finland's forests.

Kaj Barlund, the Finnish Minister of the Environment, said in an interview today that it was "the most radical" anti-pollution agreement ever signed between a Communist and a non-Communist country, but he conceded that the Soviets would probably require costly technological help from the Finns to live up to their end of the deal.

The treaty calls for reducing the two countries' 1.4 million tons a year of sulfur-dioxide emissions by half before 1995. The largest share of the noxious emissions comes from two Soviet nickel smelters a few miles east of the Finnish border.

Mr. Gorbachev also made a significant concession to Finland's pride tonight when he said at a banquet speech, "I want to greet neutral Finland."

It was the first time that a Soviet leader had given full weight to this country's policy of neutrality in world politics. Moscow's reluctance to directly acknowledge that Finland is neutral has long been resented here as an implication that Finland owes special deference to the Kremlin.

In turn, Mr. Koivisto, the Finnish President, demonstrated the kind of sensitivity to the Soviet Union that the Kremlin prizes in this relationship. He included in his banquet speech an implicit but unmistakable message of nonsupport for separatist movements in Soviet Lithuania, Latvia and Estonia, across the Baltic Sea from Finland.

Mr. Koivisto said that although tensions are now erupting in the Soviet Union, "underneath the surface, there is every reason for confidence in the ability of this community of peoples to solve its problems in a way that enables the distinctiveness of the parts to be increased while strengthening the whole."

Finland and Estonia, which face each other across the Gulf of Finland, have longstanding ties that are now expanding. Direct air connections and a new, second ferry line across the gulf are due to open this winter, adding to an already fast-growing business and tourist traffic. Finnish bankers and businessmen say they see promising investment opportunities if Estonia gets greater economic independence from Moscow.

By mid-October, in the days just before and after Gorbachev delivered the Helsinki speech, the clamor for change that had arisen in Eastern Europe was centering on East Germany. Some East Germans were fleeing while others were trying to wield suddenly unleashed emotions and yearnings into an organization. Out of the milling and shouting—chaotic by German standards—emerged New Forum, which was to focus, if not fully lead, the mounting wave of demonstrations.

East German Movement Overtaken by Followers

By Serge Schmemann   *New Forum*

WEST BERLIN, Oct. 15—It is a sign of the novelty of resistance in East Germany that the premier opposition grouping, founded only a month ago, provided a rallying cry in the streets even before it had time to become a movement.

Among the chants that echoed loudest through the streets of East Berlin, Leipzig and Dresden during last week's mass protests was "Neu-es Fo-rum! Neu-es Fo-rum!" But few of the demonstrators had met anyone from New Forum, and its leaders deliberately stayed clear of the marches.

On the eve of the Government's celebration of the fortieth anniversary of the Communist state, New Forum leaders had actually urged East Germans not to demonstrate, fearing that uncontrolled protests could turn violent.

As Sebastian Pflugbeil, one of the founding members, said on the eve of the anniversary, "We don't have any means of asking people to behave peacefully. We have no access to media, we don't have any organization, we have no group that could manage a demonstration."

That was 10 days ago, before tens of thousands of East Germans across the country took to the streets, and before the alarmed Politburo demonstrated a first, tentative readiness to discuss the problems that had fired the protest and the earlier mass exodus to the West. One hundred and twenty New Forum representatives from all parts of East Germany met and agreed to form a standing coordinating committee, to appoint a "spokesmen's council" to speak for the movement, and to publish a newspaper starting next month. They claimed to have 25,000 supporters.

New Forum also renewed its application for official registration as a political organization, which authorities rejected last month with a threatening denunciation of the fledgling group as "a platform hostile to the state."

To be sure, the Politburo made clear in its statement on Wednesday that it was prepared to have discussions only through existing channels.

But the newly stiffened New Forum declared that "real dialogue had to be institutionalized."

"With our first manifesto we tried to bring people out, to say to them, 'We want to stay,'" Barbel Bohley, the most vocal of the founding members, said in a recent interview. "Many agreed with that, but we can't remain at this point. We are interested in standing on our own feet."

Founded less than a month before the anniversary by a group of middle-aged, left-wing intellectuals and defectors from the ruling Communist Party, New Forum was born as a popular rebuttal to the mass exodus of East Germans to West Germany through Hungary, Czechoslovakia and Poland and to the talk of reunification this prompted in the West.

In their manifesto on September 12, the founders declared that they did not want to go West, they did not want German reunification, they did not want capitalism. They want to create a political platform for the "restructuring of the German Democratic Republic," for a democratic socialism.

At a time when the world's attention was focused on the exodus and the common joke was whether anyone would be left in East Germany to turn off the lights, the appearance of a group militantly bent on staying and changing the state from within attracted instant attention.

If the Government had simply ignored New Forum instead of denouncing the movement, it might have remained one of several pro-reform groups springing up in the fertile tumult of the exodus. Instead, its name spread through East Germany by West German radio and television, it became a rallying cry for the dissatisfaction catalyzed by the exodus.

"Things are moving much faster than we ever thought," said Mr. Pflugbeil. "Now even in small cities and in small factories people are joining New Forum. But you shouldn't overestimate what we are doing. You shouldn't compare us to Solidarity. This is only the beginning, on a very small scale."

With his tangled beard and large glasses, Mr. Pflugbeil seemed to fit well the profile of a New Forum founder. A physicist and at 42 a veteran of the East German peace movement, he had emerged like many other founders from the protective shadow of the Protestant churches, where East German dissenters had long huddled.

Teenagers when the Berlin wall was erected, they had cut their dissenters' teeth in the small anti-missile movements that rose after 1979 as an echo of the potent peace movement in West Germany, and the environmental activism of the early 1980's. Harassed constantly by the state, they had watched their leaders repeatedly expelled to the West, leaving their movement in a permanent state of disorganization.

Now, joined by Communist Party defectors inspired by the Soviet President, Mikhail S. Gorbachev, they represent a blend of perestroika Communism and environmentalism, a group in some ways reminiscent of the dissident writers and scientists in Moscow in the 1960's, or of KOR in Poland or Charter '77 in Czechoslovakia in the 1970's.

Speaking in a soft voice over tea in his book-lined apartment in central East Berlin, Mr. Pflugbeil talked of the difficulty of dissent in a nation still scarred by its past.

"We are now at the point where we have to openly discuss change," he said. "It is especially important that we speak openly and with no fear, because since 1933 we have forgotten that freedom of speech can be used. We all learned from our parents that to touch political things is dangerous. That is an attitude that has to change."

The attitude, it seemed last week, has changed more than New Forum or the church were prepared for. At one point during the demonstrations in East Berlin, several thousand protesters reached Gethsemane Church, a center of opposition, and filled the small square facing its entrance.

As the police advanced, the throng looked to the entrance glowing in the light of candles placed by dissenters, as if waiting for someone to appear and take charge.

Nobody did. Unlike the Polish strikers in 1980, the young East German demonstrators had neither militant workers nor an organization behind them. Their demonstrations seemed largely spontaneous eruptions of anger and frustration, catalyzed by the mass exodus and the gaudy celebrations marking the state's fortieth birthday. Mr. Gorbachev was in town, and an army of Western reporters had been reluctantly let in for the festivities.

For New Forum, the protests seemed to pose a critical challenge. To remain an intellectual forum was to risk irrelevance in the new mood. To try to take charge was to telescope an evolutionary process from intellectual dissent to power politics that had taken successful movements like Solidarity years to achieve.

"We move ahead, but we don't have an overview yet," Miss Bohley said. "We've grown up without democracy, and we honestly do not know this playing field, democracy. On one hand we reject the tutelage of the state, on the other we don't know how democracy really looks. Now some are calling for a program. We have to have patience."

As Mr. Gorbachev offered his assurances of nonintervention and the New Forum people drew more and more adherents, tens of thousands of East Germans had been streaming out of their country via Hungary and Czechoslovakia to West Germany. As numbers of these mostly young émigrés built up in the West German Embassy in Prague, the East Germans agreed to their transfer, but at the same time announced the border to Czechoslovakia would be sealed. But then in the face of protests, they relented, and once more people swarmed to Prague in growing numbers. And at home, huge rallies were taking place at which new demands were raised that went far beyond calls for freer travel.

300,000 Reported to March in Largest East German Protest

By Henry Kamm

EAST BERLIN, Oct 23—Hundreds of thousands of East Germans marched peacefully through Leipzig tonight, demanding democratic changes, including legalization of opposition movements, independent labor unions and separation of powers between the Communist Party and the state. . . .

An East Berlin worker complained not long ago that all his life he had been taught "to learn from the Soviet Union is to learn to triumph." Now that East Germans would like to follow the Soviet example, he said, they are being told that each country must follow its own path. . . .

The East German government was being forced into concessions.

East Germans Declare Amnesty for Those Who Fled

By Serge Schmemann

BONN, Oct. 27—East Germany announced an amnesty today for all citizens who have fled or tried to flee the country, as well as most of those arrested in the recent wave of anti-Government demonstrations.

The Government also announced that East Germans could again travel to Czechoslovakia without a visa. A ban was imposed on October 3 to halt a tide of East Germans fleeing to the West German Embassy in Prague hoping to win passage to the West. Almost 20,000 fled in this way before East Germany shut the border, the only one East Germans had been freely allowed to cross.

The Interior Ministry said today the ban would be lifted as of November 1. There was no indication whether the Government would take new steps to prevent another mass flight to the West German Embassy, which has continued to attract a trickle of East Germans. . . .

Another Big Rally in East Germany

By Serge Schmemann

LEIPZIG, EAST GERMANY, Oct. 30—Chanting demands for everything from free elections to the ouster of the secret police, more than

300,000 East Germans marched around Leipzig's old center in what has become the major weekly ritual of the growing popular movement for change.

A thicket of placards challenging the Communist Party's rule with slogans like "New politics with the old crowd?" offered evidence of how far the movement has evolved in the three weeks since the Communist Party first allowed a march in Leipzig to go unchallenged and so signaled a retreat from its hard line. . . .

As soon as they were able to resume their flight via Prague, they did, and on November 1 the very first day that the new rules went into effect, 8,000 crossed into Czechoslovakia, and even larger numbers swarmed in the days that followed. The policies of permissiveness were not stemming the exodus. The stream of émigrés was turning into a torrent, as was the surge of protest inside the country.

500,000 in East Berlin Rally for Change; Émigrés Are Given Passage to West

By Serge Schmemann

EAST BERLIN, Nov. 4—Four weeks to the day after a few thousand East Berliners took to the streets to demand political change, at least a half-million demonstrators jammed the heart of the East German capital today for the largest rally so far in what one speaker called a "revolution from below."

At the same time, reports from Prague, the Czechoslovak capital, said East Germany had agreed to let its citizens leave for the West from Czechoslovakia by simply producing their internal identity documents.

The decision marked the first time that East Germany allowed its citizens free passage to West Germany, and in essence it opened a door through the wall that for so long has stood as the foremost symbol of Communist control, the dividing line between East and West.

Ingrid Stahmer, the Deputy Mayor of West Berlin, who visited Prague today, indicated that she believed that the new measures meant that the Berlin wall had, in effect, passed into history. "It is just going to be superfluous," she said. The news did not seem to dampen calls for change as the throng in the East German capital marched down broad boulevards through the city center with a thicket of placards, finally engulfing Alexanderplatz, a vast plain of concrete at the heart of East Berlin, to hear a series of speeches. As the marchers passed the headquarters of the Council of Ministers, many demonstrators posted demands on the wall or laid them on the ground, and they remained there long after the demonstration ended.

Some estimates put the crowd at more than a million, and by any count it posted another milestone in a mass movement that has filled the streets of East Germany virtually daily in numbers unknown in its forty-year history.

And like all the demonstrations since the state first reined in the police on October 9 and allowed people to protest unmolested, the authorities did not interfere and the four-hour rally was disciplined and peaceful.

In the spirit of openness that has spread over the last four weeks, the demonstration was broadcast live on the East German radio and television.

Most of the placards, and the statements from the seventeen speakers that drew the loudest cheers, called for free speech, free elections, an end to the "leading role" of the Communist Party and—a demand that prompted the most boisterous whoops—a settling of accounts with the hated security police.

Only Gunter Schabowski, the Communist Party chief in East Berlin, referred directly to the renewed flight when he spoke of the "depressing news and pictures from Prague." There was also a banner linking "monopoly of power by the Communist Party" and "mass flight" by émigrés.

The agreement between East Germany and Czechoslovakia, first announced by West German officials, meant that an East German had only to show an internal identity document to cross Czechoslovakia to West Germany. Almost immediately, sputtering East German Trabant cars began arriving at the Czechoslovak–West German border, along with trainloads of East Germans who had thronged to the West German Embassy after East Berlin first lifted restrictions on travel to Czechoslovakia on November 1.

East Germans still could not travel directly to West Germany. But the announcement of the East German–Czechoslovak arrangement stressed that it would be in force only until East Germany enacts a promised new travel law, which reportedly will enable East Germans to travel abroad with relative ease.

The march in East Berlin had been organized by the official Union of Actors, and a cordon of actors and artists, wearing sashes that read "No Violence," helped keep order.

Most marchers seemed largely unimpressed by the promises of "far-reaching" changes and the dismissal of five Politburo members announced Friday evening by Egon Krenz, the new party chief. The new program and the resignations are to become formal at a meeting of the Communist Party's Central Committee next week.

It seemed a measure of the remarkable pace of events in East Germany that even while Mr. Krenz was announcing measures that would have been breathtaking only four weeks earlier, he now seemed to trail behind the demands of a popular movement still without real leadership.

"He's learned a lot, he's gaining pace, but I'm not sure whether he's quick enough to keep up with events," said Jens Reich, one of the founding members of the New Forum opposition group and a speaker at the rally. "He must become more bold."

Four weeks earlier, during celebrations of East Germany's fortieth anniversary that were attended by President Mikhail S. Gorbachev of the Soviet Union, a small group of demonstrators had begun chanting "Freedom!" and "Gorby!" on Alexanderplatz.

Before the night was over, about 5,000 demonstrators had clashed violently with the police, revealing to the Government the danger of the popular discontent and prompting the dramatic change of course both by the Communists and the public.

Many of the placards carried by the crowd were laced with a humor that seemed to reflect a growing confidence in the popular movement. "Always forward, never backward—Erich Honecker, roofer," read one, referring to the fallen party leader and his original trade. Some referred to Mr. Krenz's support for the Chinese after the June crackdown on dissent: "Krenz Xiaoping, no thanks."

Other banners called for dismantling the security police and demanded free trade unions and new faces at the top. One simply read, "Thanks, Hungary." It was Hungary's opening of its borders that prompted a mass migration last summer, which in turn was a catalyst for the movement for change at home.

The seventeen speakers included actors, opposition leaders, party officials, church leaders, writers and other prominent figures. Some drew cheers, some jeers and some both.

"I don't like the words 'change of course,' " said one of the most popular speakers, the prominent writer Christa Wolff, referring to the term by which the Communist Party has repeatedly referred to its new openness.

"It sounds like a sailor changing direction with the prevailing wind," she said. "I would rather say 'revolutionary renewal,' a 'revolution from below.' "

Some of the largest jeers were reserved for Mr. Schabowski, who has shown probably the least reticence among Politburo members in coming face to face with critics.

"What does a Communist think in the face of hundreds of thousands of demonstrators?" he asked, shouting into the microphones over a steady roar of whistles and jeers. "Bitter things have been said, directed to my address. But only if we speak to each other can we create a new East Germany."

Shouts of "Shut up!" rose from the crowd, drowning out all but snatches of Mr. Schabowski's address.

A prominent lawyer, Gregor Gysi, received a mixed reaction when he said it was Mr. Krenz, then the party secretary charged with security, who ordered the police not to interfere with marchers in Leipzig on October 9, and thus ended the violence that had marked demonstrations until then.

Among the last speakers was an elderly and popular actress, Steffie Spira, who alone stayed within the five-minute limit set on addresses and who raised a roar of laughter when she concluded her remarks by saying: "I want the Government to do what I am about to do. Step down." And she did.

The next week proved critical. Successive headlines reflected the quickening tempo.

10,000 More Flee as East Germany Vows Easy Travel
By Serge Schmemann

EAST BERLIN, Nov. 5—Thousands of East Germans left for West Germany today as the Government said that new laws making it relatively easy for citizens to travel to the West would be ready for Christmas.

The announcement by Interior Minister Friedrich Dickel on the evening news program seemed intended to halt another frenzied westward flight by East Germans afraid that the borders might once more close. . . .

A Draft Law Grants East Germans the Right to Travel or Emigrate
By Serge Schmemann

EAST BERLIN, Nov. 6—East Germany today published the draft of a law that declared for the first time that every citizen has the right to travel abroad or emigrate. But against the weekend backdrop of yet another surge of emigration to West Germany, the measure seemed to attract little excitement.

"Travel is not the primary problem anymore," said Sebastian Pflugbeil, a founding member of the opposition movement New Forum. . . .

Then on November 7 came word that the entire East German cabinet resigned and the next day the announcement was made that the Politburo was being reorganized to enable Egon Krenz, then still in his first month as party leader, to name what was described as a streamlined and younger party leadership. The day after that, on November 9, a Thursday, the East German authorities took the step that they had long thought unthinkable.

The Border Is Open; Joyous East Germans Pour Through Wall; Party Pledges Freedoms, and City Exults
By Serge Schmemann

WEST BERLIN, Nov. 10—As hundreds of thousands of East Berliners romped through the newly porous wall in an unending celebration, West German leaders today proclaimed this the moment Germans had yearned for through forty years of division.

At the same time, change continued unabated in East Berlin, where the Communist Party's Central Committee concluded a three-day session with the announcement of a program of radical changes. They included "free, democratic and secret elections," a "socialist planned economy oriented to market conditions," separation of party and state, parliamentary supervision of state security, freedom of assembly and a new law on the press and broadcasting.

"The German Democratic Republic is in the midst of an awakening," the Central Committee declared in the prologue to the newly adopted program. "A revolutionary people's movement has brought

175

into motion a process of great change. The renewal of society is on the agenda."

Though the West Berlin police could give no estimate of the numbers of East Berliners who crossed over in the last 24 hours, the authorities said that only 1,500 so far had announced their intention to stay.

Beyond Berlin, only one of many points along the border between the two Germanys where people could cross, 55,500 East Germans crossed over the border between the two Germanys since the wall was opened on Thursday, and 3,250 remained in West Germany, the West German Interior Ministry said.

Chancellor Helmut Kohl, who interrupted a state visit to Poland to come to West Berlin, told an emotional crowd of East and West Berliners gathered outside the West Berlin city hall: "I want to call out to all in the German Democratic Republic: We're on your side, we are and remain one nation. We belong together."

Speaking on the steps of the city hall, from which President John F. Kennedy had made his "Ich bin ein Berliner" speech shortly after the wall was raised, Mr. Kohl declared: "Long live a free German fatherland! Long live a united Europe!"

All through the night and through the day, East Berliners continued to flood into West Berlin in vast numbers, filling the glittering Kurfurstendamm until traffic came to a halt, forming long lines to pick up the 100-mark "welcome money"—about $55—that West Germany has traditionally given East Germans on their first time in the West, gaping at shop windows and drinking in the heady new feeling of freedom.

A festive air seized the entire city. West Berliners lined entry points to greet East Berliners with champagne, cheers and hugs. Many restaurants offered the visitors free food. A television station urged West Berliners to call in with offers of theater tickets, beds, dinners or just guided tours of the "Ku'damm."

The Hertha soccer club, popular both in West and East, offered 10,000 free tickets to the game against Wattenscheid on Saturday.

Both West and East German television gave saturation coverage to the reunion, often under titles like "The End of the Wall," contributing to a widespread sense that a great moment was in the making.

In a development that gave further evidence of the figurative crumbling of the wall, East Germany announced the opening of five new crossings. One was at the Glienicke Bridge, famed as the site of past exchanges of captured spies between East and West, and another was at Potsdammer Platz, once the heart of Berlin.

The arrival of an army bulldozer at Eberswalder Strasse to drill another new opening quickly attracted a crowd on both sides and sent rumors through the city that the East German Army was breaking down the wall. When the machine finally broke through, West Berliners handed flowers to the driver and rushed to pick up pieces of the wall for souvenirs.

At the Potsdammer Platz crossing site, West Berliners mounted the wall to chip away pieces while East German workers laid paving stones in the no-man's-land, watched by about 50 soldiers.

The East German authorities also announced that bus shuttles would connect East and West Berlin.

In the giddiness of the grand reunion, German reunification was in the air. "We've done it! The wall is open!" proclaimed the popular tabloid *Bild* in a giant headline. "This is the first step to unity."

The conservative *Frankfurter Allgemeine* tempered its excitement with caution: "Since Thursday evening that monstrous construction and barbed wire no longer divide the people. But with the joy over the end of the torment of German division, we must realize that faster German rapprochement needs a faster consideration of how politically to handle a situation changing by the hour."

A group of young men walked down the Kurfurstendamm with the two German flags, identical save for a Communist emblem at the center of the East German banner, sewn together.

The theme was there, too, in the emotional speeches from the steps of city hall. Willy Brandt, the former West German Chancellor who was West Berlin's Mayor in 1961 when the wall was raised, declared in a choked voice: "This is a beautiful day after a long voyage, but we are only at a way station. We are not at the end of our way."

"The moving together of the German states is taking shape in reality in a different way than many of us expected," Mr. Brandt said. "No one should act as if he knows in which concrete form the people in these two states will find a new relationship. But that they will find a relationship, that they will come together in freedom, that is the important point."

Walter Momper, the Mayor of West Berlin, raised cheers when he declared: "The whole city and all its citizens will never forget November 9, 1989. For 28 years since the wall was built we have yearned for this day. We Germans are now the happiest people on earth. Yesterday was not yet the day of reunification, but it was a day of reunion."

The West German Foreign Minister, Hans-Dietrich Genscher, who returned with Mr. Kohl from Poland for the gathering, opened his address by recalling his roots in East Germany, from which he fled after the war.

"My most hearty greetings go to the people of my homeland," he said. "What we are witnessing in the streets of Berlin in these hours is that forty years of division have not created two nations out of one. There is no capitalist and there is no socialist Germany, but only one German nation in unity and peace."

Evidently anticipating the anxieties of other countries, Mr. Genscher added: "No people on this earth, no people in Europe have to fear if the gates are opened now between East and West. No people have to fear that liberty and democracy have returned to the G.D.R."

Mr. Kohl was met by loud jeers from the crowd, evidently reflecting his unpopularity among many West Berliners, as he declared this "a historic moment for Berlin and for Germany."

The Chancellor appealed to East Germans to stay in their country now that it was evidently firmly on the road to political and economic change. "We are sure that when these reforms come to pass, and if the G.D.R. goes forward on this path, our compatriots there who now think of leaving will stay in their homeland," he said.

Mr. Kohl flew from West Berlin to Bonn, where he will preside over an emergency Cabinet meeting on Saturday morning before returning to Poland to continue his official visit.

In East Germany, the conclusion of the Central Committee meeting was followed by a mass rally of Communist Party members that was addressed Egon Krenz, the new party leader.

"We plan a great work, a revolution on German soil that will bring us a socialism that is economically effective, politically democratic, morally clean and will turn to the people in everything," Mr. Krenz declared.

"That's why the Council of Ministers issued new travel regulations for all mature citizens in our country as an expression that we are serious in our policy of renewal and that we reach out our hands to everyone who wants to go with us," he said.

The "action program" adopted today, Mr. Krenz said, was "a program for our people to win back trust among the people."

"We want better socialism, we want free elections, we want our people to send their best representatives to Parliament," he said.

Mr. Krenz also reaffirmed his loyalty to Moscow, as he has taken care to do since he came to power. "Our close links to the Soviet Union make us strong, and give new meaning to our slogan, that to learn from the Soviet Union is to learn to win, especially in these days," he said.

The action program outlined by the official press agency A.D.N. followed the proposals first made by Mr. Krenz on the opening day of the Central Committee meeting. The three-day meeting proved a turning point in the dramatic upheaval that has seized East Germany over the last month.

The Central Committee issued only broad directives for change. On the economic front, it called for making the planned economy sensitive to market conditions, though it did not elaborate how this would be done. With an eye to the most widespread complaints, it said the economy would concentrate on areas such as consumer goods, meat, beer and spare parts.

The proposed election law promised to be the most fateful of the new measures. The West German radio said Hans Modrow, the new Prime Minister, had discussed with Mr. Krenz the possibility of forming a coalition government with some of the small parties, including the Social Democrats and the Liberals.

Mr. Modrow said the action program of the Communist Party would not be enough without the input of the other parties, which have become more independent and vocal over the last month.

The Central Committee also strongly censured Erich Honecker, the fallen party leader, and two Politburo members ousted with him, Gunter Mittag and Joachim Hermann. "The Central Committee has learned that serious mistakes of the previous General Secretary and Politburo led the party and republic into deep crisis," the final communiqué of the session said.

The committee reserved its sharpest criticism for Mr. Mittag, who had been the secretary charged with the economy. "Comrade Mittag was excluded from the Central Committee because of the gravest violations of inner-party democracy, against party and state discipline and because of damaging the reputation of the party," it said.

The program also called for approval of freedom of assembly, legalization of new political organizations, a constitutional court and changes in criminal law to include independent juries. It also said the party would immediately take measures to lift privileges held by party leaders.

It declared, too, that military policy would be publicly discussed, and that military spending might be reduced.

The program is expected to come under more detailed discussion when Parliament meets on Monday.

Amid the euphoria there were trickles of anxiety. Would a less divided Europe become a less peaceful place? How great would be the burdens of helping the poor Eastern cousins catch up with the West, and if they did not catch up, would they remain quiet and content?

Redefining Europe; As the Revelry Goes On, Politicians Ponder the Ramifications of Changes in Germany
By Craig R. Whitney

WEST BERLIN, Nov. 10—By the simple act of forcing their Communist rulers to open the Berlin wall and allow them to go wherever they wish, the people of East Germany have irrevocably changed the way Berlin, Germany and all of Europe have defined themselves for more than forty years.

Thousands and thousands of East Berliners celebrated their triumph today by promenading up and down the elegant, tree-lined shopping boulevards of the western part of the city, which most of them had never before been allowed to see. They made the Kurfurstendamm into a street festival this evening as church bells pealed joyously into the night.

Willy Brandt, who was Mayor of West Berlin when the wall was built in 1961, said at a rally this evening, "The moving together of the German states is taking shape in reality in a different way than many of us expected.

"No one should act as if he knows in which concrete form the people in these two states will find a new relationship. But that they will find a relationship, that they will come together in freedom, that is the important point."

But the entire postwar European order has been based on the assumption that Germany, and Europe, would remain divided, and the countries of Eastern and Western Europe firmly anchored in their respective alliances.

In that assumption the United States, in the NATO alliance, guaranteed the security of Western Europe. And in that same assumption

France, West Germany and the other major industrial countries of Western Europe began the economic and political unification of the European Community.

West German politicians, including Mr. Brandt and Chancellor Helmut Kohl, who interrupted an official visit to Poland today to fly to Berlin, all insist that West Germany's commitment to West European integration and the alliance remains.

But politicians, diplomats and business leaders all over Europe are considering new implications for both institutions now that the end of German partition is at last imaginable.

"Europe, though Europeans did not always appreciate it, has been a haven of order these past 44 years," *The Economist* wrote today. "For East Europeans the price of that stability has been high: a lifetime wasted under a government you loathed. For West Europeans the stability has been marvelous. They could get rich, and start to build a new unity, within a clearly defined zone which ended at the river Elbe and the Bohemian forest."

Now, a NATO diplomat in Brussels said, "The end of the wall raises questions of what's going to happen in Europe. The whole concept of the European Community now may have to change."

So would the concept of the NATO alliance, this diplomat conceded: "Our role will be to design a new role for the alliance—maintaining a balance of stability with the East while all this change is going on.

"There's a reassessment of the Warsaw Pact going on too," he said. "This organization we rejected over the years is beginning to be seen as a possible element of stability in the future, to prevent the Balkanization of Eastern Europe."

Rudolf Witt, a 32-year-old mechanic from East Berlin who crossed over this afternoon with his wife, Barbara Rieck, and their 4-month-old baby, Susanne, said on his way back home at the Invalidenstrasse crossing point, "We're the balancing scales of Europe, and we don't want to tip them with something like German reunification."

An American diplomatic expert on Germany said, "I think the orderliness of everything that has happened so far, and the great restraint shown by the West Germans, shows that there will be an orderly transition to something else."

"I think Kohl will make a great big pledge and West German industrialists will start rebuilding" East Germany, he said. "But the price will be more political reform than the East German leadership originally intended. If they follow the Polish model, East Germans would have eight or ten years to determine whether they wanted to remain a separate country," he said.

Such uncertainties have been far from the minds of the European Community politicians who have spent the last three years trying to agree on ways to closer economic and political unity among the twelve existing members.

Chancellor Kohl has been trying to persuade his fellow European leaders to agree to make the Community into a confederation, rather than the loose collection of cooperating sovereign states that is preferred by Prime Minister Margaret Thatcher of Britain.

Mrs. Thatcher is already regarded by the other leaders in the Community as an obstacle to greater unity among the twelve. At full steam only a year ago, omentum toward closer union could falter if much of West Germany's attention in the next few years is diverted to the East. On Wednesday, Mr. Kohl promised a "completely new dimension" of economic aid for East Germany if it went ahead with promised political changes.

But even if European integration is sidetracked for the time being, it may acquire a new direction if the peoples of Eastern Europe can go on forcing democratic change in their countries. Nations like Hungary, Poland and perhaps even East Germany could become associate members of an expanded European Community, if not full ones.

The challenge would be to allow them to flourish economically in association with Western Europe without upsetting the security interests of either the United States or the Soviet Union in the process.

Both superpowers, at the moment, look more or less like passive, though benevolent, bystanders as events in Eastern Europe unfold. Moscow no longer seems to see itself as threatened by radical political or economic change in Eastern Europe, and both the United States and the Soviet Union have an interest in achieving substantial cuts in their conventional armed forces on both sides of the German divide.

What is not so clear is where Moscow's strategic bottom line lies, and what the attitude of the United States—not just the Bush Administration, but Congress as well—will be if many Americans decide the cold war is over and their troops should all come home. There are about 300,000 Army and Air Force troops in Western Europe.

The American attitude is the key to insuring that Germany does not lose its Western orientation and that Europe manages an orderly transition to whatever new future awaits it, many Germans and Western diplomats agree.

"We are at present at the creation of a new postwar era," one American official said, "and I hope the people at home will see it that way."

Jubilation in Berlin; A Day for Celebration and a Bit of Shopping
By Ferdinand Protzman

EAST BERLIN, Nov. 10—Church bells pealed, long-separated friends and family members fell into each other's arms, people wept for joy and complete strangers pressed money into newcomers' hands or offered them rides to wherever they wanted to go.

It was a day that made an indelible imprint on Berlin's collective memory. Hundreds of thousands of East Berliners crossed into West Berlin today, according to police estimates.

"The mood is just fantastic," said a woman from East Berlin. "The West Berliners have been wonderful to us. I thank them all." The East Berliners, coming from a land where nearly all prices are kept artificially low by subsidies, were also greeted by price-tag shock.

"It's all quite lovely," said a young woman from Rostock as she gazed at the display window of a women's clothing store on the Kurfurstendamm, West Berlin's main street and the city's toniest shopping area. "But cheap it's not."

The sky was a high, clear blue and the "Berliner Luft"—the air of Berlin, that is lauded by natives for its invigorating qualities—overcame the usual pollution and lived up to its reputation. It rang with the sounds of celebration. The city center of West Berlin became a giant festival grounds, forcing police to ban auto traffic because of the press of pedestrians. Some restaurants gave out free food and drink. Bottles, cans and broken glass seemed to be everywhere.

"The wall is gone!" Those slightly hyperbolic words were uttered countless times here in the last 24 hours, by people in both sides of the city. Although the forbidding concrete barrier still stands, it has fallen in the minds of East and West Berliners alike.

"I knew as soon as I heard the news on the radio last night what it meant," said Stani, a 19-year-old East Berliner, as he jostled for position in a West Berlin subway packed with East Germans on their way to celebrate on the Kurfurstendamm. "There is no turning back from this now. Allowing people to travel freely is a step that our Government can never retract. We won't be closed in again. The people will simply not allow that. Now we know the way here." . . .

Ripples in Poland; Kohl Delivers Aid and Returns Home
By John Tagliabue

WARSAW, Nov. 10—Chancellor Helmut Kohl of West Germany told Polish leaders today that he was interrupting a five-day visit to their country for 24 hours, but not until he had signed accords granting Poland the largest amount of economic aid it has yet obtained from a Western nation.

The Chancellor, responding to the political changes in East Germany, then set off by aircraft for home, to attend a huge rally in West Berlin celebrating the end of the Berlin wall, to preside over an emergency session of his Cabinet in Bonn on Saturday morning, and to seek a meeting with East Germany's new leader, Egon Krenz. . . .

The changes were again spreading. They were occurring all over Eastern Europe. The success of marchers seeking reform in one place inspired marchers elsewhere. From Bulgaria came news that the man who had ruled that country for almost 35 decades was being forced to step down. Slightly more than a year earlier, the Warsaw pact allies of the Soviet Union had been ruled by old men who had seemed to have lifetime tenure. Now Janos Kadar was gone in Hungary, Erich Honecker was out in East Germany, and Zhivkov was on his way out in Bulgaria. In Poland, General Jaruzelski, the youngest of the lot, was President, but he was sharing power with non-Communists. Only in Czechoslovakia and Rumania were the old guard holding the same posts they had when the year began.

Bulgarian Chief Quits After 35 Years of Rigid Rule
By Clyde Haberman

SOFIA, BULGARIA, Nov. 10—Todor I. Zhivkov, Eastern Europe's longest-serving leader, resigned today as Bulgaria's President and Communist Party leader, after 35 years of guiding the country with old-line orthodoxy.

Mr. Zhivkov, 78 years old, was immediately replaced as the party's General Secretary by his longtime Foreign Minister, Petar T. Mladenov, who is viewed here as likely to take a somewhat more flexible approach toward economic and political restructuring. It will be up to the politically weak National Assembly to choose his successor as President.

Since Mr. Zhivkov and other top officials recently began to talk about the need to separate state and party roles, it seemed possible that someone other than Mr. Mladenov could be selected.

Mr. Zhivkov's resignation came as a surprise but not as a total shock to Western diplomats, who said that the Bulgarian leader had apparently fallen victim to the fast-paced changes elsewhere in Eastern Europe.

Bulgarian officials reportedly said in confidence that Mr. Zhivkov did not want to stay too long and risk being forced from power in disgrace, as were Janos Kadar of Hungary or Erich Honecker of East Germany.

There were strong rumors of more shifts to come in top party echelons, but the state press agency and television network made no announcements. The prospects for genuine change here, several diplomats said, are likely to be determined by the extent of any future shake-up.

Mr. Mladenov, who is 53 and was Foreign Minister for 18 years, wasted no time as the new leader in warning that "there is no alternative to restructuring" Bulgaria's struggling economy and tightly controlled political apparatus. The present system has "handicapped progress in our society in all spheres," he told the party Central Committee, adding: "We have to turn Bulgaria into a modern, democratic and lawful country."

Despite his words, however, many Bulgarians and diplomats were not convinced that rapid changes were on the way.

Mr. Zhivkov, they said, had filled the Central Committee with people who basically followed his version of orthodox Communism, and they did not regard Mr. Mladenov as a conspicuous exception. "He's generally perceived to be more liberal than Zhivkov but not markedly so," a Western diplomat said. "I would suspect that it means policies will continue."

Another reason for the cautious assessment is that Mr. Mladenov's remarks today echoed what Mr. Zhivkov had been saying for more than two years, if with meager results. Matching words with deeds eluded him. Official tolerance for dissent remains slight, and the economy has limped along with shoddy consumer goods, poor farm production and shortages of basic food items like butter and sugar.

Mr. Zhivkov acknowledged the failure in a report today to the Central Committee, in which he calls for broad political and economic adjustments, including more power for the National Assembly and clearer divisions between the party and the Government.

"In the final account, we were unable to make a significant breakthrough in any sector of our work," he said.

Thus far, Bulgaria has been in the rear guard of the Communist world, plodding along amid the rush of events sweeping the Soviet Union, Hungary, Poland and now even East Germany, which had also been a hard-line state. But it is not immune to events elsewhere, and in recent weeks a new breed of Bulgarian dissidents has begun to speak out to a degree rarely heard in this Slavic nation.

The first known demonstration in four decades took place last week in the center of Sofia, the capital, when about 5,000 Bulgarians marched on the National Assembly building to express their grievances on environmental pollution. For many, environmental concerns were merely an excuse to give vent to broader anti-Government frustrations.

It is not clear, however, that Bulgaria has turned the corner on dissent, for the Government permitted the demonstration primarily because an international environmental conference was under way in Sofia. Now that the foreigners have gone home, dissidents say they cannot be sure that another such protest would be tolerated.

Mr. Zhivkov became Communist Party leader in 1954, a year after Stalin's death, and in recent years he has been the Soviet Union's most faithful ally. Soviet flags often fly beside Bulgarian flags in the capital, and the anniversary of the Russian Revolution in 1917, observed last Tuesday, is a Bulgarian national holiday.

Over the decades, Mr. Zhivkov consolidated his power by purging opponents. The process continued as recently as last year, when he forced out a Politburo member, Chudomir A. Aleksandrov, who had been widely considered a possible successor.

In addition to his party post, Mr. Zhivkov became chairman of the Council of Ministers, the equivalent of Prime Minister, in 1962, a position that yielded in 1971 to the Presidency. Except for a failed coup attempt in 1965, there had been no serious challenges to his leadership. His health has suffered in the last few years, but before today there was no indication that he was in immediate danger of losing power.

Bulgaria's relations with the Soviet Union have weakened in recent years, partly because of Moscow's preoccupation with its own problems and partly because Soviet restructuring under Mikhail S. Gorbachev has outstripped the pace here.

Two years ago, a new economic program was announced by Mr. Zhivkov, laying the basis, it was hoped, for a thoroughly revamped economy. But the promise of more self-management for private businesses proved greater than the reality, and the economy has only bumped along since.

It suffered a further blow, as did Bulgaria's image, when 310,000 ethnic Turkish residents of the country fled across the border into Turkey last summer to escape a campaign of forced assimilation. Since then, 60,000 of them have returned, according to estimates, but their abrupt departure from a country of nine million people had already disrupted crop harvests and factory production in predominantly Muslim provinces in eastern Bulgaria.

Dramatic as the Bulgarian changes were, they were less riveting than what was going on in the very heart of Europe, in Berlin.

The Open Frontier; East Germans Flood the West, Most to Rejoice, Then Go Home; Kohl and Krenz Agree to Meet
By Serge Schmemann

WEST BERLIN, Nov. 11—A million East Germans streamed into West Berlin and West Germany today on foot and by car, subway and train, many passing through border crossings so new that the paint was not yet dry. More important for East Germany, most were going back.

In Bonn, Chancellor Helmut Kohl announced after a telephone call to Egon Krenz, the new East German leader, that he would visit East Germany before the year's end. Mr. Kohl also presided over an emergency meeting of his Cabinet before flying back to Poland to resume the state visit he interrupted after East Germany opened its borders on Thursday night.

In East Berlin, Mr. Krenz declared after the telephone call that "German reunification is not on the agenda." He said Mr. Kohl had touched on the provisions in the West German Constitution calling for the unity of Germany through self-determination, but "that is his business."

"My business as the representative of the German Democratic Republic," Mr. Krenz said, "is to point out that there are two wholly sovereign German states that have to get on well with each other."

At a news conference in Bonn, Chancellor Kohl said that his Cabinet supported the changes taking place in East Germany and that "we are ready to offer whatever help will benefit the people." But Mr. Kohl said West German assistance would help East Germany only if "the system of state-planned economy would be substituted by a socially responsible market economy."

After 40 years of being penned in by walls and barbed wire, the East Germans seized on their new freedom to travel, creating epic jams at border crossings, highways and train stations.

Officials said half a million flocked into West Berlin today and another 500,000 to other crossing points in West Germany. More were to come. The official East German press agency A.D.N. said 2.7 million visas had been issued for foreign travel since the Government announced the new travel regulations on Thursday.

First reports indicated that the large majority of visitors were returning home after a glimpse of the West and after lining up for 100 marks, about $55, in "welcome money" from the West German Government. Interior Minister Wolfgang Schauble said that of the first 125,000 visitors, only 5 percent, or some 6,000, had applied to stay. East German television said that of the first 206,000 visitors today, 2,866 had opted to remain in West Germany. An additional 8,000 had applied through East German channels to emigrate.

Though it was too early to draw firm conclusions, the figures suggested that the decision by Mr. Krenz to throw open the gates of his country may have succeeded in slowing the exodus that had drained East Germany of almost 300,000 citizens so far this year.

The images of the baptism in freedom mesmerized both Germanys, whether in the streets or in the endless coverage on television. For the third night a vast throng of people gazed at the bright lights of the Kurfurstendamm, West Berlin's celebrated shopping boulevard. Most stores stayed open long past the usual Saturday closing time of 2 P.M. and many offered discounts or gifts to the East Berliners.

Thousands more East Germans packed the Olympic stadium for a soccer game, while others explored a West they had known only from television. Young men swarmed through the BMW showroom, gazing at models whose 12-cylinder engines seemed light-years beyond their own antiquated little 2-cylinder Trabants. A few slipped into the luxurious Kempinski Hotel to grab a "Do Not Disturb" sign for a souvenir.

Then there were the epic lines. Human rivers formed at every border crossing, including two new gateways punched through the concrete Berlin wall overnight and a subway station reopened after being sealed off for 28 years. Workers were still painting the price schedule at the Jannowitz Bridge underground station when people began flooding down for the ride to the West.

Inside West Berlin, the lines formed again outside banks for the 100-mark welcome that the West German Government allows each visiting East German once a year. Many visitors who waited hours to cross and up to four hours at a bank simply returned home exhausted with their 100 marks, saying they would return to shop and sightsee another time.

Cars stretched three abreast for 40 miles back from the border crossing at Helmstedt, reaching beyond the city of Magdeburg, and motorists reportedly waited up to 11 hours to cross into West Germany.

Long lines formed for special trains to West Germany at Leipzig, Dresden and other cities, and the rows of smiling, waving travelers hanging out of open windows seemed an especially poignant contrast with the sealed trains in September and early October sent to transport East German refugees from Czechoslovakia to the West.

The invasion posed all sorts of problems. In the northern city of Lubeck, the city council ran out of cash to pay the welcome money and had to appeal to local banks and stores for more.

Not all was sweetness and light. At the wall before the Brandenburg Gate, across which people swarmed on Thursday night, a band of West Berliners managed last night to pry away one of the thick concrete panels of which the wall is built.

East German border guards drove the West Berliners back with water hoses and put the panel back. They then mounted the section of the wall in front of the gate.

The brief confrontation created a somewhat tense mood at the gate that persisted into the night. It also led to the first open contact between the police of both sides since the borders were opened. Their meeting at Checkpoint Charlie led to the East German border guards' retreating from the wall and the arrival of the West Berlin police to prevent more damage to it.

The curious image of West Berlin policemen guarding the wall was repeated at other openings, where security officers from East and West joined to maintain an orderly flow, often side by side.

In a poll taken in both Germanys by the Wickert Institute of West Germany, 91 percent of East Germans and 89 percent of West Germans responding said they believed that the border between them would remain permeable. But when asked if the border opening meant they could trust their new leadership, only 19 percent of the East Germans said yes. . . .

The meeting between Mr. Kohl and Mr. Krenz will be only the third summit conference between leaders of the two Germanys in the 40-year existence of the two countries. . . . The Chancellor also said that the right of Germans to self-determination had not yet been fulfilled.

"Freedom was, is and remains the heart of the German question," Mr. Kohl said. "That means above all that our fellow countrymen in East Germany must be able to decide themselves what road they want to take in the future. They do not need any instructions, from whatever side. They themselves know best what they want."

It was evidently this comment that prompted Mr. Krenz to declare that reunification was not up for discussion. The East German regime, both under Erich Honecker and now Mr. Krenz, has staunchly rejected any talk of reunification. . . .

A Day Trip Through the Wall; Family Says of the West, "It's a Dream"
By Ferdinand Protzman

WEST BERLIN, Nov. 11—In the midst of the carnival fever that seized West Berlin today, 4-year-old Gregor Stephan stretched out on a bench in a small inn just off the Kurfurstendamm where his family was having lunch, put his head in his father's lap and fell asleep.

Hans Schmalfeld, 51, put down his fork and stared at his slumbering grandson. "Gregor is taking a nap in West Berlin," he said in a hushed voice. "It's unfathomable. If you had told me that one week ago, I wouldn't have believed it. Mentally, I still can't. It will take a few days before what this means sinks in."

Gregor's weariness was understandable. His parents, Joachim and

Annette Stephan, had got Gregor and his older brother Robert, 7, out of bed at 3:45 A.M. An hour and a half later, the family piled into a Wartburg automobile along with Mr. Schmalfeld and his wife, Wally, 53, and headed for East Berlin, 40 miles west of home in Joachimstal, East Germany. Their destination was West Berlin.

They were not alone. Hundreds of thousands of East Germans poured into West Berlin today, taking advantage of the East German Government's new policy of allowing free travel to the West.

As they neared the Berlin wall, the family took one look at the crush of people streaming to the border crossing points and parked their car.

"Driving was hopeless, so we decided to go on foot," said Mr. Stephan, a 23-year-old cattle farmer. "From watching the news, we thought that crossing over wouldn't take much time, but there were so many people that it took three hours in line to get the visas stamped and our personal identity cards. They aren't letting people just walk through the border like they did last night."

The family crossed into West Berlin at Checkpoint Charlie, though that name, which is one of the symbols of Berlin's division in the Western world, meant nothing to them. "Is that what it is called?" Mrs. Schmalfeld asked later.

Once across, they did what all their countrymen do: they went straight to a bank to pick up the 100 marks in "greeting money" given by the West German Government to East Germans arriving in the West for the first time. The money goes to every man, woman and child from the East, but only once a year and each identity document must be stamped.

Mr. Schmalfeld, who operates a family-owned ice cream shop with his wife and daughter on the Werbellinsee, a large lake in the Schorfheide forest east of Berlin that is a popular resort area, lived in what was then known as the Soviet sector of Berlin when the wall was built in August 1961. But he had not been back since, and the rest of the family had never set foot in the West.

After waiting three and a half hours, the family collected their money from the Deutsche Bank Berlin branch across from Checkpoint Charlie and headed for the Kurfurstendamm, the glittering shopping street in the heart of West Berlin. Although they did not want their picture in the newspaper, the family was happy to take a reporter they met outside the bank in tow.

The trip proved somewhat difficult. The crush of East Germans, most with the same destination in mind, overloaded West Berlin's usually efficient mass transit system. Subway trains were so packed that only a few people could squeeze aboard.

On the elevated S-bahn trains, the crowds were even thicker. A 20-minute wait proved futile. "Let's see if we can find a bus," Mr. Schmalfeld said. "There must be buses around here somewhere that go to the Ku'damm."

At the corner of Mehringdamm and Yorckstrasse, the family caught a No. 19 bus. As the brand-new double-decker bus rolled toward the city center, many of the East Germans on board stared out the window, eyeing the cars, stores and apartments like children at a candy counter.

A motorcyclist whizzed past, drawing oohs and aahs from passengers in the upper deck. "Woha! Hey, Achim, did you see that?" Mr. Schmalfeld yelled back to his son-in-law. Mr. Stephan groaned slightly and rolled his eyes.

Getting off at the city center, the family found themselves staring at the KaDeWe department store. "There it is," Mr. Schmalfeld cried. "I haven't seen it since 1961. The last time I was here was the day before the wall went up. Then, overnight, all this was gone for us." They wandered farther down the street, marveling at the crowds, the stores and the cars, then stopped for lunch.

"We were in church at a peace service Thursday evening when we heard the news," Mr. Stephan recalled. "I never really thought the wall would be open. Last year, we were just sitting around and I made a joke that soon people would be able to walk through the Brandenburg Gate. But I didn't really believe it."

His wife described their trip as "such a dream for us, a storybook tale. We'll look around slowly and carefully and see if there is anything we want. It's mostly the little things we don't have in East Germany, like fresh vegetables or tomato catsup. Supply has gotten a bit better lately. There is a little fresh breeze blowing, but there is still very much that must be changed."

A decisive factor in the family's decision to come today instead of waiting was mistrust of the East German Government, she added. "No one knows what will happen in the future and we were forbidden to travel to the West for so long that we wanted to take this opportunity now while it's there.

"We don't want to leave the G.D.R.," she said. "We love our home and we live quite well by East German standards. We work really hard and earn pretty well, but our money just isn't worth anything."

Mrs. Stephan also pointed out that there are many good things in East Germany that are often overlooked. Prices are state-subsidized, so the cost of living is very low. The nation also has an outstanding public health system, although it is suffering at the moment because so many doctors, nurses and nurse's aides have emigrated to the West in the exodus that began in May.

"What bothered us most was that they always treated us like idiots," she said of the Government. "That is really changed now. Before, it was always such lies. The newspapers said the plan had been fulfilled and still there was nothing in the shops."

The family viewed many of the things that the West takes for granted as luxuries. Returning from the restroom in the inn, Mrs. Schmalfeld said that she had never seen such a rest room, that even the toilets were beautiful. "Do they spin you around?" her husband joked.

Lunch finished, the family returned to the Kurfurstendamm, planning to go shopping. That plan was thwarted by one of the less free-market aspects of West German capitalism. The big department stores, like KeDeWe, were closed, despite recently passed legislation that would have allowed them to stay open.

The mood in the street was euphoric nevertheless. Cars had been banned, and East and West Berliners alike were strolling along, taking the air and window-shopping. The family looked at the Christmas displays in the show windows of the Wertheim department store, then moved on, looking mostly at household goods.

"We want to renovate our ice cream shop," Mr. Schmalfeld explained. He glanced up at a movie marquee and burst into laughter. "*Sex, Lies and Videotape*," he read aloud. "Unbelievable."

Gregor was wide awake now. In a kiosk on the sidewalk, he spotted a familiar figure. "It's Batman," he screeched, pointing to an array of Batman dolls. "It's Batman and Batman and Batman." He began humming the Batman theme song. Closed stores or not, his first day of freedom to travel in the West was made.

In Moscow, Soviet citizens drew hope from the collapse of the wall.

The Comrade on the Street; Russians See an Omen of Their Own Progress

By Francis X. Clines

MOSCOW, Nov. 11—Soviet citizens hailed the end of the Berlin wall today as an omen, if not an outright prod, for even faster Soviet progress toward genuine democracy and economic recovery.

"Every honest man wants socialism wiped out," said a strapping man talking loudly and happily near Pushkin Square. "You can't control a country with bayonets and walls."

Various countrymen easily agreed with him as they stopped to listen, to take hope from the failed wall and to express surprisingly little concern over the specter of a reunified Germany, the World War II enemy whose Nazi infamy has been inculcated for generations into the Soviet worldview.

"This is not 1941," said Vasily F. Simonenko, a 67-year-old veteran of the war, limping from old battle wounds as he took a sunny stroll on Gogol Boulevard and declared that he wished the best for East and West Germans.

"The war was horrible for us, but there is no Fascist country left there now," he said. He echoed the reassurances of other Soviet citizens that Chancellor Helmut Kohl of West Germany, as one of the earliest European leaders to support President Mikhail S. Gorbachev's liberalization proposals, would be even more helpful now toward the gasping Soviet economy because of the end of the Berlin wall.

"Political theory is one thing, and real life is quite another, and we must make practical decisions based on all these changes," Mr. Simonenko said.

In conversations around the city, ordinary Muscovites, and young people in particular, stressed that any benefits from the changes in Germany could not come fast enough to this demoralized nation.

"Even with this, it could take ten or twenty years for us to get as far," said one rather despairing student, 20-year-old Yuliana Pogosov, asserting that razing a wall, even one that was the symbol of the cold war, seemed a far simpler problem than resurrecting the depressed Soviet economy. "This is good news for Gorbachev, but I don't think such change can really happen here because he wants to do everything himself, without anyone else's help."

Her colleague, Natalya Demenko, 20, added, "And what our economy needs now is capitalist improvement."

Across from her in the garden quadrangle at the University of Moscow, another student, 17-year-old Andrei Rumyantsev, said the fall of the Berlin wall would not be likely to resonate this far into the Communist world. "There's such inertia here," he said, looking far too weary for his boyish face and crewcut hair. "We can see our Government is feverishly trying to adjust to all this."

"So far our own borders have not opened up," stressed his companion, Dmitri Zubov, 17. "This great wave of excitement seems to be going in only one direction, toward the Germans, not toward us."

"A lot depends now on what happens in our country," said Yelena N. Dobroditsky, a 66-year-old war veteran and invalid. "The problem here remains that individuals, not laws, rule our country."

Vladimir Porokhov, a 37-year-old economist, seemed to be mainly savoring the pleasing shock of the news about the wall, rather than joining in the day's running political dialogue amid the talkative crowd that always gathers lately outside the offices of *The Moscow News*. "Gorbachev could not have expected this outcome so quickly," he speculated. "His way is to go for gradual change, to pacify the people. Who knows whether such an unexpected change could happen here, too?"

But he could not resist his own question. "We have begun thinking beyond our daily bread," he said. "Take the miners' strike: They pushed for political change, not just for bread. Something similar can happen here, provided the Government does not decide to turn guns on the people."

Several people seemed to think the question of lost prestige from the Communist turmoil was one mainly for the Kremlin, not the ordinary Muscovite. "We're happy—what could be the danger in such good news?" asked Ilya B. Goldman, a 69-year-old retiree.

"We have too many real problems now," he said, dismissing national prestige as an academic aside when shop shelves are so empty.

The one noticeable note of suspicion to the news about East Germany was offered by a man who said he was an active member of the Communist Party. "It seems to have been a necessary thing, a matter of their internal business," said Nikolai D. Nekrasov, a 49-year-old Government executive. "But the role of our party remains strong here, and I don't think the wall will influence our life unless reunification actually happens. Then people would sense danger, and that would complicate life greatly for Gorbachev."

But Sergei S. Abelikchen, a 64-year-old factory inspector, disagreed. "I remember the war very well, with Moscow under constant threat, almost lost," he said.

"Germany is a different nation now based on different ideas, and by all means, the news about the Berlin wall can only influence us positively," he said, searching for fresh news from Germany amid the Moscow crowds studying newspaper bulletin boards.

From China, the official view of the events in Europe was quite different.

Disgust with the West Is Reported, but Beijing Ignores the Wall's End
By Sheryl WuDunn

BEIJING, Nov. 10—Newspaper readers in China learned of the remarkable resignations of East German leaders this week, but they also picked up another bit of news: two East Germans who had fled more than a month ago to the West found the new society too disorderly and so returned home.

Chinese official newspapers have regularly, if sparingly, reported the developments within the East German leadership this week. But the brief reports included no explanations of the pressures that led to the unusual collective resignations. Lately, there has been little coverage of the mass demonstrations for democracy or the exodus to the West.

Such matters are presumably regarded as too delicate, too reminiscent of the democracy movement in China in the spring. Instead of giving in to some of the demonstrators' demands, as the East German leadership has done, the Chinese authorities called in troops and crushed the movement.

Today, there was no mention in the press or the national television about East Germany's opening of its borders to the West, although the trip to Poland by Chancellor Helmut Kohl of West Germany was reported.

The recent articles—about one every two days, carried on the international news pages—have confined themselves to reporting excerpts from speeches by the new East German leader, Egon Krenz, about the necessity of reforming the party so that it can better exercise its leadership role.

"Democratic Germany is currently in a tense period full of contradictions," *People's Daily* today quoted Mr. Krenz as saying. "To make it through the difficult period, it is necessary to first carry out reform in the party itself." . . .

A Contrite Government; Contrite Deputies Say Party Failed the East Germans
By Craig R. Whitney

EAST BERLIN, Nov. 13—The East German Parliament, dormant and docile ever since it called the German Democratic Republic into existence 40 years ago, came to life today, with deputy after deputy agreeing that the Communist Party's failings were so great that it was no longer entitled to the leading role guaranteed in the nation's Constitution.

It was a day of contrition, anger and hangdog faces for the 478 legislators who were elected the old way, without opposition, three years ago. As one speaker after another acknowledged, they had only themselves to blame for letting the old leadership under Erich Honecker run the economy into the ground, creating a situation in which more than 200,000 people left the country in the last two months.

After hours of grim recitation of past failure, the members of Parliament did what the new Communist Party leader, Egon Krenz, had asked them to do. They elected Hans Modrow, the 61-year-old party chief in Dresden, as Prime Minister, though one lawmaker raised a hand in opposition.

Mr. Modrow, widely regarded as a proponent of liberalization, said he would lay out his new policy and name a coalition cabinet that would include members of East Germany's long-subservient non-Communist parties at the end of this week.

Last week, Mr. Modrow confided to a fellow member of the Central Committee that "I can see the end coming." His disgraced predecessor, Willi Stoph, who is 76 years old, took the floor earlier today to say: "I accept responsibility for all the failures of the former Government. We failed to account properly to Parliament and report shortcomings as they occurred."

Mr. Stoph blamed "decisions not made in the Council of Ministers"—presumably meaning interference by the Communist Party—for "severely" harming the economy.

"The deposed leadership was characterized by arrogance," said Werner Jarowinsky, the Communist Party leader in Parliament.

Mr. Krenz, who replaced Mr. Honecker last month, listened, apparently hoping that his party's promises of free elections, a freer press and freedom to travel would convince most of the country's 16.5 million people that the new leadership would earn their trust.

But in Leipzig, the hotbed of protest, mass demonstrations continued tonight. Huge crowds chanted, "We are the people!" and booed and hissed Mr. Krenz's promises of "free" elections.

Most of the one million or so East Germans who visited the West after the border was opened on Thursday night appeared to have gone back home to work today. The streets of West Berlin were almost normal this morning, although visitors from the East poured in again in smaller numbers than the vast crowds that thronged the shopping streets from Friday to Sunday.

Mr. Krenz, answering a question in Parliament, said he had told West Germany's Chancellor, Helmut Kohl, in a telephone call yesterday, "Unification, or reunification, of Germany is not on the agenda."

"I believe the existence of two German states, independent of each other, is a decisive question of stability in Europe, and that that is a decisive question of peace in Europe," he said. "Without peace there is nothing."

The East German authorities continued today to announce the opening of new border crossings up and down the 1,000-mile frontier with West Germany, and said East Germans living close to the line would no longer require special permission to have guests and visitors. The East German military authorities have also ordered troops to stop using weapons to prevent illegal border crossing.

After Parliament debated the critical situation in the country, the Communist Party Central Committee met late into the night to discuss Mr. Krenz's decision to hold the special party congress next month. He said he wanted it to elect a new Central Committee to support his program of change. Western diplomats and East Germans believe there is considerable skepticism about his sincerity among party members, who number about two million, as well as in the country at large.

All the speakers in Parliament today agreed on the need to strengthen Communism, to save the system, not abandon it, and to create what Mr. Jarowinsky called a "market-oriented planned economy."

"Our fatherland is in danger," said Hans-Dieter Raspe, a member of the small Liberal Democratic Party. "Our citizens have no confidence in the leadership of the country."

The former president of Parliament, Horst Sindermann, apologized for having waited too long to call the legislature into session after the mass emigration and police repression of demonstrators began early last month. He apologized for doing his job "not always well," but said he had tried to do his best.

Mr. Jarowinsky said: "Our party is determined to draw radical consequences from this bitter fact. We need changes in the Constitution."

The first article of the Constitution says East Germany is a Communist state of workers and farmers, "led by the working class and its Marxist-Leninist party." But speaker after speaker today agreed that the Communists had lost touch with the people.

"We see and hear encouraging things from New Forum," Mr. Jarowinsky said, referring to the biggest new opposition group. "It's time to come closer together."

Since 1950, the East German system has grouped four other parties with Mr. Krenz's Communists—officially called the Socialist Unity Party—plus the central trade-union organization, the youth league and various other political groups in a so-called National Front.

In a system that has not changed since the Communists came to power after World War II, East Germans vote every five years, with only candidates of the National Front on the ballot. The groups in the front, which all agreed in 1950 that the Communists would run things, then divide up the 500 seats, with the Communists getting the biggest share—127 seats in the current legislature, which was elected in 1986.

The Communists did not offer a candidate today for the largely ceremonial post of President of the People's Chamber. Manfred Gerlach, a 61-year-old leader of the Liberal Democrats since the beginning, was widely expected to win, since he had called for radical change before Mr. Krenz did. But in the second ballot, he lost, 230 to 246, to Gunther Maleuda, the little-known leader of the 120,000-member Democratic Farmers' Party.

The name on each of the nearly 480 ballots that were cast had to be read aloud to the chamber and the results counted by hand.

"Surely there must be more modern and scientific methods in the age of micro-electronics," the East German television announcer said to the national audience.

The chamber was closed to most journalists and to the general public.

The combustible nature of social change was reflected in the following story, which accurately captured the stolid mood of Prague. Unlike their neighbors in Poland, Hungary, and East Germany, the Czechoslovaks had remained impassive except for a handful of dissidents, mostly intellectuals. A week later things would be very different.

Little Change in Czechoslovakia; Maintaining Tight Control in Prague

By R. W. Apple, Jr.

PRAGUE, Nov. 13—Last month, 300,000 people staged a demonstration in Leipzig, East Germany's second city. Five days later, about 10,000 people gathered in Wenceslas Square, this capital's historic cockpit of protest, to call for change.

Only about 160 miles separate the two cities, and both have been ruled by Communists for four decades.

But while the protest in Leipzig and others that followed it resulted in a new East German Government, the opening of the Berlin wall and a promise of major political changes, the protest in Prague was followed by no others, provoking a show of force by the Czechoslovak Government and almost no political change. As a shopkeeper said today, "We have become the class dunces, the ones who learn their lessons slowly."

Milos Jakes, the Communist Party leader, ordered out heavily armed police officers, who bashed dozens of heads with their truncheons, to put down the October 28 demonstration. And he remains firmly in control at a time when his fellow hard-liners, Erich Honecker in East Germany and Todor Zhivkov in Bulgaria, have either stepped down voluntarily or been forced to resign.

"He will probably survive this year," a European diplomat said, "but he may not make it through the party congress next year, and he certainly won't settle in for five or ten years. He and his colleagues on the Politburo simply lack the flexibility and the intelligence to make the reforms and accept the changes that will be needed if Communism is to last here."

Shortly before the October demonstration, someone leaked a tape recording of a speech that Mr. Jakes gave at a provincial party meeting. Rambling and clumsy, the recording was broadcast into Czechoslovakia by Radio Liberty and other Western radio stations, providing what one dissident described as "a laugh a minute" that he said undercut Mr. Jakes's public standing.

Some opponents of the Government hope to stage a protest on Friday to mark the anniversary of the death of one of the political martyrs in Czechoslovak history. The protesters intend to commemorate the death of Jan Opletal, who was killed in 1939 by Nazi storm troopers while protesting the German occupation of Czechoslovakia.

Today four prominent dissidents went on trial in Bratislava on charges of sedition for urging Czechoslovaks to lay flowers for those killed in the 1968 invasion by the Soviet Union and its Warsaw Pact allies that crushed the movement for liberalization that became known as the Prague Spring. And in Prague another dissident, Jiri Jilinek, 22 years old, was sentenced to a year in prison for distributing leaflets urging a pro-democracy protest in May, the dissident Anna Sabatova said.

Mr. Jakes on Sunday told 900 delegates to a conference of the Socialist Youth Union in Prague, where other speakers were unusually critical of the regime, that he would not tolerate street protests or communicate with groups advocating abandonment of Czechoslovakia's form of Communism.

According to the official press agency, the party leader promised that restructuring of the Communist apparatus would continue. In a response unusual for Czechoslovakia but still timid by the standards common in Poland, Hungary and, of late, East Germany, Vasil Mohorita, a leader of the state-sponsored youth group, said that the Government's plans, which call for some important economic change but no real political evolution, "do not fit the expectations of young people."

"Some youths are losing faith in the possibility of Communist renewal," the official news agency quoted Mr. Mohorita as saying. "The reason for this weakening of trust is that an atmosphere of self-satisfaction has ruled in this country."

In recent months, the Czechoslovak Government had been attempting to forge closer ties with East Germany, working toward a kind of traditionalist caucus within the Warsaw Pact that would refuse to follow the lead of Poland and Hungary. Mr. Honecker had visited Prague, and Ladislav Adamec, the Czechoslovak Prime Minister, had visited East Berlin. Now those efforts are ruined.

"The way Honecker's world was swept away in two or three weeks, and the way the people got so far ahead of the leadership so fast, must have sent shivers up and down Jakes's spine," a leading Czechoslovak dissident said.

Bonn Outlines Aid for East Germany

By Henry Kamm

BONN, Nov. 14—West Germany made public the outlines of a possible economic aid program to East Germany today, but repeated a warning that the proposal would be adopted only if East Germany carried out a "thorough change" of its centralized economy and spelled out the changes it plans.

Economics Minister Helmut Haussmann said that if East Berlin met its conditions, Bonn would make loans available to West German entrepreneurs interested in investing in East Germany. The money would come from a European reconstruction fund totaling $2.5 billion.

He added that if East Germany allowed its citizens to engage in such ventures, they too might be eligible for loans from the fund.

West Germany also said it might offer tax advantages to investors in East Germany similar to those it provides for investors in West Berlin.

Other ways of helping the East German economy might include export credit guarantees for sales of capital goods to East Germany, investment guarantees for the West German partner in joint ventures and support for West German concerns acting as management consultants in East Germany.

The Economics Ministry announcement came six days after Chancellor Helmut Kohl said Bonn would be ready to provide "a new dimension" of aid to East Germany if it allowed political pluralism and made fundamental economic changes. But the statement today gave no indication of how much direct assistance Bonn was prepared to extend.

For the time being, "there are more questions than answers," Mr. Haussmann said. "Announcements of billions in aid at this time are devoid of sense."

In an "action program" adopted on Friday by the Communist Party's Central Committee, the new East German leadership under Egon Krenz said "fundamental changes" in economic policies were required and promised "far-reaching economic reform." The aims cited in the program were "constantly improving satisfaction of the real needs of the population," more honest reporting on whether the central plan's goals are being met and the speeding up of technological renewal of industry.

But neither the program nor the speeches of economists and industrial managers in the committee's three days of sessions suggested how those goals are to be achieved. Unlike other Communist countries, including the Soviet Union, whose economic reform programs have stressed the introduction of market conditions at the expense of central planning, East Germany continues to affirm the virtues of planning.

The "action program" espoused "a socialist planned economy oriented toward market conditions" but failed to explain how the two would coexist. The Central Committee said the Government, which is soon to be formed under Prime Minister Hans Modrow, named Monday, should work out plans and submit them for discussion.

Mr. Haussmann said a basic condition for West German assistance was greater freedom in East German social life and the economy. He cited difficulties experienced by West German businessmen in establishing direct contacts with their East German partners. Businessmen often complain of slow progress through a complex bureaucracy in their efforts to conclude deals in East Germany.

Mr. Haussmann also urged quick East German approval of a law governing the establishment of joint ventures.

In a television interview, Finance Minister Theo Waigel said he believed that West German capital would not flow into East Germany until a market economy was established.

Hans Peter Stihl, president of the German Industry and Commerce Organization, said, "Before we break our heads about it here, East Germany must spell out its concept for economic reform."

Mr. Haussmann announced that he would soon invite leading West German economic figures to discuss relations with East Germany and to sound out businessmen on conditions they would demand for active participation in East Germany's industry. He said that so far East Germany had failed to take full advantage of the special conditions for inter-German trade offered by Bonn and had prevented trade from rising above the level of barter.

The Minister said he was ready to meet with the East German Economics Minister and favored Mr. Krenz's suggestion for establishing a bilateral trade commission.

It was hard to imagine that the repressed calm of Czechoslovakia would endure forever as reform and democratic movements were sweeping all of the neighboring allied countries, yet this was the view to which Prague's Communist leadership was clinging despite warnings from Moscow.

Unease in Prague; A Soviet Warning on Foot-Dragging Is Given to Prague

By R. W. Apple, Jr.

PRAGUE, Nov. 15—The Soviet Union warned Czechoslovakia last week in a high-level message that further delay in introducing political change could cause serious trouble, Communist Party officials said today.

Perhaps as a result, the first major public signs of fear, tension and conflict are beginning to appear within the hard-line Czechoslovak Government.

According to reports circulating in party circles, Moscow cautioned Prague not to make the same mistakes made by Communist traditionalists elsewhere in Eastern Europe. Excessive caution or half-heartedness in putting political changes into effect, the Soviets are reported to have said, could lead to an uprising like the one that forced sweeping changes in East Germany.

The present Czechoslovak leadership descends from the one that was installed by the Soviets 21 years ago, at a time when the Brezhnev doctrine, since renounced by President Mikhail S. Gorbachev, sanctioned intervention by one Communist country in the internal affairs of another if necessary to prevent heresy.

A senior adviser to one Czech minister said that the message was similar to one sent to Bulgaria, which apparently helped to persuade Todor I. Zhivkov, that country's longtime party leader, that it was time to retire.

Although the position of Milos Jakes, the 67-year-old Czech party leader, is believed to have weakened somewhat lately, and although Prague is alive with speculation about his ability to survive until next spring's party congress, there is no sign that he plans to follow Mr. Zhivkov's lead soon.

Nonetheless, dramatic exchanges have taken place this week in Parliament here, centering on the question of political evolution. Last night, Prime Minister Ladislav Adamec quoted in a wrap-up speech to Parliament the formula repeatedly stated by Mr. Jakes, his boss: first major economic changes, and later—only later—minor political adjustments. Then, according to today's ssue of *Rude Pravo*, the official party newspaper, the Prime Minister explicitly challenged that position. The newspaper quoted him as having said: "We hold the view that economic progress cannot be separated from political progress. Economic reform cannot succeed without political reform. Especially in our situation, the political change should be somewhat in advance."

Prace, the trade-union newspaper, quoted a passage from Mr. Adamec's speech that *Rude Pravo* did not. In it, the Prime Minister went even further, asserting that "nothing can be ordered" by the Government, which, he said, "can only create favorable conditions." He added: "In the very complicated present conditions, it is possible to govern only provided that people have the necessary confidence in our central political organs."

A party official close to Mr. Adamec said today that he had "decided to throw the gauntlet down to Jakes on this, because he knows that his economic reform program has no chance unless there is some democratization." *no chance unless Dem*

One experienced politician who heard them said that the Prime Minister's words angered Vasil Bilak, the former ideological chief in Gustav Husak's regime, who is widely believed to have asked the Soviet Union to suppress the Government of Alexander Dubcek in the Prague Spring of 1968. The politician reported that Mr. Bilak said it sounded as if Mr. Adamec "thinks nothing good happened in this building in the last 40 years."

A motto in the chamber where the debate took place says, "All power resides in the people." Mr. Bilak reportedly pointed to it and demanded of Mr. Adamec whether or not he thought that had been true in the past.

When the outburst was over, the politician said, Mr. Bilak, once a very powerful figure, sat down, and no one paid the old-guard parliamentarian the slightest bit of attention.

Slowly, a party member familiar with the situation said the heretofor quiescent Parliament is moving—"not the way the Polish or the *moving slow* Hungarian Parliament has moved, toward real coalition government, not from black to white, not too far or fast, not everyone at once, but slowly and surely from black to dark gray."

What that might mean in terms of political change is not clear. Mr. Jakes has already made concessions on travel, cultural issues and religion, but he has yielded nothing to the dissidents, such as the playwright Vaclav Havel, and indeed has cracked down even harder on demonstrators and others who make their dissatisfaction public.

Mr. Havel, one of the original signers of the Charter 77 manifesto, was arrested last January and released in May after serving half his sentence. His trial helped him to become, like Lech Walesa in Poland, a powerful symbol of the opposition. But he is still seen here as more a moral force than a man likely to form a government.

"I think of him in terms of Jan Hus," said a Czechoslovak journalist, referring to the fifteenth-century church reformer who remains a national hero. "But maybe he has capacities we don't know about. Maybe he can someday become what he isn't yet—the leader of a mass movement, like Walesa, or like Tomas Masaryk, come to that."

Masaryk built and led the first Czechoslovak republic after World War I. Both Mr. Adamec, who at 62 may be a bit old, and Frantisek Pitra, 55, the party leader in Bohemia, one of the constituent parts of Czechoslovakia, are believed to be maneuvering to succeed Mr. Jakes if he steps down. Mr. Pitra is considered the more subtle, less confrontational of the two. Neither is thought by Western analysts to be an instinctive progressive; both are thought to be attempting to harness the current forces of change in Eastern Europe to help their careers.

But as East Germany showed, any change at the top can result in other, unforeseen changes at lower levels, as well as major shifts in policies.

Some Western diplomats believe that Mr. Jakes might try to save himself by throwing one of his colleagues to the wolves. If that happened, several of the diplomats said, a likely candidate would be Jan Fojtik, the tough current ideological chief. He was reported to be in trouble a year ago, but he was saved, some observers think, because events in China strengthened hard-liners and hurt reformers within the Communist Party here, as elsewhere.

As the pressure was mounting in Prague, Lech Walesa, the shipyard electrician who had first shown how Communist totalitarianism can be peacefully and successfully challenged, was in the United States, being cheered and celebrated as a prophet. The high point of his visit came when he addressed a joint meeting of Congress.

Gratitude and a Request; In Talk to Congress, Walesa Urges a Marshall Plan to Revive Poland

By Neil A. Lewis

WASHINGTON, Nov. 15—Lech Walesa, the founder of Poland's Solidarity movement, called for a second Marshall Plan today as he addressed a joint meeting of Congress. He warned that without the sort of commitment that helped rebuild Western Europe after World War II, the situation in his country could become dangerous.

The former shipyard electrician began by expressing his gratitude for the support his movement received from Americans in the years that it was suppressed and driven underground. He also gave thanks for the support the United States has given to more recent political and economic changes in Poland.

Nevertheless, to the accompaniment of repeated rounds of hearty applause, Mr. Walesa made it clear that more assistance would be needed to keep Poland from becoming so poor that it could destabilize the region.

"We are not asking for charity or expecting philanthropy," he said. "But we would like to see our country treated as a partner and a friend." He chided Americans for offering a surplus of good wishes but a paucity of money. "We have heard many beautiful words of encouragement," he said. "These are appreciated, but being a worker and a man of concrete work, I must tell you that the supply of words on the world market is plentiful but the demand is falling. Let deeds follow words now."

Mr. Walesa's entrance was announced in much the same manner reserved for the President before a State of the Union Address. "Mr. Speaker, the leader of Solidarity," said the doorkeeper. Mr. Walesa entered the chamber to a boisterous reception and as he made his way down the center aisle, members of Congress struggled to get close and shake his hand.

Among those vigorously applauding Mr. Walesa was Yuri V. Dubinin, the Soviet Ambassador to Washington, who was sitting in the audience. . . .

Senator Barbara A. Mikulski, a Maryland Democrat whose great-grandmother came from Poland to Baltimore for an arranged marriage, was one of those in the audience who wept during the address. "I never thought this day would come," she said afterward. "I just didn't think it was Poland's destiny to be free." . . .

Mr. Walesa, describing in his address the efforts of the new non-Communist Government in Warsaw, said, "Our task is viewed with understanding by our Eastern neighbors and their leader, Mikhail Gorbachev."

But he also said the imposition of a Communist economy on Poland for forty years had brought it to the "verge of utter catastrophe," and that "all the countries of the East bloc are bankrupt." He recalled that at the end of World War II, Stalin pressed Poland to reject an invitation to take part in the Marshall Plan.

"It is worth recalling this great American plan which helped Western Europe to protect its freedom and peaceful order," Mr. Walesa said. "And now it is the moment when Eastern Europe awaits an investment of this kind—an investment in freedom, democracy and peace, an investment adequate to the greatness of the American nation."

At a lunch meeting with Senators after his speech, he offered a gloomy assessment of the consequences if the new Solidarity-led Government fails to get control of the economy.

Speaking of his own turn of fortunes, which led him from the shipyard to the Nobel Peace Prize and a key political role, he said through a translator, "I was happier as an electrician and did not understand how difficult it was to make that jump to the public arena."

Mr. Walesa's remarks were underscored by reports from East Germany, which had always been regarded as the most successful of the East bloc economies, that the true state of the economy was ragged and getting worse.

Grim State of East Germany's Economy Is Disclosed to Parliament
By David Binder

EAST BERLIN, Nov. 15—East Germany's economy, battered by the flight to the West of more than 100,000 workers, many of them highly skilled, is in much worse shape than almost anyone knew, high-ranking Communist officials disclosed this week.

In the session of Parliament on Monday, the departing Finance Minister, Ernst Hofner, declared that East Germany's budget deficit amounted to 130 billion marks, causing gasps of amazement in the hall. The amount is about $70 billion at the official exchange rate of 1.85 marks to the dollar.

Mr. Hofner said further that the efficiency of factories producing goods for export had sunk by almost 50 percent in the last nine years and that this would lead to further deficits, perhaps 65 billion marks—about $35 billion at the official rate—in the 1990's. As a small consolation, he told the Parliament that East Germany's counties, cities and villages were debt-free.

The Finance Minister said he could not confirm an estimate by a member of Parliament that East Germany's inflation rate stood at 12 percent. But today a party economics expert said the rate was much higher than that. Gerhard Schurer, the departing chairman of the State Planning Commission, told Parliament that East Germany's foreign debt was a state secret. But today *Berliner Zeitung*, the organ of the Berlin party, cited the Swiss Central Bank as saying that East Germany's short-, middle- and long-term obligations to Western creditors totaled $20 billion. This sum would put East Germany's per capita foreign debt close to or ahead of those of Hungary and Poland.

Seeking to defend his performance as planning chief in the Government of the ousted party leader, Erich Honecker, Mr. Schurer said he had been unable to block excessive investments in the electronics industry and other areas of the economy.

Mr. Schurer said that all of his proposals to ease the economic situation were "rejected by the Central Committee Secretary for Economy, Gunter Mittag, with attacks and false accusation." Mr. Mittag, a Honecker associate, was dismissed from the Central Committee last week.

The planning chief was backed up by Willi Stoph, the former Prime Minister, who told the Parliament with bitterness in his voice that his own efforts in economic policy making had been subverted by Mr. Mittag, who he said had approved huge investments in the electronics and fertilizer industries without informing him or his aides.

The fresh gaps in the economy created by the flight of skilled workers and professionals was underlined in a report today by *Berliner Zeitung,* which said the departures registered since June included doctors and transport personnel. It named the Narva electrical products factory as one of the big losers. And a person knowledgeable about health personnel said today that more than 200 staff members had fled from the well-known Charité Hospital. About 1,200 East Germans fled to West Germany today, either directly or by way of Czechoslovakia.

Adding to these problems are the relatively new phenomena of large-scale smuggling and hoarding, according to Gunther Arndt, deputy head of East Germany's Customs Administration.

Edda Kaiser, an executive of the Centrum department store in Berlin, said in an interview about those problems, "It is an untenable situation for our house and surely for similar establishments, not only in Berlin." *Berliner Zeitung*, which quoted Mrs. Kaiser, said the offenders were mostly Poles and members of the American, British and French forces stationed in West Berlin. These people can purchase East German marks at a very low rate outside this country. Although the official exchange rate is 1.85 East German marks to the dollar, the currency can be exchanged outside at a black-market rate of over 10 marks per dollar.

The events in Germany were quite clearly exhilarating, spelling out as they did a further erosion of oppressive state power. They also signaled the approaching end of a divided Europe. But at the heart of any united Europe there had to be an undivided Germany, and given the modern history of Europe, this was a prospect that alarmed many. Moreover, the logistics of bringing together NATO's richest member with the Warsaw Pact's second-richest state after the Soviet Union were staggering. For one thing, West Germany was the home base to the largest concentration of NATO forces, while East Germany was the fortress of the Warsaw Pact. Sensitive to the fears of its allies, West German leaders, at first, took special care in their responses.

Kohl Says Bonn Will Not Press East Germany on Reunification
By Serge Schmemann

WEST BERLIN, Nov. 16—Chancellor Helmut Kohl presented today what has evolved into a broad West German consensus on how to approach the new developments in East Germany, declaring that Bonn would not try to influence the East Germans on reunification and would respect whatever path they chose.

Mr. Kohl also reiterated that any substantial economic aid to the East Germans would be given on the condition that they introduce a market economy.

Mr. Kohl addressed the Parliament in Bonn on the eve of a meeting of the East German Parliament at which the new Prime Minister,

Hans Modrow, is to make public an economic program that is said to call for a loosening of the central-planning system and greater possibilities for foreign participation.

Mr. Modrow is also expected to announce a new, streamlined government with almost half the ministries distributed among members of the four small parties traditionally allied with the governing Communists.

Mr. Kohl's speech, and the reactions of opposition parties to the right and left in Parliament, indicated that the Chancellor had achieved a consensus before any significant political disagreement over Bonn's policy toward the East emerged.

"We do not wish to force our conceptions upon anyone," Mr. Kohl said. "Nobody, however, could honestly argue that socialism has proven to be one single failure. It has failed throughout the world, not just in the G.D.R. By contrast, free enterprise means the freedom of decision, personal self-determination and broadly distributed wealth."

On the issue of German reunification, Mr. Kohl said, "Our compatriots in the G.D.R. must be able to decide for themselves which way they want to go in the future," and that West Germans would not try to influence their choice.

"Of course we will respect every decision that is being made by the people of the G.D.R. in free self-determination," he said.

But the Chancellor said economic assistance would be useless "unless there is an irreversible reform of the economic system, an end to a bureaucratic planned economy and the introduction of a market economy."

Mr. Kohl also sought to give strong reassurance to West Germany's Western allies that the developments in East Germany would not alter Bonn's commitments to the West. "We are and remain a part of the Western system of values," he said, adding that it would be a "fatal error" to slow the process of European integration.

Mr. Kohl's statements prompted almost no retorts from the opposition. "There is little room for party patriotism when what is being asked for is national responsibility and solidarity," said Willy Brandt, the former Social Democratic Chancellor. With their ideological affinities with socialist opposition movements in the East, the Social Democrats potentially have the most to gain from reunification.

In East Berlin, officials said that the 45 ministries would be reduced to 27, and that 11 of those would be filled by the "block parties"—

small organizations that were subsumed by the Communists when they seized power and survived to give the impression of pluralism to the one-party state.

Opposition spokesmen and Western diplomats were initially skeptical of Mr. Modrow's assertion to have formed a broad "coalition government," even though the block parties have tried to demonstrate a degree of independence in recent weeks.

They noted that no members of the new opposition movements were included and that the ministers were still drawn from a Parliament that until recently served as a rubber stamp for party directives.

"It is a beginning, but we have to wait and see how it works out," said Jutta Seidel of New Forum, the largest of the new opposition groups. "The other parties have never really been an opposition."

A.D.N., the East German press agency, said Egon Krenz, the East German leader, was also involved in the talks with the small parties. The Communist Party, which has about 2.3 million members, holds 127 of the 500 seats in Parliament, and the block parties, with a combined membership of 470,000, have 52 each. The 165 remaining seats are divided among mass organizations like trade unions and the Communist Youth League, many of whose delegates are Communist Party members.

Mr. Modrow is also expected on Friday to ask the Parliament to prepare a new election law and to form a commission to propose changes to the Constitution, which now in its first article guarantees the Communist Party a "leading role" in East German society....

But just as the wall and the party that had built it were finally brought low not by the action of governments but by the assertion of autonomy by the millions who walked and chanted, so the prospect of reunification or reassociation of the Germanys lay in the action of people who were likely to join in thousands of private economic relationships, establishing and expanding networks embracing both East and West.

The Two Countries Are Likely to Join Their Industries Before Their Politics
By Craig R. Whitney

WEST BERLIN, Nov. 16—Foreigners who worry about "reunification" as an immediate and ominous consequence of the end of the Berlin wall overlook two things. One is that East and West Germany together only constitute about two-thirds of the prewar territory of the German Reich. Another is that East and West Germany have gradually been extending and broadening ties of all kinds ever since they established diplomatic relations with each other in 1972.

For Germans on either side of the border, what is at the top of their minds is not political reunification, but an economic growing together.

"Other models are conceivable, of course," said a Western diplomat in East Berlin. "It's possible to think of East Germany being annexed someday by West Germany, or of West Germany seceding from NATO and the European Community and coming together with East Germany as a neutral country. But neither of those seems anywhere near as likely as a gradual coming together of the two economies, with later political consequences."

Not all Western politicians would agree about the unlikelihood of the first two possibilities, but the two German economies have undoubtedly been coming together over the years. Trade between East and West Germany will amount to about $7.5 billion in both directions this year. And even though nearly four million East Germans have visited the West since the border barriers were taken down a week ago, more than 2.3 million East Germans visited West Germany last year, and 5.2 million West Germans visited the East.

Germans, East and West, will increasingly read even more of the same books if censorship in East Germany continues to be lifted at the current rate. Stefan Heym, who lives and works in East Germany, has been a best-selling author in the West for much of the last 40 years. East German television is now, at times, hard to distinguish from the Western stations.

Economic differences divide the two countries more than social or cultural ones. But West German business leaders and politicians are already thinking of ways to do it, and East German economic planners and politicians are already hoping they will be allowed to start soon.

"Nothing can happen until we have thorough political reform here," a leading East German lawyer said the other day, echoing Chancellor Helmut Kohl's conditions for providing massive economic aid to the East. "That means genuinely free elections."

"If we had free elections today, the Communist Party might win 5 percent of the vote," an East German diplomat said. "But then we might at least be able to start a genuine process of economic reform."

How difficult that would be can be seen on two levels. One is daily life. East Germans live in subsidized housing and the food they buy in state stores is sold at subsidized prices. A two-bedroom apartment in the Prenzlauer Berg section of East Berlin, for example, rents for 57 marks a month, about $31 at the official rate of exchange—and $3.10 at the rate East Berliners get when they go over to a bank in the West to change their money.

Right now, East German police and customs officials are barely checking people as they go back and forth across the border. But until apartments and loaves of bread and apples and oranges cost the same and are as freely available on both sides of the border, smuggling and black-market profiteering, not rapid economic growth, will be the result in East Germany, according to East German officials.

On a larger scale, West German businesses are ready to help develop the East German economy if they can be assured of the security for their investment and of a way to make profits and get them out in freely convertible currency.

"West German enterprises enter into cooperation agreements the world over," wrote Heinz Durr, chairman of the West German electronics giant, A.E.G., in *Der Spiegel* recently. "Why shouldn't they start cooperating with plants in the G.D.R. and offer joint products on the world market? We would have cost savings, and the G.D.R. would solve its convertible-currency problem, at least to a large extent."

"The same language and culture, the same mentality, even our tendency to perfectionism all speak for such a vision becoming reality," Mr. Durr wrote. "But the new model has to be wanted by the G.D.R."

However, a West German member of Parliament, Andreas von Bulow, pointed out that even then there would be many difficulties to overcome. Volkswagen, he said, had arranged years ago to build motors for its small cars in East Germany but the East German enterprise that built them had not yet been able to make them to standards high enough for any market except East Germany's.

Mr. von Bulow has produced a list of 35 steps for revision-minded Eastern European countries to take if they want to integrate themselves more closely into the Western economic system. They include steps like those taken by Ludwig Erhard in West Germany in 1948, when the Western allies introduced a new currency in their occupation zone—the West German mark—to replace the Reichsmark.

Many West Germans point to the history of the European Community as the best precedent for the kind of slow growing together of the two German states that they think is more likely than overnight reunification.

Economic integration has been underway in Western Europe since the Treaty of Rome was signed in 1957, they say. Political unification has been a much more difficult and slower process.

Prime Minister Margaret Thatcher of Britain said that even a common European currency would require a surrender of national sovereignty by the British Government because 12 European Community countries cannot have a common currency without a common monetary policy, probably run by a common central bank.

The borders among the 12 European Community countries have become far less important than they ever were in the past. On the Belgian border with West Germany, most cars pass through without a customs inspection and the police of both countries work side by side.

Since last week, East Germany's border has not been much more complicated to pass through than Britain's Heathrow Airport. The West Berlin and East Berlin Police have had their first contacts in 28 years about how to ensure order on both sides of the wall, and the mayors of both sides have shaken hands on the Potsdamer Platz.

Sometime in the next few weeks, Chancellor Kohl and Egon Krenz, the East German leader, will meet in East Berlin to talk about where things go from here.

"If it's true that the parts of Europe are coming closer to each other," wrote the former West German Chancellor Willy Brandt today in *Die Zeit*, "who could halfway seriously suggest that it would be justified to keep the parts of Germany out of it?"

The view from China remained deeply negative.

Chinese Premier Sees No Effect from Europe

RAWALPINDI, PAKISTAN, Nov. 16—Prime Minister Li Peng of China said here today that Beijing was watching events in Eastern Europe closely but that the surge of change in East Germany and other Warsaw Pact nations would not weaken China's commitment to Communism.

On his first foreign trip since Chinese troops crushed the democracy demonstrators in Tiananmen Square in June, Mr. Li said at a news conference with Western reporters that the "drastic changes" in Eastern Europe were attracting worldwide attention, and that "China naturally is also concerned" about them. The 61-year-old Prime Minister, who has given Western reporters few opportunities to question him since the Tiananmen crackdown, rejected any comparisons between Beijing's actions and the far-reaching concessions in East Germany.

Things were happening so quickly that it was hard to maintain perspective. At times it appeared as if people in the East bloc, notably in East Germany, suddenly became emboldened and that by marching and chanting they brought down the toughest and most absolute of rulers—men like Honecker—and that these emperors were revealed as naked. As the East Germans were now adding calls for justice and accountability to their cries for freedom, some of the inner circle were ready to offer the most prominent among them in their hope of salvaging some credibility for their wounded party and for themselves. In the process it was possible for outsiders to learn what exactly had happened in the innermost circles of power as their political control unraveled, at summer's end and most particularly after Mikhail Gorbachev's visit on October 6, when Honecker was thwarted from implementing what was termed "The Chinese solution."

How the Wall Was Cracked—A Special Report; Party Coup Turned East German Tide

Based on reporting by Craig R. Whitney, David Binder and Serge Schmemann and written by Mr. Whitney

EAST BERLIN, Nov. 17—The turning point came on October 7, after the Communist Party leader, Erich Honecker, ordered security forces to be prepared to open fire on demonstrators in Leipzig—a "Chinese solution" to the rising tide of dissent in East Germany.

But violence and killing were averted when Egon Krenz, then Politburo member in charge of security, flew to Leipzig on October 9 and canceled Mr. Honecker's order, allowing the protesters to march unmolested. Mr. Krenz became the new party chief on October 18.

What could have become a bloodbath as terrible as China's June crackdown instead became a peaceful revolution that is changing the face of East Germany and Eastern Europe. Within ten days, Mr. Honecker had resigned under pressure and the Communist Party was pledging profound changes. Within a month, the Berlin wall was broken.

Although this sequence of events would tend to bolster the image of Mr. Krenz, it is supported by the accounts of several members of the East German party, most of whom do not owe their current positions to Mr. Krenz.

They said Mr. Krenz reversed the order to shoot because he feared that hundreds of dead and wounded would be a fatal blow to the East German party's standing at home and abroad. . . .

On October 7, with Mikhail S. Gorbachev in East Berlin, crowds took to the streets of the capital, chanting "Gorby! Gorby!" and "We want to stay!" With many foreign reporters looking on, the police waded into the throngs, and their actions were recorded and immediately played back to the rest of East Germany on West German television.

More violence followed on Sunday, and by Monday, October 9, the suspense was tangible. A weekly Monday peace service, held in the Nikolai Church in Leipzig, had in recent weeks become the launching point for broad protests, and after the weekend clashes, huge crowds were expected at the church.

According to Manfred Gerlach, the leader of the small Liberal Democratic Party, and others, a huge force of soldiers, policemen and secret police agents was assembled in Leipzig and issued with live ammunition. Their order was to shoot if necessary, and the order had reportedly been signed by Mr. Honecker himself.

"There was a written order from Honecker for a Chinese solution," said Markus Wolf, the retired head of East Germany's spy agencies, who has emerged as a leading advocate of reform. "It could have been worse than Beijing."

But by then many in the Politburo had come to the decision that Mr. Honecker must go, and that the situation was explosive. In Leipzig, Kurt Masur, the director of the Gewandhaus musical theater, and some local party officials opened urgent discussions on averting a clash.

Finally, Mr. Krenz and Wolfgang Herger, the Central Committee department chief under him, flew to Leipzig's Schkeuditz Airport. They drove into the city to meet with local Communist officials at the home of Mr. Masur.

"I was in Leipzig," Mr. Krenz later said. "I helped there to see to it that these things were solved politically."

When tens of thousands took to the streets of Leipzig that night, the police did not interfere. The "revolution from below" was under way.

The frustration that erupted in October had been long in gathering. Mikhail S. Gorbachev, the Soviet President, had set loose yearnings for change throughout Eastern Europe, but in East Germany the old loyalists around Mr. Honecker sat entrenched in their isolated villas on Lake Wandlitz, refusing to acknowledge any reason to change.

The words perestroika and glasnost could not be uttered over the airwaves or printed in the East German press, either in Russian or German, and Soviet publications were banned.

East Berlin continued to flaunt its rigidity. Local elections on May 7 were plainly rigged. After the massacre in Tiananmen Square in Beijing on June 4, Mr. Krenz sent a message to the authorities in China congratulating them on their firmness. . . .

Mr. Honecker [after an operation] was back at work, and his attention was on the celebrations planned for October 7, the fortieth anniversary of the German Democratic Republic. Mr. Gorbachev was to lead a retinue of Communist leaders to East Berlin. . . .

Mr. Gorbachev seemed intent, publicly at least, not to inflame the opposition. But it did not take much. It was enough that he said that East Germany had to decide its own future to signal to many that Soviet troops would not interfere. When he said that those who did not change with the times would see life punishing them, the comment was seen as a direct reference to Mr. Honecker. Wherever he went, the crowds chanted "Gorby! Gorby!" Mieczyslaw Rakowski, the Polish Communist Party leader, sat next to Mr. Gorbachev on the reviewing stand at the October 7 military parade. He later said with some irony that when he heard the chants he remarked to Mr. Gorbachev, "It looks as if they want you to liberate them again."

The Soviet leader was more direct when he met in private with the East German Politburo. An East German diplomat said Mr. Gorbachev did not try to prescribe what the East Germans should do. "He made it very clear that the spectacle of thousands of people running away from the country and of violence being the only way to keep them in was not helping him in his own difficult situation," he said.

According to a wide range of party insiders, Mr. Honecker was incapable of grasping the situation. He reacted with stubborn insistence that he was on the right course and would brook no leniency. He told a Chinese visitor that any attempt to change his course was "nothing more than Don Quixote's futile running against the steadily turning sails of a windmill."

On Saturday night, October 7, as Mr. Gorbachev was leaving for Moscow, tens of thousands of East Berliners moved from the anniversary ceremonies to Alexanderplatz, the vast square at the heart of the city. Bearing candles and torches, they began chanting slogans demanding change.

The East German police, armed with riot sticks, chased them out of the square and north into the heavily populated and dilapidated Prenzlauer Berg section, a hotbed of the growing New Forum opposition group. Hundreds were beaten and jailed. The scene was played out again on Sunday night in the same area of East Berlin, as well as in Leipzig and Dresden.

Mr. Krenz, at 52 the youngest member of the Politburo, was hardly a predictable architect of change. He had followed Mr. Honecker's path from the Communist youth league to take charge of security and youth affairs, and his statements had given no sign that he was anything but a hard-liner.

But he was considered sharp, and he was young. And it was he who took the fateful step on October 9 to avert violence in Leipzig.

Back in East Berlin, the Politburo gathered for its regular Tuesday meeting. Nobody knew how Mr. Honecker or his ideological allies would react to the unilateral order by Mr. Krenz barring the Leipzig crackdown.

It was Erich Mielke, the tough 82-year-old security chief, who told Mr. Honecker, "Erich, we can't beat up hundreds of thousands of people."

But the 77-year-old Communist leader would not be swayed. Earlier in the day, three members of the Central Committee had handed Mr. Honecker a report on the unrest among the country's youth and its causes, with a request for a special session of the leadership to deal with it. Mr. Honecker flew into a rage, calling the report "the greatest attack on the party leadership in 40 years."

Now Kurt Hager, the 77-year-old chief ideologist, raised his voice. The young people were right, he said. The mood on the streets was more defiant that he had ever seen it. Gunter Schabowski, the respected party secretary for East Belin, concurred.

Only two members firmly took Mr. Honecker's side: Gunter Mittag, the 63-year-old Economics Minister, who had dominated East German planning since the era of Walter Ulbricht, the first Communist Party chief, and Joachim Hermann, the 61-year-old secretary for propaganda.

Others wavered or kept silent. With the Politburo deadlocked, the secretaries of East Germany's 15 districts, including Hans Modrow, the party chief for Dresden who had a reputation as a reformer favored by Moscow, were called in for an unusual expanded meeting of the leadership. The meeting went late into the night of October 10 and continued on October 11.

"The district leaders said that the grassroots wouldn't stand for things to continue the way they were," a Central Committee member said.

The leaders began discussing a conciliatory statement to the nation. According to several accounts, Mr. Honecker resisted this too, fuming instead about his betrayal by Hungary.

Over his objections, the statement was issued October 11, declaring that the Politburo was ready "to discuss all basic questions of our society," and acknowledging that those who had fled may have had valid reasons.

From that day, the press suddenly became more open, with panel discussions on major public complaints. The small "parties," traditionally subservient to the Communists, suddenly gained a voice of their own, and Mr. Gerlach, the Liberal Party chairman, even suggested in his party paper that the "leading role" of the party should be reconsidered.

The Politburo met again on October 17. By now it was clear to most of the other seventeen Politburo members that Mr. Honecker no longer understood what was happening. One Communist official said Mr. Honecker had been so infuriated by Mr. Gerlach's statement and considered taking action against him.

This time, several Central Committee members said, only Mr. Mittag and Mr. Hermann still supported Mr. Honecker. Some officials said Mr. Mittag was holding out in the hope of securing the party leadership for himself, after having filled in for the ailing Mr. Honecker through the summer.

An important defector was Mr. Hager. "Without Hager, nothing would have gone through in the Politburo," a party official said.

Finally, Willi Stoph, the 75-year-old Prime Minister, told Mr. Honecker that the time had come for him to resign, a Central Committee member said.

That was the decisive push. On the next day, October 18, Mr. Honecker announced to the Central Committee that he was resigning for reasons of health, and the Politburo moved that Mr. Mittag and Mr. Hermann be ousted. Mr. Krenz was the new party chief, head of state and Defense Council chairman.

The meeting was brief. Mr. Krenz read a speech promising an "earnest political dialogue," and then urged the Central Committee to quickly close its proceedings so he could go on nationwide television.

Mr. Krenz immediately set about trying to establish himself, within the party and outside, as the leader of real change. "We see the seriousness of the situation," he said. "But we also sense and recognize the major opportunity we have opened for ourselves to define policies in dialogue with our citizens."

The pace quickened. Mr. Krenz and other Politburo members met people in factories and in the streets. On October 27, the Government announced that it would restore free travel through Czechoslovakia, for people wanting to go to West Germany. On November 1, Mr. Krenz flew to Moscow to meet Mr. Gorbachev and endorsed a version of perestroika—economic and social restructuring—in East Germany.

Still, demonstrations swelled. Huge crowds marched in Leipzig, East Berlin, Dresden and other major cities, and thousands of East Germans perhaps seeing this as their last chance to flee resumed their efforts to get into the West German Embassy in Prague.

Finally, on November 4, Mr. Krenz announced that East Germans who wanted to settle in West Germany could travel freely through Czechoslovakia. More than 10,000 a day began quickly surging across the border into the West.

That same day, more than a half million East Germans demonstrated for democracy in the largest protest that East Berlin or East Germany had ever seen. The crisis was not over.

Hoping to slow the exodus, the Government hastily drafted a law on travel that said East German citizens would be free to go abroad, but for only 30 days a year and after applying at police offices. The bill was promptly denounced, and in a sign of the rebellious mood, the Legal and Constitutional Committee of the normally docile Parliament dismissed it as unacceptable.

The pace of change gathered speed. On November 7, the entire Council of Ministers resigned and called on Parliament to choose a new government. The Central Committee convened on November 8, and this time the entire Politburo resigned, to be replaced by a smaller group, still headed by Mr. Krenz, with five new members. Among them was Mr. Modrow, the party leader from Dresden, who would soon become the next Prime Minister.

Thousands of Communist Party members demonstrated outside,

demanding a party congress to install an entirely new leadership.

On November 9, a Thursday, the Central Committee continued to sweep the ranks of the leadership. Four new members of the top leadership were swept out after their regional party organizations rejected them.

Mr. Mittag came under intense criticism and was expelled from the Central Committee for "the most egregious violations of internal party democracy and of party and state discipline, as well as damaging the reputation of the party."

In the evening, Gunter Schabowski came to brief reporters. Toward the end of the session, he announced that a new travel law had been drafted, giving East Germans the right to leave the country through any border crossings. The Berlin wall, already circumvented, was beginning to crumble.

The measures had been drafted by the Politburo, officials later said. It was still fresh, and the details were not immediately clear, although it later became evident that citizens did have to obtain exit visas from local police stations before going across. But when Mr. Schabowski was asked directly if East Germans could freely go West, his answer was yes.

Soon after, a young East German couple went to the Invalidenstrasse crossing to test the announcement. To their amazement, the guards, who had heard Mr. Schabowski and had no instructions, let them cross. After 28 years, 2 months, 27 days and, the deaths of 80 killed trying to cross it, the wall was open. The astonishing event was reported on West German television, and within an hour tens of thousands were streaming into West Berlin for one of the most extraordinary reunions ever held. Over the weekend two million visited the West, bought chocolates and for the most part, returned home to East Germany. Only a few thousand remained.

Not even the Soviet Government, one of the four World War II Allied powers who hold occupation rights in Berlin, was told of what the East Germans were doing, an East German Government official said. . . .

As events pressed forward, Hans Modrow, the man who by the virtual default of every other party figure, was leading East Germany, gave his own response to Chancellor Kohl on the question of reunification.

New Ties to Bonn Sought by Premier of East Germany

By Craig R. Whitney

EAST BERLIN, Nov. 17—Announcing a sweeping program of economic and political change, East Germany's new Prime Minister today held out the prospect of relations "on a new level" with West Germany.

In a speech broadcast live in East and West Germany, the new Prime Minister, Hans Modrow, said his nation stood by its commitments to the Warsaw Pact, but added:

"We are for supplementing the common responsibility of both German states with a complex of treaties that go far beyond the treaties and agreements signed up to now. This Government is ready for talks on this."

But Mr. Modrow, the 61-year-old former Communist Party chief in Dresden, said decisive change in East Germany would end "unrealistic and dangerous speculation about reunification."

The West German Government, which is sending an official to East Berlin on Monday to meet with the new Communist Party leader, Egon Krenz, reacted cautiously. Chancellor Helmut Kohl has promised West German economic aid on a vast scale if the East Germans carry out genuine economic and political change.

Mr. Modrow obtained unanimous approval from the 500-member East German Parliament for a streamlined, 28-member Cabinet in which the Communist Party kept control of the major portfolios, including defense, national security, foreign affairs, finance, heavy industry, planning and interior, which controls the police. . . . Twenty-seven members of the old Parliament, including the ousted Communist Party chief, Erich Honecker, and his wife, Margot, were replaced with new faces by unanimous consent this morning.

Several thousand East Germans demonstrated in front of the immense white Parliament building as deputies debated Mr. Modrow's statement of policy this afternoon. They carried banners including such slogans as "Socialism Is Dead! Long Live Socialism" and "Rehabilitate the Victims of Stalinist Show Trials." The demonstrations showed, as much of Mr. Modrow's speech did, both how far the country has come since Mr. Honecker was forced to resign a month ago and how far it has yet to go.

"A lot of things have stagnated here for a long time," said Steffen

Feiereis, one of the demonstrators. "There's been a lot of talk. Now it's time to do something." . . .

While fall was giving way to winter, radical political and social changes were underway in East Germany, Hungary and Poland. The course of reform was also zigzagging unevenly in different regions of the Soviet Union. All Europe was anticipating further changes. In this context, correspondents of **The Times** *interviewed three figures who were viewing the transformation from the perspective of dissidents, men who had spent years in jail for the efforts to bring about what now seemed to be taking place.*

Three Dissident Voices From Eastern Europe

Three Eastern Europeans with long careers as dissidents—a Pole, a Hungarian and a Czechoslovak—were asked in separate interviews what surprised them most about the recent events in East Germany, what they thought might be the next step in Eastern Europe and what they considered the greatest dangers.

Jan Litynski: Poland

Jan Litynski was thrown out of the mathematics department of Warsaw University in March 1968 and spent two and half years in jail for taking part in anti-Soviet protests. In the late 1970's he was a founder of the Committee to Defend Workers and edited underground papers.

He helped organize Solidarity, and when the movement was crushed under martial law in 1981, he was arrested and spent another year and a half in jail. He escaped into the underground when he was given a furlough to attend the communion of his daughter.

Mr. Litynski worked as an adviser to Silesian coal miners during the strike-filled summer of 1988. He was elected to Parliament as a candidate of the Solidarity-backed party.

"I guess what surpised me most is that I just did not think it would happen so soon," he said.

"The next major step? I think it should be real change in Czechoslovakia. For us, this is much more important than Germany, because it affords the chance of developing a common line for Hungary, Poland and Czechoslovakia. This would mean the end of Soviet domination in this region.

"By common line I mean we should work out a kind of common foreign policy. Now there are discrepancies, contradictions. I'm not talking about a confederation, as some have suggested, but simply to do our best to avoid the mistakes of the 1920's and 1930's.

"Dangers? Altogether, the economy, and especially the economic situation in the Soviet Union. I hope and think we can cope with our economic situation, and first symptoms are emerging that we will be able to do it. But there is the possibility of a crash in the Soviet Union, especially because of the nationalities problem. And then there is the situation in East Germany. If the Soviet Union lost its influence on East Germany it could result in a kind of military coup in Moscow."

Mr. Litynski was asked whether in his prison years he ever fantasized about the kind of changes that have taken place.

"Never, not at all. Even after I got out of prison, in the underground, I never dreamed of it. As for myself, I used to think maybe someday there'd be a role for me as a trade-union activist. But never as a politician, someone sitting in Parliament."

Miklos Vasarhelyi: Hungary

Miklos Vasarhelyi is a writer and former journalist who was sentenced to five years in prison for his role in the 1956 Hungarian uprising, which was crushed by the Soviet Army. Mr. Vasarhelyi, who was press secretary to the reformist Prime Minister Imre Nagy, was a defendant in the same secret trial in 1958 at which Mr. Nagy and three others were condemned to death. They were executed; he was sentenced to five years and released after four years.

Mr. Vasarhelyi lives in Budapest. He was interviewed in Washington, where he is doing research on the Western role and response to the Soviet invasion of Budapest in 1956.

Referring to the events in East Germany, he said: "What was most surprising was the speed with which it happened. Since last May we thought and we hoped there would be changes. But what's happening now and especially in Berlin is a major surprise. Nobody dared to think about such big changes. Even to have mentioned such things three months ago would have seemed crazy.

"What was so unusual is that it was all the will of the people. It was not figured out by intellectuals or politicians or diplomats.

"It's very different than in 1956. Then, we were crushed because we were alone. Hungary was isolated. This today is impossible to crush because it is going on almost everywhere behind the Iron Curtain. It is irreversible and I can tell you sincerely, I never expected to live to see it."

Asked what he thought would happen now, he replied: "First of all, there will really be a Europe again. The countries of Central and Eastern Europe will finally get an opportunity to unite with the West. We will begin to live under the same conditions.

"It will take time, but socially, politically and economically we will achieve what the Western countries have already achieved. The doors are open now."

On the question of dangers, he said they were fewer than they had been. "There are problems, but they don't worry me. What worried me was to live under a dictatorial system and foreign domination. All other worries are peanuts compared to that.

"Nor am I afraid of a united Germany. The Germans have changed very much. In the last century, the French wanted to take all of Europe. Now they are the most civilized and cultured of nations. The Germans had the terrible experience of Nazism for 10 years 50 years ago. Should we now have to say forever that we have to be afraid of the Germans?"

Jiri Dienstbier: Czechoslovakia

Jiri Dienstbier is one of the founders of the Czechoslovak human-rights group Charter 77. He was a Communist Party member and radio commentator on foreign affairs in 1968 when the Soviets invaded to crush the liberalization begun by the Communist Government of Alexander Dubcek. He spent three years in prison, lost his job and has not been allowed a telephone because of his work.

This is what he said in an interview this week at his home in Prague:

"What surprised everybody was the quick unraveling of things in East Germany. The opposition there wasn't very much bigger than in Czechoslovakia, which is pretty small. It was based almost completely on the evangelical church. In fact, the East German movement started outside the country, with the opening of the border between Austria and Hungary, which gave the East Germans an escape route. This shows that no matter where the rot sets in, the Communist system collapses very quickly.

"The next step? I hope it's Czechoslovakia. I think it could be. The leadership here is dead, only waiting to be carried away. Jakes is completely discredited. The party's only alternative to the status quo is to open up the system, but they know that once they open it up, they are doomed.

"As for dangers, the main problems are the potential economic collapse in Russia and Poland. Whether that pulls us all down would depend mainly on the scope and the nature of the collapse."

The enthusiasm of the three men was justified. Mr. Dienstbier's hopes that the next turn of the wheel would take place in his country was fulfilled within days of the interview. On the night of November 17, as students were taking part in a procession meant to commemorate the shootings of university students by Nazi occupiers, police attacked them. It was an officially sanctioned march, but presumably some authorities felt that what was needed was a preemptive show of force to thwart any attempt to march, chant and bring down the government on the East German model. If that was the intent, the policy backfired. For from that night on, daily rallies grew more massive with each day until in Czechoslovakia, too, the dissidents turned out the Communists. When Mr. Dienstbier gave his interview he was working as a coal stoker in a hospital, a job he had been assigned as a result of his protest. A month later, he was his country's foreign minister.

With Czechoslovakia on the verge of change, Rumania was the last holdout in the Warsaw pact. Nothing, it seemed, was likely to happen there to weaken the tight grip of its Stalinist leader, Nicolae Ceausescu.

Rumanian Leader Refuses Changes

By Alan Riding

BUCHAREST, RUMANIA, Nov. 20—Using the occasion of a major Communist Party congress, President Nicolae Ceausescu made it clear today that as long as he is in charge, Rumania will not follow other East European countries along the paths toward democracy or capitalism.

"Some socialist countries have adopted measures with a view to increasing the wealth of some people and increasing the number of poor," he said. "This focus is not socialist, and we cannot admit it in any way."

In a five-hour speech constantly interrupted by delegates who jumped up, chanted slogans, applauded and sat down in unison, Mr. Ceausescu singled out no particular Eastern bloc government for criticism, preferring instead to emphasize each country's right to pick its own political system.

But the 71-year-old President indirectly referred to widespread speculation about German reunification after the opening of the Berlin wall, noting that "the existence of two Germanys should continue to be a reality of Europe today and tomorrow."

He also raised eyebrows by calling for "the condemnation and cancellation of all the accords concluded with Hitler's Germany, practical conclusions being drawn to eliminate all the consequences of those accords and dictates."

One consequence of the Hitler-Stalin pact of 1939 was that Soviet troops occupied the Rumanian territory of Bessarabia. Although Rumania's Communist Government has never reclaimed what is now Soviet Moldavia, more than 90 percent of its population is still Rumanian, with nationalist sentiments one reason for recent unrest in the republic.

Most of Mr. Ceausescu's speech today, though, was dedicated to extolling the virtues and listing the achievements of the Government since he became General Secretary of the Rumanian Communist Party in 1965.

Only on two occasions did he abandon his prepared text and raise his voice almost to a scream to insure that Rumanians were in no doubt about his opinion of those East European Governments that are veering away from Communism.

"What do we say to those who want to lead the way to capitalism?" he asked. "What were they doing when they were in positions of responsibility? The answer is they used their jobs to block socialism and did not serve their people."

To underline his point, he said that the capitalist world was characterized today by unemployment, homelessness and growing illiteracy. "Adding to all this are crime and drugs, which have become national problems in many countries," he said.

While Mr. Ceausescu's orthodox stance came as no surprise, the long-scheduled party congress has underlined his hard-line Government's growing international isolation as well as its heightened sensitivity to foreign criticism.

With the exception of Yasir Arafat, chairman of the Palestine Liberation Organization, no prominent foreign dignitaries were present at the opening of the party congress, and other East bloc Communist parties sent low-level delegations. Western ambassadors boycotted the occasion to protest Rumania's human rights record.

In the days leading up to the congress, the Government also tightened its borders with Hungary, Yugoslavia and the Soviet Union to the point of turning away ordinary tourists. A French journalist was expelled last Friday, numerous correspondents from Western newspapers were refused visas, and reporters arriving here Sunday saw all their papers mentioning Rumania seized by customs officers at Bucharest airport.

At home, though, bolstered by a huge and notoriously effective security apparatus, Mr. Ceausescu still appears to be unchallenged, with dissidents numbering only a score of intellectuals and disillusioned party officials whose occasional protests are better known abroad than here.

Unlike other East European countries, Rumania also seems to be largely immune to pressure from the Soviet Union. Moscow has had no troops stationed here since 1957 and has viewed Mr. Ceausescu as something of a maverick ever since he criticized the Soviet invasion of Czechoslovakia in 1968.

Further, even though living conditions have steadily deteriorated over the last fifteen years, the Rumanian economy is less dependent on the outside world than that of, say, Poland because of Mr. Ceausescu's decision to dedicate the 1980's to paying off the country's $11 billion debt.

"The repayment of the foreign debt is a great success of our state's policy, and it puts an end to this country's long dependence on foreign monopolies and financial capital," he said today. "For the first time in its history, Rumania no longer pays either tribute or interest."

And although the Rumanian leader has lost much of the international influence that he enjoyed when he was viewed by the West as a critic of Moscow, Mr. Ceausescu urged the superpowers to move rapidly toward disarmament. Specifically, he called for the denuclearization of Europe by 1995 and the elimination of all nuclear weapons by the year 2000.

200,000 March in Prague as Calls for Change Mount

By John Tagliabue

PRAGUE, Nov. 20—More than 200,000 marchers called today for freedom and a change in government in the largest and most vociferous public demonstration since the euphoric Prague Spring that preceded the 1968 Soviet-led invasion of Czechoslovakia.

At the same time, party and Government officials pointedly reaffirmed their opposition to introducing political change in the face of the protests.

Nonetheless, they at least tacitly acknowledged a changed political climate by postponing an official visit here by Egon Krenz, the new East German leader, which was to have begun Tuesday. Prague's

229

official press agency said that on the "basis of a mutual agreement," Czechoslovakia and East Germany had decided to call off the visit indefinitely.

The demonstrators, most of them young people, gathered initially at Wenceslas Square, the half-mile-long pedestrian plaza sloping down from the National Museum. The square has repeatedly been the forum for expressions of Czechoslovak nationalism. And today, the crowd waved flags and chanted anti-Government slogans.

As the group, which included striking university and high school students, set out to cross the Vltava River on the way to Hradcany Castle, which houses the President's office, their shouts became bolder. Cries demanding "freedom"and "free elections" mingled with calls for a general strike and chants of "Jakes out!," a reference to the country's orthodox Communist Party General Secretary, Milos Jakes.

The gigantic crowd moved slowly through the narrow, curving streets of the baroque city. But as the marchers headed onto several bridges, they were confronted by large numbers of heavily armed police officers. The protesters reversed course and dispersed soon after they returned to the north shore, avoiding the kind of violence with which club-wielding policemen scattered a smaller group of demonstrators on Friday night.

The march through Prague was reminiscent of the mass protests in 1967 that swept out Antonin Novotny, then the hard-line Communist leader, replacing him with the reform-minded Alexander Dubcek. . . .

Though the tremendous size of the crowds—which seeped through crooked squares and broad shopping streets, and then snaked along the open stretches of the river shore—made it difficult to determine how many people marched, the official radio estimated that more than 200,000 Czechoslovaks had taken to the streets.

National television, which reported extensively on the demonstration, also gave news of similar marches in at least three other cities— the northern center of heavy industry, Ostrava; the Slovak capital, Bratislava, and Brno, the site of the second-largest protest, with several thousand marchers.

In Prague, schools of the university were closed by striking students, and banners declaring sit-in strikes appeared at institutes of higher learning throughout the city.

Dissident leaders repeated a call for a two-hour general strike on November 27. Vaclav Havel, the playwright and leading Czechoslovak dissident, reported that he had received a message from coal miners at a small pit in northern Bohemia, who expressed support for the requested stoppage. But the extent to which industrial workers might join the swelling protest remained both critical and, as yet, unanswered.

Western diplomats and Czechoslovak dissident leaders believe that if workers were to join in with students and intellectuals, it would spell the almost certain collapse of the Government.

At various sites throughout the city tonight, groups of young people, students and workers could be seen milling around columns of police vehicles, in animated discussion with the young officers. Apparently, the security authorities had given orders for the police to use restraint today. But that decision did not appear to signal any lessening of the leadership's will to resist political change.

Mr. Jakes, in a statement that rang with a sense of warning, accused the protest-march organizers of "seeking to create chaos and anarchy."

Such efforts, he said, would "seriously endanger the implementation of necessary changes and bring socialism into crisis, with unforeseeable consequences."

Even more striking than the statement by Mr. Jakes, a widely acknowledged hard-liner, was another by the Cabinet today that endorsed the measures taken by the Communist Party leadership to put down protest last Friday. Many demonstrators were injured in that action.

The Cabinet said it approved of "measures whose purpose is to renew order, protect property and protect the lives of the citizens."

Its remarks were notable because Ladislav Adamec, the 62-year-old Prime Minister, has emerged in recent weeks as the principal rival to Mr. Jakes. He has adopted a relatively moderate stance in his apparent maneuvering to succeed the party leader.

An example of the Communist Party's declining authority came last Sunday, when the leader of the hitherto satellite Socialist Party, Jan Skoda, broke ranks and turned up along with Mr. Havel and other dissidents at the founding assembly of a new political group, the Civil Forum.

That gathering, held in a Prague theater, heard another leading dissident, the Rev. Vaclav Maly, a Roman Catholic priest banned by the state from performing his priestly duties, read a declaration calling for the removal of hard-liners like Mr. Jakes and threatening a general strike.

Earlier today, Mr. Havel announced that he had refused a Government offer of a passport to travel to Sweden and accept an award there "because the situation at home is becoming dramatic."

Prague's Premier Has Initial Talks with Opposition
By John Tagliabue

PRAGUE, Nov. 21—Czechoslovakia's Communist leaders held their first talks with representatives of a newly formed opposition movement today, while more than 200,000 people joined in a fifth day of street demonstrations sustaining pressure for political changes.

In developments that at times appeared to parallel recent East German events, dissident voices were raised in the streets while Communist leaders promised new approaches and the expansion of political life beyond the ruling party.

In a televised address tonight, Milos Jakes, the hard-line Communist Party General Secretary, appealed to citizens to "depart from this present, exacerbated situation." He warned, "There are boundaries that should not be overstepped."

Mr. Jakes's address offered somewhat stern counterpoint to the news that Prime Minister Ladislav Adamec had met with opposition figures. The party leader looked despondent, but he gave no sign that he was about to step down, while acknowledging that "more than one dialogue" lay ahead of him.

Earlier, the playwright Vaclav Havel, a frequently arrested dissident leader stood on a balcony and told a huge gathering in Wenceslas Square of the meeting between Prime Minister Adamec and a delegation of the Civic Forum, a recently formed opposition group.

Mr. Adamec also promised that the Government would not impose martial law. His comments were reported by the official press agency.

The demonstrators had at times cried "Punish, punish, punish!"— urging retribution for policemen who had used billy clubs to scatter protesters on Friday. As Mr. Havel spoke, some waved Czechoslovak flags and others applauded.

The show of enthusiasm continued as the Rev. Vaclav Maly, a priest who has been barred by the Government from wearing clerical garb or performing religious duties because of his involvement with dissident and human rights groups, read a letter from Frantisek Cardinal Tomasek, the 90-year-old Primate of the Roman Catholic Church in Czechoslovakia.

"There can be no confidence in the leadership of a state that refuses to tell the people the truth and give them the rights and freedoms that are common even in third-world countries," said Father Maly, quoting the Primate. "We can wait no longer." . . .

250,000 Czechs, Hailing Dubcek, Urge Ouster of Hard-Line Leaders
By John Tagliabue

PRAGUE, Nov. 22—More than 250,000 Czechoslovaks who gathered in Wenceslas Square for a sixth consecutive day of protest shouted "Resign! Resign!" today when speakers called for the country's hard-line Communist leaders to step down.

The loudest cheers came when the urging was made in the name of Alexander Dubcek, the reformist leader who was forced from power after Soviet tanks invaded Czechoslovakia 21 years ago. Mr. Dubcek emerged today from the obscurity to which he had been officially consigned to ask that President Gustav Husak and Milos Jakes, the party leader, give up their posts.

Mr. Dubcek also spoke in public today for the first time since his efforts to introduce "Socialism with a human face" were crushed in 1968. In Bratislava, he addressed 2,000 people protesting the trial of a human-rights advocate, urging calm. Mr. Dubcek, who has been officially ignored while working in a state forestry office for much of the last two decades, was shown on state television tonight as he met protesters. Mr. Dubcek's message, read to the crowd in Prague, noted that he hoped to visit the capital soon and to appear in person at Wenceslas Square. When this was announced, the crowd began chanting, "Dubcek, Dubcek." [The Associated Press reported that citizens were able for the first time to watch a live broadcast from the square on state-run television. But the broadcast, spliced with studio film of rock bands, was abruptly halted after 50 minutes when a worker interviewed by a reporter on the square accused the Government of lying. "What is the Government afraid of?" said the worker, identified as Honza Lexa. "They might be afraid because they are lying to us for 20 years." An announcer appeared to say the broadcast was temporarily halted because some unidentified television workers disagreed with it. The broadcast from the square resumed 35 minutes later. . . .

At today's rally, Vaclav Havel, the playwright and dissident, told cheering crowds that he sought to reach "especially all the workers in our country who are for reform."

As cheers of "Long live the workers" echoed through the floodlit square, Mr. Havel continued, "Those who have been taking bloody vengeance against all their rivals for so many years are now afraid of us."

"But we are not like them," he said, from a balcony high above the square. "We don't want to take vengeance on anyone. We only ask to take control of our country."

Students in Prague who have been striking since Monday, demanding free elections and a change in government, sent hundreds of their numbers into the countryside to visit industrial plants in an effort to enlist support for the general strike. . . .

The upheavals in the East bloc were not only raising hopes; they were raising some very tricky questions as well.

The New Europe: Will It Come Apart as It Comes Together?
By R. W. Apple, Jr.

VIENNA, Nov. 22—More than a century ago, the Hapsburg Empire, based in this grand old city on the Danube, stretched across Central and Eastern Europe from the Tyrolian Alps to the Carpathian Mountains.

In a sense, its collapse under the weight of emergent nationalism led to the two great twentieth-century conflicts. The assassination at Sarajevo of Archduke Franz Ferdinand, the heir to the throne, set off World War I, and Hitler's dismemberment of Czechoslovakia, one of the "succession states" created from the defunct empire in 1918, raised European tensions to the breaking point on the eve of World War II.

Now the East European region once contested by the Hapsburg monarchy and its neighbors, with its complicated patterns of tribe and language, is in turmoil once again, with consequences that are unpredictable.

The people of Poland and Czechoslovakia, of Hungary and Bulgaria, clearly hope that once their freedom is established, once the threat of war between East and West has truly receded, they will be able to restore long-ruptured links with the rest of Europe. As a Hungarian actor said last summer, "We want so much to be Europeans again, and we think that we really have a chance, if we cross our fingers and get our politicians going."

But at the same time, the sharp reduction in Moscow's sway over what used to be called the satellite nations in Eastern Europe, a unifying influence in some ways parallel to the old empire's, could give greater play to the centrifugal forces that have proved so destructive in the past.

In the new era, in other words, with the centripetal force of ideology weakened, Poles will be able to be more Polish, Hungarians more Hungarian.

Already the Hungarians complain bitterly about Rumanian treatment of ethnic Hungarians in Transylvania, Slovaks and Czechs are more vocal in expressing resentment of each another, East Germans grouse about the fate of ethnic Germans in the now Polish region of Silesia. Everyone complains about the Poles, who can find little in their own shops, sweeping into stores in neighboring countries and denuding the shelves of shops there.

Other ancient forces have also been liberated in the drive for pluralism and free speech. In at least some countries in Eastern Europe, there has been a rise in anti-Semitism, prominent Jews say, at the same time as there is a rise in the open expression of Jewish pride.

So far, though, nationalistic rivalries have been muted in the common struggle for freedom. In a striking example of that, Anna Masaryk, the 60-year-old granddaughter of the founder of modern Czechoslovakia, Tomas Masaryk, was seen among the demonstrators this week in Wenceslas Square in Prague.

On both sides of the rapidly disintegrating Iron Curtain, older people recall a day when there was one Europe, not two, and when intellectual and cultural currents flowed freely back and forth. They remember, as the younger ones often do not, that it was the Soviet Union and not so much the Eastern Europeans themselves who cut their historical links with the West—links that made the Polish scientist Copernicus and the Czechoslovak playwright Karel Capek and the Hungarian composer Bela Bartok part of Western civilization, not a part of a separate culture that stopped at the Elbe.

When the Berlin wall was finally opened two weeks ago, Neil Ascherson wrote in a commentary in *The Independent of London*, "It wasn't just the landscape of European politics that suddenly changed; it was the European cosmos." With that act, Europe started to become whole once more, with its eastern reaches no longer enshrouded, in Mr. Ascherson's vivid phrase, in "darkness and demons."

Even far across the Atlantic, the lesson will not be long in sinking in. Americans, after all, have ethnic and religious roots in Wittenberg and Bratislava and Lodz, not just in Naples and Athens and Munich and Dublin. One of their favorite beers is named after what was once Budweis, an ethnically German brewing town in the Bohemia region of Czechoslovakia that is now called Ceske Budejovice. The Bauhaus architectural style that shaped American cities after the war was developed in Dessau, in what is now East Germany, and Haydn, as mainstream a figure in Western musical history as it is possible to imagine, wrote many of his best symphonies while serving the Esterhazy family as music-master in Hungary.

It is not so far, really, from Cracow to Chicago. At the height of the cold war, the gulf seemed enormous, but it does no longer, not with Lech Walesa drawing crowds in America and American businessmen flocking to Budapest with deal-making on their minds.

For the Europeans, the distances have been reduced even more, and events are forcing fresh thinking to the fore. The Italians are talking about—and have even held a conference to discuss—a new economic alignment in which they, the Hungarians, the Austrians and the Yugoslavs could cooperate to create a balancing force to the German sphere of influence that many expect to emerge to the north.

The Swedes, who have maintained their neutrality throughout the cold war, now see less reason to do so. With that once-central idea not so gripping anymore, they are thinking again about the possibility of joining the European Community. In Britain, debate raging over how fully that country should take part in the tighter organization of the community scheduled to take effect in 1992 has been intensified.

"We have to build mechanisms to integrate this new Europe," says Gianni de Michelis, the Italian Foreign Minister. "The new realities are social, political, economic, artistic. For a thousand years, European equilibrium was built in Central Europe, starting with Charlemagne. For the last eighty years we have lacked a workable system, with obvious results, but now we have a chance once again to build it."

In Czechoslovakia, as in East Germany, the party began to make concessions to placate the crowds. The crowds, meanwhile, kept asking for more.

Prague Party Leaders Resign; New Chief, 48, Surprise Choice; 350,000 at Rally Cheer Dubcek

By Steven Greenhouse

PRAGUE, Saturday, Nov. 25—Yielding to mass protests throughout Czechoslovakia, the Communist Party's leadership resigned on Friday, and the beleaguered Central Committee chose a younger, lesser-known Politburo member to replace General Secretary Milos Jakes.

But the election of the new chief, Karel Urbanek, a 48-year-old *not Adamec* former party leader in Bohemia, was followed by the unexpected announcement early this morning that the moderate Prime Minister, Ladislav Adamec, was resigning as well. Mr. Adamec this week had met with dissidents calling for dialogue and had been considered a likely successor to Mr. Jakes as party leader; his departure was considered a setback to the movement for change.

The makeup of a new nine-member Politburo was also announced this morning, and the new body retained several hard-liners on the 13-member Politburo that resigned on Friday.

The replacement of Mr. Jakes on Friday came just hours after 350,000 protesters crowded into central Prague in the eighth straight day of huge demonstrations.

In a striking paradox, the throng was addressed by Alexander Dubcek, whose liberal regime was overthrown by a Soviet-led Warsaw Pact invasion in 1968, and replaced by hard-line Communists of whom Mr. Jakes was one of the leaders. It was Mr. Dubcek's first public appearance in Prague since 1968.

After the news of the resignations of the old leaders spread, there was singing and dancing and scenes of jubilation throughout the center of Prague, where just a week before the police had clubbed demonstrators in a vain effort to put down the protests.

"An old wise man said, 'If there once was light, why should there be darkness again?' " Mr. Dubcek had told the crowd. "Let us act in such a way to bring the light back again." . . .

Speaking about the Politburo changes, one Western diplomat said: "It was a generational change. It is still dominated by hard-liners. I can't say it is very positive." Several diplomats said the party might have been trying to make cosmetic changes to placate protesters. The diplomats said they doubted that the changes would come close to satisfying the dissidents. . . .

The diplomats were right.

Prague Opposition Mounts Huge Protest, Denouncing New Leadership as "a Trick"

By R. W. Apple, Jr.

PRAGUE, Nov. 25—Opposition leaders redoubled their pressure on the tottering Communist regime in Czechoslovakia today, staging an immense protest rally and insisting that the shuffling of the Politburo on Friday night and further resignations this morning had failed to move the nation far enough toward democracy.

"The new leadership is a trick that was meant to confuse," said Vaclav Havel, the often-jailed playwright who to many symbolizes political dissent here. "The power remains in or is passing into the hands of the neo-Stalinists."

"Shame! Shame! Shame!" shouted thousands of his listeners, part of a huge throng of protesters estimated by Czechoslovak officials at 500,000 to 800,000. The protesters filled a large field next to a sports stadium and near Letenske Gardens, on the north side of the river and across from Wenceslas Square. Hundreds of thousands of Czechoslovaks have demonstrated in the square, a blocks-long pedestrian plaza, each night this week.

Today's crowd was the largest in the nine straight days of demonstrations.

The throng provided a powerful symbol of continuing political dissent despite the resignation of Milos Jakes, the Communist Party chief, whose leadership crumbled under the pressure of the mass rallies, and a clear lack of support from Moscow.

Karel Urbanek, the little-known Politburo member who was made Communist Party General Secretary, said on television tonight in his first address to the people that "nobody manages to create miracles from day to day." He spoke for eleven minutes, in generalities, calling himself "an honest man" who was open to dialogue with his opponents.

Mr. Urbanek did not mention a two-hour general strike that is planned for Monday. The omission was considered significant by commentators here, who saw in it a possible attempt by the new party leader to identify himself with some of the opposition's goals.

More than 24 hours after the old regime came apart, it was still not clear whether the Communists were ready for significant changes, including the abandonment of their claim to permanent control of the Government, or whether they were trying to regroup behind a new facade.

Most outsiders, including Western diplomats, leaned to the belief that Mr. Urbanek was offering the appearance of change without the reality.

"It was impossible to give Jakes a soft landing," a European envoy said. "He had to be blamed at once, and when that happens in a Communist country, it means the party is in retreat. But it doesn't mean that they're ready yet for genuine competition with other parties for power."

This was another turbulent day, not only in this fine old capital but also in Bratislava, the principal city of Slovakia; in Brno, largest city in Moravia, and in other centers. A commentator on state television spoke tonight of power struggles in party organizations nationwide. . . .

Ladislav Adamec, who lost his Politburo seat, said he had submitted his resignation as Prime Minister, but he seemed still to be functioning in that capacity. At a news conference, he said that the commandant of paramilitary forces who beat protesters on November 17 would be disciplined. He also promised a new draft constitution by the end of the year, discussed an amnesty for all political prisoners and agreed to meet again next week with the leaders of protesting students.

Pronouncing himself ready to talk with the Civic Forum, the main opposition movement, Mr. Adamec said: "Last week, I undertook such dialogue, but we cannot leave it unfinished. We must meet again and solve problems with which both sides are concerned. I think we can do it sometime next week."

A light snow was falling on Mr. Havel and Alexander Dubcek, the 67-year-old Slovak who instituted the liberalization crushed by Soviet-led tanks 21 years ago, as they spoke to the vast throng at the stadium.

People in the crowd were in an exuberant if wary mood, their confidence buoyed by the departure of Mr. Jakes. They wore ribbons in red, blue and white, the national colors, and waved Czechoslovak flags as Mr. Havel told them that he was "profoundly disturbed" by the composition of the new Politburo named at 3 A.M. today. . . .

In addition to the mass rallies, other forms of organization and protest were being planned.

Students Ask Workers' Aid in Czech Rally

By Esther B. Fein

PRAGUE, Nov. 23—Jana Markvartova is the daughter of a doctor and a lawyer, a privileged child of Czechoslovakia's elite. Before this week, she had never really talked to any of the hundreds of thousands of people who are this country's manual laborers.

Today, Miss Markvartova stood before nearly 200 workers at the Domaci Potreby household appliance factory in the polluted industrial outskirts of the city and told them how the police here had violently broken up a peaceful demonstration by students last Friday night. Then tearfully, she asked the workers to support a two-hour general strike that the students have called for Monday to demand wholesale changes in the country's leadership.

"We need your help," Miss Markvartova told the workers. "It is your work that allows us to study and to develop our minds and our ideas. But alone our ideas are nothing. We need you. We need you to join our strike."

Her efforts paid off. The workers voted overwhelmingly to support the strike.

In the last week, Miss Markvartova and students like her at Prague's universities have realized that they must reach out to workers at factories, farms and industries if their demonstrations and strikes are to succeed in forcing change on their resistant Communist Government.

Unlike Poland, where the workers themselves began the Solidarity movement that eventually unseated the Communist Government this year, the opposition in Czechoslovakia since 1968 has always been a cause of the intellectual crafts, with practically no input from workers.

To insure the complacency of the workers, Communist leaders in Czechoslovakia have consistently provided manual workers with higher salaries and greater access to such things as private cars and weekend cottages than almost anywhere else in the Eastern bloc with the possible exception of East Germany.

"We won't win if the workers are not on our side," said Jiru Masek, a 19-year-old student of foreign trade at Prague University and one of the strike organizers. "To the leaders of our country, we students are nothing. But workers are the power here. To persuade them is critical to our cause."

240

After successfully shutting down most college classes, the students set up work battalions in classrooms, gymnasiums and lecture halls. Ragged from little sleep and sporadic eating, they spend their days and nights typing up declarations and appeals to their fellow citizens, painting posters that are then plastered in store windows and subway stations and editing videotapes that show the brutal events of November 18 and the mass rallies on Wenceslas Square that have been a daily event ever since.

Then they sent teams of students out to factories and enterprises throughout the city and in the countryside, trying to bridge the vast gap between Czechoslovakia's elite and its working class and to win the support of the laborers.

Tomas Zuda, a 21-year-old economics student and a strike coordinator, acknowledged that there was not a natural line of communications betwen the impassioned young students and the workers.

"Some of us work in factories in the summer to earn money, but this is the first time most of us have actually had a dialogue with the workers," he said. "Every student who has gone to a factory, and there are hundreds of us, has had to find a common language to make the workers understand. There has been a lot of skepticism to overcome and social barriers that are usually not crossed in this country, and we don't always have success. But I think the workers see that we are more sincere than the Government when we say: 'We need you. We want you.' "

Miss Markvartova first went to the Domaci Potreby factory on Tuesday with Jan Novak, both unsure that workers there would listen to the radical pleas of two 21-year-old philosophy students asking them to stop working on Monday in a two-hour strike. They had already been thrown out of the Balirny factory across the street, where the conservative director of the packaging enterprise refused to let them speak with workers.

At Domaci Potreby, they were told to leave their literature and to come back today, when the workers would meet in the cafeteria and hear them out.

During the next two days, Miss Markvartova, Mr. Novak and thousands of students here circumvented the conservative official press to get their word out to the working people. They covered the walls of the city's subway system, bus windows, escalator railings, shop windows and street lamps with information on demonstrations and strikes and with posters proclaiming: "Workers Join Us for Freedom!" "Students Against Violence Ask for Your Help!" and "Strike for Democracy."

Overnight the students created their own "mass media" on the streets. These days virtually every public place in Prague is crowded with people reading notices, looking at pictures of the Friday night clashes and signing declarations, all surprisingly unhindered by the police.

When Miss Markvartova and Mr. Novak returned to the Domaci Potreby factory today, the workers rose in applause.

"My heart is with you," said Jitka Jeslinkova, a 30-year-old woman who has worked for two years at the plant. "I want my children to buy anything they need in the shops, to read any books they choose and watch any film they want. I want freedom for them and for me."

Monika Mlejnkova, a representative of the factory's Communist Party committee, objected to the call for a strike. "Maybe we should allow an investigation of the events on Friday, but I urge you not to strike," she said, as her colleagues began to bang the table and hiss. "The Communist Party is our strength."

Miroslav Nedorast, a burly man who has been a factory truck driver for 40 years, then shouted from the back of the room: "We want pluralism. We want free elections. I wouldn't be a Communist Party member even if I were forced. Your time is over."

The factory director called for a vote. Who supports the strike? he asked. Hands shot up across the room, already dim in the late afternoon. Who is against? Three hands were raised.

"Let's take another count," Miss Mlejnkova said.

That stirred a response from an older worker with thick glasses. "I have bad eyes," the worker said. "But it's clear even to me that most everyone here is for a strike."

But they voted again and the decision remained: Workers at the Domaci Potreby factory will join the students and lay down their tools from noon until 2 P.M. on Monday.

"This was not spontaneous support," said Jaroslava Fornuskova, a 38-year-old factory worker. "We talked about what would happen if the strike didn't work, what kind of repression there might be. But we decided we can't support a Government that beats its students. Next time it will be us, and then who will strike?"

The center of the ongoing Eastern European drama had shifted quite suddenly to Prague, but there were also major developments unfolding in Germany and gripping events almost everywhere in the bloc.

Reports of Corruption in East Berlin Shock Even the Party Rank and File

By David Binder

EAST BERLIN, Nov. 24—For the last two days, the East German press has been publishing accusations of corruption and profiteering by top officials of the former Communist leadership under Erich Honecker, and the reports are coming as a shock to the public here.

For the first time, East Germans have learned from reporters in *Neues Deutschland*, the main Communist paper, as well as *Berliner Zeitung* and *Junge Welt* about the extraordinary privileges accumulated by the Honecker regime, which was ousted a month ago. The shock is all the greater among ordinary party members because the former regime had presented itself for years as a model of Communist modesty and probity.

For the East German public, the most fascinating and revolting revelations are about Wandlitz, the heavily guarded compound of 23 houses for the Communist elite a few miles north of the capital.

A dozen or so East German reporters, photographers and television camera teams allowed into the compound for the first time disclosed such amenities as a swimming pool, a greenhouse, gardeners, maids, a tailor, a beauty parlor and a store where consumer goods unavailable to the general public in quantity or quality are abundantly stocked.

All of a sudden, the inhabitants of Wandlitz were subjected to the unwelcome scrutiny of the press. Foreign reporters are to be bused to Wandlitz on Monday for a look.

Gerhard Schurer, one of the three members of the new Communist Politburo who is still residing in the compound, though soon to move out, told a *Junge Welt* reporter that he was paid 4,735 marks a month, or about $2,250 at the official exchange rate and more than four times the average wage in East Germany. East German marks are being sold in the West for less than a tenth of that value.

Wandlitz, which East Germans have called Volvograd, an allusion to the Swedish automobile favored by the former regime leaders, is becoming a small pensioners' village. Mr. Honecker and most of his associates are apparently retaining their homes there for the time being, but without the extraordinary privileges.

Egon Krenz, who replaced Mr. Honecker on October 18, moved from Wandlitz, 15 miles northeast of Berlin, to a bungalow in the Berlin borough of Pankow earlier this week.

Equally upsetting for the public are the revelations of luxurious excesses enjoyed by other former leaders, who created their own private hunting preserves.

For example, Harry Tisch, the ousted Communist trade union chief, retained about 5,000 acres of hunting grounds in the Eixner Forest in Mecklenburg. There he maintained a preserve of about 200 acres for breeding wild boar. He also shot as many as 100 elk annually, according to *Neues Deutschland*, and maintained a richly appointed hunting ledge.

Near Gotha, in Thuringia, Gerhard Muller, a recently ousted party secretary, maintained a 700,000-mark hunting lodge. *Neues Deutschland* reported on Thursday that Mr. Muller also had a four-mile asphalt road laid into the hunting preserve to his lodge at a cost of 1.1 million marks. "We would have preferred to put the road where it was needed," said Georg Doring, the senior forest ranger in Luisenthal, site of the preserve.

In other cases related to the assertions of corruption, Gunter Mittag, Mr. Honecker's former chief aide, and the district party secretaries were expelled from the Communist Party on Thursday and apparently also face court actions.

According to *Berliner Zeitung*, Mr. Mittag had set up a dummy corporation called Commercial Coordination—it is not clear when it was established—which milked hard currency earnings from East German companies that exported valuable antiquities and books to the West.

In effect, said Gerhard Beil, the Foreign Trade Minister, the dummy corporation broke through the foreign trade monopoly of his ministry.

Among the East German enterprises named by Dr. Beil as having been co-opted by the dummy corporation set up by Mr. Mittag were Intrac Inc., Forum Trade Society, BIEC, Transinter and the International Trade Center.

Mr. Mittag apparently persuaded the directors of those enterprises to go along with his scheme by bribing them with hard currency, according to a party official.

The corruption cases were also a topic Thursday night in a public discussion in the Communist Central Committee Building in downtown East Berlin and also a subject of hundreds of letters sent to Communist Party newspapers.

Among the other new developments in the affairs of the party, the East German press reported today that the Writers Association of the German Democratic epublic had voted to readmit nine authors who

244

had been expelled from the ranks for various transgressions ten years ago. Among those readmitted is Joachim Seyppel, who has made his home in West Germany since then. Mr. Seyppel was recently found guilty by a Hamburg court of libeling Hermann Kant, the head of the Writers Association.

In an interview with *Neues Deutschland*, published today, Mr. Krenz, who is head of state as well as head of the party, said, "We are not a corrupt party," but that mistakes had been made under the former leadership, of which he was also a member. "Those who violated the law belong in front of the court," he said.

Mr. Krenz said he was in favor of the proposal that the Communist Party give up its "leading role," which is enshrined in the 1974 Constitution approved by the rubber-stamp Parliament.

Tonight Mr. Honecker's name was woven into a play being performed by the Repertory Company of the Maxim Gorki Theater on Unter den Linden. The comedy, called *The Prussians Are Coming*, by Claus Hammel, has Martin Luther and Frederick the Great among its characters. "I know everything," says Frederick the Great in the first act.

"That is what Erich Honecker thought, too," Martin Luther replies. The audience responded to the exchange with a big laugh.

There were also smaller dramas taking place.

And for Two East Germans in Love, the Changes Spell Bliss
By Henry Kamm

ERFURT, EAST GERMANY, Nov. 20—The young man with a crew cut and his fiancee held hands at the restaurant table that they shared with a foreigner and, love overcoming timidity, hugged each other and giggled happily while they studied the lunch menu.

"It's hard not to see each other for six weeks," he explained when she left the table briefly. "I'm a soldier here. She had to get up at four-thirty this morning in Karl-Marx-Stadt, and at six this evening she has to take the train back."

"I should really be in uniform," he said, "but I guess it doesn't matter now." Nowadays East Germans put a special emphasis on the word "now," as if between yesterday and today their whole lives had been altered.

The young couple regretted that they had been too late to attend the Sunday rally for democracy in the main square of this capital of the Thuringia region. Of course soldiers can and do attend such meetings, he said. "I also go to church," he added. Yes, in uniform.

They said they wished they had enough time together to join the three million East Germans who once again streamed across the border between the two Germanys for weekend visits. They have never been there, they said, but there is no hurry, the borders will stay open. Soldiers are allowed to go, he said. "We were really surprised when that was announced."

"What is happening here can't be turned back," he said, and she agreed. What is new in their lives? the foreigner asked. "We have a future," the young woman, a physical therapist, replied. "A future here," he added. Yes, they said, they had thought of leaving for West Germany. "Everybody has been thinking about it," he said.

"And a lot of people are gone," the therapist added. "People where I work and many others. But now, after the turnabout, they are not leaving anymore. Maybe some will start coming back."

"Funny, a few weeks ago I wouldn't have talked like we do now," the soldier mused. "And now it's quite natural. It was always natural with friends who knew each other, but not with strangers, especially from the Federal Republic."

Learning that the stranger was not West German but American, the couple looked at each other and burst out laughing in wonderment at what they said; it was something that had never happened to them before.

"But now everything is possible," she said, and both looked pleased. Politically, the therapist said, East Germany is now a free country. "We say what we want and to whom we want," her fiancé said.

Not all is as it should be, he continued, as if to compensate for his euphoria. "What's happening should make the world more peaceful, but I'm told the English are stepping up rearmament by mounting medium-range missiles on planes, cleverly contravening the treaties," he said. "And the Republicans in West Germany are very strong," he said, referring to a right-wing party.

"Maybe they would be strong here, too," the therapist said. "A lot of people here don't like foreigners, just like the fascists over there."

The foreigners who are unpopular, they said, are students, especially from Arab and African countries, who show off their wealth in dollars and West German marks and deal on the black market, as well as Mozambican and Cuban workers who have been sent here to make up for a chronic labor shortage.

There are also many Polish black-market traders and Vietnamese workers, who the therapist said have discovered that by feigning illness one can be excused from work for weeks and then use the time to sew jeans and sell them at high prices. About 50,000 Vietnamese work in East German factories, and Vietnamese-sewn black-market jeans have become a desired, if expensive, fashion item.

"I guess you're right," the young woman said, when the foreigner asked whether to make jeans that people want to buy was not economically more useful than working in a factory that produces second-rate goods, as many state enterprises are known to do. "Our one-sided education has confused our minds."

They ordered the most expensive things on the menu, including bird's-nest soup for the young woman, which came in a demitasse cup. "It's not that we eat like that every day," the soldier said, as if to apologize for unearned luxury. Their pay is very low, they said.

"I earned a lot more as a building worker, without a specialized education, than she does after three years of school learning a difficult profession," the soldier said.

They said East Germany's economic problems would be much harder to solve than the political questions. "It's only now that we are learning how bad our situation is, and we don't know all of it yet," the therapist said. "We have been told so many lies," the soldier added.

The couple agreed that, bad as the economic situation might be, it was far better than Poland's deep crisis.

"Maybe that's because we made our revolution after working hours," the young woman said, voicing a widespread pride that East Germans have succeeded, unlike other Communist countries, in producing political upheaval without hampering economic production.

And there was the stuff of thrillers,

Old Master Spy in East Berlin Tells Why He Backs Changes
By Serge Schmemann

EAST BERLIN, Nov. 21—Among the artists, intellectuals, clerics and other former dissidents at the forefront of those in East Germany calling for changes, Markus Wolf clearly stands out.

A big, dapper man given to well-cut tweed suits, Mr. Wolf was for 33 years East Germany's master spy. In fact, he is one of the few East Germans who cannot take advantage of the new travel freedoms because his espionage coups in West Germany have made him a wanted man there.

But three years after his retirement from the Ministry of State Security, Mr. Wolf, 66 years old, has become a leading proponent of change, appearing on television talk shows and opposition panel discussions, and he was a featured speaker at the huge rally in East Berlin on November 4.

Now there is talk that the man who bedeviled the West German Government with his spies—including the celebrated Gunter Guillaume, who became a personal aide to Willy Brandt and whose uncloaking brought about the fall of the Social Democratic Chancellor in 1974—may himself become part of a new party leadership selected when the Communist Party holds its congress next month.

Mr. Wolf denies any such ambitions. But after decades of toiling in the shadows, he seems to savor the limelight, and he is not unaware that spymasters in both superpowers have risen to the top—his "good friend" the late Yuri V. Andropov in Moscow and President Bush in Washington.

His own emergence as a reformer, he insists, was not a metamorphosis. His position in the East German Ministry of State Security, where he headed foreign intelligence, gave him access to information and license to ponder the growing problems in his homeland.

And his wartime years spent in the Soviet Union left him friends among Russians who later emerged at the forefront of perestroika and glasnost, including Vladimir A. Kryuchkov, the man President Mikhail S. Gorbachev chose to head the K.G.B.

Through Mr. Kryuchkov, he knew what was happening inside Mr. Gorbachev's Moscow. And through him, Moscow evidently kept abreast of what was happening in East Germany.

"A year ago I was telling the Russians we could still turn things around here in respect to glasnost and perestroika," Mr. Wolf said in an interview, casually acknowledging a close working relationship with Moscow.

He was saying the same things at home. "From the beginning of this year I told all our leaders that this would happen," he said, reflecting on the dramatic demonstrations that had forced the Communist Party into retreat.

248

"I didn't know it would be so powerful, or that there was such pressure. But even a half year ago there was still a chance for the party to take charge of these events. As it turned out, it was impossible with the old leadership."

Mr. Wolf's public debut as a reformer was a book published this year. Called *The Troika,* it described the lives of three families who lived together in Moscow before World War II and followed separate paths during the war—the families of Mr. Wolf's father, Friedrich, the American historian Louis Fisher and Wilhelm Bloch, who fought in Hitler's army and ended up a businessman in West Germany. .

The biggest sensation, however, was that the celebrated spymaster took a highly critical view in the book of Stalinism, a view then still taboo in East Germany, and of East Germany's policies in the 1970's, when many artists were purged. Mr. Wolf became an overnight celebrity, now as a champion of change.

"The huge interest in my book was not linked to its content but to the new demand for the truth, not to hide past errors," he said. "These demands were very strong in the party. Whoever I met demanded change—I never met anyone, in fact, who did not demand fundamental reform. But we were unable to act in good time."

Mr. Wolf professes to be proud of the peaceful and disciplined way East Germans handled their quiet revolution.

"Gorbachev's was a revolution from above," he said. "Ours was from below. To those who know the history of Germany, this is a phenomenon, that the people have been so wise, so reserved."

His great regret, he insists, is that this initiative did not come from the party. He repeatedly refers to the Socialist Unity Party, as the East German Communist organization is formally known, as "my party," and when he talks of reform, he leaves no doubt that he is talking of changes that would preserve a Communist system.

"If we want to preserve socialism—and for that we'll fight—we must have a precise concept of how we should move ahead," he said.

Mr. Wolf said academics at Humboldt University in East Berlin were already at work on concepts for reforming the party and the economy, while the opposition, including New Forum, had no expertise in these matters.

"If the leadership of the party is capable of again taking charge of the party, I'm convinced the party will not disappear," he said.

In an interview with West German television on Monday night, however, Mr. Wolf acknowledged that the Communist Party might eventually be forced into opposition. "Considering that most opposition groups are aiming at some kind of socialism, whatever they understand by socialism, we might have to say goodbye to the thought that the future of socialism has to be bound to one single party," he said.

Mr. Wolf does not exclude his former organization from the need for change. He outlined several changes he would demand, including examination of every reported violation of law by the State Security organization and compensation for its victims; a "new thinking, especially in regard to dissidents," and tight controls over the security apparatus.

Rehabilitating the State Security apparatus stands to be a major challenge. The hated Staasi have been a major target of virtually every demonstration, and Mr. Wolf himself faced prolonged jeers when he rose to address the demonstration on November 4.

"Workers of my former ministry must appear in public and fight for public confidence," he said. "If the public believes that this organization really takes care of state security, and that the rights of individuals are protected, it should accept it."

Only in Rumania did it appear that the old guard was in full control.

In Rumania, the Old Order Won't Budge
By Alan Riding

BUCHAREST, RUMANIA, Nov. 24—In a huge display of government control, tens of thousands of workers were marched to a demonstration here today to celebrate the reelection of President Nicolae Ceausescu as General Secretary of the Communist Party.

But while flags fluttered cheerfully amid a sea of posters of Mr. Ceausescu and his wife, Elena, and of banners proclaiming the people's joy, the Government was unable to inject the least enthusiasm into the crowd, which stood solemnly in the cold awaiting the chance to go home.

Until the 71-year-old President had spoken, though, burly secret policemen, militiamen and members of the Patriotic Guard blocked all exits to the plaza in front of the Communist Party headquarters to insure that no one left. Finally, after a four-hour wait for a 10-minute message. the ritual was over.

Like everything else that occurred during this week's Communist Party Congress, the demonstration had gone as planned. Not a squeak of dissidence was heard, and tonight Rumanians could see television pictures of "the people" expressing gratitude for Mr. Ceausescu's willingness to remain in charge.

Earlier, the party congress also dutifully elected a new 467-member Central Committee, which named a 47-member executive committee, which in turn picked Mr. Ceausescu as party leader. The votes took place behind closed doors, but it was later announced that each election was unanimous.

The composition of the executive committee, which is equivalent to the Politburo in other Communist countries, and Mr. Ceausescu's final address to the congress both confirmed what had long been expected: After 24 years of what is known here as the Ceausescu Era, nothing had changed.

Only two new full members of the executive committee were named. As in the recent past, Emil Bobu, a longtime Communist leader, was listed immediately after Mr. Ceausescu, while Elena Ceausescu was ranked third in the party hierarchy. The President's son, Nicu, was also reelected as an alternate member of the committee.

In his closing speech to the 3,500-member congress, Mr. Ceausescu said the party had prepared a 20-year program that would lead the country to "shining horizons" as "multilaterally developed socialism" is strengthened. "By the beginning of the third millennium, we will be ready for the next stage, which is Communism," he said.

In contrast to his opening address on Monday, when he referred disapprovingly to those socialist governments that favor moving toward capitalism, Mr. Ceausescu avoided even indirect reference to events elsewhere in Eastern Europe today. But he stressed the need for "still greater unity" in the country's Communist Party.

In a meeting with foreign delegates attending the Congress on Thursday, though, he reiterated his call for the annulment of the Hitler-Stalin pact that led to the redefinition of some European frontiers, including those of Rumania with the Soviet Union, at the beginning of World War II.

Referring to the coming meeting off Malta between President Bush and the Soviet President, Mikhail S. Gorbachev, he added: "That is why today, too, mankind is highly sensitive to a possible new accord between the United States and the Soviet Union to the detriment of other peoples. And you know well that this is something of concern to many states."

In his address to the Congress today, he focused on internal affairs, leaving no doubt that he planned to continue ruling Rumania indefinitely. "Almost sixty years ago I first joined the party," he said, "and in the future I will always be a soldier in the ranks of the Rumanian Communist Party."

Interrupted constantly by well-orchestrated applause and chants of "Ceausescu Heroism! Rumanian Communism!" he went on: "The job of General Secretary is not honorific but one of great responsibility. It is not easy to be General Secretary of a party that wants to construct socialism. But I will respond with all my strength."

If at times the congress seemed to respond to him more out of discipline than spontaneity, the short, graying party chief gave every impression of believing what he was saying, holding up the "golden dream" of Communism with the energy and emotion of a fundamentalist preacher.

When the rousing sound of the Communist Party's anthem was piped into the congress hall, only Mr. Ceausescu seemed to be singing, drumming his fingers on the podium and waving his right arm to the rhythm of the song as if each epic phrase was something to be taken literally.

As the Czechoslovaks marched and threatened strikes and as the East German Communists purged their more prominent leaders, the Hungarians went about the business of dismantling communist forms. Earlier in the year the party removed its hard-line leader and then voted to abandon its communist name, effectively declaring itself bankrupt. Now the whole country was voting in a referendum to determine the manner in which it would choose its President. At issue was whether the planned free election was to take place before or after countrywide balloting to elect a parliament in fully competitive multiparty elections. The ruling party, the successor to the Communists, were hoping to have the presidential vote before those elections, when they would still control Parliament. To that end they were favoring a boycott of the referendum; if less than 50 percent of the electorate voted, then the results would be nullified, enabling them to be free to pursue their own schedule.

Hungarians Hold First Free Vote in 42 Years, Shunning a Boycott
By Henry Kamm

BUDAPEST, Nov. 26—In the first free national vote in 42 years, Hungarians went to the polls today for a referendum on when a presidential election will be held.

Contrary to pessimistic forecasts, they did so in sufficient numbers to make the referendum valid, insuring the failure of the ruling party's silent boycott of the referendum. The vote was forced by some of the country's new opposition groups, although it was opposed by others. . . .

Participation of at least half of Hungary's 7.8 million voters was required to make the referendum valid. Two hours after most polling stations closed, the national election commission announced that an estimated 53.6 percent of eligible voters took part.

Election officials said many people were unfamiliar with voting procedures and asked how to fill out the ballots. After four decades of one-party rule by the Communists, some even asked what answers to give to the questions on the timing of the election. . . .

And when the votes were counted, it was clear that the voters had dealt another rebuff to those who had so recently been Communist but were now calling themselves something else.

Hungarians Reject Election Timetable of the Ruling Party
By Henry Kamm

BUDAPEST, Nov. 27—Voters rejected the election timetable of the ruling party by the narrowest of margins in a referendum on Sunday, forcing it to abandon its plan to elect the first President of the republic while it retained full control of the Government.

In today's counting of Hungary's first free national vote since World War II, a narrow Government lead wilted steadily until Minister of State Imre Pozsgay conceded that the opposition proposal to delay the presidential voting had carried the day. Mr. Pozsgay was to have been the ruling party's presidential candidate. Under the plan adopted by the Communist-controlled Parliament, presidential elections would have been held on January 7, before a new, democratically chosen Parliament is elected. Parliamentary elections are to be held by June, with late March considered the most likely time.

The ruling party, which until last month was known as the Communist Party, has renamed itself the Socialist Party in an effort to remain in power despite the unpopularity of Communists in Hungarian society.

"We can be certain that the number of yes votes was higher than the no votes," Mr. Pozsgay said at a news conference. A yes vote was in favor of delaying the presidential election.

The mechanics of the referendum were complicated. The most important question the voters were asked to decide was whether the presidential election proposed for January 7 should proceed.

A turnout of less than 50 percent, regardless of the vote outcome, would have meant that the referendum was null and that the election would be held as scheduled in January.

Once it was clear that enough people had voted to validate the referendum, the question became whether they would confirm the election date or vote it down, in effect delaying the choice of a President until after Parliament is elected.

The cancellation of the January 7 election works in favor of the opposition and against the Government and its candidate, Mr. Pozsgay. If he had been able to run in January, he would have had the advantages of incumbency of the Government and party.

Now the choice of President appears to go to a new Parliament, once it is elected. Most of the opposition feels that this will make it easier for the opposition to field and elect its own candidate.

As Mr. Pozsgay conceded defeat, the official count still showed the no votes ahead with 50.2 percent of those counted. But the Hungarian state radio said that in the final count the yeses would carry by a few thousand.

"It's an enormous victory," said Miklos Haraszti, a leader of the Alliance of Free Democrats, the party that had imposed the referendum on the Government.

The Free Democrats, supported by three other parties, opposed the Government's schedule on the ground that it was undemocratic to choose so important an official while the ruling party still controlled all essential offices and access to state-run television and most of the press. . . .

In Prague, it was still too early for formal referendum, so opinions were being registered by shouts of acclamation, placards and graffiti.

If the Party Has Its Back to the Wall, It's a Wall with New Posters on It

By Esther B. Fein

PRAGUE, Nov. 26—The underground press is thriving in Prague these days. The rare clandestine documents of previous generations have given way to a flood of homemade handbills and posters that adorn the city's walls and windows, subway cars and stations.

If you want to know what is going on in Prague, you have to read the walls, and the windows, and the sidewalks, and the railings, and the bumpers of city buses, all of which are covered with print.

Typed by students on home computers and typewriters, or in some cases hand painted, this "subway samizdat" has been the most effective means of spreading the word about the opposition movement and of informing the public about coming events like today's human chain, Saturday's mass at St. Vitus Cathedral and the weekend change of venue for a daily demonstration.

Even the subway workers have got involved. Today, announcers in the stations let people know the time and place of the rally where people were to hold hands and form chains of human solidarity. The announcers, who normally give the routings of trains, added the information that subway workers would be honoring the general strike from noon till 2 P.M. on Monday.

"It's a war on walls," said Jan Urban, one of the leaders of Civic Forum, the recently formed umbrella opposition group. "In a system where the state owns and controls the mass media, this is the only way to begin a campaign against the regime." . . .

In the last 48 hours, state television has metamorphosed from a tool of the Government into a vehicle for the opposition. The daily mass rallies are televised live and uncensored, including calls for an end to the Communist Party monopoly on political power. The television even broadcast an interview with Ivan Lendl, the tennis star who defected from Czechoslovakia and now lives in the United States, saying he would be delighted to return for a visit if true change took root here.

But the most innovative and provocative program is one shown on a television set placed in the window at the Magic Lantern Theater, headquarters for the Civic Forum, and on one in the window at the Gallerie Manes, an art studio and another informal gathering place for dissidents.

Both sets offer regular showings of a student-produced video that depicts the violent breakup by police of a student demonstration on Friday, November 17. The video also shows the daily rallies in Wenceslas Square that followed that night of violence. Also included are interviews with opposition leaders and snippets from the official press that have been exposed as lies.

These new forms of expression, which just two weeks ago would have been cause for arrest, have become so widespread and accepted that a worker who attended the Prague Communist Party meeting on Saturday said he overheard one member of the leadership asking another what time today's demonstration was scheduled for.

"I don't know," the official was overheard to say. "Why don't you go outside and check the wall?" . . .

There is a small, poignant sign of the new mood here on the faces of public clocks in town. Many have been deliberately stopped at 5 minutes before 12, and there are posters around showing a clock with its hands in the same position.

"It is a symbol that time is up for the Communist Party," explained Petr Krechler, a student who has been attending the daily rallies. "It's time for a new shift to come on.". . .

Since the days of Franz Kafka into the time of Milan Kundera, Prague has been a literary city. Its best known dissident, Vaclav Havel, is a playwright known for works of irony. Therefore it was not so strange that a longtime resident used the imagery of fiction to explain that for the last forty years, since Communists came to power here, people have become soured, feeling like a woman forced to marry the wrong man.

"It is like a young woman who is very much in love but she is made to marry another man," said the woman. "But she lives, she has children and she carries on in a kind of muted way, as if it were a normal life, even though in her heart, she knows it isn't normal. Then one day she sees her youthful lover on a bridge and suddenly, she comes alive.

"We are like that woman, and our lover may still be on the other side of the bridge, but at least he is now visible."

Millions of Czechoslovaks Increase Pressure on Party with Two-Hour General Strike

By R. W. Apple, Jr.

PRAGUE, Nov. 27—Millions of Czechs and Slovaks walked off their jobs and into the streets at midday today, bringing Prague and the rest of the country to a standstill. It was a powerful demonstration of national solidarity in support of free elections and opposition to Communist domination.

Rivers of people flowed down boulevards and into main squares, not only here and in Bratislava, the nation's second city, but also in Brno and Ostrava and Rosice, industrial towns where the party ruled supreme until a week or so ago.

The meticulously organized and nonviolent general strike, which lasted from noon to 2 P.M., seemed a stunning rebuke to the Communists, whose legitimacy as a party is rooted in the support of those who laid down their tools in protest today. It was the largest outpouring of dissent in this country of 15 million people since February 1948, when demonstrations orchestrated by the Communists toppled what was then the only functioning multiparty democratic government in Eastern Europe.

"It has become an unstoppable wave," a senior Western diplomat said after viewing the throngs. "One wants to avoid overexcitement, but the party has clearly fallen apart, except for some cardboard faces who meet every other day. It has no program and no response to the strike, except wishing it away. Now it is in danger of crumbling like the Polish party and finding itself excluded from power altogether."

The Communist leadership, appearing to lose strength by the hour, seemed to be moving closer to talks with Civic Forum, the new opposition group led by Vaclav Havel, the playwright and longtime dissident, who was repeatedly jailed by the Communist authorities in the 21 years after the crushing of the liberal Government led by Alexander Dubcek.

Seeking to keep the pressure on while at the same time trying to reflect a sense of responsibility, Civic Forum said in a statement issued tonight that it would negotiate with the Government if the Government responded positively on Tuesday to its demands but that, if not, it would call for the Government's resignation. The statement said the organization had "come to the conclusion that the original demands made by Civic Forum have essentially been met or are being met," and it was time to move on to larger issues, like the Communist monopoly on power.

"What is needed is a cooling down of emotions," said Vaclav Maly, a spokesman for the Forum, but he and other representatives of the group said they could restart strikes and demonstrations at once if the negotiations proved fruitless.

It seemed highly unlikely that the talks could await the special Communist Party congress scheduled for January 26 that was announced Sunday night.

A second shake-up in the Politburo in three days, announced late Sunday night, appeared to have done nothing to halt the momentum of the opposition. Three hard-liners were dropped, leaving only one hard-liner and two relatively moderate members of the old guard on the thirteen-member body. Seven new members were named, including three or four who back pluralism in one way or another.

Prague Evening, the newspaper of the city community committee, said the party could not survive because it had no program.

Rude Pravo, the organ of the national party, spoke of the paralysis of the Central Committee and of "political mummies" who were blocking action. It urged the party to prepare for "free democratic elections" by developing a new program "that will be supported by all."

On a new television program called *The Government Speaks to You,* ministers said that they favored a free-market economy—yet another departure from party orthodoxy.

Some Communist elements, including grass-roots organizations, still seemed prepared to fight for survival, and Karel Urbanek, the new party leader, appeared on television tonight, urging a group of miners to stand fast.

But Prime Minister Ladislav Adamec—who seems to have become a rival of sorts to Mr. Urbanek and whose job is believed by some to be in jeopardy as a result—has already begun negotiations with Civic Forum, and is to report to the group on Tuesday on the Politburo's reaction to its demands.

Bitter strife between hard- and soft-line factions was reported at Sunday night's Politburo meeting, but no one proposed using violent means to suppress the demonstrations. Government figures said no one had urged that since last Friday, when the party leadership started to crack.

It was hard even to spot a Communist between noon and 2 P.M.

today. A whole nation seemed to be in the streets, with more than 900 factories and other businesses closed, urban mass transit halted everywhere and only hospitals, nursing homes, food stores and a few other enterprises continuing to operate.

At exactly noon, the lights went off and doors clanged shut in cafés, bookstores, souvenir shops and airline offices around Old Town Square, a baroque complex in central Prague considered one of the most beautiful architectural settings in Europe. High in the fantastic turrets of Tyn Church, a deeply toned melancholy bell tolled.

In the middle of the square, hundreds of young women with babies in carriages gathered around the statue of Jan Hus, the religious reformer. They had been sent there, where they could be protected, lest the babies be hurt in the crush elsewhere.

The pressure was greatest in Wenceslas Square, but there were throngs as well on Narodni Avenue, where the country's leading actors and actresses gathered to wave to the strikers and shout encouragement.

The distinctive Czechoslovak flag—a blue triangular field at the left, with a band of white and a band of red on the right—hung from balconies, fluttered from poles and decorated windows everywhere. Flag-colored ribbons were pinned to every lapel and even to the collars of dogs.

On every window—even that of the Beryiozka, a restaurant run by the Soviet Government, even that of the headquarters of Cedok, the state travel agency there were signs announcing "Generalni Stavka," general strike.

In Bratislava's main square, they danced. In the old ghetto in Prague, high school students marched beneath their banners, chanting slogans of freedom as they passed historic synagogues. At the Inter-Continental Hotel, they hauled down the foreign flags in the courtyard and ran Czechoslovak flags up all ten poles. A convoy of taxicabs, lights on and horns honking, snaked through the streets of the capital. . . .

"Today's events show that the whole nation supports the students," one of their leaders, Martin Mejstrik, said in a speech this afternoon.

State television carried pictures of the strike from all over the country—from the brewing town of Ceske Budejovice in Bohemia, the mining town of Banska Bystrica in the Tatra Mountains, and from Kavci Hory, the mountain overlooking Prague where the television transmitters are situated.

In East Germany, the disclosures about the private lives of the party oligarchs brought cries of shame and calls for punishment.

Where East Berlin's Elite Lived It Up

By David Binder

WANDLITZ, EAST GERMANY—For the last three decades, the ladder to the top of what might sarcastically be called a workers' paradise ended here in a heavily wooded compound surrounded by a 1.5-mile concrete wall. The compound was the home of the 23-member Communist Politburo that ruled this country until six weeks ago.

It was something highly unusual in the Communist world, a ghetto for the elite designed to protect the leadership from any rebellion or terrorist action.

The order for its construction a few miles north of the capital came from Walter Ulbricht, who ruled the German Democratic Republic from its inception until he was ousted in 1971. His successor as Communist Party chief and head of state was Erich Honecker, who was deposed on October 17 as a result of mass demonstrations across the country and the sudden flight—at that time illegal—of close to 200,000 citizens to the West.

The rationale for the compound encompassing 23 houses, a small department store, medical clinic, swimming pool and movie theater, as explained here today by a state security officer, was "the events in Hungary in 1956 and other factors that resulted from the cold war."

Although Gunter Wolf, who ranks as a lieutenant general in East Germany's State Security Service, did not touch on the subject, one of those Cold War factors was the popular uprising of June 17, 1953, which compelled Mr. Ulbricht and fellow members of the Communist leadership to flee East Berlin in the trucks of the Soviet Army, some riding to safety in Potsdam, others flying all the way to Moscow.

The Hungarian uprising, in which a number of Moscow loyalists were killed, was not something the East German leaders wanted repeated here.

Completed in early 1961, the so-called Wandlitz Residential Object Forest Settlement was in some ways a forerunner of the Berlin wall: the border fortifications begun on August 13, 1961, to seal in East Germany.

The difference is that the wall around Wandlitz, guarded at all times by 24 armed soldiers of the Feliks E. Dzerzhinsky regiment, named for Lenin's secret police chief, is painted forest green. The Berlin wall was not painted, except for graffiti.

In the low fog that hangs over the slush of a late German November, the Wandlitz wall is scarcely visible among the thick stand of white and red pines, beeches, birches and rhododendrons here.

So, how well did the Communist elite live all these years? The department store had Western electronic products and clothes and cosmetics and toiletries that were unavailable to the general East German public until last month. The narrow elite of 23 families wanted for nothing. Two maids were provided free for each house. The rents ranged from 300 to 600 marks a month, or $168 to $336 at the official exchange rate. They could choose to view Western movies banned for the East German public.

What is surprising about Wandlitz, which is the name of the nearest village on this sandy flatland, is its banality. It is as if every member of Germany's petite bourgeoisie had voted on the architecture and furnishings: red-tile roofs topping cream-colored stucco two-story houses, a few marble tiles, parquet floors, big (but not picture) windows, pink tablecloths in the restaurant and artificial palms and magnolias on the edges of the modest swimming pool.

There are narrow asphalt roads, few toilets or bathrooms, gateposts but no fences for the houses, several aquariums with exotic fish and a bronze sculpture of a waitress carrying a tray under her right arm in front of the department store—sculptor unknown.

"As you see," General Wolf said, "no Italian marble, no silk wallpaper, no African wood." In fact, he said, everything to be seen now in the Wandlitz was "made in the German Democratic Republic."

Only two members of the past and current Politburo are living here now, Gerhard Schurer and Werner Jarowinsky, and they are moving out soon, General Wolf said. Mr. Honecker and other former members of his Politburo will leave "soon," he said.

"It can only help us to expose this," General Wolf said. "I accompanied Erich Honecker on almost all of his foreign journeys, and I can tell you that I have seen far more luxury in foreign capitals than you see here. I was there at the home of the President of Mexico in Mexico City. He had a whole stable of horses. I can only say that, compared with that, we are, as we say, in German, orphans."

The lieutenant general, a slender man in his 60's, said that since he had been under military orders, he could not and did not raise his voice against the practices of Wandlitz. He said he was unable to estimate what the compound had cost because the files were in the hands of the ministerial consul of East Germany. But he estimated that its upkeep ran into several hundred thousand marks a year.

Until today, only a handful of foreigners had been allowed through Wandlitz's modernistic blue-and-black-painted gates. Last week, the Government admitted hordes of journalists from the country's Communist news media.

"The situation for us, women and men in Wandlitz, is not easy," General Wolf said.

They were marching and remonstrating all over the lands over which the Soviet empire had held sway since war's end. Old satraps who had ruled in ways learned from Moscow were being toppled and the dogma and ideology they had intoned were being ridiculed. In the heart of the empire, Mikhail Gorbachev, the man who had urged the old satraps to reform, now seemed concerned that too much might be changing.

Marxism Will Revive, Gorbachev Insists
By Bill Keller

MOSCOW, Nov. 26—Faced with a growing clamor from Communist Party conservatives, President Mikhail S. Gorbachev published a manifesto today insisting that Marxism will be revived in the Soviet Union, and under the leadership of the Communist Party.

With Communist governments in headlong retreat throughout Eastern Europe, the document, spread across two full pages of *Pravda*, was apparently intended to reassure the party faithful at this uneasy juncture that Communism is not collapsing, at least not here.

"Today we face the difficult challenge of reviving the authority of Marxist thought, the Marxist approach to reality," he wrote, and asserted that "at this complex stage" the party must keep its monopoly on political power.

Mr. Gorbachev described his goal as "humane socialism," a clear echo of the "socialism with a human face" promoted by the Communist liberalizers of the Prague Spring in Czechoslovakia in 1968.

Mr. Gorbachev's manifesto—essentially his revisionist view of Marxism—seemed intended to counter conservatives, who have recently shown signs of trying to consolidate their forces against what they view as heresies in the party.

Tonight, the central television showed excerpts from a rally sponsored last week by Leningrad party leaders in which the crowd poured out their anger at the Politburo and legislature for tolerating a drift toward capitalism.

As the crowd waved banners denouncing private businessmen as "crooks" and warning Mr. Gorbachev, "Mikhail Sergeyevich, pay attention to the party," speakers bitterly lamented the party's loss of authority.

"Maybe we're in this situation because of the coldbloodedness and absence of emotions that prevail in our Politburo," yelled one speaker.

The Politburo has had its chance, shouted another, "now let us steer."

Aleksandr N. Yakovlev, a Politburo member who is Mr. Gorbachev's senior ally in rethinking Communism, appeared to have the Leningrad gathering in mind when he told a Soviet television interviewer tonight that the country must guard against "these dangerous conservatives."

"When they say, 'let us steer,' sometimes I wonder if they're really saying, 'let us shoot,' " Mr. Yakovlev said.

In addition to the restive party regulars, Mr. Gorbachev has recently witnessed the growing influence of new "worker fronts." These groups, backed by party and trade union functionaries, are demanding protection against the economic insecurity certain to come with moves toward a market economy.

Responding to this new lobby, the Soviet legislature last week approved a freeze on the prices of soap, nylons, cigarettes and other consumer goods.

Mr. Gorbachev's article in the party newspaper was presented as "a synthesis and development" of several recent speeches, and was aimed at emphasizing his program's Marxist-Leninist roots and working-class orientation.

He said, however, that Lenin might have been wrong about one central point of his philosophy, that there can be no intermediate phase between capitalism and socialism.

This was Mr. Gorbachev's most explicit suggestion that the "new socialism" he has in mind for the Soviet Union will be a hybrid, incorporating aspects of capitalism.

Such speeches have little appeal to those who favor more far-reaching changes and who chafe at Mr. Gorbachev's caution. But the Soviet leader seems to feel a need to shore up his defenses against the conservatives as he heads off on visits to Italy and the Vatican and prepares for his Malta meeting next weekend with President Bush.

The article appeared as the Polish Prime Minister, Tadeusz Mazowiecki, the first non-Communist to lead a government in the Soviet bloc, was leaving Moscow after a remarkably warm reception, and as the Communist Party in Czechoslovakia was wobbling under public pressure.

Often criticized for falsely raising public expectations of quick results, Mr. Gorbachev today conceded that the remaking of socialism "is a process that will stretch beyond the decade into the 21st century."

For Kremlinologists, the television interview with Mr. Yakovlev tonight was a tantalizing hint of further shifts in the Politburo.

Mr. Yakovlev, regarded as Mr. Gorbachev's main intellectual ally, is nominally in charge of foreign affairs. But his comments tonight dealt exclusively with ideology, a portfolio that belongs to the more conservative Vadim A. Medvedev.

Mr. Medvedev has recently been under open attack for trying to fire the editor of the country's most popular newspaper, and for intervening to limit the freedoms outlined in a new draft law on the press.

As in East Germany, the crowds in Prague also prevailed.

Czechoslovakia's Moment in Time
By Serge Schmemann

PRAGUE, Nov. 28—It seemed somehow appropriate that when the old regime in Czechoslovakia formally agreed to cede its monopoly on power, the deed was done between a caretaker Prime Minister and an opposition lacking even a formal headquarters.

So dizzyingly swift was the downfall of Milos Jakes and his associates in the Communist leadership that when Prime Minister Ladislav Adamec met today with Vaclav Havel and the other opposition leaders of the Civic Forum, the participants seemed to be sweeping away some unpleasant remnants before plunging into the next and far more complex phase in the shaping of a post-Communist Czechoslovakia.

As a Civic Forum representative told a news conference today, "The meeting of the demands today is just a recognition of the de facto situation on the part of the Government."

To be sure, much remained to be resolved and prepared. Mr. Adamec's pledge to delete the "leading role" of the Communist Party from the Constitution still left the Communist apparatus very much in place, running the factories, schools, courts and Government bureaus. There were still free elections to secure, ministries to fill, economic plans to forge.

But the vast force of humanity so strikingly mobilized over a week and a half of demonstrations and yesterday's two-hour general strike—a power manifest in the red, white and blue ribbons worn by every second Czechoslovak, in the flags decorating every house, in the myriad notices plastered to the shop windows of Prague and in the jubilant air pervading the old capital—seemed to preclude any chance of a comeback by the old guard.

Twenty-one years earlier, it required Soviet tanks to stifle the Prague Spring reform period. Now the Kremlin seemed almost irrelevant, Russians totally absent from the demonstrations or the slogans except for the rare tribute to Mikhail S. Gorbachev. And without Moscow, the old guard had proven to be only a flimsy facade.

Just as the Czechoslovaks followed their neighbors in the march to freedom, so too did they copy them in savoring their moment of triumph. Like the East Germans dancing through the newly opened Berlin wall, or the Hungarians cheering the restoration of the republic, Czechoslovaks also found themselves at that euphoric moment in their revolution before the heady wine of freedom began to exact its inevitable price.

The glow was almost tangible in the streets. People seemed unusually polite, even affectionate toward one another. At an impromptu public discussion in the small Ypsilon studio theater, an actor drew laughs when he said he saw a tram grind to a halt and come back in reverse to pick up a tardy passenger.

Students went around to shops with razor blades and sponges to rub off dated notices from among the hundreds plastered in virtually every shop window. Others posted large signs urging people not to spray-paint slogans onto walls.

"Democracy is fine," said 21-year-old Pavel Strida as he looked at the word "democracy" sprayed onto a stucco wall, "but it's the people who will have to clean and repaint the walls."

The Czechoslovak colors seemed to be everywhere, demonstrating a welling up of national pride. The symbol for the Civic Forum, the umbrella group of the opposition, included a leaf from the national tree—the lime in its design.

"Before this, I was afraid of what would come next, afraid that we would become poor like the Poles," Mr. Strida said. "Our professor told us recently that our country was turning into a memorial display of Communism. But now we have taken our own way."

At any rate, they had taken the first step along the way, shedding the yoke of a system that had dragged Czechoslovakia from the front ranks of industrialized Europe to the sidelines.

But already now, even while the Civic Forum searched for a head-quarters and Mr. Adamec looked for new ministers, the faint outlines of the future were taking shape—pointing, many here thought, to a pluralistic social democracy and a market-oriented economy.

A central role in the future seemed likely for Walter Kamarek, the director of the Economic Forecasting Institute, who had argued for years that Czechoslovakia needed to inject market forces and to accept democratic pluralism if it was to reform its economy.

Another economist, Vladimir Karlez of the Academy of Sciences, was reported preparing a plan for the opening of the economy to domestic entrepreneurs and foreign investors.

How Czechoslovakia would fare in a post-Communist order was, at this stage, impossible to predict. But in comparison with Poland, Hungary and East Germany, at least, it seemed reasonably well positioned.

Czechoslovakia could not boast of East Germany's special links to a prosperous Western patron. But that also safeguarded it from the rush for West German marks and goods that has seized the East Germans since the border between the two Germanys fell open.

A well-developed industrial base, even one allowed to grow decrepit under forty years of Communist mismanagement, still afforded the Czechoslovaks a disciplined labor force and a base to build on.

With the population at a manageable 15 million and a foreign debt nowhere near the level of Hungary's or Poland's, Czechoslovakia seemed free of imminent economic crisis.

And a rich cultural tradition, coupled with a lingering faith in socialism, seemed to preclude any major social problems—at least in the immediate future.

The very swiftness of its revolution seemed to be in Czechoslovakia's favor. Though the bloodshed during the police attacks on November 17 still hung heavy in the public memory, the subsequent pace of events gave these days an improvisational character that seemed to sustain idealism and a party-like atmosphere.

There was not the fatigue of Poland's long series of strikes, nor the demoralizing exodus of East Germany. Rather, there was still energy to burn and the glow on the horizon was still bright.

By one of those lovely quirks so prevalent in these heady days, Civic Forum was given the Magic Lantern experimental theater for its temporary headquarters. For their evening news conferences, leaders of the opposition sat before a newly built set representing the last tunnel of the Minotaur—a maze guarded by a mythical creature with the head of a bull and the body of a man—with the light at the end of it glowing behind.

They had not planned it that way, nor had the theater, nor had Czechoslovakia. But in the spirit of the moment, improvisation and destiny seemed to blend in wondrous ways.

And, in the city that was Kafka's birthplace, the bargain was sealed by an often-imprisoned ironic playwright.

Prague's Unlikely Collaborators for Change: Party Stalwart and Ex-prisoner Havel, Often-Jailed Dramatist, Became Symbol of Dissent
By Serge Schmemann

PRAGUE, Nov. 28—If proof is needed that the pen is mightier than the sword, then Vaclav Havel is a veritable smoking gun.

In and out of prisons over the last twenty years, his plays banned in his native land, the playwright today accepted the figurative surrender of his tormentors at a meeting with Prime Minister Ladislav Adamec.

In a coincidence that seemed to close the symbolic circle, it was also today that *Rude Pravo*, the main party newspaper, announced that the Czech and Slovak ministries of culture had lifted twenty-year-old bans on many works of art, including the writings of Mr. Havel.

Mr. Havel, to be sure, did not achieve his role in a vacuum. There is a tradition in this part of the world that intellectual integrity and independent art translate into raw political power.

Writers and artists have played major roles in dissident movements in the Soviet Union and throughout Eastern Europe. In Prague, the release of censored works also freed, for example, the writings of Milan Kundera, and among several prominent Czechoslovaks returning from exile was an actor, Pavel Landovsky.

"In our country there has been a tradition since the nineteenth century that social movements were always ignited by the intelligentsia," Mr. Havel said in an interview in the current issue of the West German weekly magazine *Spiegel*. "That was the case in 1968, and this time is no different."

But few writers or intellectuals have been thrust to the forefront of their nation's destiny quite as dramatically as Mr. Havel, the sardonic 53-year-old playwright and essayist. As uncompromising in his resistance to the totalitarian state as he is in his ironic plays, he withstood censure, prison and the muzzle to become the premier symbol of Czech dissidence in the years after the Soviet Union intervened to crush the Prague Spring of 1968.

Active in 1968 as chairman of an unsanctioned Club of Independent Writers, he subsequently helped found the Charter 77 dissident movement and through his clashes with the authorities was repeatedly sent to prison.

Mr. Havel was on one of his stints in prison only last May, this time for trying to lay a wreath at the grave of Jan Palach, a student who burned himself to death when the Warsaw Pact forces invaded in 1968. As recently as a month ago, the police dragged Mr. Havel from his sickbed to put him in detention on the eve of anticipated demonstrations marking the October 28 National Day.

Now, at the huge demonstrations that have abruptly routed Czechoslovakia's neo-Stalinist regime, the crowds have chanted "Havel! Havel!" as the writer has proclaimed the demise of the system he fought with pen in hand and his willingness to join a government that would guide Czechoslovakia to democracy.

"If someone spends his life writing the truth without caring for the consequences, he inevitably becomes a political authority in a totalitarian regime," Mr. Havel said in the magazine interview. "I am willing, and may be able, to assume a role for a short time. This transitional phase may need symbolic representatives, who are not politicians but who represent the hopes of society."

What was good for democracy, however, was not conducive to his art. "I confess I'd like to arrange with the Interior Ministry to be free three days a week and to go to prison for two days a week to take a break from freedom," he said in the interview.

Vaclav Havel was born on October 5, 1936, in Prague, where his father was a well-to-do building contractor and restaurant owner. Legend holds that his father tried to evict the Soviet newspaper

Pravda from one of his buildings. Mr. Havel stlll lives in a building built by his father.

The "bourgeois" background blocked Mr. Havel in his education, and his early postwar years included work as a taxi driver and study of traffic-control automation. But from his early years he wrote, and in June 1967 he caused a stir at a writers' congress when he criticized as absurd censorship and the Communist apparatus.

After the 1968 invasion, he left Prague and settled in a remote farming village near Troutnova, where he worked in a brewery. His growing body of plays was banned across East Europe, but they rapidly gained him critical notice in the West.

Mr. Havel was among the chief theoreticians of the movement, and his essay setting out his ideas on national resurgence in a totalitarian state, "The Power of the Powerless," was widely studied inside and outside Czechoslovakia. In it, he argued that citizens "living in truth" could successfully confront and overturn dictatorial rulers.

His involvement with Charter 77 led to the first of Mr. Havel's several stints in prison. The longest was from October 1979 to February 1983, for founding a group called the Committee for the Defense of the Unjustly Persecuted and for "keeping up contacts with émigrés." He later collected the letters he wrote from prison to his wife in a widely read volume, *Letters to Olga.*

Last January, Mr. Havel was sentenced to eight months in prison for trying to lay the wreath at the tomb of Jan Palach. But after an international outcry, the sentence was reduced to four months.

The authorities also tried to get Mr. Havel to emigrate, but he refused. He refused even to travel abroad to accept international drama prizes in the Netherlands and Sweden for fear he might not be permitted to return home.

At one point, the recently ousted Communist Party leader, Milos Jakes, privately admitted that the harassment of the playwright had only made him better known. The comment was secretly taped and further added to Mr. Havel's renown.

Mr. Havel's plays—the better-known include *Protest, Temptation, The Saviors* and *Audience*—are generally marked by strong irony, which sometimes strikes audiences as absurdist.

Many of these satirical comedies center on the dumb mechanization of man in a totalitarian world. In an interview last March, Mr. Havel said his satires should not be understood as "satire coined to some concrete conditions," but rather as "parables for human life itself."

In a very short time Europe had become an uncertain place. As Communist power eroded, new possibilities emerged for those people and states that had until recently been subject to predictable rigors. Political aspirations often translated into geographic visions. The old postwar Europe was giving way to a new, not yet clearly defined continent. The shaping of this emerging Europe was proving to be the critical issue, supplanting earlier concerns with disarmament, the third world and regional conflicts. What were the competing visions of Europe that were forming in Moscow, in Western Europe and Washington as the binding force of Communism weakened?

Gorbachev's Hope for Future: "A Common European Home"
By Bill Keller

MOSCOW, Nov. 29—When it comes to the future of Europe, no one accuses President Mikhail S. Gorbachev of lacking vision.

The Soviet leader's vision—he calls it "a common European home"—is in some respects utopian. It has been shaped in large part by the tumult of events beyond the Kremlin's control, including economic desperation at home and explosive popular aspirations in Eastern Europe.

From the time Mr. Gorbachev first broached the "common home" notion on a visit to France in 1985, it has been regarded in the West as more a speechwriter's conceit than a basis for serious discussion.

But as Mr. Gorbachev and President Bush prepare to survey together the wreckage of the postwar order in Europe, both Soviet and Western specialists have begun to look more seriously at the Soviet leader's vision of what might replace it.

In interviews conducted as successive spasms of democracy struck Eastern Europe, Soviet officials and scholars and Western diplomats here said the West had not yet grasped the magnitude of what Mr. Gorbachev wants in Europe, of the overall vision toward which he would like to maneuver Mr. Bush in their meeting this week.

In effect, what Mr. Gorbachev seeks is a huge exchange, in which Moscow surrenders its costly ambitions of expansionism—at least beyond its postwar borders.

In return, Moscow wants admission to the club of Western industrial countries, bringing with it technology and a period of calm in which to focus on the problem that really threatens Soviet security:

an economy that cannot compete in the world or satisfy the growing wants of its own people.

"The common European home means decomposition of the empire, in our own interest," said Andranik Migranyan, an analyst at one of the most influential research groups, the Institute for the Economy of the World Socialist System.

"In the end, it means the return to a single European civilization," said Fyodor M. Burlatsky, chairman of the human rights panel of the parliamentary committee on foreign relations.

As Mr. Burlatsky suggests, this Europe is not so much a geographical concept as a cultural one—it means Western civilization, including the United States. What follows is a rough floor plan, based on these interviews and Mr. Gorbachev's own comments, of the Soviet leader's European home.

The first and most startling feature of this new Europe is the breakup of the Communist bloc.

"Of course, there is still a bloc of Eastern European states, in which the Soviet Union is clearly the most formidable partner," said a Western European diplomat. "But it is no longer uniformly Communist, and it seems even Communist parties within those countries are not bound by Moscow."

Although Soviet officials do not like to advertise it, they agree that the freedom of Eastern European countries to run their own affairs includes the right to reject Communism altogether, to adopt multiparty democracies and market economies and even to call themselves capitalists.

"Once you've determined the principle of freedom of choice, I don't see how any limit can be set," said a Foreign Ministry official, interviewed on the condition he not be named. "You cannot say 'This is socialism; this line you cannot cross.' "

Mr. Gorbachev has been increasingly categorical about a policy of noninterference in the internal affairs of his allies, and has backed up his words by accepting—even applauding—the dislodging of Communist regimes in Poland and Hungary.

"One can argue about the degree to which Gorbachev had a choice, and about his motives," said a Western diplomat. "But it is hard to make the case any longer that he doesn't mean it."

This diplomat speculates that if Mr. Gorbachev had any lingering qualms about a hands-off policy, they were erased this year as he watched the horrified reaction to China's suppression of its democracy movement, and the bitter domestic backlash after troops killed demonstrators in Soviet Georgia.

At the same time, Soviet officials and Western diplomats generally agree that Mr. Gorbachev had not engineered the tumbling of Eastern Europe's dominoes, nor foreseen the pace and sequence of events.

He has, rather, played the role of catalyst, both publicly, by opening a vigorous debate of Communism's failures at home, and privately, by making it clear Moscow would not intervene to prop up old regimes.

"A signal may be either indirect or indirect," Gennadi I. Gerasimov, the Foreign Ministry spokesman, observed the other day when asked to describe Moscow's role in Eastern Europe. "We are not waving a conductor's baton."

Perhaps the best metaphor for Mr. Gorbachev's approach to his restive allies is the opening of the Berlin wall.

Just as East Germany opened its borders to slow the headlong defection of its citizens—by assuring them they could wait awhile, size up the changes at home, and leave whenever they wanted—Mr. Gorbachev's policy is to open the bloc in hopes that the members will remain together voluntarily.

So far the more independent voices in Eastern Europe have been careful to pledge their allegiance to the Warsaw Pact and to the postwar boundaries of Europe—and not only because they worry how Moscow would respond if a country bolted from the pact.

"Now the governments in Poland and Hungary have changed," said Marshal Sergei F. Akhromeyev, the former chief of the armed forces general staff and now an adviser to Mr. Gorbachev in the Soviet legislature. "There are non-Communists at the heads of the governments. But the state interests of Poland and Hungary have remained the same, to a significant degree."

"First of all, there's the stability of the territory and state boundaries," he continued. "Second, there are the economic interests of the states. After all, they've been linked for many decades. That is why the military-political alliance remains."

The next stage, already under way, is a transformation of the eastern military and economic alliances—the Warsaw Pact and the Council for Mutual Economic Assistance.

While Soviets once talked of disbanding NATO and the Warsaw Pact simultaneously—a bluff the West did not take seriously—they now tend to agree that it is better to preserve the alliances for the foreseeable future, since on its own each country might be tempted to renew historical disputes with its neighbors.

In Mr. Gorbachev's vision, the military alliances that now face off across a central European front will evolve into political alliances, in which the military role has withered.

Beginning with a meeting of Warsaw Pact leaders in Bucharest, Rumania, last July, where the group for the first time declared a policy of noninterference in its members' internal affairs, the Eastern alliance has begun to take on some trappings of a more political, NATO-style fraternity.

According to Western and Soviet specialists, the Soviet side has signaled that it will accept changes in the Warsaw Pact Constitution that would ban use of troops in internal affairs, declare that the pact does not include promoting Communism, and make membership more equal and voluntary.

In the Soviet vision, the remaking of the pacts would include a rollback of military forces on both sides.

"The state interests of both alliances still remain, and the contradictions remain," Marshal Akhromeyev said. "And a certain quantity of arms and armed forces will remain. But what matters is that it be such a quantity which would not permit the country to start a war, even if it wanted to."

Mr. Akhromeyev and Mr. Gorbachev publicly insist these reductions must be mutual, worked out at the conventional arms talks under way in Vienna between the sixteen NATO allies and the seven members of the Warsaw Pact.

But among the Soviet researchers, some theorists now argue openly for more dramatic, one-sided moves.

Vladimir N. Chernega, vice rector of the diplomatic academy of the Soviet Foreign Ministry, suggests that the Soviet Union could withdraw its troops entirely from Eastern Europe without demanding that America match it.

"If the governments of Eastern Europe want it, we must withdraw our troops from their territory," he said, stressing that this was a personal opinion. "We can do this even unilaterally. As for American troops—I would leave that up to the Western European governments. I know that some circles in Western Europe feel their security is greater with American troops. It's an understandable position. Let them have it."

"We have a historical chance now and we have to make the most of it," he said. "In this context, a certain presence of Americans troops—a limited presence—poses no danger."

Like Mr. Gorbachev's own series of announced military budget cuts, "the pact will dissolve, that seems irreversible," said a Polish journalist who visited Moscow last week with Tadeusz Mazowiecki, Poland's new non-Communist Prime Minister. "So why waste our energy pushing it? The only thing we have to do is avoid posing a threat to the Soviet Union, and we are not that stupid."

"For us, this is not just reducing military spending and reallocating resources to civilian purposes," Mr. Chernega noted. "It is a matter of structural reorganization of our whole economy. Forty percent of our machine-tool industry and 75 percent of our spending on science go to the military. This is no basis for a normal economy."

Ultimately, after the withering of military confrontation, some Soviet analysts expect that some of the Soviet allies will become neutral-but-careful neighbors like Finland.

On his visit to Helsinki in October, Mr. Gorbachev hailed Finland as a model neighbor. Mr. Migranyan predicts that Finlandization of the Eastern bloc will come more quickly than anyone in the West anticipates.

Mr. Burlatsky, a legislator close to the leadership, is more cautious, but he says neutrality is entirely possible.

"If Austria can be neutral, then why not Hungary?" he said. "But that's in the future, after radical structural changes in the two blocs."

If the Warsaw Pact is being revamped, the Eastern economic alliance seems to be quickly coming apart, as budding market economies like Hungary and Poland find it harder to coexist with the older, planned economies.

The more market-minded members of the alliance, including the Soviet Union, are aggressively seeking to open new relationships with the European Community, and with individual Western countries.

But the Eastern European countries are so bound together by common backwardness and mutual trade dependencies that economic integration with the West may prove more difficult than reducing military confrontation.

"There is an asymmetry between the disintegration of Eastern Europe and the growing integration of Western Europe," Mr. Burlatsky said, noting the Western European countries' planned 1992 market consolidation.

"It seems there is a danger of Eastern Europe and the Soviet Union turning into an economic appendage of the West, a supplier of raw materials," he said. "That would create political problems, because a great superpower such as the Soviet Union will not feel comfortable in such a role."

Mr. Burlatsky argues for "a common market on the entire European continent," but he predicts a difficult decade or two before that is possible.

In the meantime, Mr. Gorbachev seems to accept, even welcome, the flow of Western credits, guarantees and investment to Eastern European countries. Although he warns against "exporting capitalism," he realizes that Western capital relieves him of an unbearable economic burden, and he hopes that it will help Eastern Europe become a bridge by which the Soviet Union can reach Western technology and markets.

Some portions of Mr. Gorbachev's design remain deliberately unfinished.

One is Germany. The Soviets are uneasy about the potential clout of a reunified Germany, and they are reluctant to be seen undermining the authority of their allies in East Berlin.

But some Soviet analysts say privately they are not alarmed about some new arrangement short of complete reunification, with security guarantees to reassure the neighbors.

And Soviet officials say they do not rule out reunification in the future, after "overcoming the division of Europe," as the Foreign Ministry spokesman Yuri Gremitskikh said today.

Another gray area in the blueprint is the fate of the Baltic republics, Lithuania, Latvia and Estonia, which yearn to rejoin Europe as independent states. Moscow is willing to concede these republics greater autonomy and closer economic links with the West, but balks at complete independence.

So far, most Western governments seem to accept this as Mr. Gorbachev's domestic problem, and they have not pressed him on behalf of the Baltics. But the three republics are pushing ahead without foreign encouragement.

The overriding question about Mr. Gorbachev's vision is how widely it is shared within the Soviet power structure. Clearly there are conservatives here who chafe at the retrenchment of Soviet power and the flouting of Communist verities, but they are understandably quiet about it.

Mr. Migranyan, for one, contends that the collapse of territorial ambitions has now very nearly reached the point where it would be impossible to reverse even if Mr. Gorbachev were replaced by a conservative.

"Even the most conservative government here will have to accept the changes in Eastern Europe," he said. "It would cost too much to reverse them."

The concerns and visions in Western Europe varied considerably.

Unease Fills Western Allies over Rapid Changes in East

By Craig R. Whitney

LONDON, Nov. 28—The joyous revolution of freedom sweeping Eastern Europe is confronting Western Europe with some of its gravest decisions in forty years.

Among the most daunting challenges is how to maintain the movement toward European unity if, as most Western European leaders expect, the West Germans become distracted from that old goal by the newly aroused prospects of achieving German unification—a vision spelled out by Chancellor Helmut Kohl in Bonn on Tuesday.

Another concern questions where the United States and the Soviet Union will fit in the suddenly shifting European landscape. Many Western Europeans think the natural course of events will bind them more closely to the new Soviet Union, which after all shares the same continent, and pry them loose from their security and economic ties to the United States.

The biggest worry of all, to many Europeans, is West Germany itself, increasingly inclined to take charge of its destiny in ways that would have been unthinkable a decade or even a year ago. Mr. Kohl, for example, outlined his ideas for German unification Tuesday without any prior consultation with his allies, though the United States, Britain and France share with the Soviet Union a treaty responsibility for "Germany as a whole" that dates back to 1945.

Conversations with politicians, business leaders, students, writers and ordinary people from Wales to West Berlin in recent weeks leave a clear impression of unease, a sense that without wise actions the dream come true in Eastern Europe could easily turn into unpleasant realities.

What is also becoming apparent is that rapid changes can bring long-submerged cultural, historical and political differences of the twelve members of the European Community to the surface. Indeed, this risk has appeared just as those nations are poised to eliminate the remaining trade barriers among their 320 million people by the end of 1992.

The unease is compounded by a feeling that Western leaders have not been saying what they really think about the central problem of a united Germany. For four decades, when reunification appeared impossible, all of them implicitly accepted it by saying that a truly free, united Europe, East and West, was the ultimate goal. Now that the reintegration of Europe and the Germanys no longer looks so distant, said Klaus Bolling, a former head of West Germany's mission to East Berlin, "We're seeing a tremendous outbreak of hypocrisy."

"It seems a little bit insulting to Germany to say that it needs to be anchored into Europe," Prime Minister Margaret Thatcher of Britain said on BBC television Monday night, clearly hoping to anchor the West Germans even more firmly with such expressed sentiments.

"I am not afraid of reunification," President François Mitterrand of France said in Bonn earlier this month. "If the Germans want to be a single nation in a single state, this must be founded on the will of the German nation, and nobody can oppose it." But officials in Paris now explain that what the President intended by the statement was to calm the fears of many French people over unification, and to encourage the Germans not to be distracted from the unfinished work of building the European Community.

Mr. Kohl tried to reassure other European leaders, in Paris on November 18, that West Germany saw "no alternative" but to work for German unity within the existing European context.

"We agreed not to raise the question of the existing borders," Mrs. Thatcher acknowledged, but diplomats in Bonn, Paris and London all agree that the reason German reunification was left off the agenda was the fear that forcing the issue could bring down President Mikhail S. Gorbachev, on whom they think all the fragile changes in the Soviet Union and Eastern Europe continue to depend. All the Western European leaders agreed over dinner in Paris on November 18 that Mr. Gorbachev was at a critical juncture and that they should do nothing to undermine his position.

Officially, reunification will not be on the agenda when President Bush sees Mr. Gorbachev off Malta this weekend, but hardly anyone in Europe thinks it can stay off forever.

"To talk about the breakup of NATO does no one any good at all," Mrs. Thatcher said Tuesday night. But questions are even beginning to surface at the popular level all over Western Europe about whether there will be any need for an American-dominated military alliance against possible Soviet attack, when or if that threat no longer exists.

Ordinary people, as well as their political leaders, sense that a historical turning point is being reached. "We thought we had everything perfect in the Common Market," said Janet Semper, who lives in Westminster Abbey with her husband, Colin, a resident canon there. "We were letting in one country at a time—Spain, Portugal, Greece, and then in comes this wonderful rabble through the Berlin wall and now we have to rethink the whole thing."

"The instant the Berlin wall comes down, France is no longer the center of Europe—it's on the periphery," said François Barbey, a 48-year-old real estate salesman in Paris. "People say we've won. We've come to the end of one world, but we haven't found the key to the next."

John le Carré, whose master spy George Smiley got his Soviet counterpart, Karla, to defect across the Berlin wall in his 1980 novel, *Smiley's People,* put it this way in a recent essay: "Smiley had won, as the West has won now. But the sweets of victory elude us—as they eluded Smiley, partly because he had forgotten what he was fighting for, partly because he feared that his masters preferred the comforts of permanent aggression to the hardship of new choices and alignments."

"We really invent the enemies we need," the novelist, whose real name is David Cornwell, explained later. "We could be making the discovery that Russia, once the military threat is removed, is a huge, untidy third world problem that will demand time, effort and money—lots of money—to fix. It could be a terrible headache."

To many people, the German question already is "I don't know what will become of this land," Mr. Bolling said in his home in West Berlin. "There'll be bound to be a cooling off vis-à-vis America as the prospect of a united Germany comes into view. Already the people of West Berlin are complaining about how the three allied military commanders have just bought ten new Mercedes cars with their money, and they're asking how much longer they have to go on paying for such things."

Already Lufthansa, the West German airline, is demanding that Britain, France and the United States relinquish their monopoly on flying between West Germany and West Berlin.

"The division into Eastern and Western Europe was a construction of the cold war," Heinz Ruhnau, Lufthansa's chairman, told *Die Welt* the day before the wall came down. "East and West have to recognize that their status positions can't be maintained any longer after forty years."

"We all want a relationship with the United States," said Sergio Romano, a former diplomat who was Italy's Ambassador to Moscow until earlier this year."But I imagine we would all prefer that it not be so hierarchical as it has been."

NATO diplomats in Brussels say that the organization, like the Warsaw Pact, will have to convert itself into an instrument for managing change and monitoring complex negotiated arms control agreements over the next few years, but in London, Paris and Bonn, diplomats complain that such thinking is only in its embryonic stage, and not well coordinated.

If events in Eastern Europe are only beginning to spark a rethinking of NATO's role, they have uncovered contradictions about the European Community that have existed since the Treaty of Rome established it in 1957. In those early days, President Charles de Gaulle of France insisted that Europe not be federation but a collection of sovereign, cooperating nation states. De Gaulle called it "l'Europe des patries," and used it as an excuse for keeping out Britain in the early 1960's, because he feared the British would turn the European Community into an Anglo-Saxon United States of Europe.

Now all the European leaders but one—the British Prime Minister—have agreed that the changes in the East require urgently forging ahead to more federalism in the community. "For the European Community to remain the center of gravity that it is, we must accelerate," said Jacques Delors, its executive president, two weeks ago.

Mrs. Thatcher wants to complete the 1992 program, but is wary of surrendering more British sovereignty to the community's executive commission in Brussels, which she says is not fully accountable to any democratic parliament. As Eastern European countries evolve toward political and economic democracy, her close advisers believe, the community should stay loose and flexible. "This isn't the time to become more exclusive," one of them explained.

"I do not believe in a federation of Europe, a United States of Europe," Mrs. Thatcher said again on television Monday. "I believe it will work far better if we cooperate together as twelve sovereign states."

French officials expect that Mrs. Thatcher will be alone in opposing a call at the next European Community summit in Strasbourg, France, December 8–9, for a conference that would consider changes in the Treaty of Rome to permit full monetary union, though they say they are not sure the Germans will not have developed second thoughts as well.

But if changes in the East continue, the European Community will no longer be limited to the twelve, and one of the main subjects on the agenda in Strasbourg will be how to respond to the clamor in Eastern Europe to get in on the prosperity.

The twelve agreed in principle in Paris earlier this month to provide economic aid to all Eastern European countries, but only if they make clear progress toward economic and political democracy. Separately or together, *Le Monde* calculated the other day, the Europeans and the other industrial democracies have given or pledged more than $6 billion in aid or loans to Eastern Europe, mainly Hungary and Poland, this year.

West German and French officials believe that Bonn is prepared to offer even more than that to East Germany. "It wouldn't be hard to make a success out of East Germany," one French diplomat observed. "It could be more prosperous than Portugal in five years."

The larger question behind this is whether Poland and Hungary, and now possibly East Germany and Czechoslovakia, should be allowed or encouraged to join the European Community, with associate membership as a first step.

"The E.C. already has various bilateral 'association agreements' with other countries; more can be struck in Eastern Europe as reform takes hold," *The Economist* newspaper wrote last week, a suggestion that was endorsed by Mrs. Thatcher. A former President of France, Valery Giscard d'Estaing, has suggested that the community tailor these association agreements country by country, and tie them to price reform, privatization and currency convertibility in each one.

Some European leaders speak of a Marshall Plan for Eastern Europe, with a leading role for the West; *Le Monde* said that Marshall aid from the United States from 1947 to 1948 totaled $13 billion, worth $171 billion today.

"A Marshall Plan now is impossible," Prof. Alfred Grosser, a French expert on Germany, said. "You have hardly anyone in the Soviet Union, and not many in Eastern Europe, who know how to manage a market economy."

In addition, all Eastern currencies have been pegged at wildly artificial rates against Western ones for years, and to get them down to realistic exchange values will be painful. In West Germany, the mark, now one of the world's strongest currencies, was introduced in June 1948 at a rate of one for every 10 old German reichsmarks, causing tremendous resentment and pain until people regained confidence in their money and the economy started functioning again.

Representatives of 24 industrial democracies, including the European Community, the United States, Japan and South Korea, will meet in Brussels on December 13 for more discussions about how to help. "The socialist models are collapsing," said François Perigot, head of the French employers' federation in Paris. "If all they get from our system is black markets, petty corruption, unemployment and social indifference, they could turn away from our model. Europe shouldn't give them a bad example."

But essentially Europe is confused. No journalist, politician, professor or economic expert saw that change would come so suddenly to so many countries all over the East. What has happened has left many of them in breathless bewilderment.

All ordinary people can see for sure is that a Soviet threat that made them dependent on the United States has receded, and that for better or for worse the Europe they have known for forty years will rapidly change into something else.

"Everyone everywhere is talking about it, of course," said Raymond Kingsley-Taylor, chapter clerk of Hereford Cathedral. "There's relief, sheer stunned surprise, and apprehension."

"Europe will become more and more aggressively competitive against Japan, and distance itself from the Americans," said Jacques Seguela, a French advertising executive and author in Paris. "The Soviet Union will be part of this new Europe." He will open an advertising agency in Moscow January 1 and two in Hungary and Poland.

Anke van der Valk, a 38-year-old social worker in Delft, the Netherlands, agreed. "Those Eastern lands belong to Europe," she said. "I think they should join the Common Market." But, she added, "I'm a bit afraid of a united Germany. Better for the two Germanys to remain separate, and let both of them be members of the European Community."

"All the French public opinion polls show that between 60 and 70 percent of the French people say German reunification wouldn't bother them," said Professor Grosser, France's leading expert on

Germany. But in the Quai d'Orsay, some diplomats speak of the shelling of Rheims Cathedral in the Franco-Prussian War of 1870 as if it were yesterday.

"National pride caused all the problems we're seeing today," said Markus Doll, a 22-year-old student in Hamburg. "The people who used to say 'We are Germans' now say 'We are Europeans.' For me it's no better. They should say 'We are people, just like everybody else.' "

In Washington the realization was dawning that while the Soviet Union would remain in Europe as at least a neighbor whether it had troops in the East bloc or not, the U.S. role on the continent was becoming less obvious in the new configurations of power. In the beginning of December, President Bush had met with Mr. Gorbachev in Malta to discuss essentially European issues.

Changes in East Call for a U.S. Balancing Act
By Thomas L. Friedman

WASHINGTON, Dec. 6—A senior policy maker was explaining the other day that the Bush Administration had two sets of policies for Eastern Europe—one for that night's network news and one for the year 2010. But the real challenge for Washington, he said, will be developing approaches to Europe not for tonight and not for the next century, but for next year, 1992 and 1995.

"Our internal debates are either very technical or very cosmic," the policy maker said. "Look, our long-term goal, the 'vision thing,' is obvious. It doesn't glitter. It doesn't blind you. It isn't a new Jerusalem. It is something very simple: all the countries in Eastern Europe should have democratic institutions and not go to war with each other. It isn't any more complicated than that."

"What is complicated," he said, "is getting there. It is that middle distance—the policy for 1995—that's the problem. It has to be something more than a Polish aid package and something less than the vision of a 'Europe whole and free.' "

Ultimately, it will be policies for the middle distance that will determine how effectively the United States can help Europe make its transition from the barbed-wire-divided landscape of the recent past to a continent whole and free. In addressing the NATO allies in Brussels this week after his meeting in Malta with President Mikhail

S. Gorbachev of the Soviet Union, President Bush acknowledged this challenge.

"The United States will remain a European power, and that means that the United States will stay engaged in the future of Europe and in our common defense," Mr. Bush said. But he was quick to add that the task required a reversal of old approaches almost as great as that being tried in Moscow.

"As I watched the way in which Mr. Gorbachev has handled the changes in Eastern Europe, it deserves new thinking," the President said. "It absolutely mandates new thinking."

But if the United States is to be involved in drawing the Europe of the 1990's, as the President vowed, what are the immediate goals it is seeking there? With budgetary pressure mounting for a reduction in the number of American troops in Europe, what form will the United States presence take over the middle distance? At a time when American officials themselves admit they have little leverage to influence the pace and scope of change in Eastern Europe, how can the United States develop a blueprint for the future that will not be overwhelmed by events? Finally, is there a threat that the emerging unity of Eastern and Western Europe may lead to a growing disunity in the Western alliance?

The time available for answering these questions may be less than anyone imagines. Administration officials say that although President Bush and Mr. Gorbachev never really got around to exchanging detailed plans for a new Eastern Europe, what the Soviet leader did say left the Bush team feeling that he was not only pleased with the nature of change there, but intended to continue promoting it. In other words, events are likely to move faster before they move slower.

The fact that senior Administration decision makers have not yet produced clear-cut blueprints for the middle distance appears to be more a result of their being overwhelmed by events than a lack of imagination. It seems that too much is changing too fast in too many unexpected ways for the leadership to get too far beyond the day-to-day.

"I don't think people genuinely have recovered their breath from what has happened," said a top Administration policy maker. "I have spent my entire grown-up life not knowing the difference between Latvia, Lithuania and Estonia. They were like Central African lakes to me. There was never any reason to think about them. If you had told me two years ago that I would now be drawing careful political distinctions between Estonia and Lithuania, I would never have believed it."

Nevertheless, interviews with a range of officials, scholars, policy analysts and historians made clear that there is no shortage of ideas on how the Administration should act toward Europe in the middle distance.

At the heart of all the "new thinking" about Europe in Washington lies the German question. How the United States relates to the North Atlantic Treaty Organization and the European Community will be shaped to a large extent by whether East and West Germany are reunited and if so, how.

The Bush Administration has made a strategic decision in recent months not to oppose German unification in principle provided it is done through free elections. But in his Brussels speech the President sketched out for the first time other conditions Washington would insist on.

"Unification should occur in the context of Germany's continued commitment to NATO, an increasingly integrated European Community, and with due regard to the legal role and responsibilities of the Allied powers," Mr. Bush said. "In the interest of general European stability, moves toward unification must be peaceful, gradual and part of a step-by-step basis. And lastly, on the question of borders, we should reiterate our support for the Helsinki Final Act"—which declared that Europe's postwar borders were inviolable.

But the question remains how the Administration should go about imposing these conditions.

"We would be nuts to try to oppose German reunification—there is nothing to be gained by antagonizing Germany—but we would be equally nuts to keep our hands off and say that German reunification is only a question for the German people," said Burton Yale Pines, an expert on Europe at the Heritage Foundation, a Washington-based conservative research center.

"Because of the instabilities a united Germany has created in this past century, it is absolutely appropriate for Moscow and Washington to begin talking now, along with Britain and France, about how Germany should be reunified—what sorts of weapons it should be allowed to have, what limitations on its troops should be imposed and how it would relate to its neighbors."

Administration officials say they are concentrating their energies now on insuring that there is a unified Western approach to the

German question before they begin talking with the Soviets. Washington's nightmares here are two. The first is that East Germany will literally collapse tomorrow, fostering a popular momentum for unification and possibly prompting the Soviets, who have some 400,000 troops in East Germany, to intervene to halt the process.

The Administration's view is that keeping East Germany propped up so that it can make a gradual transition to unification is primarily the job of West Germany, the only country with the resources and contacts to make it happen.

Which leads to the Administration's second nightmare: As East and West Germany inexorably grow closer together, even if step by step, deeply rooted fears about a united Germany will set off an earthquake in the NATO alliance, with its epicenter in London, where Prime Minister Margaret Thatcher has opposed unification at this time.

Secretary of State James A. Baker 3d will be going to Europe next week for meetings in Bonn and Brussels with the aim of obtaining a NATO consensus on Mr. Bush's approach. At the last minute he added London to his itinerary to try to ease Prime Minister Thatcher's anxieties.

In Bonn, Mr. Baker will try to continue the Administration's approach of hugging the West Germans to the Western camp. That means, an official said, letting Bonn know that Washington has "total confidence" in the prudent way West Germany has handled the situation up to now and wants to consult with Bonn at every step of the way. At the same time, the official said, Washington will need to reaffirm by words and with arms around the shoulder that it believes Bonn must continue consulting with the West and reiterating its unshakable ties to NATO and the European Community.

Such commitments are necessary both to reassure the rest of Western Europe and to send a signal to Mr. Gorbachev. Administration officials left Malta with a sense that while the Soviets continue to oppose total German unification, they too may be starting to recognize that it may be inevitable and hence they may begin insisting that such a unified entity be "neutral."

In London and in Brussels, Mr. Baker will try to promote Mr. Bush's position that German unification in the context of continued membership in NATO and the European Community is nothing the allies need to fear.

"This is a policy that is going to require a lot of handholding," a

State Department official said. "Once we have a framework agreed on with the British, French and West Germans, then we can start talking to the Soviets."

The longer-term question, policy analysts say, is how can the United States insure that a unified Germany is firmly anchored in the Western alliance when the lessening of the Soviet threat will feed budgetary momentum in Congress to bring the bulk of the 317,000 American troops in Europe home?

The answer, said Stephen F. Szabo, a German expert at the National War College, is for the United States to take a much more active role in promoting European integration, not only the plans of the twelve members of the European Community to turn themselves into a single market by the end of 1992, but also their proposals for a European monetary union and for a defensive structure of their own to augment NATO. This would both dilute the power of a unified Germany and keep it enmeshed in the West.

"We are going to be playing a declining military role, so we better have something there in place when we leave that can both maintain an overall balance of power with the Soviets and at the same time be a firm anchor holding Germany to the West," Mr. Szabo said. "This means trying to promote more European control of NATO."

Even over the long term, Administration officials are convinced that Mr. Gorbachev does not want the United States out of Europe, but instead sees a continued American presence there as the ultimate guarantor that neither the German question nor intra-European antagonisms will get out of control. Administration officials say it is premature to even begin talking about a changed American relationship to NATO, let alone the United States' leaving Europe.

"NATO provides the single greatest institutional tie the United States has to Western Europe, and no one wants to see that relationship attenuated," said Deputy Secretary of State Lawrence S. Eagleburger. "Over time I am sure we will have to adjust our relationship, but we are not there yet. I don't think anyone at this point can envisage how the relationship will change."

If there is any real threat from Eastern Europe to American interests in the middle term it is no longer the threat of a Warsaw Pact invasion but rather a Warsaw Pact economic collapse. When Administration officials talk about their "worst case scenario" for Eastern Europe, it always begins with economics, not politics.

"The worst case," a senior State Department official said, "is that the Eastern Europeans get bogged down and can't make the structural changes in their economic and political systems and then you see pessimism and cynicism set in. That could get ugly."

It is often forgotten that in the first few years of the cold war, American policies in Europe were not primarily military but economic. The Marshall Plan was intended primarily to strengthen European countries, which had been devastated by the war, so that they could resist decay, instability and Communist subversion. NATO and the policy of military containment came into their own only after the Korean War raised the specter of a Soviet-led strike across Central Europe.

"With the diminished threat from the East, American European policy no longer has to emphasize military containment," said Michael Mandelbaum, an expert on East-West relations at the Council on Foreign Relations. "We are back to the situation of 1947—helping fledgling democracies, devastated in this case by the calamity of forty years of Communist rule, trying to get on their feet."

For the short term, the Bush Administration, prodded by Congress, has come up with a package that provides $938 million in grants, investment funds, bank credits, scholarships, job-training schemes and environmental protection projects for Poland and Hungary. But this package will expire in three years, and does not even address changes in Czechoslovakia, Bulgaria and Yugoslavia.

For the middle distance, Felix G. Rohatyn, a senior partner in the investment bank Lazard Frères & Company, has suggested that the United States should take the lead in creating a permanent Eastern European Development Bank.

"For the longer haul," Mr. Rohatyn said, "it seems to me that some kind of multinational development institution should be created by the Europeans, Japanese and ourselves along the lines of the Reconstruction Finance Corporation of the 1930's."

The capital, Mr. Rohatyn said, should be held by Japan, the United States and the European Community.

"I would begin with $5 billion, which would allow them to borrow much more, and put the bank in Vienna," he said. "Any country that has made the political reforms—that is, free elections and recognition of the principle of private property—but not yet the economic ones could apply."

Such a bank, he said, would act as a permanent provider of financing for infrastructure projects, like telecommunications and irrigation systems, and for developing free-market instruments and skills, like accounting systems, mortgage institutions, copyright laws, credit and banking systems.

To transform the economies of Eastern Europe in a stable manner from planned economies to more free-market systems "is going to take a long time, so we need institutions that can work over the long haul," Mr. Rohatyn said.

And there is the rub, some American officials say.

"I represent a great power and we reach into our pockets and all we have is loose change," a State Department official said. "I am not saying you should substitute check writing for policy making. But let's face it: student exchanges, leadership grants, banking credits, new consulates—these are the network of things that bring us influence on the ground. You have to put your money where your mouth is, and we're broke."

Administration officials concede that they will have to influence economic development in Eastern Europe with a small purse, at best. Their policy for the middle distance is to make a virtue of necessity and share leadership on the aid front with both the European Community and the group of 24 leading Western industrial nations.

"There is a lot we can do without money—providing technical assistance, or incentives for reform or intellectual capital," an Administration official said. "We're going to have to do more of that. Look at all we offered Gorbachev in Malta. Did that cost us any money?"

Out of all these loose threads today's decision makers will somehow have to weave a policy for the middle distance. Those who will have to carry it out greet the task with excitement and humility, dread and awe, said Raymond G. H. Seitz, the Assistant Secretary for European Affairs, whose father was a United States Army general in command of American forces in Munich when the Berlin wall went up in 1961.

"When I was 20, I came home from college for the summer to visit my family in Munich," he recalled. "I remember very well the night when the red phone in the house rang and my father was told that the East Germans are putting up a wall in the middle of Berlin. Now his son is one of those dealing with the implications of that wall coming down."

"I guess history comes in waves," he added, "and this is one that is clearly cresting. It is not coups we are talking about. It is mass movements, people in the streets. What it has lacked up to now, thank goodness, is a feature that always gives history its real pungency, though. That is violence and barricades—*Les Misérables.* So we may not get on-Broadway plays out of this moment, but we'll definitely get off-Broadway."

When asked how he was instructing his staff to go about planning for the middle distance, Mr. Seitz mulled the question over for a moment before answering.

"Everything goes back to square one now," he said. "No assumptions are valid, nothing is ruled out anymore. Of course that is exciting. Bureaucracies are meant to operate within a framework. In terms of European policy we have had that framework established for a very long time. There was NATO, the Warsaw Pact, the wall, the spending levels. They were all thought to be immutable."

"The bureaucracy is not like academe, where you are trained to question assumptions," he continued. "Around here you don't have time to question assumptions, and anyway you know that they are valid. Right? Now everything is back to square one. Nothing is immutable. It requires a total intellectual retooling."

On his way to Malta, Mr. Gorbachev stopped in Italy, where he was cheered wildly by people who regarded him as the man who more than any other had brought about the piercing and toppling of Europe's divisions. But the highlight of this part of the trip was the first meeting ever between a Soviet leader and a Pope.

Gorbachev Lauds Religion on Eve of Meeting Pope
By Clyde Haberman

ROME, Nov. 30—On the eve of an encounter with Pope John Paul II, President Mikhail S. Gorbachev said tonight that the Soviet Union had erred in long rejecting religion and now needed its moral force to help make his plans for a restructured society work.

"We have changed our attitude on some matters, such as religion, for example, which admittedly we used to treat in a simplistic manner," said Mr. Gorbachev, whose meeting with the Pope on Friday will be the first between a Soviet Communist leader and the spiritual guide to the world's 850 million Roman Catholics.

"Now we not only proceed from the assumption that no one should interfere in matters of the individual's conscience," he said. "We also say that the moral values that religion generated and embodied for centuries can help in the work of renewal in our country, too."

"In fact," Mr. Gorbachev added, "this is already happening."

His thoughts on religion came in a multi-themed speech that was as much a philosophical reflection as a political statement. In it, the Soviet leader offered a vision of a new Europe, one that would be "a commonwealth of sovereign democratic states," based on spiritual values, pluralism, religious tolerance and mutual understanding. . . .

The Kremlin and the Vatican; Gorbachev Visits Pope at Vatican; Ties Are Forged
By Clyde Haberman

ROME, Dec. 1—With an agreement to begin official relations and a pledge of expanded religious freedom for Soviet citizens, President Mikhail S. Gorbachev joined hands today with Pope John Paul II.

Seven decades of spiritual and philosophical conflict came to a symbolic end as the two talked for more than an hour in the heart of Vatican City, the first encounter between a Soviet Communist leader and a Pope.

Both men agreed in principle to establish diplomatic ties, and Mr. Gorbachev invited the Pope to make a return visit to the Soviet Union.

The Pope's reply to the invitation was noncommittal. It appeared that before saying yes, he intended to keep on pressing Moscow to restore religious liberties to Soviet Catholics. According to a spokesman, the Pope "cordially thanked" his guest, and said he hoped that "developments would make it possible for him to accept."

Much will apparently depend on what happens to the four million to five million Eastern Rite Catholics in the Ukraine, in which the Polish-born Pope has a special interest. Much of the western Ukraine was once part of Poland, until it was incorporated into the Soviet Union after World War II.

The Ukrainian Catholic Church was driven underground by Stalin in 1946. It was forcibly dissolved, and its parishes were closed or merged into the Russian Orthodox Church. Centered in the western Ukraine, the Ukrainian Catholics follow the Eastern liturgy but profess allegiance to the Pope.

The Pope has insisted repeatedly that the Ukrainian Catholic Church be made legal again, and he got an important start toward that goal when Mr. Gorbachev promised him today that a new law guaranteeing freedom of conscience would soon be enacted.

In turn, the Soviet leader won something he had come for: legitimacy from the leader of the world's 900 million Roman Catholics. It came in the form of a papal blessing for his plans to restructure Soviet political and economic life. John Paul said the Holy See "wishes you success and declares itself ready to support every initiative that will better protect and integrate the rights and duties of individuals and peoples."

But the Pope's main concern was religious liberty, and he stuck to that point tenaciously, reminding Mr. Gorbachev that Moscow had signed international treaties guaranteeing freedom of worship. "I express the fervent hope," he said, that Catholics in the Ukraine, the Baltic republics and Armenia will be able "to practice freely their religious life."

In his brief remarks, the Soviet leader said all believers "have a right to satisfy their spiritual needs." On Thursday, he told Italian leaders that his country had made the mistake of treating religion in "a simplistic manner."

Developments such as these, the Pope said to him today, "lead us to hope that the situation will change."

Indeed, in the Ukrainian city of Lvov, the layman who leads the Ukrainian Catholic Church reported that a major shift had already occurred. The leader, Ivan Hel, said that Ukraine officials had announced that the church could register like any other accepted religious organization.

Beyond the immediate agendas of each leader, the meeting today in the ceremonial library of the Vatican's Apostolic Palace contained a symbolism of almost epic proportions.

At an earlier time, Stalin had scornfully asked how many divisions the Pope had. Now, a successor intent on undoing Stalin's legacy has crossed St. Peter's Square in open recognition that he must reckon with the Vatican as a moral and political force.

Certainly, the significance was not lost on either of the participants, who have many points in common. Both are Slavs. Both say spiritual values must go hand in hand with material gains. Both talk of a Europe unified by a common civilization despite political diversity. And both can maintain, in different ways, that their separate visions helped trigger the tumultuous changes under way across the Continent.

The two symbol-conscious men were also aware of the power of photographs and televised images showing them clasping hands and appearing in the relaxed company of each other.

"A truly extraordinary event has taken place," said the Communist leader, who was baptized as a boy in the Russian Orthodox Church. "It has become possible due to the profound changes that are sweeping many countries and nations. What is more, we can expect it to help assure their positive continuation."

"Our meeting today," the Pope said, "will hardly fail to have a powerful impact on world opinion. Not only is it something new and unusual, It will also be interpreted as singularly meaningful, a sign of the times that have slowly matured, a sign that is rich in promise," he said.

For the Vatican, the Gorbachev visit crowned a year of dramatically improved relations with the Eastern bloc.

The church has been permitted to make long-prohibited ecclesiastical appointments in Czechoslovakia and in the Soviet republics of Lithuania and Byelorussia. Four months ago, it established diplomatic relations with Poland, its first with a Warsaw Pact nation. Last week, Hungary announced that it was ready to follow suit.

But full Vatican relations with the Kremlin are expected to take considerably more time. Even so, it was a giant stride today when Mr. Gorbachev said, "We have reached agreement in principle to give official status to our interstate relations."

Asked later if this was a move toward full diplomatic relations, the chief Vatican spokesman, Dr. Joaquin Navarro-Valls, said it was.

While the meeting today was friendly—punctuated with smiles and occasional laughs—the two leaders did not show true warmth in public. Still, the special nature of the occasion shone through, even in small gestures.

Mr. Gorbachev called the Pope "Holy Father." For his part, John Paul varied his routine in a significant way.

Normally, he greets visitors at the door of his library, which is on the second floor of the Apostolic Palace, one floor below his private apartment. To show his esteem for this guest, he came out several dozen yards from the library, to the Throne Room.

Then they entered the library, sitting on either side of a wooden desk during a 70-minute conversation. For the first five minutes, according to Dr. Navarro, they were alone, speaking in Russian. But then they brought in interpreters, with Mr. Gorbachev continuing in Russian and the Pope alternating between Polish and Italian.

While the two men talked, Mr. Gorbachev's wife, Raisa, toured the Sistine Chapel and the Raphael rooms of the Vatican Museum. Then she returned to meet the Pope, raising eyebrows by turning out in a bright red suit. It is customary for women to wear black at private papal audiences. But if the Vatican was displeased, it kept its feelings to itself.

In an exchange of gifts, John Paul presented Mr. Gorbachev with a reproduction of an early Christian mosaic showing Christ on St. Peter's tomb, and gave Mrs. Gorbachev rosary beads of gold and mother of pearl. In return, he received two fourteenth-century Psalm books from Kiev.

Just before this exchange, Dr. Navarro said, the Soviet leader told the Pope, "Holy Father, we are aware that we are dealing not only with the highest religious authority in the world but also someone who is a Slav."

"Yes, I'm the first Slav Pope, " John Paul reportedly replied, adding, "I'm sure that Providence paved the way for this meeting."

After the meetings in Rome Mr. Gorbachev went on to Malta to discuss matters of European security and Soviet plans for progress and modernization with President Bush in a stormy setting that contrasted with the developing show of superpower amity.

The Malta Summit; Bush and Gorbachev Proclaim a New Era for U.S.-Soviet Ties; Agree on Arms and Trade Aims

By Andrew Rosenthal

VALLETTA, MALTA, Dec. 3—President Bush and President Mikhail S. Gorbachev ended their first summit meeting today with an extraordinary public affirmation of the new relationship between their countries.

Mr. Gorbachev said he and Mr. Bush agreed that "the characteristics of the cold war should be abandoned."

"The arms race, mistrust, psychological and ideological struggle, all those should be things of the past," he said.

Mr. Bush said: "With reform under way in the Soviet Union, we stand at the threshold of a brand-new era of U.S.-Soviet relations. It is within our grasp to contribute each in our own way to overcoming the division of Europe and ending the military confrontation there."

In the most substantial agreements reached at the meeting, the two leaders said they would strive to conclude treaties on long-range nuclear weapons and conventional arms in 1990. They also agreed to hold another summit meeting in June in the United States.

But the significance of the first summit meeting between the leaders seemed to lie more in the tone than the substance.

They ended their rain-soaked two-day meeting with the first joint news conference by Soviet and American leaders.

There had been some annoyance aboard Mr. Gorbachev's ship, the *Maxim Gorky*, on Saturday night when Mr. Bush canceled an afternoon session and a dinner because of a gale. The tension lingered in the background today but it melted under the television lights in a 65-minute display of cordiality that ended with Mr. Bush reaching over to grasp Mr. Gorbachev's right forearm. The news conference was remarkable for its lack of conflict over issues that have long divided East and West, including arms control, the Middle East and economic relations.

For all the cordiality, the meeting did not produce any new treaties or specific agreements, or even a joint statement.

After eight hours of intimate discussions, the two leaders were still far apart on the issue of sea-based nuclear cruise missiles, a major point of disagreement on a strategic arms treaty. They remained at odds on Central America, and Administration officials said Mr. Gorbachev did not give a definitive answer to Mr. Bush's proposals on an agreement reducing chemical weapons.

But Mr. Gorbachev, clearly pleased that Mr. Bush had shown some initiative on economic issues, registered approval on most of the proposals offered by Mr. Bush on Saturday, and the two leaders expressed broad optimism about the course of their relations.

Although they said they did not reach any specific accord on how to deal with the unraveling political power structure in Eastern Europe, Mr. Bush and Mr. Gorbachev seemed optimistic even about that problem.

"We searched for the answer to the question of where do we stand now," Mr. Gorbachev said. "We stated, both of us, that the world leaves one epoch of cold war and enters another epoch."

The two leaders did not dwell on Eastern Europe at length in their news conference, and American officials said the subject did not take up as much of the summit talks as they had expected. In response to a question about the two Germanys, Mr. Bush adopted what had long been the Soviet position. He said the conference on European security that began in Helsinki "spells out a concept of permanent borders."

Mr. Gorbachev said "any artificial acceleration" of the unification process would make it more difficult to carry through the changes taking place in Eastern Europe.

At times, the cautious Mr. Bush seemed to make an effort to show that all was not settled between the two nations. Even then, the statements from both sides were far more mild than the political oratory that has characterized the Soviet-American relationship for much of the last four decades.

Mr. Bush said his conversation with Mr. Gorbachev stayed cordial even on human rights. "I remember a time when I first met Mr. Gorbachev and we talked about human rights and he became visibly agitated with me for raising it," Mr. Bush said.

"And I think there's been a great evolution in his thinking on that question, and certainly on his relations with the United States, just as there had been an evolution in my thinking," Mr. Bush said, noting that he had once opposed holding the very type of meeting he had with Mr. Gorbachev here.

Indeed, when it came to what American officials said was the most troublesome policy dispute between the two leaders during the shipboard meeting—American charges that Nicaragua is sending arms to the leftist rebels in El Salvador—Mr. Gorbachev said, "We understand the concerns of the United States."

Mr. Bush, for his part, said he was "angry" about the issue but was not accusing Mr. Gorbachev of anything. Noting that Nicaragua had assured the Soviet Union that the arms shipments had ended, Mr. Bush said, "I do not believe the Sandinistas have told the truth to our Soviet friends."

Mr. Bush and Mr. Gorbachev talked to reporters aboard the *Maxim Gorky*, a Soviet cruise liner, before Mr. Gorbachev returned to Moscow.

Later in the day President Bush flew to Brussels, where he is to meet with heads of state and government of the North Atlantic Treaty Organization on Monday. At the airport this evening, he paid tribute to NATO's role in maintaining stability in Europe, noting that "this alliance of free nations remains the bedrock of peaceful change in Europe." . . .

On Saturday, Mr. Bush outlined 18 proposals to Mr. Gorbachev that ranged from nuclear arms control to educational exchanges. A senior American official who sat in on the talks said Mr. Gorbachev responded positively to almost all of them.

The notable exceptions, he said, were Mr. Bush's proposal that the two nations negotiate and sign an agreement in 1990 limiting their chemical arsenals to 20 percent of the present American level and that they call jointly for the holding of the 2004 Olympic Games on both sides of Berlin.

The official said that Mr. Gorbachev did not give Mr. Bush a clear no on those points but rather did not register the approval that he offered on the other issues.

In the news conference, Mr. Gorbachev said he had agreed with a suggestion by Mr. Bush that Secretary of State James A. Baker 3d and the Soviet Foreign Minister, Eduard A. Shevardnadze, meet in the Soviet Union in January to discuss arms control issues in preparation for a summit conference in the United States that the two leaders agreed to hold in the last two weeks of June.

He reaffirmed Mr. Bush's hope that the two leaders could sign a strategic arms control treaty, cutting long-range nuclear arsenals in half, at the next summit meeting. Barring that, he said, he hoped the two ministers would be able to resolve enough outstanding problems that at the next summit they could "agree on the provisions of the treaty and later in the coming months it might be ready for signature."

Mr. Gorbachev said he also hoped that a treaty limiting conventional weapons in Europe could be signed in 1990 in Vienna. Mr. Bush told reporters that he and Mr. Gorbachev had discussed in general what further cuts might be made in conventional arms, but did not talk about specific numbers.

On strategic arms, Mr. Gorbachev outlined some major obstacles to an accord. He said he was particularly concerned about remaining differences on air-launched cruise missiles and added that he had not dropped his insistence on opening negotiations on sea-based nuclear cruise missiles. Noting the progress that has been made in a number of other areas, Mr. Gorbachev said, "The time has come when we should begin discussing naval forces."

Mr. Gorbachev did not make it clear whether he was still setting forth a side agreement on naval weapons as a condition for concluding a strategic arms treaty. But Mr. Bush did suggest that he has not eased his opposition to negotiating about such weapons.

"The chairman knows that I could not come here to make deals in arms control," said Mr. Bush, who has repeatedly promised to consult his allies before making any major new treaty proposals or reaching any substantive agreements with Mr. Gorbachev on reducing nuclear or conventional arms.

Mr. Gorbachev was especially appreciative in public—and in private too, American and Soviet officials said—about Mr. Bush's proposals on trade and economic relations, which included his expression of support for Soviet observer status in the General Agreement on Tariffs and Trade. Mr. Bush also said he would begin immediate negotiations on lifting American barriers to trade with the Soviet Union and would recommend most-favored-nation status as soon as new Soviet emigration laws are enacted.

Mr. Gorbachev, who has long been seeking these moves and had viewed the lack of progress on economic issues as a major problem in the superpower relationship, said Mr. Bush's ideas and the discussion in Malta "could be regarded as a political impetus which we were lacking for our economic cooperation to gain momentum."

Mr. Bush called trade "one of the most fruitful parts of our discussion" and said he would "like to have a climate in which American businessmen can help with what Chairman Gorbachev is trying to do in terms of reform and glasnost."

On Central America, Mr. Bush said there were still clear differences between himself and Mr. Gorbachev. But he said, "I'd like to feel that if there are some differences between the two of us, then they have been narrowed."

Turning to the Middle East, Mr. Bush moved away from the often-expressed American view that the Soviet Union is impeding the peace process or, at best, trying to gain influence in the region at American expense.

"The Soviet Union is playing a constructive role in Lebanon and there is common ground there," Mr. Bush said, noting that it had "not always been the case in history" for an American President to take such a position.

New Spur for a New Journey Together
By R. W. Apple, Jr.

VALLETTA, MALTA, Dec. 3—George Bush finished one political journey today and started another.

Mr. Bush began his Presidency seeming more skeptical than his predecessor, Ronald Reagan, of Mikhail S. Gorbachev and his ideas. But the meeting in September between the Soviet Foreign Minister, Eduard A. Shevardnadze, and Secretary of State James A. Baker 3d marked a turning point, and two days of meetings here apparently convinced Mr. Bush and Mr. Gorbachev not only that they could trust each other but also that they needed each other to achieve their political goals.

So what their foreign ministers began amidst the scenic splendors of Wyoming in September was completed this weekend in the gales of Malta, as the leaders agreed to link their political fortunes in an effort to build a world free, as Mr. Gorbachev put it, from the "psychological and ideological struggles" of the last four decades.

No formal agreements were reached here; there was not even a written joint statement, let alone anything as formal as a communiqué. But the summit conference generated a sense of momentum, an intangible but important dynamic element, that the Soviet-American relationship had heretofore lacked.

As he had promised before arriving, Mr. Bush took the Soviet leader to task for his nation's Central American policy. But at the joint news conference given by the two men in lieu of individual sessions, the American President vividly demonstrated how eager he is to make the new relationship work.

Mr. Gorbachev had denied sending arms to El Salvador, Mr. Bush noted, while the United States had hard evidence that Soviet arms were reaching the insurgent forces there. Other American Presidents might have left the matter there, with the implication that the Soviets were being less than candid. But Mr. Bush reached a completely different conclusion.

The Sandinista Government in Nicaragua, the President said, must have shipped the Soviet weapons to El Salvador and then lied about their activities "to our Soviet friends."

Only at a time when the American attitudes are undergoing a profound change, with more and more Americans looking upon the Soviet Union not as an enemy but almost as the ally that it was during World War II, could Mr. Bush so clearly signal his willingness to give Mr. Gorbachev the benefit of the doubt. It will be more difficult now for his critics at home to accuse him of halfheartedness in his approach to the changes wrought by the Soviet leader.

The most important achievement here, one of Mr. Bush's advisers said, was to put "a new political impetus, a new impetus of personal leadership," behind United States–Soviet relations. The clear feeling among White House staff members and senior Kremlin officials was that this, plus an accelerated timetable for two sets of arms-reduction talks, plus good chemistry between the two leaders, made success in their summit conference next year in the United States a probability, not merely a possibility.

"I couldn't have asked for a better result from this non-summit summit," President Bush said. For Mr. Gorbachev, the broad spectrum of economic assistance offered by his friend in the White House, from better access to the Western trading bloc to lower tariffs on Soviet products in the United States to (improbably enough) American help in setting up a Soviet stock market, could not have been more welcome as the Soviet Union begins a long, cold winter.

Most of all, a Soviet official said, Mr. Gorbachev was greatly relieved that Mr. Bush now seemed fully engaged in the relationship in a way that he had not been before, and seemed disposed to look for ways he could help the Soviet program of perestroika, or restructuring, toward success.

In the early months of the Bush Administration, some officials questioned whether Mr. Gorbachev was really a reformer and asked whether the White House should help him. Those in favor of Mr. Gorbachev argued that Ronald Reagan, in the last years of his Presidency, had become more trustful of Mr. Gorbachev.

The mood generated here may prove less transitory than earlier waves of good feeling generated by summit meetings, but there are still problems with regard to regional conflicts, as in Central America, and with regard to arms control, with both sea-launched cruise missiles and chemical weapons.

"Look, we've got some differences," President Bush acknowledged. Both leaders seemed eager to sidestep the German question, for an evident reason: any move by the two Germanys to amalgamate or confederate will tend to undercut the North Atlantic Treaty Organization or the Warsaw Pact or both, and Mr. Bush and Mr. Gorbachev are counting on those two organizations, perhaps in changed form, to give them leverage in Europe.

Mr. Bush, furthermore, was at some pains to avoid giving offense to the Western Europeans—at least according to the accounts of his aides. He may have told Mr. Gorbachev of plans to cut United States troop strength in Europe; if so, he will presumably tell his allies in Brussels on Monday.

The plan to hold the conference on board Soviet and American warships, which was a White House idea, designed perhaps to generate public-relations echoes of the Roosevelt-Churchill talks during World War II off Newfoundland, didn't work out as planned, having failed to take into account the unpredictability of the weather. The meetings had to be shortened and moved to the cruise liner *Maxim Gorky*, docked nearby, because of mountainous seas.

Unlike Mr. Gorbachev, President Bush made no claim that the cold war was over, and unlike Mr. Reagan, he made only modest claims for the nature of his relationship with the Soviet leader.

"I don't think that he has me down as a total negativist," said Mr. Bush of Mr. Gorbachev, "and I certainly don't have him down as one."

In the end, Mr. Bush proposed more here than his staff had indicated that he would, and Mr. Gorbachev proposed less than expected. But then, it was Mr. Bush's turn, since the Soviet leader has been springing surprises almost weekly in recent months, and Mr. Bush must have been dying to do something unexpected, given his almost obsessive delight in keeping secrets.

Surprising as the turnaround in superpower relations had been, they were still not as startling as the almost daily events taking place in Eastern Europe. It appeared at times that the all the countries except Rumania were leapfrogging each other as they raced to democracy. Poland had been the first to challenge the party's political power; Hungary had been the first to have its party rename itself. Bulgaria was the first to take up the elimination of constitutional guarantees of the Communist Party's leading role. Under such onslaughts, the once all-powerful Communists were abasing themselves, offering concessions and self-criticism and sacrificing their more prominent leaders in vain attempts to appease the crowds who were calling for the end of a system. One of the more bizarre developments came when the Czechoslovak Communists moved to condemn the very act that gave them their authority.

Czech Party Calls '68 Invasion Wrong
By Serge Schmemann

PRAGUE, Dec. 1—The new Politburo of the Czechoslovak Communist Party declared today that the Soviet-led invasion that choked the Prague Spring of 1968 was wrong.

"We are of the opinion that the entry onto our territory of five armies of the Warsaw Pact in 1968 was not justified, and the decision to do so was wrong," said Vasil Mohorita, one of the reform-minded officials elevated to the 13-member Politburo last weekend, reporting at a news conference on today's meeting of the party's ruling body.

As the Politburo made the declaration, President Mikhail S. Gorbachev of the Soviet Union acknowledged that the Czechoslovak uprising of 1968 resulted from a yearning for democracy, and East Germany joined Hungary and Poland in apologizing to Czechoslovakia for participating in the military attack.

Mr. Gorbachev told a news conference in Milan, Italy, that the Czechoslovak reform movement in 1968 was "a process of democratization, renewal and humanization of society."

"It was right at that time and it is right now," he said.

But he stopped short of condemning the Soviet intervention, saying that the action had to be seen in the context of the tense East-West relations of the time.

By their condemnation of the Warsaw Pact invasion, the ten new appointees and the three Politburo holdovers basically undermined the position of all the Communists who have ruled here until last week. None of the members are old enough to have profited directly from the invasion, but their elders and patrons in the party were installed in their posts by the 1968 intervention that Moscow described at the time as "fraternal assistance."

One of the principal beneficiaries of this action was Gustav Husak, long the party leader and now Czechoslovakia's head of state. . . .

Four days later, the '68 invasion was formally condemned by the invaders.

Warsaw Pact Condemns '68 Prague Invasion
By Bill Keller

MOSCOW, Dec. 4—The Soviet Union and four Warsaw Pact allies made a common break with the past today by jointly condemning the Soviet-led 1968 military suppression of the Czechoslovak experiment in political liberalization called the Prague Spring.

The Kremlin also agreed today to open discussions with Czechoslovakia on the withdrawal of Soviet troops from that country, linked to broader East-West disarmament negotiations.

Meeting as several of their governments were still reeling from democratic upheavals, the leaders of the Eastern bloc called the 1968 invasion "illegal" and pledged a strict policy of noninterference in each other's internal affairs, the Soviet press agency Tass reported tonight.

The statement was signed by the five countries that took part in the invasion: the Soviet Union, East Germany, Poland, Hungary and Bulgaria. The Soviet Union also issued its own, separate declaration of repentance for contriving to stifle change in Czechoslovakia, its first official admission that the invasion was wrong. The Warsaw Pact statement today was in contrast to one issued on August 21, 1968, by the same countries saying they had sent armed forces to Czechoslovakia at the invitation of the Czechoslovak Communist Party and Government leaders to deal with "the threat emanating from the counter-revolutionary forces that have entered into a collusion with foreign forces hostile to socialism."

The crushing of the Prague Spring had already been condemned by the two alliance members that did not take part, Rumania, which refused to join the invading force, and Czechoslovakia itself. They reportedly endorsed today's statement by the invaders.

Rezso Nyers, chairman of Hungary's Socialist Party, told Hungarian journalists tonight that the declaration marked a formal repudiation of the Brezhnev doctrine, the Kremlin principle of intervening to prevent a retreat from Communism. . . .

Admissions of error and concessionary promises of freely contested elections, an end to the legally entrenched dominance of the Communist Party and the withdrawal of Soviet troops, while welcome, failed to silence the clamor of aroused nations. In East Germany, the party was withering in plain sight.

East Germans Fear New Freedom Could Outstrip Ways to Control It

By Craig R. Whitney

EAST BERLIN, Dec. 2—The position of Egon Krenz, who took over as Communist Party leader on October 18, appeared to be unraveling rapidly tonight on the eve of an emergency meeting of the party's Central Committee, scheduled for Sunday.

A crowd outside party headquarters this evening demanded Mr. Krenz's resignation and that of the rest of the Politburo, booing Mr. Krenz when he arrived. Many in the crowd said the new leadership under Mr. Krenz had failed to react strongly enough to reports of corruption and misuse of office by the country's old-guard leaders.

News of the growing clamor for Mr. Krenz's departure was broadcast on the East German television, which said the demonstrations would resume on Sunday night if the leadership did not quit.

Mr. Krenz, hearing the calls for his resignation, said, "I will report to the Central Committee of our party about the atmosphere here." He was sweating in the cold night air.

The demonstration reflected an intensifying mood of anger and disgust at a spate of revelations of abuses of power and authority. Mr. Krenz, responsible for internal security under Erich Honecker, the party chief ousted in October, has been criticized as one of the "new old men," as one party critic put it in an article published on Thursday in the East German newspaper *Berliner Zeitung*.

The Central Committee meeting was called without explanation on Friday. Several members said tonight that they expected Mr. Krenz and the entire Politburo brought in with him in the last month to resign, staying in office in a caretaker role until a special party congress, which begins on December 15.

A wide range of party members, diplomats and others here say the only figure who appears to have enough authority to take Mr. Krenz's place is Hans Modrow, the former party leader in Dresden, who became Prime Minister on November 13. The youngest member of the leadership, 37-year-old Hans-Joachim Willerding, a nonvoting member of the Politburo, resigned tonight, saying he no longer felt able to represent the party membership adequately, East German television reported.

The growing political crisis makes it clear that the Communist Party leaders, trying to save the system that has run the country for forty years by opening the Berlin wall and lifting most restrictions on public debate, set off a chain reaction that rapidly escaped their control, diplomats, party officials and ordinary citizens here say. . . .

The collapse of the authority of the Communist Party is accelerating, and its constitutionally prescribed leading role was eliminated on Friday by the East German legislature after forty years. The newspapers and television, newly free to report and comment on the failings and even crimes of its leading officials, are doing so with a vengeance, astonishing even longtime observers of the country's affairs. . . .

In Czechoslovakia, the Communists having promised to share power with non-Communists, came up with a coalition that reserved the lion's share of power for themselves while promising to do better and condemning the '68 invasion. This approach was denounced and essentially vetoed by the people, who once again turned out in Wenceslas Square.

Protest Rallies Resume in Prague in Effort to Oust New Government
By Henry Kamm

PRAGUE, Dec. 4—About 200,000 people poured into Wenceslas Square today to shout their rejection of a new Government formed on Sunday and to applaud a call for a general strike next Monday if it is not replaced.

Renewing protests suspended last Monday after Prime Minister Ladislav Adamec promised a multiparty Cabinet and other concessions, the marchers denounced the new Government as a betrayal.

The Cabinet presented by Mr. Adamec on Sunday is made up of sixteen Communists, two members of parties that had historically been aligned with the Communists and three independents. Opposition spokesmen said the Cabinet would keep intact the "leading role" for the Communist Party that Parliament struck from the Constitution last week as part of the concessions.

Responding to Sunday's announcement, student opposition leaders today reversed a decision to scale back a strike that is keeping all places of higher learning occupied and inactive. Actors and other performers called off an announcement that theaters and concert halls would reopen tonight. Since last month, theaters have been used for political discussions in which members of the Civic Forum opposition group replace actors onstage and discuss the upheaval with the public.

"We are forced to continue our strike," Miroslav Machacek, an actor and director, said in remarks to the demonstrators today.

"Long live the actors!" the protesters replied.

For the first time, a representative of industrial workers called for the formation of independent trade unions. The workers' representative, Igor Pleskov, said committees maintaining a strike alert throughout the country should be converted into the cores of independent unions. "Let's take our affairs into our own hands," he said.

In addition, leaders of Civic Forum, the main opposition group to emerge from the demonstrations of recent weeks, declared for the first time that it would function like a political party. Forum leaders and representatives of Public Against Violence, a similar organization that emerged in the Slovakian region of the country, announced at the rally that they would be offering a common list of candidates for parliamentary elections that the opposition has demanded for no later than July. The crowd cheered in the cold and darkness of the afternoon.

It was the first time Civic Forum representatives spoke publicly of turning the group into a competitive political party. Forum leaders had insisted that the group saw its role solely as stimulating free political expression and assisting fledgling political groups. . . .

The gathering today turned into a passionate dialogue, in which speakers' demands and declarations were greeted not with chants or slogans, as before, but with pointed comments from those gathered in front of the balcony. Those words were taken up by others standing farther away, until they rolled to the farthest fringes.

"Undoubtedly a number of members of Parliament have betrayed our confidence," said Radim Palous, a spokesman of Civic Forum. Then he began reciting a list of offenders. "Jakes," he began, referring to the deposed Communist chief, Milos Jakes.

The crowd responded, "Throw him out immediately."

He continued, naming Vaclac David, a former Foreign Minister; Jan Foitik, the ousted curator of ideology; and Alois Indra and Vasil Bilak, former party presidium members who had supported the Soviet-led invasion of 1968.

"Send them to work" came the chorus.

At Mr. Palous's next listing of deputies, the crowd roared, "Give them a shovel."

"They have lost the right to be deputies," the speaker said. "Mafia," the crowd responded. "You no longer have our mandate," the speaker said of the deputies.

"They don't have it," the chorus crowed.

What was happening in Prague was that the crowd was coalescing into a political force. Unlike Poland, where Solidarity had forged programs and structures during nearly a decade of clandestine activities, Czechoslovakia had no mass dissident movement. Nor were the churches able to serve as sanctuaries for protest, as was true in both Poland and East Germany. Essentially there were only a handful of often-persecuted dissidents associated with groups like Charter 77 and the Committee for the Defense of the Unjustly Accused. And yet, when the dam of repression began to give way, these few people—a playwright. a priest,

and a number of coal stokers—formed a political nucleus that very
quickly attracted a mass of followers.

Civic Forum: Politics on a Shoestring
By Henry Kamm

PRAGUE, Dec. 5—Civic Forum, which in scarcely two weeks has assumed the mantle of Czechoslovakia's political opposition, is a mass movement whose members simply declare themselves by shouting for freedom at demonstrations and whose leaders serve by acclamation.

And yet despite such loose organization, the group has forced and shaped greater changes in the country than what has taken place in two decades.

The group has no master plan, no bylaws, and its strategy is not drafted by professional consultants. Instead, its leaders, a group clustered around Vaclav Havel, the dramatist and human rights campaigner, conduct marathon crisis sessions in temporary headquarters in a dingy downtown theater, altering their plans from hour to hour. The group is in the process of moving to quarters that until recently housed the Czech-Soviet Friendship Society.

As the discussions continue into the night, new people come in while weary participants head elsewhere. For instance, as Mr. Havel and some others crossed the Vltava River to meet with Prime Minister Ladislav Adamec, others headed to a balcony on Wenceslas Square to address crowds or to attend concerts to be cheered by young supporters, or to go to news conferences and interviews.

The atmosphere is hectic and informal. Even distinguished visitors get only cursory attention. When Alexander Dubcek, who led the Prague Spring of 1968, called on Mr. Havel last week, the playwright, who had others waiting for him, had Mr. Dubcek sit in on a staff meeting. The former leader listened to the discussion, which continued as if he were not there, for two and a half hours and then left quietly.

Meals are taken on the fly or not at all. Most participants are clearly in need of sleep. The wife of a principal leader, asked if she needed anything available from the West, replied, "We're running short of vitamin pills to keep him going." The Forum is run on a shoestring, with all of its leaders and volunteer workers paying their own way. They all continue to go to their regular jobs while they debate and shape the future of their nation.

One example of the activities that have been going on in the basement of the Laterna Magica theater is reflected in the efforts of three men who have been pondering and discussing what kind of program and what kind of priorities Forum should propose to the nation, once the machinery is set up for national dialogue and public discourse.

"In three days—which for this period is a very long time—of very intense discussions, we worked out our principles," said Josef Vavrousek, an economist and ecologist, who worked with Petr Pithart, a lawyer and political scientist, and Ivan Havel, Vaclav's brother, a computer specialist.

The principles, made public last Wednesday, state broad goals under the headings of law, politics, foreign policy, economy, social justice, environment and culture. The statement sets the objective of turning Czechoslovakia into a democratic state of laws that will "again assume its honorable place" in the world.

Currently nine subcommittees are at work to put flesh on these bare bones. In addition to the seven principles, there is one charged with recording today's history and that of 1968 and the Soviet-led invasion, and another that is concerned with planning the internal organization of Forum.

In an interview in a café above his windowless "office," Mr. Vavrousek emphasized that there would be no revenge. "We don't want another genocide of the Czech intelligentsia," he said, referring to the mass firings and expulsions of professionals who refused to approve the invasion in the months after the tanks arrived. He also referred to the purges and persecutions of intellectuals in the last fifty years, the first carried out by Nazis in 1938–39, and the other by the Communists in 1948.

"We can't say, 'You're a Communist, so you're no good,' " Mr. Vavrousek said. "There are 1.7 million party members. That would mean another decline of Czechoslovakia."

Mr. Vavrousek added that of the various impulses that have brought the adherents of Forum together "the ethical level is the most important consideration." He noted that the group, which came together so quickly and suddenly, embraces many different points of view. "Ethics is the integrative factor for all of us," he continued.

Moreover, said Mr. Vavrousek, ethical pressure is the major mechanism by which the mass membership influences those who have assumed leadership. "They criticize extremely hard" when they believe a speaker for the Forum is showing intolerance, he said.

He said Mr. Havel held a special position. "We are respectful to each other, but he gets slightly more respect than all the others," said Mr. Vavrousek, attributing the high esteem for Mr. Havel to the commitment to moral positions that the playwright showed through years of imprisonment.

"We can only understand this by the history of Czechoslovakia," he said when asked to explain the exceptional tolerance shown to representatives of a repressive regime during its decline. He said it grew from "a culture of mutual understanding" that kept the Czech nation alive in three centuries of subjugation to Austria.

Mr. Vavrousek said Mr. Havel was directly linked to the ethics of Thomas G. Masaryk, the founding President of Czechoslovakia, who anchored the nation's political character in the tradition of humaneness.

He said the Communist regime had driven people into "inner emigration" by violating these values. To be in contact with those of common values, which was politically impossible, Mr. Vavrousek said, people found each other in churches or sports clubs and other innocuous groups. "Even people in the party joined," he said.

"These became the cells of the Civic Forum," said Mr. Vavrousek. "Together, they have set off a chain reaction of mutual trust."

On December 6 Egon Krenz, who had replaced Erich Honecker as a younger, ostensibly less tainted, more acceptable leader, bowed out like his predecessor, who by this time was under detention facing charges of abusing his power and enriching himself. In Prague, Ladislav Adamec, the new and ostensible liberal Communist Prime Minister, threatened to quit. And Vaclav Havel, the ironic playwright and much imprisoned dissident, declared that he was willing to serve as President.

East German Out as Chief of State; Party in Disarray

By Serge Schmemann

EAST BERLIN, Dec. 6—East Germany's fallen Communist chief, Egon Krenz, gave up his remaining state positions today amid the continuing political turmoil. The foundering Communist Party advanced its emergency congress to Friday and is expected to shed its Stalinist structures and even its name.

The developments added to a sense of a political whirlwind, fed by the rapid disintegration of the Communist Party before the anger of the nation over revelations of widespread corruption at the top.

Mr. Krenz was replaced as the head of state on an interim basis by Manfred Gerlach, the head of the small Liberal Democratic Party, which until recently was subservient to the Communists but like other small parties has broken away. . . .

The caretaker committee formed Sunday to steer the Communist Party toward the emergency congress announced today that the meeting would start Friday instead of December 15.

The committee gave no reason for the shift, but several party members said a tide of resignations by members, coupled with the collapse of party authority, had made it imperative to hold the congress as soon as possible. Delegates have already been selected by local organizations.

Members said the congress would almost certainly change the name of the Communist Party, whose official name is the Socialist Unity Party, and could well transform it along the lines of Western social democracy, possibly abandoning the factory cells that have traditionally been its primary base.

Neues Deutschland, the official Communist organ, asked in an editorial whether the party needed a Politburo any longer and urged the congress to "radically end structural Stalinism." The *Berliner Zeitung* urged a new name for a "new socialist party."

But given the tempo of the time, no one dared to predict what the congress would do, or how long it would last. . . .

At the East Berlin City Hall, a government committee opened public hearings on the violent clashes between the police and demonstrators in early October. The clashes led to the mass demonstrations that toppled Mr. Honecker.

At today's session, the East Berlin Police Chief, Friedhelm Rausch, said the former Minister of State Security, Erich Mielke, had given the direct order "under all circumstances not to permit demonstrations and to disperse them."

Czech Premier Quits as Dissidents Press to Control Cabinet

By John Tagliabue

PRAGUE, Dec. 7—Ladislav Adamec resigned today as Czechoslovakia's Communist Prime Minister and was replaced by his relatively unknown 43-year-old deputy. Mr. Adamec reportedly felt that the new leader would find it easier to put together a cabinet acceptable to the opposition led by Civic Forum.

The 63-year-old Mr. Adamec announced his resignation as he met with the increasingly independent members of once-docile parties allied to the Communists. According to some of these non-Communist politicians, Mr. Adamec told them that a new, younger leader would be better able to achieve a compromise on the composition of a Government.

Shortly thereafter, President Gustav Husak, among the hardest of Czechoslovak hard-liners, asked Marian Calfa, a Slovak, who was named deputy Prime Minister when the current Government was empaneled five days ago, to take over for Mr. Adamec and continue seeking a solution.

In the meantime, Civic Forum sustained its pressure on the Government, once again raising the prospect of renewed mass demonstrations and a general strike, as its leaders publicly offered the names of recently imprisoned and ostracized dissidents on lists of those it wanted to be included in a Government that would diminish the power of the Communists.

Spokesmen for the Forum said that shortly before Mr. Adamec resigned he had been given a list of people favored by the Forum for ministerial appointments that included Jiri Dienstbier, a man who has spent most of the last two decades forced to work as a coal stoker; Jan Carnogursky, a Catholic human rights campaigner released from prison two weeks ago; and Petr Miller, a worker at a large industrial plant in Prague.

The opposition group spokesman said the group had nominated Mr. Dienstbier to be Foreign Minister, Mr. Carnogursky to be deputy Prime Minister, and Mr. Miller as Minister of Social Affairs.

As pressure on the Government mounted, some people within the small People's Party, which has recently allied itself more and more with Civic Forum, said that the goal of negotiations between the opposition and the Government should be the replacement of the Communist President, Gustav Husak, and the formation of a cabinet in which Communist Ministers would be a minority.

As the demands on the Government seemed to increase, Civic Forum leaders renewed their warnings that a general strike, similar to a two-hour nationwide work stoppage they staged last week, would be held this Monday unless talks produced some significant progress. . . .

310

Havel Makes It Official: He'd Accept Top Billing

By Henry Kamm

PRAGUE, Dec. 7—Vaclav Havel, the playwright and opposition leader, declared his readiness tonight to become President.

His announcement, in reply to a barrage of questions at a news conference, marked a quantum jump in a meteoric political career. In less than a month, the modest 53-year-old writer has gone from being a bookish and persecuted symbol of resistance to totalitarianism to become the acclaimed leader of the Civic Forum mass movement, which is shaking the foundations of a 41-year-old Communist regime.

The boyish-looking Mr. Havel, who until recently was often conveyed in police cars and police wagons, has since last week been riding in chauffeured Government limousines to meetings with the top leaders of the Communist Party and state structure.

And tonight, after fencing wittily with several reporters and refusing to deny his availability, he finally owned up to it.

"I have repeatedly said my occupation is writer," he replied to an American correspondent. "I have no political ambitions. I don't feel myself to be a professional politician. But I have always placed the public interest above my own.

"And if, God help us, the situation develops in such a way that the only service that I could render my country would be to do this, then of course I would do it." . . .

The whirlwind pace of change had most Czechoslovaks concentrating on where they were headed, wondering what new twists lay ahead. But from the west of the country came a story that underscored how far they had already come.

For Hidden Slovak Dissidents, a Guide

By Brenda Fowler

BRATISLAVA, CZECHOSLOVAKIA—When a visitor rings the doorbell at the apartment of Bishop Jan Korec, there is no sound inside, but a small light goes on in the kitchen. He would not want frequent ringing to be heard by the neighbors upstairs, who for the last eight years have been assigned to keep tabs on Bishop Korec, the leader of the underground church in Slovakia.

Prohibited from celebrating Mass because his secret ordination in

1950 is not recognized by the state-sponsored organization of priests, the 64-year-old Bishop has worked quietly since then, waiting for a time when he might openly practice his faith again.

His life underground parallels that of many dissidents in Slovakia, where 60 percent of the population is Catholic. Less oriented toward the West and its media than their statesmen in Prague, many Slovaks have worked quietly within the Catholic Church, publishing illegal books and newspapers and sometimes going to prison. Unlike best-known opposition figures in Bohemia—the region that includes the capital—such as the Civic Forum leader Vaclav Havel, few Slovak dissidents are members of human rights groups like Charter 77.

"In Slovakia, the leaders of the movement were ordinary people in the church and only a few intellectuals," said Jan Carnogursky, a Catholic dissident here who was the only person from Slovakia at a meeting between Mr. Havel and Government officials in November.

"And even the intellectuals weren't interested in publicity," Mr. Carnogursky said. "Mostly they were just interested in working among young people and they felt that publicity would hurt them."

The most common form of protest in Slovakia is the pilgrimage, dozens of which are held each year, he said. Last year, 500,000 Slovaks took part in pilgrimages, and one to the thirteenth-century town of Levoca drew more than 100,000 people.

But there have also been demonstrations. Slovak Catholics maintain that the student protest on November 17 in Prague was not the first occasion that police intervened brutally at a large demonstration in the last twenty years.

In March of last year, they said, several thousand Catholics, including many elderly people, gathered with candles in front of the National Theater here to call for greater religious freedom. The police closed off the area and began harassing the protesters, finally using water cannon to disperse them.

For Bishop Korec, the mass demonstrations and changes in the Communist Party and Czechoslovak Government have brought a sense that his own personal struggles and those of all Slovak Catholics may finally be nearing an end.

As a young seminary student in 1950, he was briefly interned when the Government liquidated all monasteries and seminaries. An interned bishop secretly ordained him a priest in 1950. Less than a year later his superiors decided to make him a bishop, and he was secretly consecrated on August 24, 1951.

"Then I began fulfilling my mission," the Bishop said, though at that time not even his mother knew he was a bishop. He spent the next ten years doing manual labor until he was arrested in 1960 on a charge of treason for having helped to educate seminary students. Sentenced to 12 years in prison, and led out of the court handcuffed to a murderer, Bishop Korec worked on a lathe shaping crystal for chandeliers, a job that ground away the fingertips of those not trained for such a craft.

During the liberalization movement of 1968 he was released from prison and met Pope Paul VI at the Vatican, though he was still not allowed to work as a priest. Since 1970 the Bishop has lived in the apartment of a friend, working in a small room crammed with books. In that time he has written the bulk of his 65 manuscripts and books, most of them published abroad.

The authorities have continued to harass him, and he has been interrogated by police 30 times in the last ten years. This interview, Bishop Korec said, indicating his informant-neighbors upstairs, was only the second time in eight years that he has spoken in a normal voice.

Then, his voice dropping to a whisper, his eyes opening wide, he asked, "Can you imagine what kind of a total physical stress it was to speak like this? Can you imagine?"

Farther to the northeast, another people were pursuing their own plans for establishing democratic pluralism. The Lithuanians were advancing their challenge not on the streets but through parliamentary and Constitutional means.

Lithuania Legalizes Rival Parties, Removing Communists' Monopoly
By Esther B. Fein

MOSCOW, Dec. 7—Lithuania became the first Soviet republic to abolish the Communist Party's guaranteed monopoly on power when its parliament voted overwhelmingly today to legalize rival political parties.

Rejecting repeated Kremlin pleas and warnings to curb its political defiance, the Lithuanian parliament changed the republic's constitution to abolish the guarantee of power for the Communist Party.

With the vote of 243 to 1 with 39 abstentions, Lithuania, one of 15

Soviet republics, joined the majority of Eastern bloc nations in legalizing a multiparty system.

In neighboring Estonia, the central committee of the Communist Party agreed at a meeting today that Article Six of the republic's constitution, which guarantees the Communist Party's pre-eminence, should be annulled, setting the stage for a similar constitutional amendment in that republic.

Both decisions today are clear signs that the tensions tearing at the former strongholds of Communist power elsewhere in Eastern Europe are growing in the Soviet Union itself.

The actions are sure to anger President Mikhail S. Gorbachev, who while not interfering with such moves by the Soviet Union's East European allies, has said the Communist Party is the only force capable of seeing the country through its current economic and political crises.

A leading Lithuanian Communist Party official said today that Mr. Gorbachev had "without a doubt" contacted the Lithuanian party leader, Algirdas Brazauskas, to try to prevent the legislature's move and to censure it. But Mr. Brazauskas clearly resisted the pressure, which Mr. Gorbachev has brought to bear on several previous occasions, and voted for the constitutional amendment.

The parliaments of Poland, Hungary, Czechoslovakia and East Germany have all voted recently to deny the Communist Party its long-guaranteed "leading role" in political, educational and social spheres.

According to people who attended or listened to the Lithuanian parliamentary session today, several deputies spoke of the changes elsewhere in Eastern Europe and urged the legislators to continue the progressive path that Lithuania had already begun. . . .

Amid the decay so evident in the Communist world, the only appeal for the retention of orthodoxy came from an island ninety miles from Florida.

Castro Says He'll Resist Changes Like Those Sweeping Soviet Bloc
By Larry Rohter

MEXICO CITY, Dec. 8—In his bluntest public rejection yet of the profound political and economic changes now sweeping the rest of the

Soviet bloc, President Fidel Castro of Cuba has vowed to resist all such reforms even if it means a parting of the ways with his allies.

"If destiny assigns us the role of one day being among the last defenders of socialism in a world in which the Yankee empire has succeeded in embodying Hitler's dream of world domination, we will know how to defend this bulwark to the last drop of blood," President Castro said in a speech delivered on Thursday in Havana and monitored here.

Mr. Castro's remarks were his first public comment on the state of East-West relations since last weekend's summit talks between President Bush and President Mikhail S. Gorbachev of the Soviet Union and reflected his growing ideological isolation within the Eastern bloc. At the meeting off Malta, Mr. Bush called on Mr. Gorbachev to do more to prevent Cuba from shipping arms to Nicaragua and to leftist guerrillas in El Salvador and also offered to assist Mr. Gorbachev in carrying out economic reforms.

Speaking at ceremonies honoring Cuban combatants killed in the course of "internationalist missions" in Angola, Ethiopia and other African countries, Mr. Castro did not criticize Mr. Gorbachev or any Eastern European leader by name. But he complained of the difficulty of building a Communist state when others are "slandering socialism, destroying its values, discrediting the party and liquidating its leading role, doing away with social discipline and sowing chaos and anarchy everywhere."

Mr. Gorbachev's policies of perestroika and glasnost, or restructuring and openness, have aroused interest in Cuba, which experimented briefly with a degree of economic liberalization early in the decade but then reversed course with a "rectification" program after Mr. Castro decided that some people were making too much money and egalitarianism was eroding. The Soviet leader received a warm popular welcome when he visited Cuba in April, but Mr. Castro has rejected many of Mr. Gorbachev's innovations as violations of Marxist-Leninist orthodoxy.

The transformations taking place elsewhere in the Soviet bloc coincide with Cuba's most serious political and leadership crisis in years. In July, several senior Cuban military officials were executed for drug trafficking in circumstances that have yet to be fully explained, and economic and morale problems have also forced Mr. Castro, who is 63 years old and has been in power for more than thirty years, to shake up his Cabinet.

The Cuban leader has long feared that the lessening of tensions between the United States and the Soviet Union will translate into changes in the military status quo in Europe that would increase Washington's ability to impose its own views elsewhere, including the Caribbean. He also remains firmly committed to the principle of "proletarian internationalism," a justification for intervention abroad that he fears is on the wane elsewhere.

According to reports from Managua, the Soviet Ambassador there met with Nicaraguan and Cuban officials on November 28, just days after Mr. Bush had blamed the Soviet Union for supplying arms to Mr. Castro that eventually ended up in the hands of rebels in El Salvador. "We are hearing that he really read them the riot act," said a European diplomat based in the Nicaraguan capital.

The official Cuban news agency Prensa Latina reported on Thursday that American forces at Guantanamo Bay Naval Station had fired twice on Cuban sentries outside, calling the incident "serious and of unpredictable consequences." Today, a Pentagon spokesman denied the charge, saying "no weapons or rounds ever crossed the fence line."

In his address, Mr. Castro justified the prohibition in Cuba of some Soviet publications, such as *Sputnik* and *Moscow News*. He said the measure was necessary because such publications were "filled with venom against the U.S.S.R. itself and against socialism" and have "demanded the cessation of just and equitable commercial relations between the U.S.S.R. and Cuba."

Since the early 1960's the Soviet Union has heavily subsidized the Cuban economy through such measures as the purchase of Cuban sugar at prices well above market levels and the sale at bargain rates of petroleum, some of which Cuba then resells to gain hard currency. Those subsidies, amounting to as much as $5 billion a year, have increasingly been questioned by Soviet officials as part of the economic restructuring that is under way.

"From the crisis that has emerged in the socialist camp, we can only expect negative economic consequences for our country," Mr. Castro said.

Just hours before Mr. Castro's appearance at the war commemoration ceremonies, during which he was accompanied by President Jose Eduardo dos Santos of Angola, the Cuban Government for the first time announced casualty figures for the more than 400,000 soldiers and "technical advisers" it has sent to fight in Africa over the last fifteen years. According to official statements, 2,289 Cubans have died abroad, more than 2,000 of them in Angola.

If there were any in East Germany who heard Mr. Castro's counsel, they may well have regarded the advice as either outdated or absurd. Instead of resorting to old slogans, the beleaguered party hunkered down in an emergency congress, and after rejecting a motion to dissolve itself, voted in Gregor Gysi as its new leader, citing among his virtues the fact that as a lawyer he had defended members of the amorphous New Forum opposition when they were persecuted three months earlier.

• • •

The paramount issue for those who had marched to bring down old Communist leaders had been liberty. The paramount issue for the leaders still plying their trade in both the East and the West was becoming the maintenance of stability, limits and borders. At the heart was the German question, and Helmut Kohl, who had earlier offered his vision of an amalgamated German nation without consulting any allies, now spoke in less definite terms.

Bonn Leader Softens His Plan for German Unity
By Craig R. Whitney

WEST BERLIN, Dec. 11—Taking account of foreign concerns, Chancellor Helmut Kohl of West Germany softened a vital element of his vision of German unity today as representatives of the four wartime occupying powers met here and insisted on "the importance of stability" in Eastern Europe.

In a speech to members of his Christian Democratic Party, Mr. Kohl eased away from his notion of an early "confederation" of the two German states—an idea that has worried the European allies, the United States and the Soviet Union by suggesting that German reunification could come without international approval.

"For several reasons, I am consciously not talking about a 'confederation,' " he said. "One of these reasons is that such a step raises questions that we cannot yet answer today because of the fact that both states in Germany belong to different alliances."

Mr. Kohl, who now says West Germany will not move toward unification without consulting with the Western alliance and the Soviet Union, said, "The goal of our policy never has been and never will be to establish an overpowerful Germany in the middle of Europe, as many in the Council of Europe, in London, Rome and Paris fear—just look at the newspapers," he said. But he added, "Reunification—that

317

is, regaining the state unity of Germany—remains our political goal."

While openly acknowledging the uneasiness of Germany's neighbors, Mr. Kohl also spoke with a view toward domestic politics on the issue of unification, which has become the central theme of West Germany's 1990 election campaign. As the Chancellor encouraged his Christian Democrats to run as the party that encouraged East Germans to march for freedom, the Social Democratic opposition in Bonn announced its own plan for a confederation of the two Germanys and accused the Kohl forces of plagiarizing its ideas. Mr. Kohl suggested today that many people had misunderstood his proposals, but he also said that German policy was being made not in the chancelleries but in the streets. And in protests tonight in the East German cities of Leipzig and Dresden, as many as 300,000 people took to the streets in a huge demonstration marked by insistent calls for unification, more so than in previous weeks. . . .

Since the upheavals began, the United States had been either slow or deliberate in its reactions. But as the year was ending, Secretary of State Baker visited both Germanys and outlined a comprehensive plan reaffirming a U.S. role in the new Europe that was yet to emerge.

Baker, in Berlin, Outlines a Plan to Make NATO a Political Group
By Thomas L. Friedman

POTSDAM, EAST GERMANY, Dec. 12—Seeking to give some American direction to the rapidly changing events in Europe, Secretary of State James A. Baker 3d today outlined proposals for transforming NATO from a primarily military organization to a political alliance.

Mr. Baker's proposal, made in a speech to the Berlin Press Club in West Berlin, was part of the most comprehensive and detailed set of ideas to emerge from the Bush Administration to deal with the upheavals that are reshaping the European political landscape.

Mr. Baker said he hoped that his ideas for recasting existing institutions like NATO, the European Economic Community and the Helsinki process could help channel the "peaceful revolution" under way in Europe into a stable, democratic new order.

Mr. Baker, in his speech, also proposed that the United States and the European Community work together to strengthen their ties. He urged support for changes in Czechoslovakia, Bulgaria and East Germany and suggested that the 35-nation Conference on Security and Cooperation in Europe be reshaped into a framework for "openness" between NATO and the armies of Eastern Europe.

Directly after his speech, Mr. Baker slipped into a Mercedes limousine and traveled to East Germany to deliver another message in a previously unannounced round of talks with East Germany's Communist Prime Minister, Hans Modrow, as well as with several East German opposition leaders.

Those talks were held in Potsdam, not far from the hall where Truman, Churchill and Attlee gathered to meet with Stalin in 1945 to frame Germany's postwar occupation, and they were made at the first visit of an American Secretary of State to East Germany. Potsdam lies just 20 miles southeast of Berlin.

While American officials would not say so explicitly, they left a clear impression that Mr. Baker's primary purpose in seeing Mr. Modrow was to do what he could to shore up his Government in the hope that it might survive long enough to conduct free elections, now scheduled for May. In other words, after refusing to visit East Germany for 45 years because it was considered to have an illegitimate, unrepresentative regime, an American Secretary of State finally made such a trip. Officials also said that Mr. Baker wanted personally to urge the opposition to keep its movement nonviolent and to approach the issue of German reunification with sober restraint. . . .

At about the same time, Mikhail Gorbachev was analyzing the tumult in Eastern Europe for his own Central Committee.

Excerpts from Speech by Gorbachev on Bloc

MOSCOW, Dec. 11—Following are excerpts from the speech by President Mikhail S. Gorbachev to the Communist Party Central Committee last Saturday, as translated by the Soviet press agency Tass:

Comrades, implementation of the long-term course of perestroika not only exerts a revolutionary influence on all the spheres of life of Soviet society, but also influences other socialist coutries and developments in the world. At the same time, perestroika itself comes under the influence of the world, and needs favorable international conditions.

This year signified major changes in Eastern Europe. In fact, processes there are developing swiftly. . . . The truth, about which we spoke so often in the past few years, has been reaffirmed once again: Where there is a delay in dealing with overripe problems, excesses are inevitable.

What is taking place in socialist countries is the logical outcome of a certain stage of development which made the peoples of these countries aware of the need for change. This is the result of internal development, the result of choice by peoples themselves.

For all the specificity of deep changes in socialist countries, one cannot deny the fact that they proceed in the same mainstream as our perestroika, although we in no way encouraged these processes.

In some socialist countries the situation has been unconventional. Fraternal parties are no longer ruling in Poland and Hungary. Our friends in the German Democratic Republic and Czechoslovakia have largely lost their positions. New political forces have emerged on the arena. They include both those who support the socialist idea and those who seek other ways of social development. . . .

The Soviet Union is building its relations with East European countries—whether they have been carrying out transformations for quite some time, or have only embarked on that road, or are yet to do it—on a single position of respect for sovereignty, noninterference and recognition of freedom of choice. We proceed from the fact that any nation has the right to decide its fate itself, including the choice of a system, ways, the pace and methods of its development. . . .

We firmly declare that we will see to it that no harm comes to the G.D.R. It is our strategic ally and a member of the Warsaw Treaty. It is necessary to proceed from the postwar realities—the existence of the two sovereign German states, members of the United Nations. Departure from this threatens . . . destabilization in Europe.

Naturally this is not to say that relations between the G.D.R. and the F.R.G. cannot change. Peaceful cooperation between them can and must develop. As for the future, it will take shape in the course of history, in the framework of the development of the general European process. . . .

Despite the image of tractability that Mr. Gorbachev was so eager to project abroad, at home he was growing more and more impatient with those who wanted to move faster and further than he thought appropriate.

Gorbachev Blocks Debate on Ending Party Supremacy

By Francis X. Clines

MOSCOW, Dec. 12—President Mikhail S. Gorbachev, appearing wary and temperamental, today beat back attempts by the national Congress to question the Communist Party's constitutional monopoly on power and politics in the Soviet Union.

In the vote rejecting the proposal to take the issue up now rather than later, Mr. Gorbachev was supported by 1,139 deputies, while 839 others favored enlarging the agenda to include debate over the existing Article Six, which gives Communists dominance. Fifty-six other legislators abstained.

The issue, an echo of the rush from Communism now under way in the Soviet Union's once-obeisant Eastern European satellites, was settled early and quickly by Mr. Gorbachev in the Congress's opening winter session.

The Soviet leader's obvious concern veered toward testiness at times, as he allocated most debating time to his own insistence on the party's necessary primacy and cut off some speakers, waving his hand dismissively and snapping, "That's all, that's all."

The debate demonstrated Mr. Gorbachev's overwhelming, near-bullying parliamentary dominance of the 2,106-member assembly. The Congress of People's Deputies, the nation's new lawmaking forum, is trying to come to grips with the limited democratic initiatives introduced last spring by Mr. Gorbachev in the nation's first partly competitive elections under its one-party system.

Only a few deputies came forward to present a call for multiparty politics and an end to Communism's seven decades of monopoly over society.

Among them was Andrei D. Sakharov, the Nobel laureate and human rights champion, who was unceremoniously cut short by Mr. Gorbachev. But the final vote still managed to put a considerable measure of minority interest in the issue on the public record, indicating, as Mr. Gorbachev conceded, that it likely would return if only as part of a less timely, more drawn out attempt to revise the Constitution.

"I think a way will be found," he declared, while tenaciously defending for now the party supremacy that the Eastern European nations have been typically shedding in their first days of poltical revolt.

The vote took place in the Palace of Congresses.

In a long, emotional, at times desk-slapping defense of Communist hegemony, Mr. Gorbachev contended the issue was a choice between remaining on an intensified quest for his perestroika program of national review while guided by the party, or veering off on a "hasty" political tangent.

"We would be making the biggest mistake," he said. He argued that he did not necessarily disagree with the proponents of change in the long run, but that changes should come "in the framework of the normal constitutional process."

That is a framework for procrastination, in the view of critics, but Mr. Gorbachev dismissed their attempt to raise the issue in the Congress as a "bell-ringing" fire brigade.

"We must not involve society in clashes," he told the lawmakers, some of whom predicted there would be repeated future attempts to debate the party's privileged status.

One leader of the nationalist movement in Estonia, Marju Lauristin, cautioned Mr. Gorbachev that the issue, now flaming with popular sentiment in Eastern Europe, had arrived. "It has ripened for discussion," she said in a direct, brief summary. "It's obsolete for our political system and now has become an obstacle."

Mr. Gorbachev, a lawyer and ever-vigilant master of the Congress's agenda, worked hard to hold the debate to the procedural question of changing the agenda and to rule out substantive statements questioning the party's monopoly on politics and power.

"I'm asking you two to leave," he told two deputies, ruling even before they spoke that their points were not germane.

"All deputies who do not have something new to propose may return to their seats," he announced, waving his hand in frowning contrast to the beaming, cooperative summit leader that so recently was on display in his role more familiar to the outside world.

One deputy who did reach the rostrum, Yevgeny Yevtushenko, the poet, spoke directly as a non-party member to the many Communists in the hall, warning them that in these times the party would be wise to take up the fight to open up the pluralism debate.

"You cannot gain prestige from a single paragraph," he said, referring to Article Six. "Such authority should be earned daily."

At the last minute, after Mr. Gorbachev had winnowed the speaker's line away, Dr. Sakharov arose from his sixth-row seat and walked slowly toward the microphone.

His approach prompted groans from some party stalwarts as he advanced to speak. Leaning to the microphone, he pleaded in his characteristic sharp-toned voice for the fullest congressional debate of such amendments crucial to revamping Communism as property ownership and party pluralism. "We have to open up a way for the Parliament to adopt these laws without amending the Constitution," Mr. Sakharov said, speaking of the urgency of the nation's needs.

"This will not do," Mr. Gorbachev interrupted at one of Dr. Sakharov's points, for a brief moment no longer taking his usual care to appear courtly toward a man respected in the West as a voice of conscience.

Dr. Sakharov sought to raise Article Six by citing telegrams from the public, but Mr. Gorbachev, unimpressed, interjected: "I can show you three folders of them with thousands. Let's not manipulate public opinion."

"That's all," he said, waving Dr. Sakharov back from the microphone.

That exchange marked the last public appearance by Dr. Sakharov. The old dissident, human rights campaigner and renowned physicist died of a heart attack two days later.

Government That Exiled Him Hurries to Mourn Sakharov

By Francis X. Clines

MOSCOW, Dec. 15—The Soviet Government, which once exiled Andrei D. Sakharov for being a human rights champion, today embraced him in death. President Mikhail S. Gorbachev mourned the national loss of "a man of conviction and sincerity."

The Government moved swiftly to seek a state funeral and marshal Politburo tributes for the tart-tongued humanist who died on Thursday night, only hours after delivering another denunciation of the Communist monopoly of the nation.

But the Sakharov family was reported working on other plans for the burial of the 68-year-old Nobel laureate and deputy to the new national legislature who collapsed from a heart attack and died alone in his study.

The sudden news swept this hard-pressed nation with much of the political and emotional power that Dr. Sakharov wielded in two decades of singular criticism of the Kremlin.

Many Soviet citizens felt that with his death President Gorbachev had lost a badly needed, greatly respected moral goad. And Dr. Sakharov's nation had lost another embattled individualist who demonstrated the virtue of resisting the regime at personal risk in the service of others' freedom.

"As long as he was alive, we all felt safe," said a woman who stood mourning on the street below his apartment, her face wet with tears and snow.

"*Uzhasna,*" she muttered in Russian: terrible.

No less lamentable than the death of the physically frail, spiritually relentless man were the political ironies that ensued before the eyes of Muscovites: guards of the K.G.B., who once kept Dr. Sakharov at bay in his apartment, cleared a path to his front door this afternoon so a quickly assembled Government funeral commission could express sad-faced grief to his widow, Yelena G. Bonner.

Tass, the Government press agency, which once denounced Dr. Sakharov as a traitor deserving his six years of internal exile in Gorky, issued warm posthumous descriptions of him as a civil rights battler and even offered videotapes of his final days for sale to foreign correspondents at $1,500.

Dr. Sakharov's death was the opening story on the evening television news program *Vremya*. The account focused briefly on the moment of silence observed in the Congress rather than on a detailed biography of Dr. Sakharov and his long history of resisting the Kremlin. *Izvestia,* the Government newspaper, had no mention in its evening edition.

Zglyad, the alternative Friday television program of current events, now the most popular in the nation, devoted considerable time and sympathy to Dr. Sakharov in the recollective style reminiscent of American television's treatment of the assassination of Senator Robert F. Kennedy and the Rev. Dr. Martin Luther King, Jr. Most poignant was a moment when Dr. Sakharov's widow paused in mid-interview as it dawned on her what she was discussing.

"My God," she said, her eyes welling with tears. "My God."'

"They did all they could to kill him," lamented Boris Fayants, one of the many ordinary Soviet citizens who seemed clearly to feel that Soviet political life, with its fresh seeds of hope born when President Gorbachev ended Dr. Sakharov's exile, had been drastically altered by the death.

"For us, it was wonderful to see him elected to the Congress, but for him it was a terrible mistake," Mr. Fayants, a mathematician, said, grasping at his own heart.

Mr. Gorbachev said, "This is a big loss," choosing to comment not from the Congress rostrum but in a corridor outside in a brief interview with reporters. "This was not some sort of a political intriguer, but a person who had his own ideas, his own convictions, which he expressed openly and directly."

The death of Dr. Sakharov, a physicist who evolved from designing the Soviet hydrogen bomb to leading the nation's antiwar movement, deprives the Soviet leader of a badly needed force for credibility.

Mr. Gorbachev was obviously peeved at times to see Dr. Sakharov arise regularly from his sixth-row congressional seat to deliver sharp-toned blasts at Gorbachev programs. But the President seemed far more mindful of the fact that he gained credit for having invited such political change and goading in the first place.

It was credit from the outside world more than from the members of the Communist majority in Congress. After Dr. Sakharov's death, they all had to stand for a moment of silence in his memory this morning.

Sakharov associates complained that the funeral commission included prominent party officials who did nothing to help him a decade ago when the Government ostracized him for refusing to cease his criticism of the Soviet combat role in Afghanistan, and he was exiled to Gorky.

The body of the slender, stoop-shouldered physicist was discovered by his wife. He had returned to their eighth-floor apartment near the center of the city after another long day of congressional debate and caucusing with the opposition group he helped to found.

Needing to work further on a congressional speech on the economic crisis, Dr. Sakharov had gone down to his study, a separate apartment on the seventh floor.

"He was in his undershirt, probably getting undressed, and he fell to the floor with a heart attack," said a friend, the poet Vladimir Kornilov.

Dr. Sakharov's body, wrapped in a green sackcloth and strapped to a stretcher, was carried down to a waiting ambulance at 1:30 this afternoon. Wet, thick snow fell on the city. "There is no one in the Congress to take up his leadership," said Igor Belkov, a passerby watching the scene. "He was the real leader in the real perestroika."

In Congress, Dr. Sakharov's admirers had the same thought. Anatoly A. Sobchak, normally a steely-eyed analyst of things politic, was teary-eyed in conceding the enormous loss of Dr. Sakharov.

"This was a man whose uncompromising fight in the period of

stagnation—one on one against the whole Government apparatus, beaten down, betrayed—was maintained with all his strength so that this day, today, would come," he said. . . .

Dr. Sakharov died in the midst of a campaign to demonstrate to the nation the value of opposition voices in the one-party legislature. The stilling of his own special voice now makes this point most dramatically, but raises questions of how the nebulous early opposition caucus he helped found, the Interregional Group, will carry on without him.

Both the opposition and Mr. Gorbachev seemed to benefit from Dr. Sakharov's treks to the rostrum. The last public exchange of the two men on Tuesday was typical. Legislators groaned as Dr. Sakharov came up to speak. Mr. Gorbachev had been busy brushing aside other speakers, but not Andrei Dmitrivich.

In one sentence, squinting and craggy-voiced, Dr. Sakharov ripped into the Government's failure to move toward its promises on land reform. In the next, he turned toward Mr. Gorbachev wielding a sheaf of telegrams like a fiery sword, speaking for citizens demanding that Congress repeal the Communist Party's power monopoly.

"That's all," Mr. Gorbachev snapped, growing short with the man he freed from exile. Dr. Sakharov retreated from the uncertain new legislature for the last time looking unsurprised and unsatisfied, as if he harbored every intent of complaining another day.

Despite the changes that have already taken place in East Germany, the level of national yearning had not abated. Though travel restrictions had been removed, the pace of emigration to the West had not slackened once the novelty of free movement wore off. In the face of this, the Communists followed the same general formula that had been pursued first in Poland and Hungary and was now also taking place in Czechoslovakia—that is, they gave up their monopolies in successive stages. They abandoned the leading role that they had held by fiat, they changed the symbols, they eased censorship, they tinkered with economic reform, in some cases they even changed the name of the party. With each such step came the hope that since they had lost de jure omnipotence, society might now be willing to grant them some de facto credibility. Indeed, what seemed to be happening was that society was simply demanding unlimited freedoms.

Berlin Communists Outline Platform

By Craig R. Whitney

EAST BERLIN, Dec. 17—Acknowledging a struggle for the country's continued existence as well as its own, the Communist Party of East Germany said today that it would give up the formal trappings of power and declared itself ready to compete in elections next May with other emerging democratic forces.

And the Communist-controlled Cabinet, acknowledging the failure of an earlier plan to rename the Ministry of State Security, one of the most feared institutions of control, announced today that it would dissolve the secret police agency.

It said a new civilian administrator would be named to supervise the assignment of legitimate intelligence functions to two new and separate organizations reporting directly to Prime Minister Hans Modrow.

Today's developments seemed to reflect a turning point in the way the East German authorities have responded to the revolution on the streets that swept the country's hard-line leader, Erich Honecker, out of power in October. They apparently realize that the popular mood will not accept superficial changes, but demands real ones.

Egon Krenz, who briefly replaced Mr. Honecker, tried the first course, failed and was forced to resign along with the entire party leadership on December 3.

And both Gregor Gysi, the 41-year-old lawyer who became Communist Party Chairman last weekend, and Mr. Modrow also recognize that their country could quickly be swallowed up by its larger, economically more powerful Western neighbor unless they can persuade East German voters next spring to stand by their country as a separate, "socialist" alternative.

"Like it or not, the election campaign has already begun," Mr. Gysi said today in a speech outlining policy positions to 2,654 delegates at a resumed special party congress here. "On December 3," he concluded, two and a half hours later, "a party leadership that had failed resigned, and there was a serious danger that the party, and with it the country, could go under."

To a standing ovation before the delegates ended the congress by singing the "Internationale," he said, "We're all ready now to raise our heads high and fight for the party and for the country."

They also decided to drop the party statute defining the Communists as "the conscious and organized shock force of the working class," and on Saturday night amended the party's formal name to add a commitment to socialist democracy, producing the jawbreaking title of Socialist Unity Party of Germany–Party of Democratic Socialism, or, in German, S.E.D.-P.D.S., for short.

Mr. Gysi read a remarkable catalog of confessions of past party and state failures, and the delegates eagerly assented to all of the criticisms.

By way of giving up the trappings of power, he proposed turning part of the giant party headquarters in East Berlin into a public conference center with a library, a movie theater and hotel rooms. He called for dissolution of established party organizations in the armed forces, and he said military uniforms should be replaced because they resemble those of the Nazi Wehrmacht. Military parades and goose-stepping, he suggested, should also go.

"And we'd be doing not only ourselves, but more important all soldiers, a favor," he said.

Concern over the danger to the continued existence of East Germany as a nation was never far from Mr. Gysi's mind in his long speech this morning.

"Supporting the Modrow coalition Government is of life-and-death importance for our country and our citizens," he said. "We all have to be clear that whether our ship of state can steer clear of the reefs of anarchy and annexation by West Germany depends essentially on this Government." Mr. Modrow, a Communist, formed the Cabinet last month with twelve non-Communist members from previously subservient smaller parties. . . .

Mr. Gysi was applauded when he criticized East Germany's professional sports machine, a source of Olympic medals, international recognition and prestige under the Honecker leadership.

"In sports we see an important, but no longer the only cultural achievement of our country," he said, "and we urge that it be supported but not elevated to a question of national prestige."

More important for his party's future constituency, he seemed to say, were things like grocery stores. "After forty years, it must be possible for us to have vegetable stores that it's a pleasure to go to and, more important, to come out of," he said to laughter. "And for that, the permanent choice between cabbage and apples just won't do."

WINTER 1989–90

Within the last two weeks of the year, the general pace of reform seemed quick and steady throughout the East bloc. In Poland, where the non-Communist-led government was completing its fourth month, the emphasis shifted from political reforms to the massive reorganization of the economy. A proposal was drafted and enacted just before the new year calling for an end of subsidies, a free float of prices and other measures that would be certain to bring painful unemployment and high prices, at least in the short run. The plan was being sold to the nation as the bitter medicine needed to finally escape from the stranglehold of central planning and structural inefficiency. Implementation of the package was certain to prove the greatest challenge for the new government but if it worked, Poland, the first of the bloc countries to have moved toward pluralism and democracy would be the first also to achieve an economy where the value of money, time and labor as well as goods would be determined by markets and not fiat.

In Czechoslovakia, the pressure from the nation was forcing the leaders of party and state to concede on the composition of the newly emerging government and to move toward free elections. Facing the prospects of strikes and demonstrations, the Communists in the parliament were preparing to accept as the country's leaders two men whom their party had persecuted and scorned for more than twenty years— Alexander Dubcek and Vaclav Havel.

These events were all remarkable, but they were no longer quite so startling for a world that had seen the Berlin wall come down. The bloodless revolutions of the East bloc appeared to be playing themselves out with a steady march toward greater democracy and freer markets.

Leaders of the Two Germanys Meet; Symbolic Reconciliation Cheered

By Serge Schmemann

DRESDEN, EAST GERMANY—The leaders of the two Germanys met today for the first time since the East fell into the throes of protest and change, and in a symbolic reconciliation agreed to reopen the Brandenburg Gate in Berlin and introduce free movement across their border for all Germans by Christmas.

The announcement was the centerpiece of the first official visit to East Germany by Chancellor Helmut Kohl, an emotional journey on which he was greeted at every stop by thousands of East Germans, many waving West German flags and clamoring for the reunification still opposed by their leaders.

In the sort of public adulation that has usually eluded him at home, the crowds often broke into chants of "Helmut! Helmut!" Their cheers were loudest when the Chancellor mounted a platform in front of the memorial ruins of the Frauenkirche at dusk and declared to a throng of about 10,000:

"My goal, when the historic moment makes it possible, is the unity of our nation. I know we can reach this goal. It is a difficult way, but it is a good way in our common future, though it won't happen overnight."

At the end of his address, Mr. Kohl wished the East Germans a merry Christmas and then, his voice breaking, concluded, "God bless our German fatherland."

At a news conference earlier, the East German Prime Minister, Hans Modrow, announced that he and Mr. Kohl would join the mayors of the two Berlins to inaugurate a pedestrian crossing at the Brandenburg Gate. East German state television later said the ceremony would take place on Christmas Eve.

The eighteenth-century triumphal arch has stood for the last 28 years as the premier symbol of German division, a war-damaged relic of past glory stranded in the no-man's-land on the eastern side of the Berlin wall. The West German President, Richard von Weizsaecker, once declared that as long as the gate was closed the "German question" would remain open.

The opening would unite the divided halves of what was once Berlin's premier boulevard, Unter den Linden. The avenue is still among the most elegant in both Berlins, lined with embassies in the

East and with parkland in the West, where it was renamed "17 June" in honor of the 1953 anti-Communist uprising in East Berlin.

Mr. Modrow and Mr. Kohl also moved up the ending of all restrictions on the movement of West Germans across the border, originally scheduled for January 1, to Christmas Eve. That would effectively end any hindrance to the free movement of Germans across the line that has divided their nation for the last forty years.

The two leaders also announced plans to sign a treaty by next spring establishing future forms of social, economic, cultural and other ties. The treaty plans are a response to Mr. Modrow's call for a "community of treaties" between the two Germanys, as well as to Mr. Kohl's call for the establishment of "confederative structures" as a prelude to reunification. . . .

The chants of "Helmut! Helmut!' were not only a personal tribute, they were also typical of the familiarity East Germans have come to feel for West German public figures. Similar cheers have met Willy Brandt, the former Chancellor; Hans-Dietrich Genscher, the Foreign Minister and President von Weizsaecker.

Mr. Kohl, who rarely prompts such a spirited reaction in his own Germany, seemed to revel in the televised cheers, especially with West German national elections now less than a year away and German unity looming as the dominant issue.

Before the ruins of the Frauenkirche in this city, which was destroyed by Allied bombers in 1945 and then painstakingly rebuilt, he said: "I stand here to bring the greetings of fellow citizens in West Germany, and also to express my recognition and admiration for the nonviolent revolution in the G.D.R. It is the first time in German history, and I thank you for it."

While most of Eastern Europe was approaching the year-end holidays with an enthusiasm touched off by the accelerating pace of social and political change, another sudden and unexpected event erupted in Rumania, the country that until then had seemed impervious to the reforms sweeping Europe's Communist states, remaining in the very tight grasp of its Stalinist dictator, Nicolae Ceausescu. The first news of any stirrings there reported that on December 17 security forces were battling protesters in the city of Timisoara, near the Yugoslav border. As details slowly emerged, it turned out that a pastor of the Hungarian Reform Church, a man named Laszlo Tokes, was about to be forcibly deported from his home for having openly preached against the Ceau-

sescu policy of razing old villages and replacing them with agricultural factories where families were to live in giant dormitories. As the police came to seize him, his Hungarian-speaking parishioners sought to protect him and they were joined by students and others from the city's Rumanian majority. There was a protest rally. The security forces fired into the crowd. Ceausescu went on a state visit to Iran. The protests continued and intensified. The security forces received orders to kill. Ceausescu returned and summoned another of his state-managed demonstrations in the capital. This time when he denounced counterrevolutionaries, he was booed. The shock on his face was shown on television just before the transmission was cut off. Very quickly, the Rumanian revolution had begun and the clamor for freedom had spread to the last holdout in the Warsaw Pact.

Hatred of Security Forces Growing as Rumanian Atrocities Increase

By Celestine Bohlen

ARAD, RUMANIA, Dec. 23—"It's the Securitate," yelled a burly man, leaning out of the open door of the small white car as it careened, horn honking and lights blazing, down a dark and empty boulevard. "They're shooting again, the bastards."

It was after midnight and fighting had broken out between the security forces and the army in Rumania outside the capital city of Bucharest. After a day of euphoria of celebrating the fall of the hated tyrant, people stood silently in knots, listening to the spates of gunfire and the air-raid sirens. One woman sobbed. A young man clenched his fists.

"This is just another case of the Securitate to fight and kill more people," he said fiercely.

In the last few days, with former President Nicolae Ceausescu in hiding, the people's fear, anger and hatred has concentrated on his security forces, the main corps of forces now fighting the provisional government. The most despised group is the Securitate's black-shirted elite, said to number 10,000 to 15,000.

As they fight from hidden perches, machine-gunning the population from helicopters, rooftops and running cars "Capone-style," as one witness described it, the Securitate's reputation for brutality has only grown. The odd part is that this hated group still hopes to regain control of the country even as evidence of its atrocities are being brought to light.

In Timisoara, a city to the south of here where the revolt began last Friday, citizens early this morning silently filed by a gruesome lineup of naked corpses, dug up the day before from one of several mass graves for the victims of last Sunday's massacre, now estimated here at 4,500.

Given the horrors of this scene—a pregnant woman's belly ripped open, scars from barbed wire on the bodies' bare legs—the people's grief seemed strangely contained. But as a visiting Hungarian noted, these things are not new for Rumanians.

No one knows why, but it seems that people picked up from the demonstrations last Sunday were tortured before they were killed. Those who found the bodies, after getting tipped that trucks had appeared at a potter's field late last Sunday night, say the torture must have taken place in a pink stucco house at the back of the cemetery, on a makeshift autopsy table.

"They're worse than Hitler," said a middle-aged man who had helped to dig up the 23 bodies found in the potter's field grave. "Compared to them, Hitler looks wonderful."

One man, giving further testimony, described how agents of the Securitate went to local hospitals after Sunday's bloodletting, collected some of the wounded and took them to a morgue where they were killed. He quoted irate witnesses who said the security forces, mingling with regular army soldiers, could be seen executing those soldiers who refused to fire on the crowd.

In the days since the collapse of the Ceausescu regime, people are wary about saying that the Securitate's days are over.

"Be careful," an old man warned two travelers as they drove through the deserted, dimly lit streets of Arad after 3 A.M. this morning. "Remember, they are like a snake."

In this western Rumanian city as in other populated centers outside of Bucharest, the dreaded security forces—well trained, well paid and intent on keeping the population in fear—waited until the dead of night to strike back at the popular revolution that had defeated them and their patron, Mr. Ceausescu.

In Timisoara, they laid low until midnight. Then as bells, horns and sirens sounded in honor of the thousands they had killed last Sunday, the Securitate agents fired into a crowd of more than 100,000 people gathered on Opera Square, killing an estimated 160 people.

Even today, as crowds gathered anew in the square, the shooting continued. One witness said the Securitate's forces were even shooting at ambulances as they attempted to approach victims lying on the ground.

Stories of the Securitate's cunning and resourcefulness continued to spread. One report circulating in Timisoara told of a woman Securitate agent who smuggled arms in her small Rumanian-built car to the children's hospital, where "terrorists," as the security forces are now called, were gathering.

This and other reports of arms smuggling are cited as reasons for the dozens of roadblocks that have been set up on roads leading to the battle-scarred urban centers by young supporters of the new Government.

In Arad, one family spoke of how the Securitate had infiltrated a Red Cross convoy, using one of its trucks to store guns.

"They have secret apartments, secret caches of ammunition, places where they can hide all over the country," said Alexander Hernea, a chemical engineer who today for the first time set aside the fear instilled by this awesome police force and invited a foreigner to his apartment.

The fighting between the Securitate and the army, which has now come out in support of the anti-Ceausescu revolution, seems shrouded in mystery. Accurate body counts are hard to come by and the fighting is so scattered that many people continue to go about their daily business as though a civil war were not taking place in their midst.

In Timisoara, the Securitate forces were holed up in several central locations—a fourteenth-century castle opposite the opera house and the Botanical Gardens, the Children's Hospital and a downtown fashion store where a handful were flushed out earlier today.

On December 23, as Western correspondents were still trying to get to Bucharest, East bloc correspondents reported that Nicolae Ceausescu, who fled from his besieged party headquarters in a white helicopter, had been captured. Meanwhile fighting was continuing between the Securitate people and units of the army that joined the revolutionary effort.

Rumanian Army Gains in Capital but Battle Goes On

By John Kifner

BUCHAREST, RUMANIA, Dec. 24—Bursts of gunfire sounded through this exultant but tense capital today and into the night as secret police officers loyal to the ousted dictator, Nicolae Ceausescu, held out and harassed the new provisional government claiming power in what had been the most rigorously controlled state in Eastern Europe.

Heavy-weapons fire echoed through the university district around the Inter-Continental Hotel throughout the night.

There were also reports tonight that widespread shooting had resumed after a lull during the day in the western city of Timisoara, where the uprising began nine days ago.

In Timisoara as well as in Bucharest, army units siding with the insurgents clashed with members of the Securitate, the secret police who carried out the Ceausescu policies of terror.

Somewhat incongruously, as shots rang out and sniper attacks continued in the capital, the state television tonight broadcast Christmas carols for the first time in more than four decades of Communist rule.

"But it has been bloody," a Rumanian said, staring at the unfamiliar televised image of Christmas tree bulbs on an evergreen.

It appeared certain that thousands have been killed in the fighting here, with some reports putting the toll of the dead in Bucharest at 5,000 since Friday. Rumanians are only beginning to calculate the number of dead in the countryside.

There were indications that the provisional government, calling itself the Council of National Salvation, was gaining the upper hand. The international airport, the scene of heavy fighting in recent days, where the cafeteria had been turned into a morgue, was reported reopened tonight.

Mr. Ceausescu's whereabouts remained uncertain today.

On Saturday afternoon, the state radio and television said he had been captured by the army, but the television has yet to show pictures of him.

Yugoslav press reports said that in Timisoara about forty secret policemen had surrendered and that the army had prevented people from lynching them.

The new government's radio and television stations, protected by army tanks, stayed on the air.

The state television repeated assertions that the army was in control of the city. The state television and radio carried a communiqué by the provisional government calling on the holdouts to turn in their arms by Monday or "face the consequences."

In the broadcasts, the provisional government urged calm, saying there should be no retribution because "enough blood has been shed."

The decree further declared that the "downfall of the odious dictatorship of the Ceausescu clan" had taken place but that "elements who had remained loyal to the tyrant were trying to go ahead with the terrorist practices of the old regime."

The television, which regularly displays its new name—Free Rumanian Television—has become a symbol of revolution here, having broadcast almost continuously since Friday. Before then, state television programming was limited to two hours a day, devoted almost entirely to the activities of Mr. Ceausescu.

Now the screen is filled with scenes of battles and demonstrations in the streets, interviews with excited citizens, musical programs and round-table discussions with intellectuals and suddenly reformed Government officials, all wearing armbands of red, yellow and blue, the national colors. Tonight scenes were shown from churches.

Earlier the television showed images of Zoia Ceausescu, the dictator's daughter, who was reported captured today. Nicu Ceausescu, a son of the deposed leader, had been shown after his seizure on Friday, his face bearing the signs of beating.

The 71-year-old former dictator and his wife, Elena, who had served as his chief deputy, have not been shown. But a spokesman for the Council of National Salvation said the couple were in custody and would be given a "strict and fair" trial. . . .

On Christmas Day the Ceausescus were executed by firing squad and the fighting began to wind down.

Army Executes Ceausescu and Wife for "Genocide" Role, Bucharest Says

By John Kifner

BUCHAREST, RUMANIA, Tuesday, Dec. 26—Nicolae Ceausescu, absolute ruler of Rumania for 24 years, and his wife were executed on Monday by the army that he once commanded, the Free Rumanian Television of the new provisional government said.

A first brief announcement said an "extraordinary military court" had tried Mr. Ceausescu and his wife, Elena, who was widely viewed as the country's second most powerful figure until widespread demonstrations forced the pair to flee the capital on Friday morning. They were reportedly captured on Saturday in Tirgoviste.

At 1:30 this morning, a few hours after the report of the executions, the television showed its first footage of the Ceausescus in captivity.

Some of the footage appeared to be from Monday's trial. The words "condemned to death" were barely audible on the fuzzy sound track. At one point, Mr. Ceausescu slammed his fur cap on the table. At times he seemed contemptuous. His wife appeared frightened.

The film, which opened with a doctor taking Mr. Ceausescu's blood pressure, was the first solid evidence that he had indeed been captured. The sound track also referred to the billion dollars he was said to have secreted abroad.

"The sentence was death and the sentence was executed," said the television announcement. It was proclaimed in the name of a largely faceless revolutionary government, the Council of National Salvation, which took power after the Ceausescus fled. It has not been made clear exactly when, where, how or on whose authority the Ceausescus were put to death, and their bodies had not been shown.

The charges against the Ceausescus, according to the television announcement, included the "genocide" of 60,000 people, many of whom died in the last week of fighting; undermining state power; destroying the country's economic and spiritual values; and trying to escape the country to claim $1 billion reportedly hidden abroad.

The Rumanian television said this morning that fighting near its studios in the capital was preventing staff members from getting footage of the execution on the air, Reuters reported.

The television studio has been the focus of heavy fighting between the Rumanian Army, which has sided with the popular uprising, and the security police, which is loyal to the Ceausescu regime. It is not known whether the security forces will fight on after the death of their leaders, but the insurgents clearly hope to demoralize them by showing proof of the executions.

The announcement of the execution came as Rumanians celebrated a bittersweet Christmas, treasuring their newfound and tentative liberties but mourning the many hundreds and perhaps thousands slain in the uprising.

The capital was calmer on Monday, with Rumanians strolling the boulevards and only an occasional burst of gunfire. The army appeared to be consolidating control over the remaining bands of now-renegade secret policemen, the backbone of the old order.

A Christmas tree stood on the balcony of the Communist Party headquarters this afternoon. It was placed in the spot where only last Thursday Mr. Ceausescu was hooted into shocked silence, jeered by a crowd that had been summoned to hear him condemn protests in a western city, Timisoara.

Sightseers wandered where fighting took place over the weekend between diehard security forces, who had sustained the reign of the Ceausescus, and a spontaneous coalition that united army units and irate civilians. Among those who turned out were several hundred people who gathered in front of party headquarters early this morning chanting, "We want Ceausescu hanged here at the palace!"

New newspapers have been printed in the last few days with names like *Freedom*, *Liberty* and *Free Rumania*. One paper that appeared as *Spark* when it was put under sanctions by Mr. Ceausescu renamed itself *Truth*. On Monday, when truckers drove by tossing out copies of the new papers, crowds rushed into the streets to grab them. "We had cold, hunger and terror" was the way one of the papers, *Free Youth*, described the past regime.

At a Christmas Mass at the Rumanian Orthodox Cathedral, the center of the major religion, Patriarch Teoctist Arapafu hailed "these brave young people, these young boys and girls who have died for freedom."

"They will live in our hearts forever," he said. At the same time, the Patriarch, who had cooperated with Mr. Ceausescu's Government, acknowledged that despite what he called shocking times, "I did not have the courage these children have shown."

Although orthodox, the Rumanian Church observes the same calendar of holy days as does Catholicism, the next-largest denomination in the country. But under the old regime, observances of Christmas were celebrated in private or in secrecy.

The reported execution of Mr. Ceausescu and his wife, along with the capture of his brother, son and daughter, ended nearly a quarter-century of absolute power. Mr. Ceausescu was routinely idolized as the "leader for life," with accounts of his daily routine dominating the local newspapers and the two hours each day that Rumanian television was on the air.

His harsh rule, enforced by a hated secret police and a system in which one in four Rumanians was said to be an informer, included drastic measures to pay off the foreign debt. Those included cutting off heat and electricity during the fierce Central European winter and exporting harvests of food while keeping citizens on meager rations.

But as in other Communist countries, a privileged inner circle of the party elite enjoyed amenities like ski and hunting resorts and special food shops.

The television made much of the luxurious circumstances in which Zoia Ceausescu, the ousted leader's daughter, lived, noting that $100,000 had been found in her home after she was captured over the weekend.

As in several other parts of the Soviet bloc, rigid and seemingly entrenched one-man and one-party rule has collapsed in the face of popular protest. Here the process was tougher and more violent both during the years of oppressive rule and in the days that have seen it toppled. . . .

The membership of the new government has not been made public for what its spokesman says are security reasons. But it is known to include a number of members of recent governments, some of whom had fallen out with Mr. Ceausescu.

Those include Corneliu Manescu, a former Foreign Minister; Ion Iliescu, a onetime member of the Politburo who had quarreled with the former President; and two top military figures: the chief of the general staff, Gen. Stefan Gusa, and the Deputy Foreign Minister, Ion Stanculescu.

All along the main boulevard, thousands of people strolled today, pausing to look at handbills hailing the revolution that were posted in store windows. They barely flinched as bursts of gunfire sounded a few blocks away, although at one point a group took refuge in doorways when the gunfire sounded too close.

As the new year approached, the revolutionary government gained breathing room and a modicum of legitimacy, calling for elections to be held in the next year. The leaders, men and women who were hardly well known when the revolt erupted, were making their case to the nation through television, which, it turned out, had been the most powerful of weapons.

The Airwaves; Rumanian Revolt, Live and Uncensored

By John Kifner

BUCHAREST, RUMANIA, Dec. 27—"This is the first revolution on live television," said Ion Todan, proud and tired this afternoon amid the chaotic but businesslike clutter at the heart of the videocracy that has replaced the dictatorship of Nicolae Ceausescu.

Studio 4 of Free Rumanian Television, a chamber about 12 feet square with antiquated cameras and black-and-white monitors, has been the real seat of power since Mr. Ceausescu tried to bolt the country on Friday after 24 years of harsh, absolute rule.

Rapt audiences watched again and again as the television studio repeatedly broadcast videotape of the military trial of Mr. Ceausescu and his wife, Elena, and showed the pictures of the executed ruler's body.

The broadcasts are profoundly political acts, calculated to consolidate support for the provisional government, the Council of National Salvation, and to show that further resistance by die-hard security agents is pointless.

Beginning with the poet Murica Dinesco's sudden appearance on the air on Friday morning, shouting, "We've won! We've won!" the once-soporific state television has become the pivotal instrument and embodiment of the revolution. It has struggled against sniper fire, commando attacks and its own outdated gear to keep broadcasting.

Even today, two days after Mr. Ceausescu and his wife were executed, his security police again tried to storm the station. The Bucharest radio said the agents were beaten back after a half-hour firefight.

"We knew we had to stay on the air," said Eugenia Bogdan, her face lined with fatigue, as she spoke of the station's importance to the uprising. Like the other workers, she has been living in the station since Friday. "If television falls, the revolution falls," she said. "That's for certain."

Outside, the blocks of luxurious villas and embassy buildings in the station's neighborhood sit empty, bullet-scarred and broken from the fire of the tanks and soldiers who have defended the broadcasting center. Inside, the monitors showed scenes unimaginable in Rumania just a week ago. Among them were people singing Christmas carols.

The tale of Studio 4 reveals much about power in the electronic age. Once, those who plotted revolutions and coups took aim at radio stations to gain a monopoly on the flow of information. In the Iranian revolution, new technology spread the word of Ayatollah Ruhollah Khomeini, first through tape cassettes telephoned from abroad and played over mosque loudspeakers. Later, when Khomeini was in power, the state television became his pulpit.

Conversations with ordinary Rumanians underscored the impact of the news broadcasts, not only in the last two weeks in Rumania but throughout Eastern Europe, where images of popular uprisings have penetrated borders, apparently sharpening yearnings for freedom and shaping official and public action.

Small shortwave radios can pick up foreign broadcasts. And in relatively prosperous East Germany, the people for years caught seductive glimpses of a richer society, as depicted on the West German television.

Here, where Rumanian television was once so dull that the schedules for Bulgarian programming, which can be tuned in, are a hot item for smugglers, the new freedom in the rest of the Eastern bloc could be seen on broadcasts from neighboring countries.

"The whole people see changes coming in Eastern Europe," Sergei Secuescu, a student, said on the street the other day. "We can see TV from Bulgaria, from Yugoslavia. We listen to the foreign radios, to Voice of America, Radio Free Europe, BBC. The phone was working. People have brothers, friends."

But the impact of television in the last two weeks goes far beyond that level. Viewers have seen the formation and defense of a revolutionary government, often as it happens.

For a week, Rumanians huddled around television sets and watched the demonstrations and gun battles between the army, which is supporting the popular revolution, and the renegade security forces, who propped up the old order. Then they saw the first tentative steps of the provisional government.

In a sense it was like watching live coverage of the storming of the Bastille or the Battle of Yorktown, interspersed with debates from the Constitutional Congress. But in this case the focus of the violence and struggle was the television studio itself. Sovereignty, it seemed, was reduced to the ability to convey what was happening just outside the studio door.

Early on Saturday morning, as security forces loyal to Mr. Ceausescu began their first attacks on the station, a family in the western city of Arad sat spellbound before their television, watching announcers force smiles as gunshots echoed in the studio. Soldiers were battling the security police, or Securitate, in the lobby of the television station.

Behind the announcer, a helmeted soldier with a rifle stood watch. Paratroopers who repelled the attack were brought to the studio as heroes. The announcer broadcast an appeal for help.

The television screen showed a panel of revolutionaries sitting around tables draped in red, yellow and blue, the national colors. The panel included a tank driver, two men in suits, one in a denim jacket and a student in a parka and turtleneck. At 3 A.M., the student was reading from a new broadsheet issued by an angry group of students. He stopped and began singing a song, only to be interrupted by the appearance of one of the country's biggest soccer stars.

In Arad, 265 miles northwest of Bucharest, the mother of the family watching the televised revolution—she would give only her first name, Ann—said, "We will not sleep tonight"

At another point, the television showed ten soldiers in a circle with their rifles pointing at the building's elevators, fearful that the security police had infiltrated. And in another remarkable segment, the anchorman on the news during much of the Ceausescu era told his audience that he had been forced to lie for years. He apologized and stayed on the air.

Mr. Todan, who in earlier times bought and translated the station's meager store of foreign films, recalled that on Friday morning, "The first mass movement was for the youngsters to come to the television, and Studio 4 became the heart of the revolution."

"But in the evening, the shooting started and we called for help," he said. "Crowds were surrounding the station and thousands of students were sitting under fire. If we went off the air, it meant it was over."

Perhaps the greatest threat to those inside the station came on Saturday, when security policemen assigned to the television suddenly turned on the workers. Six paratroopers were killed inside the station by knives or silencer-equipped pistols. One of the policemen got into the basement and cut off the electricity, which was restored only ten minutes before air time.

Besides bullets, the television workers had to worry about their outmoded equipment, sometimes shutting it down to avoid overheating.

"We have no spare parts," said Mikhail Bucauanu, the technical chief. "We just patch what we have." "We recently got three new cameras," he said. "They were only for filming him." He was referring to the late Mr. Ceausescu, whose activities dominated the few hours a day the television was on the air under the old regime. Now it is on long into the night.

The last few days of broadcasts have been dominated by Christmas programs.

"It was the first time we were even allowed to pronounce the word on television," Mr. Todan said. "Before, if it was in a foreign film, and somebody said 'Merry Christmas,' we had to translate it as 'Happy New Year.' "

A scrawny Christmas tree, tinsel in its few branches, stood in one corner of Studio 4 this afternoon, behind two peasants wearing knee-high boots, wide leather belts, smocks and high fur hats and carrying huge loaves of bread, proclaiming loyalty to the new Government.

The programming also included a speech by the Rev. Laszlo Tokes, the ethnic Hungarian clergyman whose persecution set off the initial protests; Christmas carols by teenage girls walking through the snow; new government decrees calling for military trials and executions of any secret policemen who did not turn themselves in by tomorrow, and the Chicago Philharmonic Orchestra playing the overture to *The Flying Dutchman.*

"At Christmas, for 17 people, we had just a round of cheese, some crackers and 200 grams of salami," Mr. Todan said. "The terrorists had infiltrated and the fight started inside the building. It was the most fantastic Christmas of my life."

In the final days of the year most attention was focused on Rumania, where revolution had flared so suddenly and violently. But in Czechoslovakia another great drama was also coming to a remarkable, though far less bloody resolution. Faced with the prospect of continuing protests and strikes, the Communist-dominated parliament gave the nation's top two posts to the two most prominent opponents of the old regime. First, Alexander Dubcek was named as Premier, and then just before the year lapsed Vaclav Havel was chosen to be President.

Czechoslovakia: Havel, Long Prague's Prisoner, Elected President

By Craig R. Whitney

PRAGUE, Dec. 29—Vaclav Havel, the Czechoslovak writer whose insistence on speaking the truth about repression in his country repeatedly cost him his freedom over the last 21 years, was elected President by Parliament today in an event celebrated by the throng outside the chamber as the redemption of their freedom.

In a speech formally nominating the 53-year-old playwright who until May 17 was serving a jail term, the country's Communist Prime Minister, Marian Calfa, praised Mr. Havel.

"He has won the respect of all," Mr. Calfa told the legislators assembled in the medieval Hradcany Castle high above the city. "He never accepted the suggestions of friends or foes that he go into exile, and bore the humiliation of a man oppressed and relegated by those in power to the margins of society. Your vote for Vaclav Havel will be a vote for insuring the human rights of every citizen of our country."

Mr. Calfa said Mr. Havel had insisted on free parliamentary elections next year as a condition for accepting the mostly symbolic post and would serve only until a new Parliament could be elected to choose a new President for a regular five-year term.

Alexander Dubcek, the country's Communist leader during the liberalizing Prague Spring of 1968 and now rehabilitated as the chairman of Parliament, called for other nominations. But there were none; Mr. Havel's election had been agreed to beforehand by the Communist leadership and the opposition Civic Forum.

Completing the formality, all 323 deputies in the heavily Communist legislature voted for Mr. Havel, Czechoslovakia's first non-Communist President since 1948.

Mr. Dubcek and Mr. Calfa left the sixteenth-century hall to fetch the new President, somber in a dark blue suit, and swear him in with an oath revised by Parliament on Thursday to delete a promise of loyalty to the cause of socialism.

After a 20-gun salute and a military parade, he addressed the joyous crowd that thronged the castle courtyard.

"Dear friends," he said. "I promise you I will not betray your confidence. I will lead this country to free elections. This must be done in an honest and calm way, so that the clean face of our revolution is not soiled. That is the task for all of us. Thank you."

After his short speech, Mr. Havel went into St. Vitus Cathedral, within the castle walls, for a Te Deum Mass presided over by 90-year-old Frantisek Cardinal Tomasek, the country's Roman Catholic Primate and Archbishop of Prague. The Gothic cathedral was jammed with people of every age. The Czech Philharmonic Orchestra and choir performed Dvorak's *Te Deum*.

Cardinal Tomasek, who celebrated the Mass, said, "We have come today to the cathedral to thank God for the great hope that has opened up for us in the last few days."

This evening, tens of thousands of people streamed into the center of Prague's Old Town in what amounted to a street celebration of Mr. Havel's election. He appeared along with the visiting Portuguese President, Mario Soares, and greeted them.

Mr. Havel, son of an upper-class civil engineer, was not allowed to go to university by the Communist Government after he finished his compulsory schooling in 1951, because of his class background. Today the students of Prague, many of them children of the Communist ruling class, have made Mr. Havel their intellectual hero, and they have been on strike since demonstrations on November 17 sparked the peaceful revolution that overthrew the long repression.

"Havel is the only guarantee that the changes here will be of a permanent character," said one of them, Ludek Vasta, 21, an economics student.

The student strike was expected to end today with his election.

President Havel, whose most recent prison term was for participating in a demonstration last January in memory of a student who immolated himself in protest against the crushing of the Prague Spring of 1968, is expected to address the nation by television on New Year's Day. He has told friends he will not move into the splendid presidential residence in the castle as his retired predecessor, Gustav Husak did, but will remain in the flat in the center of town where he and his wife, Olga, have lived for years, and commute to work in his car.

He is a man who wrote, in a 1984 acceptance speech for a French university award that the Czechoslovak authorities would not allow him to pick up, "The slogan 'better Red than dead' does not irritate me as an expression of surrender to the Soviet Union, but it terrifies me as an expression of the renunciation by Western people of any claim to a meaningful life and of their acceptance of impersonal power as such. For what the slogan really says is that nothing is worth giving one's life for."

Through much of Mr. Havel's work runs the thread of what he calls "the absolute horizon"—the moral and philosophical judgments that give human life its meaning. He repeatedly warned his persecutors that by their repression of human freedom they were ultimately undercutting their own existence as well.

When the Soviet-led invasion began in August 1968, Mr. Havel took part in Free Czechoslovak Radio broadcasts. A year later, he signed a declaration condemning the post-Dubcek policy of "normalization." His published works were withdrawn from public libraries, and his new works were banned.

In April 1975, he sent a letter to the man he has now succeeded as President, Mr. Husak, warning that ultimately a repressed people would demand a price for "the permanent humiliation of their human dignity."

"I fear the price we are all bound to pay for the drastic suppression of history, the cruel and needless banishment of life into the underground of society and the depths of the human soul, the new compulsory 'deferral' of every opportunity for society to live in anything like a natural way," he wrote then, more than a decade before the facade crumbled in Czechoslovakia and elsewhere in Eastern Europe.

"No wonder, then, that when the crust cracks and the lava of life rolls out, there appear not only well-considered attempts to rectify old wrongs, not only searchings for truth and for reforms matching life's needs, but also symptoms of bilious hatred, vengeful wrath and a kind of feverish desire for immediate compensation for all the endured degradation," he wrote.

For writing that letter, and for organizing the Charter 77 human rights movement at the beginning of January 1977, Mr. Havel was arrested and charged with "subversion of the republic." Convicted that October, his fourteen-month sentence was conditionally deferred, but he was in and out of jail again until arrested in May 1979 for supporting the Committee for the Defense of the Unjustly Accused. With Jiri Dienstbier, now Foreign Minister of Czechoslovakia, and four other defendants, he was tried again for subversion that October and sentenced to four and one-half years in prison, but he was released for health reasons in February 1983.

His refusal to break with the Charter 77 movement led to other brief periods of detention in jail. But in January of this year, defying police orders to stay away from a demonstration in memory of Jan Palach, the young man who burned himself alive in protest after the 1968 invasion, cost him four months' imprisonment.

After his release, Mr. Havel called for restraint in commemorating the invasion's twenty-first anniversary in August, but he had to hide from the police anyway to keep from being arrested. He and three associates organized a petition, called "A Few Words," which soon gathered tens of thousands of signatures, calling for the release of all political prisoners and an end to discrimination on religious and other grounds.

The presidency of independent Czechoslovakia was first held by Tomas G. Masaryk, from 1918 to 1935. Eduard Benes, his successor, resigned in 1938 when the Western Allies signed Czechoslovakia over to Nazi Germany in the Munich Pact, but served again from 1946 to 1948. After that all presidents had to be members of the Communist Party, and they were until President Husak resigned on December 10.

E P I L O G U E
Michael T. Kaufman

This remarkable year of 1989, which began with the withdrawal of Soviet troops from Afghanistan, ended with the fall of Ceausescu. In the intervening months democratic movements brought revolutionary changes and sharply altered the course set by many Communist governments over many decades.

As the year drew to a close, Poland was being led by an elected, representative Government in which non-Communists dominate. In Czechoslovakia, dissident figures who led a fragile long-persecuted opposition are serving as President and Prime Minister until promised elections take place. Free competitive multiparty elections are also due to be held in Hungary, East Germany, Bulgaria and in a still chaotic Rumania. Constitutional clauses that had guaranteed a special role to the Communist parties of Eastern Europe have been repealed. Communist symbols have been erased in many of these countries and calls have been issued for the removal of Soviet forces stationed in some of them. At the same time, these states have appealed for the restructuring of trading schedules and planning from Moscow that bound their economies to the Soviet Union.

Within the Soviet Union itself, appeals for political pluralism are being raised in several Republics, though it remains unclear whether these are impelled primarily by yearnings for greater democracy or by desires for national self-determination and separatism, though the two are related. But in Moscow, at the very heart of Communism, Mikhail S. Gorbachev is pursuing modernity by shedding old dogma. He is "stopping short of an outright acceptance of multiparty democracy," but he seems to be considering new federal formulas that could give greater economic and cultural autonomy to the Soviet Union's increasingly restless components. Indeed, as the year drew to a close, the only Communist countries in Europe where democratizing and pluralistic changes had not yet shaken ruling regimes were Albania and Yugoslavia, neither of which are members of the Warsaw Pact or Comecon, and thus lie outside Moscow's ambit. In China, for the moment, all seems quiet, though the memory of the military's crushing of student-led protests haunts some and may yet inspire others.

Does all this mean that the collapse of Communism is final and irreversible and that the cold war is over? Certainly evidence that is accumulating tends to support such conclusions. Still, one of the developments that has accompanied the obvious decline of Communism has been the refutation of claims that history is a science and that deterministic formulas could foretell the world's destiny. It is useful and humbling to recall that just a year ago no one, not the greatest of political scientists, not the most powerful of politicians, nor the best informed of diplomats, was able to envision a fraction of what has taken place. Actually, as this book has shown, it was a better time for journalists than for political scientists, primarily because journalists work in shorter time frames dealing with change in daily increments. In this year, these daily doses confounded the experts.

In light of this lesson, it would be foolhardy to proclaim that the clear democratic thrust of the last twelve months is unstoppable. In fact, it does not take a great deal of imagination to spin bleak scenarios. As the previous pages have shown, Gorbachev's role in many of the changes has been central. But what happens if he is brought down by the nationalist forces he helped unleash? What if, in the absence of old binding dogmas, some general or group of generals take over in Moscow vowing to stop the decay of Soviet power? If Gorbachev was able to override and replace the Brezhnev doctrine, is it really unthinkable that some as yet unknown figure may one day reverse Gorbachev's pledge of nonintervention?

And in the newly pluralistic states, is steady, democratic development a certainty? Obviously not. Few of them have great democratic traditions on which to draw. All of them have woefully impoverished economies that can be reformed only through the kind of painful dislocations that can easily ignite the kind of social upheavals that in the past have paved the way for demagogues and dictators. In most of these countries there are national minorities linked by language and culture to neighboring states, and the prospect of old-fashioned European conflicts is not very remote. Indeed, it can be argued that as totalitarian Communism recedes, ending the divisions of Europe, so too does the specter of a rekindled World War II. But the specter of World War I looms somewhat greater.

In the opening pages of this book, figures from the Hoover Foundation at Stamford were quoted to show that 88.6 million people around the world were thought to be Communists or adherents of Communism when the year began. No new survey has been concluded, but it is a pretty fair assumption that the number has dropped sharply everywhere. In Eastern Europe it has plummeted. In Hungary the party changed its name and went into something like bankruptcy. In Rumania it went from being the only party to being a shameful nonentity within a single month. Lithuanian Communists want to withdraw from the Moscow-led Soviet party. The reverberations of such events are being felt both in the West and in the third world, where Communist ideology has lost its power to inspire with claims of inevitable growth and triumph.

In the African country of Benin, where a one-party Marxist state had been proclaimed, a statue of Karl Marx was toppled by mobs and the country's leader reversed himself to declare that Communism was invalidated and that henceforth no one should use the term "comrade" as a term of address. Other third world countries, among them Vietnam, Angola and Ethiopia, were less dramatically retreating from their once-avid rush to embrace Communist doctrine and old Soviet-style strategies for development. Such reversals were in large measure brought on by Moscow's growing inability and unwillingness to continue high levels of economic support for countries whose leaders affirmed the ideological line of the Kremlin.

Not only was there less money available for such subsidies, the line itself had become frayed, confused and much more difficult to follow. What were third world Communists to make of Mr. Gorbachev's visit to the Vatican? Was atheism no longer the correct course? Similar confusion stemmed from Mr. Gorbachev's overtures of friendship to the democratic West in general and to the United States in particular. How was one to maintain hostility or aloofness to what had recently been viewed as the class enemy if the foremost leader of the vanguard Communist state was making his peace with the foe? What was the sense of being nonaligned when the familiar bipolar world was growing less bipolar everyday? Among world leaders, only Fidel Castro was clinging to old formulations depicting Mr. Gorbachev and his disciples as apostates and heretics.

These strains were widely evident, from Nicaragua, where Soviet arms supplies to the Sandinista government were reportedly slackening, to Mongolia, where calls for democratic reforms were being raised.

There were areas of the map, however, where such trends were not advancing. The largest of these was China, where the pro-democracy movement that blossomed in the spring had been cut off by military force. As the year ended, martial law remained in effect and it was unclear whether hopes that stirred in May were dead or just lying dormant, ready to burst forth when opportunities arose. What was clear was that the Chinese government had paid a very high price for its assault on the students. In China, as in other parts of the Communist world, the link between liberal politics and liberal economics was proving critical. It was impossible, it seemed, to seek economic change, to advance productivity, initiative, technological adaptation, unless citizens saw their own advantage involved in the process, and that by definition involved political changes. Moreover, it was hard to get the capital, the know-how and the management skills needed to assure rapid growth and restructuring if those foreigners who commanded such things were watching television footage of protesting university students being shot down.

It was not just foreigners whose reactions were shaped by such images. Along with the image that Gorbachev created for himself, the mass media served as the most significant catalyst for change. Not very long ago, it was widely assumed that revolutions like those that shaped the United States or the French Republic were probably impossible in modern industrialized societies, let alone in totalitarian dictatorships. The assumption was that the centralized power of the state was so strong that any attempt to overwhelm it was doomed, as was the case in the Budapest uprising of 1956. Perhaps, some argued, such romantic challenges might still prevail in rural-based societies like Afghanistan, but what chance of success did they have when the state commanded tanks and the people had only sabers or hunting rifles?

It turned out that a few dissidents using nonviolent means, and exploiting the freedom of the press and airwaves beyond their borders, could in this increasingly interconnected world bring down autocrat after autocrat. Foreign correspondents wrote for their own papers, but their reports were translated and beamed back to countries where such information as they were writing was banned. The spread of portable radios and videos made such information more accessible. The official press was forced to offer more information, more truth, as it was forced to compete for credibility with the outsiders. East Germans watched West German television and learned what had been achieved in Poland. In Rumania people were moved to boldness when they learned from Yugoslav stations that their countrymen had been killed by Ceausescu's security forces. Once informed, they were mobilized. In most places, they marched and chanted and drew placards, and with the world press watching such means proved sufficient to expose previously forbidden truths and to make revolutionary changes that had so recently seemed impossible.